Go Fundamentals

Go Fundamentals

Mark Bates
Cory LaNou

♦♦Addison-Wesley

Boston • Columbus • New York • San Francisco • Amsterdam • Cape Town
Dubai • London • Madrid • Milan • Munich • Paris • Montreal • Toronto • Delhi • Mexico City
São Paulo • Sydney • Hong Kong • Seoul • Singapore • Taipei • Tokyo

Cover image: T-flex/Shutterstock

Figures 7.1, 7.2: Microsoft

For information about buying this title in bulk quantities, or for special sales opportunities (which may include electronic versions; custom cover designs; and content particular to your business, training goals, marketing focus, or branding interests), please contact our corporate sales department at corpsales@pearsoned.com or (800) 382-3419.

For government sales inquiries, please contact governmentsales@pearsoned.com.

For questions about sales outside the U.S., please contact intlcs@pearson.com.

Visit us on the Web: informit.com/aw

Library of Congress Control Number: 2022943902

ISBN-13: 978-0-13-791830-0
ISBN-10: 0-13-791830-5

1 2022

Pearson's Commitment to Diversity, Equity, and Inclusion

Pearson is dedicated to creating bias-free content that reflects the diversity of all learners. We embrace the many dimensions of diversity, including but not limited to race, ethnicity, gender, socioeconomic status, ability, age, sexual orientation, and religious or political beliefs.

Education is a powerful force for equity and change in our world. It has the potential to deliver opportunities that improve lives and enable economic mobility. As we work with authors to create content for every product and service, we acknowledge our responsibility to demonstrate inclusivity and incorporate diverse scholarship so that everyone can achieve their potential through learning. As the world's leading learning company, we have a duty to help drive change and live up to our purpose to help more people create a better life for themselves and to create a better world.

Our ambition is to purposefully contribute to a world where

- Everyone has an equitable and lifelong opportunity to succeed through learning.

- Our educational products and services are inclusive and represent the rich diversity of learners.

- Our educational content accurately reflects the histories and experiences of the learners we serve.

- Our educational content prompts deeper discussions with learners and motivates them to expand their own learning (and worldview).

While we work hard to present unbiased content, we want to hear from you about any concerns or needs with this Pearson product so that we can investigate and address them. Please contact us with concerns about any potential bias at https://www.pearson.com/report-bias.html.

For Rachel, Dylan, Leo, and Ringo.
—Mark Bates

For Karie, Logan, and Megan.
—Cory LaNou

Contents

Foreword

I feel excited, honored, and a bit shocked to be writing these words.

I've known Mark and Cory for more than a decade, and as the Go project has evolved beyond our 1.0 vision, I've really been hoping for someone to write a follow up to the excellent Go 1.0 books. I'm really grateful for the good fortune I've had to be so deeply involved in the Go project and community. What began with me typing the first few lines of code into Hugo,[1] Cobra,[2] and Viper[3] over 10 years ago has exploded in ways I couldn't have dreamed of. It's been the privilege of a lifetime to lead the Go project alongside my partners Russ Cox and Sameer Ajmani and to work alongside the luminary programmers both on the Go team at Google and across the Go community.

I met Mark when we both spoke at the first Gotham Go.[4] I was instantly drawn away from him. I found his on-stage persona to be a bit too much. Later that year, the organizers of GopherCon[5] asked me to lead the lightning talk program and said they had the perfect partner for me. You guessed it—Mark. I learned that Mark's stage persona was indeed who he was off stage. I also learned that he was a loyal friend who would do anything for the Go community, whose humor and courage was boundless… limitless… maybe a bit too much. Mark and I have paired on many stages and projects over the past 10 years, and Mark injected a spirit of excitement into everything he did. He's become a dear friend, and I'm grateful to have been on so many adventures with him.

I met Cory at the second GopherCon and instantly was drawn to him. Cory is a natural teacher—captivating and empathetic. He cares deeply about the Go community and ensuring that Go is accessible to all, especially the folks new to Go. I've worked with him on a variety of community efforts, and I've always come away impressed with the depth he shows in his knowledge about Go and the learning experience.

Mark and Cory have been working together for many years now as the dominant training duo for Go under the name Gopher Guides. Together they have produced excellent training programs for clients that include many notable brands found on the Fortune 500. They have expertise in both Go and in empathic learning, forged over thousands of hours of classroom-style instruction. They are the perfect pair to author what is destined to become "The Go Book" for Go's second phase (Go with Modules & Generics).

This book leans on Mark and Cory's years of experience in the field and in the Go community to take a very grassroots approach to learning, and it is the guide for

---

1. https://gohugo.io/
2. https://pkg.go.dev/github.com/spf13/cobra
3. https://pkg.go.dev/github.com/spf13/viper
4. https://gothamgo.com/
5. https://www.gophercon.com/

programmers to become gophers. It also leverages their practical experience writing Go libraries and applications to present to the reader pragmatic solutions and simple explanations.

This book guides you like an old friend would, telling you the technical approaches to things but also relaying the cultural norms and idioms. It answers questions that the majority of books don't even think of because Mark and Cory have heard these questions asked by real people in a classroom so many times. Through reading and applying what is in this book, more than any other of its kind, you will progress from becoming a programmer to being a programmer who writes Go to being a gopher.

I am excited for the journey you are about to take with this book. I'm sure that you will sense the same excitement and empathy through these pages that I have experienced through all the adventures I've had with Mark and Cory. My hope for you is that as you learn Go, you will, as I did when I first discovered Go over a decade ago, fall in love with programming again.

—*Steve Francia*
  @spf13

Preface

Over the years, we have been fortunate to have trained thousands of developers in Go. It has been an incredible experience for us. We are developers who care about developers, so to be able to help developers grow is a great honor for us. This book is a culmination of that experience.

With nearly a half-century of experience between us, we both love Go. Go is fast, efficient, and fairly straightforward. We both believe that Go is a great first language to learn.

Unlike previous languages we have both used, there is relatively little "magic" in the language. Developers are rarely left scratching their heads as to where a function or type came from. Although the language does offer tools, such as the `reflect`[1] package, those tools are not used often. As part of this philosophy, the general consensus in the community is to favor using the standard library over third-party libraries. Again, this stems from experience with languages where bloated dependencies caused all sorts of problems. Also, early in the language's history, there was no package manager, so managing dependencies was a challenge.

The Go compiler is another reason why Go has become so popular. The speed of the compiler is a huge factor in the development of Go. Fast compilation times mean a faster feedback cycle for developers. Large Go applications can be compiled in seconds. Small Go applications, when using `go run`, compile and execute so quickly that it makes Go feel like a scripting language. This fast compilation and execution time extends to the running of tests as well. It is not uncommon for a Go developer to run the entire test suite every time they save a file. This is not something that can be done with other languages.

The Go compiler, the language's type system, and its fast compiler mean that a lot of common bugs are very quickly caught. This is a great advantage for Go developers. We are able to focus on business logic, knowing that the compiler will catch any stupid mistakes we might make, such as using a variable before it is defined or forgetting to use the `range` keyword in a loop.

For example, in Listing P.1, we are doing just that. You can see from the output that the compiler caught the error and did so very quickly.

---

1. https://pkg.go.dev/reflect

Listing P.1   Quick Feedback Cycle Thanks to the Go Compiler

```go
package main

import (
    "fmt"
    "os"
    "os/exec"
    "time"
)

func main() {
    letters := []string{"a", "b", "c"}

    for _, l := letters {
        fmt.Println(l)
    }
}
```

```
$ go run .

# demo
./main.go:13:11: syntax error: cannot use _, l := letters as value
```

```
Duration:    64.341084ms
Go Version: go1.19
```

We discuss more about looping in Chapter 3 and more about how the Go compiler and runtime work as we progress throughout the book.

Finally, Go has a great concurrency story. The language was built from the ground with concurrency in mind. This means you don't need to worry about threading, spawning processes, or anything like that. You can write concurrent code quickly and easily.

In the code snippet in Listing P.2, we are using goroutines, channels, and synchronization types, such as sync.WaitGroup[2] to create an application that properly handles concurrency.

Listing P.2   Go Concurrency in Action

```go
func main() {
    // create a channel of type int
    ch := make(chan int)
```

---

2. https://pkg.go.dev/sync#WaitGroup

```go
    // create a wait group to track
    // the goroutines
    var wg sync.WaitGroup

    // create some goroutines to
    // listen for messages on the
    // channel
    for i := 0; i < 4; i++ {

        // increment the wait group
        wg.Add(1)

        // create a goroutine
        // to call the sayHello function
        go func(id int) {

            // call the sayHello function
            sayHello(id, ch)

            // decrement the wait group
            // when the sayHello function
            // exits
            wg.Done()
        }(i + 1)
    }

    // send messages on the channel
    for i := 0; i < 10; i++ {
        ch <- i
    }

    // close the channel to signal
    // the goroutines to exit
    close(ch)

    // wait for all goroutines to finish
    wg.Wait()
}

func sayHello(id int, ch chan int) {

    // listen for messages on the channel
    // loop exits when the channel is closed
    for i := range ch {
```

```
        fmt.Printf("Hello %d from goroutine %d\n", i, id)

        // simulate a long-running task
        sleep()
    }
}
```

```
$ go run .


Hello 2 from goroutine 4
Hello 1 from goroutine 2
Hello 3 from goroutine 3
Hello 0 from goroutine 1
Hello 4 from goroutine 1
Hello 5 from goroutine 2
Hello 6 from goroutine 1
Hello 7 from goroutine 1
Hello 8 from goroutine 4
Hello 9 from goroutine 3

Go Version: go1.19
```

You can read more about Go's concurrency model in Chapters, 11, 12, and 13.

How to Read This Book

We have laid this book out with the idea that it is meant to be read from start to finish. Each chapter, and each example, build on previous examples. While those with some experience with Go might be tempted to jump straight to later chapters, we really recommend reading the whole book.

We have gone through great effort to try to make sure that examples and chapters don't contain any new information that we haven't covered up to that point. In Chapter 9, for example, we cover errors in Go. To understand how errors work, you first need to learn about interfaces, which we cover in Chapter 8. Occasionally, we do have to break this rule, though. In those instances, we try our best to explain the concept or point to the chapter where it is explained.

About the Examples

As mentioned, we spent considerable time designing the examples in this book and our training materials to be as clear and concise as possible. We also wanted to make sure that all of the code, output, and documentation were accurate.

To ensure that all of these things are true, we used a system designed give us this accuracy. Knowing that every code snippet is from a real file, every command is actually executed, every output is exact, and every piece of documentation is up to date means we can be confident in the materials we present.

In Listing P.3, you see an example of what one of these documents looks like.

Listing P.3 Sample of How the Book Was Written

```
### Commands and Documentation

In <ref>exit</ref>, we see a snippet of code.

This will execute the command 'go run .' in the 'src/bad' directory.
This command is expected to exit with a code of '1'.
The output of the command is automatically captured and inserted into
➥the document.

<figure id="exit" type="listing">
<code src="module.md#exit" esc></code>
<figcaption>Handling a non-successful exit code.</figcaption>
</figure>

In <ref>panic</ref>, we can see the output of the non-successful program.
➥Notice, at the top of the output we see the command used that was executed,
➥'$ go run .'. At the bottom we can see that the program was executed with,
➥Go version '1.19'.

<figure id="panic">
<go src="src/bad" run="." exit="1"></go>
<figcaption>Output of a non-successful program.</figcaption>
</figure>

While this book was written with Go version '1.18', all of the final
➥examples, and documentation, were run with Go version '1.19'.

In <ref>appendf.doc</ref>, we can see an example of documentation that is
➥being inserted into the document. In this case, we are inserting the
➥documentation for the new Go '1.19' function, 'fmt.Appendf'. Again, just
➥like the command output in <ref>panic</ref>, the command used to get the
➥documentation and the Go version is shown at the bottom of the output.
```

(continued)

```
<figure id="appendf.doc">
<go doc="fmt.Appendf"></go>
<figcaption>The 'fmt.Appendf' function documentation.</figcaption>
</figure>
```

The output of Listing P.3 is included in the next section.

Commands and Documentation

Listing P.4 shows a snippet of code.

It executes the command go run . in the src/bad directory. This command is expected to exit with a code of 1. The output of the command is automatically captured and inserted into the document.

Listing P.4   Handling a Nonsuccessful Exit Code

```
<go src="src/bad" run="." exit="1"></go>
```

In Listing P.5, you can see the output of the nonsuccessful program. Notice that the top of the output, you see the command used that was executed: $ go run . At the bottom, you can see that the program was executed with Go version 1.19.

Listing P.5   Output of a Nonsuccessful Program

```
$ go run .

panic: Hello, World!

goroutine 1 [running]:
main.main()
        ./main.go:5 +0x2c
exit status 2
```
```
Go Version: go1.19
```

While this book was written with Go version 1.18, all of the final examples and documentation were run with Go version 1.19.

In Listing P.6, you can see an example of documentation that is being inserted into the document. In this case, we are inserting the documentation for the new Go 1.19 function, fmt.Appendf. Again, just like the command output in Listing P.5, the command used to get the documentation, $ go do fmt.Appendf, is shown at the top of the output, and the Go version is shown at the bottom of the output.

Listing P.6 The `fmt.Appendf` Function Documentation

```
$ go doc fmt.Appendf

package fmt // import "fmt"

func Appendf(b []byte, format string, a ...any) []byte
    Appendf formats according to a format specifier, appends the result to the
    ➥byte slice, and returns the updated slice.
```

Go Version: go1.19

Summary

Contained within these pages are the concepts, types, packages, idioms, and other features of Go that we believe to be the most fundamental to understanding the language.

Go, its ecosystem, and its community are large, complex, and vibrant. Although we wish we could have included more in this book, it would've been impossible to print, and we would have never finished it.

Our goal, by the end of this book, is to help you be a knowledgeable Go programmer—one who not only feels confident using the language but understands how to write idiomatic Go code, tests, and is a good community member.

Finally, dear reader, thank you for your support. We consider it a privilege to be able to share this book and our knowledge with you. We love Go, and we hope you do, too.

—*Mark Bates and Cory LaNou*
 August 2022

Acknowledgments

Authoring a book is incredibly hard work, whether you are self-publishing or working with a great publisher like Addison-Wesley. It requires long hours of writing, creating just the right sample code, and refactoring. This is usually where the self-publishing author stops. When working with a publisher, however, this only the start of a new phase in the process.

After a book is written and submitted, a team of people jump in to try and make the book the best it can be. There are technical reviewers who are there to make sure the code and the discussion of the code are correct. There are copy editors who drill into the minutiae of grammar, spelling, punctuation, and other stylistic issues. There is the production team who is responsible for the final delivery of the book. There is the cover designer, the proofreader, the indexer, and more. As the adage says, "It takes a village."

Gopher Guides would like to thank Kim Spenceley, our editor, and Debra Williams-Cauley, our managing editor, for all of their incredible support since we first started this journey. Their optimism and excitement has kept us going through this process. Without Kim and Debra, there would be no book. Thank you two so very much.

In addition to Kim and Debra, Gopher Guides would like to the following people at Addison-Wesley for their help in the process of making this book a reality:

Copy editor and project manager: Charlotte Kughen

Production manager: Sandra Schroeder

Production editor: Julie Nahil

Cover designer: Chuti Prasertsith

Development editor: Chris Zahn

Indexer: Cheryl Lenser

Proofreader: Sarah Kearns

The rest of the village at Addison-Wesley

The Go community has been a huge supporter of Gopher Guides over the years. We would like to thank everyone on the Go team for their dedication and hard work in creating a language that is loved by so many. Thank you to all those who have committed to the Go project over the years. Again, it takes a village.

In particular, Gopher guides would like to thank the following Go community members who have helped us along the way.

Steve Francia

Ashley Willis (McNamara) (who designed
   the Gopher Guides logo)

Mat Ryer

Carmen Andoh

Johnny Boursiquot

Tim Raymond

Antonio Pagano

Renee French (for creating the Gopher
   logo)

Ron Evans

Bill Kennedy

Brian Ketelsen

Bryan Liles

Ben Johnson

Dave Cheney

Matt Aimonetti

Francesc Campoy

From Mark Bates

In addition to everyone that Cory and I have thanked already, I would like to make a few acknowledgments of my own.

First, I would like to thank my business partner and friend, Cory LaNou. Cory and I knew each other well in the community, but we really got to know each other and became good friends on a trip to GopherCon India in Bengaluru (Bangalore), India, and in Dubai, United Arab Emirates. We both spoke at the conferences, which were great, but it was the extra curriculum that truly bonded us. We rode camels, drove dune buggies, and went to a desert oasis. It was a great experience.

About a year later, in 2017, Cory and I decided that we wanted to start a company to help people learn Go. With that, Gopher Guides was born. I have never worked anywhere for longer than two and a half years. Gopher Guides, at the time of writing, has been going for more than five years. That is more than double the time I've worked at any job. The reason for this is simple: Cory LaNou is an excellent partner and a great friend. I have never felt as supported and as understood while working at any other company as I do working with Cory.

Cory, thank you for your patience, understanding, and support. I couldn't be prouder of what we have built together—this great company and our enduring friendship.

Next, I want to thank Kim Spenceley and Debra Williams-Cauley. I have known both of them for a long time. Debra was the editor on my first two books for Addison-Wesley in 2009 and 2012. Kim was the publishing coordinator of the first book. Both of these strong women have been of great support to me over the years. I always feel lucky that I was able to find a publishing company like Addison-Wesley—with editors like Debra and Kim—that is so focused on author success. Thank you both for helping me to first realize my dream of having a book published, and then for encouraging me to continue writing.

Finally, I would like to thank my family. There is no better partner, friend, and supporter than my wife, Rachel. She is an actual wonder woman. The saying "behind every good man is a great woman" is about her. She is a ball of energy, enthusiasm, and spirit. She has a goal of running a half marathon in every U.S. state, and she's more than halfway there. I get winded driving 13.1 miles. She is the morning person to my night owl. Rachel is a successful business woman who has spent her career being an advocate for women in the workplace. She is the mentor that she never had to a generation of women in business. I know several of these women, and to hear them talk about Rachel with such respect and appreciation is heart-warming.

Lastly, in addition to all of her support, love, and dedication over the years, Rachel has given me the greatest gift of all; our two sons, Dylan and Leo, are wonderful people. They are kind, caring, and honest. They are both very smart, talented, and hilarious people who continue to amaze me and make me glow with pride. Each night, we eat dinner together and then settle in, as a family, to watch TV. Our dog Ringo curls up at the end of the sofa, and we all enjoy each other's company. It's at those moments I feel truly thankful and happy to be surrounded by their love.

Thank you Rachel, Dylan, and Leo (and Ringo—the dog, not the Beatle—though he's cool, too!) for all of your support and love. I love you all to the very depths of my heart.

From Cory LaNou

First, and most obvious, my thanks go to my business partner, Mark Bates. Mark and I met through the Go community and have become not just great partners in our business but also great friends. We both share a passion for Go and training, which is why I believe we have been so successful together.

A big thanks to Levi Cook for introducing me to the Go language in March 2012 and encouraging me to start one of the first Go meetups in the world in Denver, Colorado. Levi not only introduced me to Go but also to open source and, most important, VIM!

I also want to recognize some of the brightest and most talented developers I have ever worked with on the InfluxDB project. Ben Johnson for having an ability to name the impossible things. Jason Wilder for opening my mind to taking the most complex of issues and breaking them into their smallest components. Philip O'Toole for challenging every new concept I introduced to the Go code base. David Norton for being the nicest person I've ever worked with (and giving the best SQL presentation ever!). Joe LeGasse for never hesitating to pair program with me. And all the other amazing people I worked with on the InfluxDB team.

When I moved back to Wisconsin to be around all my family, I knew I would miss Denver's rich technology community. Thankfully, Doug Rhoten was heading up the Chippewa Valley Developers meetup and made me feel incredibly welcome. Thank you, Doug, for working so hard for the local technology community!

And lastly, but certainly not least, my family! My wife, Karie, has been nothing but supportive, even when I have done the craziest of business ventures. Without her support and belief in me, I would not be where I am today. My son, Logan, and daughter, Megan, who thank me for all the long hours I put in so that they can have bacon for breakfast!

About the Authors

Mark Bates is cofounder and instructor at Gopher Guides, the industry leader for Go training, consulting, and conference workshops. After graduating with a degree in music from the Liverpool Institute for Performing Arts in 1999, Mark joined the original dot-com boom as a software engineer and began his career as a technologist. Since then, Mark has been fortunate enough to work with some of the world's largest and most innovative companies, including Apple, Uber, and Visa.

When he first discovered Go in the summer of 2013, Mark was immediately drawn to the language and its ecosystem. In 2014, Mark attended the first GopherCon, where he met Cory LaNou. For seven years, Mark hosted the GopherCon lightning talks and has been proud to introduce hundreds of new speakers to the community. Mark has spoken at conferences around the world and is a regular on the *Go Time* podcast.

When not coding or writing about coding, Mark enjoys spending time with his family, traveling, and recording music. Mark is currently completing a master's degree in music production from Berklee College of Music in Boston, Massachusetts.

Cory LaNou is a full stack technologist who has specialized in start-ups for the last 20 years. Cory has started several technology companies over the years, including companies such as Pulsity, a web consulting firm that operated in the late 1990s. From that company, Local Launch (an Internet marketing technology company) was formed and later sold to RH Donnelly in 2006.

Cory has deep experience in the Go world, having worked on the Core engineering team that contributes to InfluxDB, which is a highly scalable, distributed time series database written in Go. Cory has worked on several other Go projects with a focus on profiling and optimizing applications, using advanced profiling concepts such as torch graphs and tracing profiles.

Cory has deep ties to the Go community and started Denver Gophers, one of the very first Go meetups in the world, and he assisted in the very first GopherCon. Cory has created and led numerous Go workshops and training courses and has several published online articles related to Go. He continues to help organize and lead several community technology meetups and mentors new developers. Cory is also a partner at Gopher Guides, the industry leader for Go training and conferences.

When Cory isn't working on writing new Go training material, he volunteers his time to help local entrepreneurs start up their businesses by offering free services and business advice—such as how to incorporate their business and get their web presence set up—and giving them the moral support they need to make their dreams a reality.

1

Modules, Packages, and Dependencies

In this chapter, we begin our exploration of Go by looking at how it manages modules, packages, and dependencies. We first look at modules, which are a way to organize a set of packages for distribution under a specific version number for seamless dependency management. We then cover the concept of packages, which is the unit of code that can be imported into other packages. Finally, we look at importing packages from both the standard library and third-party packages.

Modules

A Go module[1] is a collection of Go packages[2] and their dependencies that can be built, versioned, and managed as a unit. An example of a Go module file layout can be found in Listing 1.1.

Listing 1.1   Listing of Files in a Go Module

```
$ tree


.
|__ go.mod
|__ pkga
|    '__ pkga.go
|__ pkgb
|    '__ pkgb.go
'__ pkgc
     '__ pkgc.go

3 directories, 4 files
```

At the root of a Go module is a `go.mod` file, Listing 1.2, which specifies the module's dependencies, required minimum version of Go, and other metadata.

---

1. https://golang.org/ref/mod
2. https://golang.org/ref/spec#Import_declarations

Listing 1.2   The go.mod File

```
module demo

go 1.19
```

Toolchain

Modules are built into the heart of Go's toolchain and are used to build and manage Go packages. Commands such as go build, go test, and go get have been written to work with modules. As a result, the process of working with modules is transparent to the user.

When, however, you need to work with modules directly, you can use the go mod command to interact with them. The go mod command has a number of sub-commands that can be useful for managing modules. The go help mod command will print a list of these commands, and their uses, as shown in Listing 1.3.

Listing 1.3   The go mod Command

```
$ go help mod

Go mod provides access to operations on modules.

Note that support for modules is built into all the go commands,
not just 'go mod'. For example, day-to-day adding, removing, upgrading,
and downgrading of dependencies should be done using 'go get'.
See 'go help modules' for an overview of module functionality.

Usage:

        go mod <command> [arguments]

The commands are:

        download    download modules to local cache
        edit        edit go.mod from tools or scripts
        graph       print module requirement graph
        init        initialize new module in current directory
        tidy        add missing and remove unused modules
        vendor      make vendored copy of dependencies
        verify      verify dependencies have expected content
        why         explain why packages or modules are needed

Use "go help mod <command>" for more information about a command.

Go Version: go1.19
```

Initializing a Module

To initialize a new module, you can use the go mod init command. This command requires the name of the module and will create a go.mod file in the current directory with that name. Listing 1.4 shows the help output for the go mod init command.

Listing 1.4   The go mod init Command

```
$ go mod help init

usage: go mod init [module-path]

Init initializes and writes a new go.mod file in the current directory, in
effect creating a new module rooted at the current directory. The go.mod file
must not already exist.

Init accepts one optional argument, the module path for the new module. If the
module path argument is omitted, init will attempt to infer the module path
using import comments in .go files, vendoring tool configuration files (like
Gopkg.lock), and the current directory (if in GOPATH).

If a configuration file for a vendoring tool is present, init will attempt to
import module requirements from it.

See https://golang.org/ref/mod#go-mod-init for more about 'go mod init'.
```

```
Go Version: go1.19
```

The name of the module follows the same naming rules as Go packages. In Listing 1.5, we are creating a new module named "demo" using the go mod init command. The result is a go.mod file with the module name "demo."

Listing 1.5   The go.mod File after Running the go mod init Command

```
$ go mod init demo
```

```
module demo

go 1.19
```

VCS and Modules

Nowadays, developers use services like GitHub, GitLab, and Bitbucket to manage their code. As a result, the Go tooling has support for the underlying VCS systems, such as Git and Mercurial, used by these services. This means that you can use the Go tooling to work with modules in these VCS systems.

If you are planning on hosting modules on one of these services, or an internal VCS system, you will most likely want to use a module that can be fetched using the VCS system through the go get command.

For example, if you were to host your module at https://github.com/user/repo, your module name would be github.com/user/repo, as shown in Listing 1.6.

Listing 1.6   The go.mod for a Module Named github.com/user/repo

```
module github.com/user/repo

go 1.19
```

Then you, or someone else, could use the go get command to fetch that module from the VCS system, as shown in Listing 1.7.

Listing 1.7   Using go get to Get the github.com/user/repo Module

```
$ go get github.com/user/repo
```

Packages

A package is a collection of Go files that share the same import path. These files are *almost always* in the same directory as each other, and the directory name is *almost always* the same as the package name.

Consider the folder structure in Listing 1.8 that has two folders, smtp and sound. Each of these folders contains Go source files, .go; therefore, they are considered packages.

Listing 1.8   A Folder Structure with Multiple Go Packages

```
$ tree

.
|__ go.mod
|__ smtp
|   |__ smtp.go
|   '__ template.go
'__ sound
    |__ analyzer.go
    '__ sound.go

2 directories, 5 files
```

Code within a package can reference any identifier, such as a function, variable, or type, within the package, regardless of whether that identifier is exported. Any exported identifier can be used by any other package.

Naming Packages

The name of the package *must* be declared at the top of *every* Go source file using the `package` keyword.

Naming packages[3] properly is very important. The "package" is the fundamental unit of code organization in Go.

There are naming rules, and conventions, for naming packages in Go. Package names are lowercased and should contain only contain letters and numbers. You are not allowed to start package names with a number. Listing 1.9 shows examples of both good and bad package names.

Listing 1.9 Examples of Good and Bad Package Names

```
// Good
package http
package sql
package oauth2
package base64

// Bad
package 1_is_The_loneliest_number
package help!
package structured-query-language
package structuredQueryLanguage
package Structured_Query_Language
```

Short and Simple

First, your package name should be short and descriptive. For example, `sql` is a good package name, but `structured-query-language` is not. The name of your package is going to be used in the import path, so it should be short and simple. Those using your package will also have to use your package name to reference any identifiers within your package. Listing 1.10 shows how awkward it is to use a long package name in your code.

Listing 1.10 Examples of Short and Long Package Names

```
package main

import(
```

(continued)

---

3. https://go.dev/blog/package-names

```
    "sql"
    "structured-query-language"
)

func main() {
    sql.Query("SELECT * FROM users")
    structured-query-language.Query("SELECT * FROM users")
}
```

Abbreviation

To keep package names short, you may have to use an abbreviation. When abbreviating package names, you should make sure that the abbreviation is something that will be easily recognized by the reader of your code. For example, `sql` is a good abbreviation, but `structql` is not.

Naming Conflicts

You want to try to avoid naming conflicts with other packages, although this is not always going to be possible. To help prevent these clashes, you should *always* try to avoid using the names of popular packages already in the Go standard library or names used for popular variables, such as `user`, `conn`, `db`, etc.

Avoid Generic Packages

Don't use generic, or "catch-all" packages, such as `util`, `helpers`, `misc`, etc. These are not good names for packages. They are not descriptive, and they are an open invitation for dumping random code. The contents of these catch-all packages are, more often than not, able to be refactored into more appropriate places.

> Your packages should be focused on the specific functionality and problem space they provide.

Folders, Files, and Organization

With a few exceptions, the name of the folder and the name of the package are the same.

In Listing 1.11, you see a file system containing two folders: `smtp` and `sound`. Each of these folders contains Go code, and each one is its own package. If you look at `sound/sound.go`, Listing 1.12, the folder name is `sound`, and the package name is also `sound`.

Listing 1.11 A Folder Structure with Multiple Go Packages

```
$ tree

.
|__ go.mod
|__ smtp
|    |__ smtp.go
```

```
|    '__ template.go
'__ sound
     |__ analyzer.go
     '__ sound.go

2 directories, 5 files
```

Listing 1.12 The sound Package

```
package sound

// Sound is a package for working with sound.
```

If you look at `smtp/smtp.go`, Listing 1.13, the folder name is `smtp`, and the package name is `smtp`.

Listing 1.13 The smtp Package

```
package smtp

// SMTP is a package for working with SMTP
```

While the folder name and the package name don't always have to match, it is generally a good idea, and idiomatic, to follow this convention. By following this convention, you can easily find the files that belong to a package.

Multiple Packages in a Folder

With rare exceptions, a folder can *only* contain one package. Look at the file structure in Listing 1.14.

Listing 1.14 Listing of Files in a Folder Named good

```
$ tree

.
|__ a.go
'__ b.go

0 directories, 2 files
```

Both of the files in Listing 1.15 declare their package name as good.

Listing 1.15 The `.go` Files in the good Folder

```
package good

// a.go

package good

// b.go
```

Now, look at the file structure in Listing 1.16.

Listing 1.16 Listing of Files in a Folder Named bad

```
$ tree

.
|── a.go
'── b.go

0 directories, 2 files
```

Both of the files in Listing 1.16 *should* declare their package name as bad, but they do not.

If you look at the file, a.go, in Listing 1.17, you can see that the package name is bad. However, b.go, Listing 1.18, declares its package name as sad.

Listing 1.17 Source Code for a.go

```
package bad

// a.go
```

Listing 1.18 The b.go File

```
package sad

// b.go
```

Two different package names are declared in the same folder.

When trying to build the package bad, as shown in Listing 1.19, we get an error telling us that we cannot build the package bad because two different files have declared different package names.

Listing 1.19   Building the bad Package

```
$ go build .

found packages bad (a.go) and sad (b.go) in .

Go Version: go1.19
```

All files within the same directory/package have to have the same `package` name in the file.

File Names

File names are less strict than package names. The convention is to use lowercase letters and underscores, as shown in Listing 1.20.

Listing 1.20   Examples of Good and Bad File Names

```
$ tree

.
|__ bad
|     |__ ServiceManagerTest.go
|     |__ USER_test.go
|     |__ User.go
|     '__ serviceManager.go
|__ go.mod
'__ good
      |__ service_manager.go
      |__ service_manager_test.go
      |__ user.go
      '__ user_test.go

2 directories, 9 files
```

Package Organization

There are a lot of different ways to organize packages in Go. A quick Internet search returns numerous blog posts, articles, and conference presentations that discuss the various ways to organize packages in Go. All of these ways have their pros and cons. These patterns are often extracted from one particular use case that worked well for the author in that case. However, not everyone is writing the same applications and libraries, so there can't be any one best way to organize packages.

When organizing packages, you should consider the following important factors:

- Code organization
- Documentation
- Maintainability
- Reusability
- Testing

Focus

Packages should be singularly focused. For example, if you have a package that contains tools for working with time and for working with HTTP, then that package should be split into two packages: one for time and one for HTTP. Now the packages have a clear, singular purpose.

API Scope

Package APIs should be clean, simple, and easy to use. Export only the most necessary identifiers, such as types, functions, and variables. It is always easier to expose more of a package's API later than it is to hide it after it's been exposed and is in use.

File Organization

Package files should be organized in a way that is clear and obvious to the reader. Avoid using one or two large files for a package. Instead, break the package into smaller files, with each having a clear purpose.

If you look at the file in Listing 1.21, you can see that the file contains three different type definitions and their methods. This file is difficult to read, and, as the file grows, it will become even more difficult to read and maintain.

Listing 1.21   The bad.go File

```go
package bad

import "sync"

type User struct {
    Name string
}

func NewOrder(u User) *Order {
    return &Order{
        User: u,
    }
}
```

```go
type Order struct {
    User
    products []Product
    sync.Mutex
}

type Product struct {
    Name string
    Cost int
}

func (p Product) String() string {
    return p.Name
}

func (o *Order) AddProduct(p Product) {
    o.Lock()
    o.products = append(o.products, p)
    o.Unlock()
}

func (u User) String() string {
    return u.Name
}
```

If, instead, we split the code into more files, Listing 1.22, one for each of the types declared, then you can see that each file is now easier to read and maintain. In addition, the file names are now clear and easy to understand, which makes finding the code you need that much easier.

Listing 1.22   The good Folder and Its Files

```
$ tree

.
|-- order.go
|-- order_test.go
|-- product.go
|-- product_test.go
|-- user.go
'-- user_test.go
0 directories, 6 files
```

(continued)

```go
package good

import "sync"

type Order struct {
    User
    products []Product
    sync.Mutex
}

func NewOrder(u User) *Order {
    return &Order{
        User: u,
    }
}

func (o *Order) AddProduct(p Product) {
    o.Lock()
    o.products = append(o.products, p)
    o.Unlock()
}

package good

type Product struct {
    Name string
    Cost int
}

func (p Product) String() string {
    return p.Name
}
```

```go
package good

type User struct {
    Name string
}

func (u User) String() string {
    return u.Name
}
```

Organizing your code into smaller files that have clear and specific purposes will make it easier to navigate your project as it grows. It will also make it easier for developers new to your project to find the code they are looking for.

Importing Packages and Modules

When writing code, you often need support from other modules or packages. These can be third-party modules from a source such as GitHub, another package within the same module, or a package from the standard library.

Import Path

The import path for a package is the relative path from the module root to the package directory. The import path for a package, or module, always starts with a module name.

Consider the folder structure in Listing 1.23.

Listing 1.23   Listing of Files in a Folder Named names

```
$ tree


.
|－－ cmd
|    '－－ main.go
|－－ foo
|    '－－ foo.go
'－－ go.mod

2 directories, 3 files
```

The file foo.go, Listing 1.24, is in a package called foo and exports a function, Greet().

Listing 1.24   The foo.go File

```
package foo

import "fmt"

func Greet() {
    fmt.Println("Hello, world!")
}
```

The `main.go` file, Listing 1.25, is in the `main` package but still in the same module. The `main` package has to import the `foo` package by its fully qualified import path.

Listing 1.25   The `main.go` File

```
package main

// import the foo package using
// its fully qualified name
// starting with the module name
import "github.com/user/repo/foo"

func main() {
    foo.Greet()
}
```

Using Imports

The `import` keyword is used along with the fully qualified package name to import, as shown in Listing 1.26.

Listing 1.26   Importing Multiple Packages

```
import "time"
import "os/exec"
import "github.com/user/repo/foo"
```

Multiple import statements can be condensed into a single import statement, as shown in Listing 1.27.

Listing 1.27   Condensing Import Statements for Multiple Packages

```
import (
    "time"
    "os/exec"
    "github.com/user/repo/foo"
)
```

Resolving Import Name Clashes

It is not uncommon to run into a naming collision between two packages with the same name when importing. Consider Listing 1.28.

Listing 1.28   Listing of Files in the demo Module

```
$ tree

.
|-- bar
|   '-- bar.go
|-- cmd
|   '-- main.go
|-- foo
|   '-- bar
|       '-- bar.go
'-- go.mod

4 directories, 4 files
```

There are two packages named `bar` in the `demo` module.

The `demo/bar` package defines a `Bar` type, Listing 1.29. This package would be imported as `demo/bar` and would be accessed within our code as `bar`, such as `bar.Bar`.

Listing 1.29   The bar/bar.go File

```
package bar

type Bar struct{}
```

The `demo/foo/bar` package defines a `Pub` type, Listing 1.30. This package would be imported as `demo/foo/bar` and would be accessed within our code as `bar`, such as `bar.Pub`.

Listing 1.30   The foo/bar/bar.go File

```
package bar

type Pub struct{}
```

If we try to import these packages into our code, Listing 1.31, Go will not be able to resolve the naming collision, and the compilation will fail.

Listing 1.31   Trying to Build a Program with a Naming Collision

```
package main

import (
    "demo/bar"
```

(continued)

```
        "demo/foo/bar"
)
func main() {
    var _ bar.Pub
    var _ bar.Bar
}
```

```
$ go build ./...

# demo/cmd
cmd/main.go:5:2: bar redeclared in this block
        cmd/main.go:4:2: other declaration of bar
cmd/main.go:5:2: imported and not used: "demo/foo/bar"
cmd/main.go:9:12: undefined: bar.Pub

Go Version: go1.19
```

We can fix this collision by using an import alias for one, or both, of the packages. In this case, we can alias the demo/foo/bar package to pub when importing. This will allow us to import the demo/bar package as bar and the demo/foo/bar package (see Listing 1.32) as pub and avoid the naming collision.

Listing 1.32   Successfully Building the Application

```
package main

import (
    "demo/bar"
    pub "demo/foo/bar"
)

func main() {
    var _ pub.Pub
    var _ bar.Bar
}
```

```
$ go build ./...

Go Version: go1.19
```

Dependencies

Although the Go standard library is a great starting point for building applications, it is not uncommon to reach out to other libraries to get the functionality you need. Go modules were designed to make it easy to import and use third-party libraries.

Additionally, Go modules allow for reliably reproducible builds.

Using a Dependency

Consider the application in Listing 1.33.

Listing 1.33 The `main.go` File

```
package main

import (
    "fmt"

    "github.com/gobuffalo/flect"
)

func main() {
    s := "Hello, World!"
    d := flect.Dasherize(s)
    fmt.Println(s, d)
}
```

The application imports the `github.com/gobuffalo/flect`[4] package, which provides a set of utilities for manipulating strings. In particular, the application is using the `flect.Dasherize`[5] function to convert a string to be lowercase and hyphenated, as shown in Listing 1.34.

Listing 1.34 The `flect.Dasherize` Function

```
$ go doc github.com/gobuffalo/flect.Dasherize

package flect // import "github.com/gobuffalo/flect"

func Dasherize(s string) string
    Dasherize returns an alphanumeric, lowercased, dashed string

        Donald E. Knuth = donald-e-knuth
        Test with + sign = test-with-sign
        admin/WidgetID = admin-widget-id

Go Version: go1.19
```

If we try to run the application, however, we will get a compilation error, as in Listing 1.35.

---

4. https://pkg.go.dev/github.com/gobuffalo/flect
5. https://pkg.go.dev/github.com/gobuffalo/flect#Dasherize

Listing 1.35   Error Trying to Compile Listing 1.33

```
$ go run main.go

main.go:6:2: no required module provides package github.com/gobuffalo/flect;
        to add it: go get github.com/gobuffalo/flect

Go Version: go1.19
```

The error tells us that no required module provides the github.com/gobuffalo/flect package. If we look at the go.mod file, Listing 1.36, we see that we are not requiring the github.com/gobuffalo/flect package in our module.

Listing 1.36   The go.mod File Accompanying Listing 1.33

```
module demo

go 1.19
```

Requiring with Go Get

To add dependencies to our module, we can use the go get command, Listing 1.37.

Listing 1.37   The go get Command

```
$ go help get

usage: go get [-t] [-u] [-v] [build flags] [packages]

Get resolves its command-line arguments to packages at specific module
versions, updates go.mod to require those versions, and downloads source code
into the module cache.

To add a dependency for a package or upgrade it to its latest version:

        go get example.com/pkg

To upgrade or downgrade a package to a specific version:

        go get example.com/pkg@v1.2.3

To remove a dependency on a module and downgrade modules that require it:

        go get example.com/mod@none
```

See https://golang.org/ref/mod#go-get for details.

In earlier versions of Go, 'go get' was used to build and install packages.
Now, 'go get' is dedicated to adjusting dependencies in go.mod. 'go install'
may be used to build and install commands instead. When a version is specified,
'go install' runs in module-aware mode and ignores the go.mod file in the
current directory. For example:

```
        go install example.com/pkg@v1.2.3
        go install example.com/pkg@latest
```

See 'go help install' or https://golang.org/ref/mod#go-install for details.

'go get' accepts the following flags.

The -t flag instructs get to consider modules needed to build tests of
packages specified on the command line.

The -u flag instructs get to update modules providing dependencies
of packages named on the command line to use newer minor or patch
releases when available.

The -u=patch flag (not -u patch) also instructs get to update dependencies,
but changes the default to select patch releases.

When the -t and -u flags are used together, get will update test
dependencies as well.

The -x flag prints commands as they are executed. This is useful for
debugging version control commands when a module is downloaded directly
from a repository.

For more about modules, see https://golang.org/ref/mod.

For more about specifying packages, see 'go help packages'.

This text describes the behavior of get using modules to manage source
code and dependencies. If instead the go command is running in GOPATH
mode, the details of get's flags and effects change, as does 'go help get'.
See 'go help gopath-get'.

See also: go build, go install, go clean, go mod.

Go Version: go1.19

When we use the go get command, Listing 1.38, the go.mod file is updated to include the dependency, its version, and any other dependencies that it requires.

Listing 1.38   The go.mod File after Adding the github.com/gobuffalo/flect Package

```
$ go get github.com/gobuffalo/flect
```
```
Go Version: go1.19
```
```
module demo
```
go 1.19
```
require github.com/gobuffalo/flect v0.2.5
```

In Listing 1.39, we see the application now compiles and runs without errors.

Listing 1.39   Successfully Running Listing 1.33

```
$ go run main.go
```
```
Hello, World! hello-world
```
```
Go Version: go1.19
```

The Go Sum File

When adding a third-party dependency to the module, the Go toolchain will generate and manage a go.sum file. See Listing 1.40.

Listing 1.40   File Structure for an Application with External Dependencies

```
$ tree

.
|__ go.mod
|__ go.sum
'__ main.go

0 directories, 3 files
```

The go.sum file contains a list of all the dependencies, direct and indirect, that are required by the module. Additionally, the go.sum file contains a hash of the source code and go.mod file for each dependency. The go.sum file in Listing 1.41 shows the dependencies and their checksums after importing a third-party dependency.

Listing 1.41   The go.sum File for the Listing 1.33 Application

```
github.com/davecgh/go-spew v1.1.0 h1:ZDRjVQ15GmhC3fiQ8ni8+
➥OwkZQ04DARzQgrnXU1Liz8=
github.com/davecgh/go-spew v1.1.0/go.mod h1:J7Y8YcW2NihsgmVo/mv31Awl/
➥skON4iLHjSsI+c5H38=
github.com/gobuffalo/flect v0.2.5 h1:H6vvsv2an0lalEaCDRThvtBfmg44W/QHXBCYUXf/
➥6S4=
github.com/gobuffalo/flect v0.2.5/go.mod h1:
➥1ZyCLIbg0YD7sDkzvFdPoOydPtD8y9JQnrOROolUcM8=
github.com/pmezard/go-difflib v1.0.0 h1:4DBwDE0NGyQoBHbLQYPwSUPoCMWR5BEzIk/
➥f11ZbAQM=
github.com/pmezard/go-difflib v1.0.0/go.mod h1:
➥iKH77koFhYxTK1pcRnkKkqfTogsbg7gZNVY4sRDYZ/4=
github.com/stretchr/objx v0.1.0/go.mod h1:HFkY916IF+
➥rwdDfMAkV7OtwuqBVzrE8GR6GFx+wExME=
github.com/stretchr/testify v1.7.0 h1:
➥nwc3DEeHmmLAfoZucVR881uASkOMfjw8xYJ99tb5CcY=
github.com/stretchr/testify v1.7.0/go.mod h1:
➥6Fq8oRcR53rry900zMqJjRRixrwX3KX962/h/Wwjteg=
gopkg.in/check.v1 v0.0.0-20161208181325-20d25e280405/go.mod h1:
➥Co6ibVJAznAaIkqp8huTwlJQCZ016jof/cbN4VW5Yz0=
gopkg.in/yaml.v3 v3.0.0-20200313102051-9f266ea9e77c h1:
➥dUUwHk2QECo/6vqA44rthZ8ie2QXMNeKRTHCNY2nXvo=
gopkg.in/yaml.v3 v3.0.0-20200313102051-9f266ea9e77c/go.mod h1:
➥K4uyk7z7BCEPqu6E+C64Yfv1cQ7kz7rIZviUmN+EgEM=
```

The go.sum file should be checked into version control. The go.sum acts both as a security measure to prevent malicious code from being added to the module and as a source of truth for the dependencies that are required by the module.

> The go.sum file is managed by the Go toolchain and should *not* be modified by the module author.

Updating Dependencies

To update a direct dependency of our module, we can use the go get command, Listing 1.42, with the -u flag.

Listing 1.42   Updating a Dependency with go get

```
$ go get -u github.com/gobuffalo/flect
```

When we use the go get command with the -u flag, the go.mod and go.sum files are updated to include the dependency, its version, and any other dependencies that it requires.

If we want to update all direct dependencies of our module, we can use the go `get` command with the `-u` flag, Listing 1.43, without specifying a dependency.

Listing 1.43   Updating All Dependencies with go `get`

```
$ go get -u
```

Semantic Versioning

Go modules are versioned using semantic versioning.[6] For example, `v1.2.3` is a semantic version that tells us the major version of the release, `1`, the minor version of the release, `2`, and the patch version of the release, `3`.

In addition to semantic versioning, Go modules also include a concept known as semantic import versioning.[7] When a breaking change is introduced in a module, that module should increase its major version by 1. For example, if the module is currently on `v1.2.3`, and a breaking change is introduced in the module, the module should now be tagged as `v2.0.0`.

Semantic import versioning states that if your major version changes, the import path to that new version should also change.

Consider the example in Listing 1.44.

Listing 1.44   A Module That Imports a Third-Party Module

```
package foo

import "github.com/user/repo"
```

When we import the `github.com/user/repo` package, Go modules will automatically find the latest version of the package that is less than `v2.0.0` and use that version. For example, if the latest version of the package is `v1.2.3`, the import path should be `github.com/user/repo`.

If the `github.com/user/repo` module is updated to `v2.0.0`, then we need to change the import path to reflect the new version, as shown in Listing 1.45.

Listing 1.45   Importing a Module Using Semantic Import Versioning

```
package foo

import "github.com/user/repo/v2"
```

---

6. https://semver.org/
7. https://research.swtch.com/vgo–import

Multiple Versions

Because of semantic import versioning, we can have multiple versions of a package in our module.

Consider Listing 1.46. We are importing two versions of the `github.com/gofrs/uuid`[8] package: the first version is `v1.x.x`, and the second version is `v3.x.x`.

When importing the two, we can assign import aliases to the two versions to allow us to use them side by side.

Listing 1.46 Importing Two Versions of the `github.com/gofrs/uuid` Package

```
package main

import (
    "fmt"
    "log"

    one "github.com/gofrs/uuid"
    three "github.com/gofrs/uuid/v3"
)

func main() {
    id1 := one.NewV4()
    fmt.Println(id1)

    id3, err := three.NewV4()
    if err != nil {
        log.Fatal(err)
    }
    fmt.Println(id3)
}
```

The `go.mod` file in Listing 1.47, for Listing 1.46, shows the specific versions for each module being used in our application.

Listing 1.47 The `go.mod` File for the Listing 1.46 Application

```
module demo

go 1.19

require (
    github.com/gofrs/uuid v1.0.0
    github.com/gofrs/uuid/v3 v3.1.2
)
```

8. https://pkg.go.dev/github.com/gofrs/uuid

Finally, as you can see from Listing 1.48, we are able to use both versions of the package side by side and generate different UUIDs.

Listing 1.48   Output from the Listing 1.46 Application

```
$ go run main.go

939addf2-66a1-4d17-ac0b-7e02d1fd06f8
aad010af-ac3f-429e-8a78-bd4b964e09e3
```
```
Go Version: go1.19
```

Cyclical Imports

Care must be take to avoid cyclical imports. Cyclical imports can cause a package to import itself, which is not allowed by the Go language.

Consider the Go module in Listing 1.49.

Listing 1.49   Listing of Files in a Go Module

```
$ tree

.
|__ bar
|    '__ bar.go
|__ foo
|    '__ foo.go
'__ go.mod

2 directories, 3 files
```

In the bar package, the function `Convert`, Listing 1.50, takes a `foo.Foo` as a parameter and returns a `Bar`. The bar package imports `demo/foo` to be able to use the `Foo` type.

Listing 1.50   The `bar.go` File and the `Convert` Function

```
package bar

import "demo/foo"

type Bar int

func Convert(f foo.Foo) Bar {
```

```
    return Bar(f)
}
```

In the `foo` package, we create a type alias[9] called `Foo` that is an alias of the `bar.Bar` type. The `foo` package imports `demo/bar` to be able to use the `Bar` type, as shown in Listing 1.51.

Listing 1.51   The Foo Type

```
package foo

import "demo/bar"

type Foo = bar.Bar
```

The result, Listing 1.52, is a cyclical import as the two packages are dependent on each other.

Listing 1.52   Trying to Build a Program with Cyclical Imports

```
$ go build ./...

package demo/bar
        imports demo/foo
        imports demo/bar: import cycle not allowed

Go Version: go1.19
```

Summary

In this chapter, we shared that packages are the unit of code that can be imported into other packages. We discussed good and bad package names, as well as various strategies for file organization and naming. We explained the Go module system and how you can use it to manage your application's dependencies. Finally, we discussed how to resolve import issues such as cyclic dependencies and conflicting package names.

---

9. https://golang.org/ref/spec#Type_declarations

2

Go Language Basics

In this chapter, we begin by understanding the basics of the Go language. We cover topics such as variable declaration, the type system, built-in data types, and the basic control flow constructs of the language.

While some of this material might be familiar to you already, we *strongly* recommend you read through all of the material carefully. Properly understanding these basics is necessary to getting the most out of this book.

Go Language Overview

Go is a statically typed,[1] garbage collected,[2] compiled[3] language that is capable of producing highly concurrent, thread-safe programs that will scale as needed. Go binaries are statically linked and self-contained. This means they don't need any runtime or development libraries to run. These binaries can be compiled to run a variety of architectures and operating systems.

Static Typing

In a statically typed language, each statement in the program is checked at compile time, when the binary is built, rather than at runtime. It also means that the data type is bound to the variable. In dynamically typed languages, the data type is bound to the value.

For example, in Go, Listing 2.1, when declaring a new variable, you must also define the type of the variable (int, string, bool, etc.).

Listing 2.1   Example of a Variable Declaration in Go

```
var pi float64 = 3.14 // pi is a float64
var week int = 7      // week is an int
```

---

1. https://en.wikipedia.org/wiki/Type_system#Static_type_checking
2. https://bit.ly/3AyIn0Y
3. https://en.wikipedia.org/wiki/Compiled_language

In a dynamically typed language, such as PHP,[4] Listing 2.2, the data type is bound to the value and not the variable. When a new value is assigned to a variable, the data type of the variable is inferred from the value.

Listing 2.2   Example of a Variable Declaration in PHP

```
$s = "gopher";        // $s is a string
$s = 123;             // $s is now an integer
```

Garbage Collection

Managing memory and applications can be tedious, and many times they are a source of bugs in programs. Because of this, Go employs the use of a garbage collector to manage memory. This means that developers do not need to explicitly allocate and deallocate memory for storing variables.

Instead, developers use a garbage collector to monitor the program's memory usage. The garbage collector periodically determines which memory is still in use, and which is not, and releases the memory that is no longer being used by the program.

Although using a garbage collector makes it easier for you to write code because you don't need to be concerned about managing memory, there is a cost in terms of performance. As you generate more memory usage (or "garbage"), the garbage collector needs to spend time releasing that memory later. This is time that your program will not be spent running the business logic. As such, excessive garbage can lead to poorly performing programs.

Since Go runtime provides little in the way of controlling garbage collection, you need to know some basic concepts about how Go identifies memory as garbage and when it may impact your program's performance.

Many articles and conference talks have been devoted to the Go garbage collector over the years. The reason is the Go garbage collector is continually being improved and tuned with each new release of Go.

As you move through this book, you will find little talk of memory management or the garbage collector. We instead focus on the concepts of the Go language, stopping where necessary to discuss memory. Such is the case when we discuss pointers later in Chapter 6.

Compilation

Before a Go program can be executed, you must first compile it. This varies from interpreted languages, such as Ruby,[5] where code is being interrupted, and executed, at runtime.

---

4. https://en.wikipedia.org/wiki/PHP
5. https://bit.ly/3rRrnPS

Traditionally, compiled languages such as C[6] and C++[7] take a long time to compile a large program. As a result, getting immediate feedback to program changes was a lot more difficult. Interrupted languages helped in this respect by featuring no upfront compilation time. The downside is that the program is not as fast as it could be because each line of code is being executed at runtime. With interpreted languages, you also lose the ability to know before you go to production that you are about to run a program that might crash because of a typo.

One of the original design goals behind the Go language was fast compile times. The advantage of this is that it allows you to get immediate feedback to program changes and retain the benefits of a compiled language.

Consider a simple Go program, Listing 2.3, that attempts to add two different types together, such as int and string.

Listing 2.3   A Go Program That Attempts to Add Two Different Types Together

```go
package main

import "fmt"

func main() {
    fmt.Println("Hello, World!")
    x := 1 + "one"
}
```

Before this code can be executed, it must first be compiled. This is done by the go build command, which we explore in greater detail later. When we attempt to compile the program, Listing 2.4, we are given an error informing us that we cannot add the two types together.

Listing 2.4   An Error When Trying to Compile Listing 2.3

```
$ go build .

# demo
./main.go:7:7: invalid operation: 1 + "one"
➥(mismatched types untyped int and untyped string)

Go Version: go1.19
```

Now, consider a similar Ruby program, Listing 2.5, that does the same thing. The difference is that this code won't be checked until it is being run by the end user.

---

6. https://bit.ly/3r4XbBI
7. https://en.wikipedia.org/wiki/C%2B%2B

Listing 2.5   A Ruby Program That Attempts to Add Two Different Types Together

```
puts "Hello, World!"
s = 1 + "one"
```

It is only when we attempt to run the program, Listing 2.6, that we get an error, which ripples back to the user.

Listing 2.6   An Error When Trying to Run Listing 2.5

```
$ ruby main.rb

Hello, World!

main.rb:2:in '+': String can't be coerced into Integer (TypeError)
        from main.rb:2:in '<main>'
```

Keywords, Operators, and Delimiters

As with all programming languages, Go features a selection of keywords that are reserved by the language and cannot be used as an identifier, such as a variable name, in the program. Following is a list of keywords in Go that are reserved and may not be used as identifiers:

any	default	func	interface	select
break	defer	go	map	struct
case	else	goto	package	switch
chan	fallthrough	if	range	type
const	for	import	return	var
continue				

The following is a list of the operators[8] (including assignment operators[9]) and punctuation in Go:

+	&	+=	&=	&&	==	!=	(	)
-	|	-=	|=	||	<	<=	[	]
*	^	*=	^=	<-	>	>=	{	}
/	<<	/=	<<=	++	=	:=	,	;
%	>>	%=	>>=	--	!	...	.	:
	&^		&^=					

---

8. https://golang.org/ref/spec#Operators
9. https://golang.org/ref/spec#assign_op

You find out more about many of these operators and keywords as you move through this book.

Numbers

Go has two types of numeric types. The first type is an architecture-independent type. This means that regardless of the architecture you compile for, the type will have the correct size, bytes, for your type. The second type is an implementation-specific type, and the byte size of that numeric type can vary based on the architecture the program is built for.

Go has a number of architecture-independent numeric types, shown in the following list:

```
uint8       unsigned  8-bit integers (0 to 255)
uint16      unsigned 16-bit integers (0 to 65535)
uint32      unsigned 32-bit integers (0 to 4294967295)
uint64      unsigned 64-bit integers (0 to 18446744073709551615)
int8        signed  8-bit integers (-128 to 127)
int16       signed 16-bit integers (-32768 to 32767)
int32       signed 32-bit integers (-2147483648 to 2147483647)
int64       signed 64-bit integers (-9223372036854775808 to
            ➥9223372036854775807)
float32     IEEE-754 32-bit floating-point numbers (+- 10-45 -> +- 3.4 * 1038)
float64     IEEE-754 64-bit floating-point numbers (+- 5 * 10-324 -> 1.7 *
            ➥10308)
complex64   complex numbers with float32 real and imaginary parts
complex128  complex numbers with float64 real and imaginary parts
byte        alias for uint8
rune        alias for int32
```

As mentioned earlier, in addition to the implementation-specific numeric types, Go has a couple of architecture implementation-specific types, listed here:

```
uint     either 32 or 64 bits
int      same size as uint
uintptr  an unsigned integer large enough to store the uninterpreted bits
         ➥of a pointer value
```

Implementation-specific types have their size defined by the architecture the program is compiled for. For example, on a 64-bit architecture, uint will be 64 bits and int will be 64 bits, whereas on a 32-bit architecture, uint will be 32 bits and int will be 32 bits.

Picking the Correct Numeric Type

In Go, picking the correct type[10] usually has more to do with performance for the target architecture you are programming for than the size of the data you are working with. However, without needing to know the specific ramifications of performance for your program, you can follow some basic guidelines when first starting out.

For integer data, it's common in Go to use the implementation types like int or uint. This typically results in the fastest processing speed for your target architecture.

If you know you won't exceed a specific size range, picking an architecture-independent type can both increase speed and decrease memory usage. Integer types come in two flavors: int and uint. An int is a signed integer, meaning it can store positive and negative numbers. An uint, on the other hand, is an unsigned integer, meaning it can only store positive numbers. The following list shows some examples of integer types in Go:

```
int8 (-128 -> 127)
int16 (-32768 -> 32767)
int32 (- 2,147,483,648 -> 2,147,483,647)
int64 (- 9,223,372,036,854,775,808 -> 9,223,372,036,854,775,807)

uint8 (with alias byte, 0 -> 255)
uint16 (0 -> 65,535)
uint32 (0 -> 4,294,967,295)
uint64 (0 -> 18,446,744,073,709,551,615)
```

Floats are available in two flavors: float32 and float64. float32 is a 32-bit floating point number, and float64 is a 64-bit floating point number. Here are a couple of examples:

```
float32 (+- 10-45 -> +- 3.4 * 1038 )
(IEEE-754) float64 (+- 5 * 10-324 -> 1.7 * 10308 )
```

Now that we have looked at some of the possible ranges for numeric data types, we can show you how they will be affected if you exceed those ranges in your program.

Overflow versus Wraparound

Go has several numeric data types. For integer data types, there are boundaries to what the maximum and minimum values can be. Because of this, when performing mathematical calculations on these data types, there is a potential to either "overflow" a number or "wraparound" a number.

---

10. https://golang.org/ref/spec#Types

At compile time, if the compiler can determine a value will be too large to hold in the data type specified, it will throw an overflow error. This means that the value you calculated to store is too large for the data type you specified.

Consider Listing 2.7, which has a uint8 data type that is already set to its maximum value of 255.

Listing 2.7 An uint8 That Is Already at Maximum Capacity

```
func main() {
    var maxUint8 uint8 = 255 // Max Uint8 size
    fmt.Println("value:", maxUint8)
}
```

```
$ go run .

value: 255
```

```
Go Version: go1.19
```

In Listing 2.8, we are adding 5 to the uint8 value of 255 *after* the variable has been declared.

Listing 2.8 An uint8 That Is Already at Maximum Capacity but Is Then Incremented by 5

```
func main() {
    var maxUint8 uint8 = 255 // Max Uint8 size
    fmt.Println("value:", maxUint8+5)
}
```

As shown in Listing 2.9, the output unexpectedly shows the value as 4 instead of 260. This is an example of "wraparound."

Listing 2.9 Incrementing an uint8

```
$ go run .

value: 4
```

```
Go Version: go1.19
```

In Listing 2.10, we are assigning a value *greater* than that of maximum capacity to the uint8 data type.

Listing 2.10   Overflowing a uint8

```
func main() {
    var maxUint8 uint8 = 260
    fmt.Println("value:", maxUint8)
}
```

The compiler can determine that the given value will not fit into the uint8 and will throw an overflow error, Listing 2.11.

Listing 2.11   Compilation Error Compiling Listing 2.10

```
$ go run .

# demo
./main.go:7:23: cannot use 260 (untyped int constant)
↪as uint8 value in variable declaration (overflows)
```

```
Go Version: go1.19
```

Based on the previous examples, you can see that an overflow happens if the compiler can determine the value when compiling the code. However, a wraparound only happens at runtime because the compiler doesn't know the resulting value, leaving the runtime to properly handle the calculation. Understanding the boundaries of your data helps you avoid potential bugs in your program in the future.

Saturation

Go does not saturate[11] variables during mathematical operations such as addition or multiplication. In languages that saturate, if you have a uint8 with a max value of 255 and add 1, the value is still the max (saturated) value of 255.

In Go, however, it always wraps around, as shown in Listing 2.12.

Listing 2.12   Demonstrating Lack of Saturation in Go

```
func main() {
    var maxUint8 uint8 = 11
    maxUint8 = maxUint8 * 25
    fmt.Println("value:", maxUint8)
}
```

---

11. https://en.wikipedia.org/wiki/Saturation_arithmetic

```
$ go run .

value: 19
```

```
Go Version: go1.19
```

Strings

A string is a sequence of one or more characters (letters, numbers, symbols) that can be either a constant or a variable. Strings exist within either back quotes (`) or double quotes (") in Go and have different characteristics depending on which quotes you use.

If you use the back quotes, you are creating a raw string literal. If you use the double quotes, you are creating an interpreted string literal.

Interpreted String Literals

Interpreted string literals are character sequences between double quotes, as in "bar". Within the quotes, any character may appear except newline and unescaped double quote.

You will almost always use interpreted string literals because they allow for escape characters, such as \t and \n, as shown in Listing 2.13.

Listing 2.13 Interpreted String Literals

```
package main

import "fmt"

func main() {
    a := "Say \"hello\"\n\t\tto Go!\n\n\nHi!"
    fmt.Println(a)
}
```

```
$ go run .

Say "hello"
            to Go!


Hi!
```

```
Go Version: go1.19
```

Raw String Literals

Raw string literals are character sequences between back quotes, often called back ticks. Within the quotes, any character may appear except a back quote. Listing 2.14 shows an example.

Listing 2.14   Raw String Literals

```go
package main

import "fmt"

func main() {
    a := 'Say "hello" to Go!'
    fmt.Println(a)
}
```

Backslashes have no special meaning inside of raw string literals. For example, trying to insert newline or tab characters will not work, as shown in Listing 2.15. Those characters will be interpreted as part of the string.

Listing 2.15   Raw String Literals with Escape Characters

```go
package main

import "fmt"

func main() {
    a := 'Say "hello"\n\t\tto Go!\n\n\nHi!'
    fmt.Println(a)
}
```

```
$ go run .

Say "hello"\n\t\tto Go!\n\n\nHi!

Go Version: go1.19
```

Raw string literals can be used to create multiline strings, unlike interpreted string literals. This makes raw string literals very useful for creating multiline templates, mock JSON data for testing, and so on. In Listing 2.16, we are using a multiline string literal to create JSON content for testing.

Listing 2.16   Raw String Literals with Multiline Strings

```
package main

import "fmt"

func main() {
    a := '# json data for testing
{
    "id": 1,
    "name": "Janis",
    "email": "pearl@example.com"
}
'

    fmt.Println(a)
}
```

```
$ go run .

# json data for testing
{
    "id": 1,
    "name": "Janis",
    "email": "pearl@example.com"
}

Go Version: go1.19
```

UTF-8

Go supports UTF-8[12] characters out of the box, without any special setup, libraries, or packages. In Listing 2.17, we are using English characters for the word "Hello" and Chinese characters for "World." In this example, Go is simply printing the output to the console. In the "Iterating over UTF-8 Characters" section, you see how Go is able to properly iterate correctly over both the English and Chinese characters.

Listing 2.17   A Simple Program That Prints the String "Hello, 世界"

```
func main() {
    a := "Hello, 世界"
```

(continued)

---

12. https://en.wikipedia.org/wiki/UTF-8

```
    fmt.Println(a)
}
```

```
$ go run .

Hello, 世界
```

```
Go Version: go1.19
```

Runes

A rune is an alias for `int32` and is used to represent individual characters. A rune can be made up of 1 to 3 `int32` values. This allows for both single and multibyte characters. A rune can be defined using the single quote (') character. In Listing 2.18, we are creating a new rune from the letter A. Then we print the value of the rune using the `%v` formatting verb. Finally, we print the type of the rune using the `%T` formatting verb.

Listing 2.18   Printing Information about a rune

```
func main() {
    a := 'A'
    fmt.Printf("%v (%T)\n", a, a)
}
```

When printed as a value, a `rune` will be printed as an `int32` corresponding to the UTF-8 encoding of the character,[13] Listing 2.19.

Listing 2.19   Printing a rune as an `int32`

```
$ go run .

65 (int32)
```

```
Go Version: go1.19
```

Iterating over UTF-8 Characters

When iterating over a string, Listing 2.20, and trying to access individual characters, you encounter issues with UTF-8 characters, if you're not careful. One approach is to use a traditional `for` loop, where you iterate over the string's bytes.

---

13. https://www.charset.org/utf-8

Listing 2.20 Iterating over Each Character in a UTF-8 String

```
func main() {
    a := "Hello, 世界" // 9 characters (including the space and comma)
    for i := 0; i < len(a); i++ {
        fmt.Printf("%d: %s\n", i, string(a[i]))
    }
}
```

However, when iterating this way, Listing 2.21, the output is unpredictable.

Listing 2.21 Unpredictable Output When Iterating Characters in a UTF-8 String

```
$ go run .

0: H
1: e
2: l
3: l
4: o
5: ,
6:
7: ä
8: ,
9: ▯
10: ç
11: ▯
12: ▯

Go Version: go1.19
```

Notice the unexpected characters in Listing 2.21 that were printed for index 7-12. This is because we were taking part of the rune as an int32, not the entire set of int32's that make up the rune.

When iterating through each character in a string in Go, the proper way is to use the range keyword in the loop, Listing 2.22.

Listing 2.22 Properly Iterating over Each Character in a UTF-8 String

```
a := "Hello, 世界"
for i, c := range a {
    fmt.Printf("%d: %s\n", i, string(c))
}
```

(continued)

```
$ go run .

0: H
1: e
2: l
3: l
4: o
5: ,
6:
7: 世
10: 界

Go Version: go1.19
```

The `range` keyword ensures that we use the proper index and length of `int32s` to capture the proper rune value. We discuss the `range` keyword in more detail later in Chapter 4.

Variables

In Go, there are several ways to declare and initialize a variable. In some cases, there is more than one way to declare the exact same variable and value. Each method of declaration or initialization has its own place in the Go language.

Variable Declaration

Go is a statically typed language, meaning that the type of a variable is known at compile time. This means that the type of a variable must be specified when the variable is declared. New variables can be declared with the `var` keyword and given a name and a type. In Go, when you declare a variable or ask for an argument to a function, the name of the variable comes first, followed by the type of the variable: `var <name> <type>`. In Listing 2.23, we are creating four variables all using this same pattern. For example, `var i int` is declaring a new variable, named `i`, that is of type `int`.

Listing 2.23   Declaring Variables in Go

```
func main() {
    // var
    var i int     // declare i as an int
    var f float64 // declare f as a float64
    var b bool    // declare b as a bool
    var s string  // declare s as a string
}
```

Variable Assignment

Once a variable has been declared, any value of the variable's type can be assigned to it using the = operator, Listing 2.24.

Listing 2.24 Assigning Values to Variables in Go

```
func main() {
    var i int      // declare i as an int
    var f float64 // declare f as a float64
    var b bool     // declare b as a bool
    var s string   // declare s as a string

    i = 42              // assign 42 to i
    f = 3.14            // assign 3.14 to f
    b = true            // assign true to b
    s = "hello world" // assign "hello world" to s
}
```

When trying to assign a value to a variable that is not the same type as the value being assigned, Listing 2.25, the compiler reports an error.

Listing 2.25 Assigning Value to a Variable That Is Not the Same Type as the Value Being Assigned

```
func main() {
    var i int      // declare i as an int
    var f float64  // declare f as a float64
    var b bool     // declare b as a bool
    var s string   // declare s as a string


    i = "42"
    f = true
    b = 3.14
    s = 42
}
```

```
$ go build .

# demo
./main.go:10:6: cannot use "42" (untyped string constant) as int value in
➥assignment
./main.go:11:6: cannot use true (untyped bool constant) as float64 value in
➥assignment
```

(continued)

```
./main.go:12:6: cannot use 3.14 (untyped float constant) as bool value in
➥assignment
./main.go:13:6: cannot use 42 (untyped int constant) as string value in
➥assignment
```

Go Version: go1.19

Zero Values

If a variable has been declared but no value has been assigned to it, the variable will have a zero value. A zero value is a value that is the same type as the variable. For example, a variable of type int has a zero value of 0. Complex types, such as a struct, have a zero value that is composed of the type's individual fields' zero values.

The fmt[14] package has several useful printing verbs and functions that you can use to inspect a variable. The %T verb, for example, prints the type of a variable, Listing 2.26.

Listing 2.26 Zero Values in Go

```
func main() {
    var i int
    var f float64
    var b bool
    var s string

    fmt.Printf("var i %T = %v\n", i, i)
    fmt.Printf("var f %T = %f\n", f, f)
    fmt.Printf("var b %T = %v\n", b, b)
    fmt.Printf("var s %T = %q\n", s, s)
}
```

```
$ go run .

var i int = 0
var f float64 = 0.000000
var b bool = false
var s string = ""
```

Go Version: go1.19

Nil

There are certain types in Go, such as maps, interfaces, and pointers, that have no obvious zero value. For these types, the zero value is nil. We explore nil in more detail as we explore other concepts in this book.

---

14. https://pkg.go.dev/fmt

Zero Values Cheat Sheet

Listing 2.27 shows types and their corresponding zero values. There are some types we
have not covered yet, but we cover them in more detail later.

Listing 2.27 Zero Values Cheat Sheet

```
var s string     // defaults to ""
var r rune       // defaults to 0
var bt byte      // defaults to 0
var i int        // defaults to 0
var ui uint      // defaults to 0
var f float32    // defaults to 0
var c complex64  // defaults to 0
var b bool       // defaults to false
var arr [2]int   // defaults to [0 0]
var obj struct {
    b   bool
    arr [2]int
}                // defaults to {false [0 0]}
var si []int     // defaults to int
var ch chan string // defaults to nil
var mp map[int]string // defaults to nil
var fn func()    // defaults to nil
var ptr *string  // defaults to nil
var all any      // defaults to nil
```

```
$ go run .

string              : ""
rune                : 0
byte                : 0
int                 : 0
uint                : 0
float32             : 0
complex64           : (0+0i)
bool                : false
array [2]int        : [0 0]
struct              : {false [0 0]}
slice []int         : []
channel chan string : <nil>
map map[int]string  : map[]
function func()     : <nil>
```

(continued)

```
*string              : <nil>
any                  : <nil>
```

```
Go Version: go1.19
```

Variable Declaration and Initialization

When declaring a variable, we often want to initialize that variable with a value. This is done by assigning a value to the variable at declaration time, Listing 2.28.

Listing 2.28   Declaring and Initializing Variables in Go

```go
func main() {
    var i int = 42
    var f float64 = 3.14
    var b bool = true
    var s string = "hello world"
}
```

When declaring and initializing a variable at the same time, Listing 2.29, you can use the := operator to shorten the declaration and initialization process.

Listing 2.29   Declaring and Initializing Variables with the := Operator

```go
func main() {
    i := 42
    f := 3.14
    b := true
    s := "hello world"

    fmt.Printf("var i %T = %v\n", i, i)
    fmt.Printf("var f %T = %f\n", f, f)
    fmt.Printf("var b %T = %v\n", b, b)
    fmt.Printf("var s %T = %q\n", s, s)
}
```

```
$ go run .

var i int = 42
var f float64 = 3.140000
var b bool = true
var s string = "hello world"
```

```
Go Version: go1.19
```

When using the `:=` operator, the variable is declared and initialized at the same time, with Go inferring the type of the variable from the value being assigned. For most types, the Go compiler has no trouble inferring the correct type for the variable. When it comes to numbers, however, the compiler has to guess the type and by default assumes that the variable is of type `int` or `float64`, if there is a decimal point in the value being assigned.

If a number type other than `int` or `float64` is desired, Listing 2.30, you can use the `var` keyword to declare the variable and specify the type. Alternatively, casting can be used with the `:=` operator to explicitly cast the value to the desired type.

Listing 2.30   Casting Values in Go

```go
func main() {
    i := uint32(42)
    f := float32(3.14)

    fmt.Printf("var i %T = %v\n", i, i)
    fmt.Printf("var f %T = %f\n", f, f)
}
```

```
$ go run .

var i uint32 = 42
var f float32 = 3.140000

Go Version: go1.19
```

Assigning Multiple Values

Go allows you to assign several values to several variables within the same line. Each of these values can be of a different data type. In Listing 2.31, we are declaring new variables, i, f, b, and s, and assigning them each a value. For example, the variable i has the value of 42, f has the value 3.14, and so on. When we run this code, we see that each of the variables was correctly assigned the appropriate value and type.

Listing 2.31   Assigning Multiple Values in Go

```go
func main() {
    i, f, b, s := 42, 3.14, true, "hello world"

    fmt.Printf("var i %T = %v\n", i, i)
    fmt.Printf("var f %T = %f\n", f, f)
    fmt.Printf("var b %T = %v\n", b, b)
    fmt.Printf("var s %T = %q\n", s, s)
}
```

(continued)

```
$ go run .

var i int = 42
var f float64 = 3.140000
var b bool = true
var s string = "hello world"

Go Version: go1.19
```

This approach to assigning multiple variables to multiple values in one line can keep your lines of code down, but make sure you are not compromising readability for fewer lines of code.

Multiple assignment is most often used when capturing the results of a function call, Listing 2.32.

Listing 2.32   Assigning Multiple Variables from a Function Call in Go

```go
func main() {
    i, f, b, s := Values()

    fmt.Printf("var i %T = %v\n", i, i)
    fmt.Printf("var f %T = %f\n", f, f)
    fmt.Printf("var b %T = %v\n", b, b)
    fmt.Printf("var s %T = %q\n", s, s)
}

func Values() (int, float64, bool, string) {
    return 42, 3.14, true, "hello world"
}
```

```
$ go run .

var i int = 42
var f float64 = 3.140000
var b bool = true
var s string = "hello world"

Go Version: go1.19
```

Unused Variables

The Go compiler does not allow for unused variables or imports, Listing 2.33. Go also requires that you capture all of the results of a function call, even if you do not use the results.

Listing 2.33   Unused Variables in Go

```go
func main() {
    i, f, b, s := Values()

    fmt.Println(s)
}

func Values() (int, float64, bool, string) {
    return 42, 3.14, true, "hello world"
}
```

```
$ go run .

# demo
./main.go:7:2: i declared but not used
./main.go:7:5: f declared but not used
./main.go:7:8: b declared but not used

Go Version: go1.19
```

We can tell the Go compiler to discard a variable by assigning it to the blank identifier _. The _ identifier acts as a placeholder for the variable that is not being used, allowing the compiler to run successfully. In Listing 2.34, for example, the Values function returns four different values. In this example, we only want the last of these four values. To ignore the first three values, we can use the blank identifier (_) to tell Go to ignore that value. The result is a variable s that has the value hello world.

Listing 2.34   Discarding a Variable in Go

```go
func main() {
    _, _, _, s := Values()

    fmt.Println(s)
}

func Values() (int, float64, bool, string) {
    return 42, 3.14, true, "hello world"
}
```

```
$ go run .

hello world

Go Version: go1.19
```

Constants

Constants are like variables, except they can't be modified once they have been declared. Constants can only be a character, string, boolean, or numeric value. Constants are declared using the `const` keyword, Listing 2.35.

Listing 2.35 Defining a Constant

```
func main() {
    const gopher = "Gopher"
    fmt.Println(gopher)
}
```

```
$ go run .

Gopher
```

```
Go Version: go1.19
```

If you try to modify a constant after it was declared, you will get a compile time error, as shown in Listing 2.36.

Listing 2.36 Attempting to Modify a Constant

```
func main() {
    const gopher = "Gopher"
    gopher = "Bunny"
    fmt.Println(gopher)
}
```

```
$ go run .

# demo
./main.go:8:2: cannot assign to gopher (untyped string constant "Gopher")
```

```
Go Version: go1.19
```

Values that can be modified, such as maps and slices, *cannot* be constants, and neither can the result of a function call, Listing 2.37.

Listing 2.37 Attempting to Modify a Variable

```
func main() {
    const gopher = func() string {
        return "Gopher"
```

```
    }()

    const names = []string{"Kurt", "Janis", "Jimi", "Amy"}

    fmt.Println(gopher)
}
```

```
$ go run .

# demo
./main.go:7:17: func() string {...}() (value of type string) is not constant
./main.go:11:16: []string{...} (value of type []string) is not constant

Go Version: go1.19
```

Typed Constants

If you declare a constant with a type, it will be that exact type. In Listing 2.38, leapYear is defined as data type int32. This means it can only operate with int32 data types.

Listing 2.38 Typed Constants

```
const (
    leapYear = int32(366) // typed
)
```

In Listing 2.39, hours is declared with no type, so it is considered untyped. Because of this, you can use it with any integer data type. If you try to use a typed constant with anything other than its type, Go throws a compile time error.

Listing 2.39 Attempting to Use a Typed Constant with a Variable of a Different Type

```
func main() {
    hours := 24
    fmt.Println(hours * leapYear) // multiplying int and int32 types}
}
```

```
$ go run .

# demo
./main.go:15:14: invalid operation: hours * leapYear (mismatched types int
➥  and int32)

Go Version: go1.19
```

Untyped Constants (Inferred Typing)

Constants can be untyped, meaning that their type is inferred by the value assigned. This can be useful when working with numbers such as integer type data. If the constant is untyped, it is explicitly converted, whereas typed constants are not. For example, in Listing 2.40, the year constant is "untyped," which means it can act as any of the integer types in Go. When we try to multiply the "untyped" year constant with the hours variable, of type int, Go casts the year constant to the int type. When multiplying year against the minutes variable, of type int32, Go casts the year constant to an int32.

Listing 2.40   Constants with Inferred Typing

```
package main

import "fmt"

const (
    year     = 365          // untyped
    leapYear = int32(366) // typed
)

func main() {
    hours := 24
    minutes := int32(60)
    fmt.Println(hours * year)       // multiplying an int and untyped
    fmt.Println(minutes * year)     // multiplying an int32 and untyped
    fmt.Println(minutes * leapYear) // multiplying both int32 types
}
```

```
$ go run .

8760
21900
21960
```

Go Version: go1.19

Type Inference

It is important to remember that the untyped const or var will be converted to the type it is combined with for any operation for that type. In Listing 2.41, you can see that the constants a and b, as well as the variable d, all of which are "untyped," are cast to the appropriate integer type needed for the operation.

Listing 2.41 Type Inference

```go
const (
    a = 2
    b = 2
    c = int32(2)
)

func main() {
    fmt.Printf("a = %[1]d (%[1]T)\n", a)
    fmt.Printf("b = %[1]d (%[1]T)\n", b)
    fmt.Printf("c = %[1]d (%[1]T)\n", c)

    fmt.Printf("a*b = %[1]d (%[1]T)\n", a*b)
    fmt.Printf("a*c = %[1]d (%[1]T)\n", a*c)

    d := 4
    e := int32(4)

    fmt.Printf("a*d = %[1]d (%[1]T)\n", a*d)
    fmt.Printf("a*e = %[1]d (%[1]T)\n", a*e)
}
```

```
$ go run .

a = 2 (int)
b = 2 (int)
c = 2 (int32)
a*b = 4 (int)
a*c = 4 (int32)
a*d = 8 (int)
a*e = 8 (int32)

Go Version: go1.19
```

Naming Identifiers

The naming of identifiers is quite flexible, but there are some rules you need to keep in mind:

- Variable names are case sensitive, meaning that userName, USERNAME, UserName, and uSERnAME are all completely different variables.

- Variable names cannot be reserved words.
- Variable names cannot begin with a number.
- Variable names cannot contain special characters.
- Variable names must be made up of only letters, numbers, and underscores (_).
- Variable names must only be one word (as in no spaces).

Bad Identifier Names

Listing 2.42 demonstrates several bad identifier names and the resulting compiler errors.

Listing 2.42   Examples of Bad Identifier Names

```
func main() {
    var !i int
    var $_f float64
    var 5b bool
    var b!!! bool
    var user-name string
    var #tag string
    var tag# string
    var user name string
    var "username" string
    var interface string
}
```

```
$ go build .

# demo
./main.go:7:6: syntax error: unexpected !, expecting name
./main.go:8:6: invalid character U+0024 '$'
./main.go:9:6: syntax error: unexpected literal 5, expecting name
./main.go:10:7: syntax error: unexpected !, expecting type
./main.go:11:10: syntax error: unexpected -, expecting type
./main.go:12:6: invalid character U+0023 '#'
./main.go:13:9: invalid character U+0023 '#'
./main.go:14:16: syntax error: unexpected string at end of statement
./main.go:15:6: syntax error: unexpected literal "username", expecting name
./main.go:16:6: syntax error: unexpected interface, expecting name
./main.go:16:6: too many errors

Go Version: go1.19
```

Naming Style

The most important thing about style is to be consistent, and that the team you work on agrees to the style.

It is common in Go to use very terse (or short) variable names. Given the choice between using `userName` and `user` for a variable, it would be idiomatic to choose `user`.

Scope also plays a role in the terseness of the variable name. The rule is that the smaller the scope the variable exists in, the smaller the variable name. Listing 2.43 demonstrates this with the short variable names, `i` and `n`, contained within the scope of the `for` loop.

Listing 2.43   Using Short Variable Names

```
names := []string{"Amy", "John", "Bob", "Anna"}
for i, n := range names {
    fmt.Printf("index: %d = %q\n", i, n)
}
```

The variable `names` is used in a larger scope, so it would be common to give it a more meaningful name to help remember what it means in the program. However, the variables `i` and `n` are used immediately in the next line of code and never used again. Because of this, someone reading the code will not be confused about where they are used or what they mean.

Finally, some notes about style. The style is to use `MixedCaps` or `mixedCaps` rather than underscores for multiword names. Table 2.1 demonstrates the difference between the two.

Table 2.1   Examples of Conventional and Unconventional Naming Styles

Conventional Style	Unconventional Style	Why Unconventional
userName	user_name	Underscores are not conventional.
i	index	Prefer `i` over `index` as it is shorter.
serveHTTP	serveHttp	Acronyms should be capitalized.
userID	UserId	Acronyms should be capitalized.

Conflicting with Package Names

Occasionally, you may want to use a variable name that is the same as a package name. Go allows this; however, from that point on in the `.go` file that has the conflict, you are no longer able to access that package.

Consider the `path`[15] package, Listing 2.44. The `path` package is used to manipulate paths, such as URLs.

Listing 2.44   The path Package

```
$ go doc path

package path // import "path"

Package path implements utility routines for manipulating slash-separated
➥paths.

The path package should only be used for paths separated by forward slashes,
➥such as the paths in URLs. This package does not deal with Windows paths
➥with drive letters or backslashes; to manipulate operating system paths,
➥use the path/filepath package.

var ErrBadPattern = errors.New("syntax error in pattern")
func Base(path string) string
func Clean(path string) string
func Dir(path string) string
func Ext(path string) string
func IsAbs(path string) bool
func Join(elem ...string) string
func Match(pattern, name string) (matched bool, err error)
func Split(path string) (dir, file string)
```

Go Version: go1.19

The identifier path is a great candidate for a variable name when working with the
path package. Consider Listing 2.45.

Listing 2.45   Conflicting with Package Names

```
package main

import (
    "fmt"
    "path"
)

func main() {
    name := "file.txt"

    ext := path.Ext(name)

    fmt.Println("Extension:", ext)
```

```
    path := "/home/dir"

    path = path.Join(path, "file.txt")

    fmt.Println("Path:", path)
}
```

In Listing 2.45, we are able to access the `path.Ext`[16] function before we define the variable `path`. After the variable is defined, we can no longer access functions on the `path` package, such as `path.Join`.[17] Listing 2.46 shows the compiler error when we try to access the `path.Join` function after overwriting the `path` package with a local `path` variable.

Listing 2.46   Error while Trying to Compile Listing 2.45

```
$ go run .

# demo
./main.go:18:14: path.Join undefined
➥(type string has no field or method Join)
```

Go Version: go1.19

Resolving the Conflict

The *best* way to resolve this problem is to use a different name for the variable, Listing 2.47.

Listing 2.47   Resolved Conflict with Package Names

```
package main

import (
    "fmt"
    "path"
)

func main() {
    name := "file.txt"

    ext := path.Ext(name)

    fmt.Println("Extension:", ext)
```

(continued)

---

16. https://pkg.go.dev/path#Ext
17. https://pkg.go.dev/path#Join

```
    fp := "/home/dir"

    fp = path.Join(fp, "file.txt")

    fmt.Println("Path:", fp)
}
```

```
$ go run .

Extension: .txt
Path: /home/dir/file.txt
```

```
Go Version: go1.19
```

Resolving the Conflict with a Package Alias

The conflict prevented in Listing 2.45 can be resolved by using an alias for the `path`
package, Listing 2.48. This, however, is considered *bad* practice and should be avoided. It is
far easier, and less prone to error, to change the name of a local variable than to rename a
package for the entire `.go.` file.

Listing 2.48   Resolving the Conflict with a Package Alias

```
package main

import (
    "fmt"
    gpath "path"
)

func main() {
    name := "file.txt"

    ext := gpath.Ext(name)

    fmt.Println("Extension:", ext)

    path := "/home/dir"

    path = gpath.Join(path, "file.txt")

    fmt.Println("Path:", path)
}
```

```
$ go run .

Extension: .txt
Path: /home/dir/file.txt
```

```
Go Version: go1.19
```

Exporting through Capitalization

The case of the first letter of an identifier has special meaning in Go. If an identifier starts with an uppercase letter, that identifier is accessible outside the package it is declared in (or exported). If an identifier starts with a lowercase letter, it is only available within the package it is declared in.

In Listing 2.49, `Email` starts with a uppercase letter and can be accessed by other packages. `password` starts with a lowercase letter and is only accessible inside the package it is declared in.

Listing 2.49   Exporting Identifiers through Capitalization

```
var Email string
var password string
```

Printing and Formatting

Most often when we need to print or format a value or type, we use the `fmt`[18] package. The `fmt` package provides a number of functions for printing and formatting values. Go uses a formatting style similar to C, but simpler.

The scope of the `fmt` package is rather large, so we only cover the most common functions and formatting verbs. The documentation for the `fmt` package outlines all available verbs and their usage.

Formatting Functions

When examining the `fmt` package documentation, Listing 2.50, notice there are many functions that are nearly identical, such as `fmt.Sprintf`,[19] `fmt.Printf`,[20] and `fmt.Fprintf`.[21] The core of these functions is to generate a formatted string based on user input. These function groups differ in how they output the formatted strings.

---

18. https://pkg.go.dev/fmt
19. https://pkg.go.dev/fmt#Sprintf
20. https://pkg.go.dev/fmt#Printf
21. https://pkg.go.dev/fmt#Fprintf

Listing 2.50   The fmt Package

```
$ go doc -short fmt

func Errorf(format string, a ...any) error
func Fprint(w io.Writer, a ...any) (n int, err error)
func Fprintf(w io.Writer, format string, a ...any) (n int, err error)
func Fprintln(w io.Writer, a ...any) (n int, err error)
func Fscan(r io.Reader, a ...any) (n int, err error)
func Fscanf(r io.Reader, format string, a ...any) (n int, err error)
func Fscanln(r io.Reader, a ...any) (n int, err error)
func Print(a ...any) (n int, err error)
func Printf(format string, a ...any) (n int, err error)
func Println(a ...any) (n int, err error)
func Scan(a ...any) (n int, err error)
func Scanf(format string, a ...any) (n int, err error)
func Scanln(a ...any) (n int, err error)
func Sprint(a ...any) string
func Sprintf(format string, a ...any) string
func Sprintln(a ...any) string
func Sscan(str string, a ...any) (n int, err error)
func Sscanf(str string, format string, a ...any) (n int, err error)
func Sscanln(str string, a ...any) (n int, err error)
type Formatter interface{ ... }
type GoStringer interface{ ... }
type ScanState interface{ ... }
type Scanner interface{ ... }
type State interface{ ... }
type Stringer interface{ ... }
```

Go Version: go1.19

Sprint Functions

Functions starting with Sprint, such as fmt.Sprint,[22] all return a formatted string,
Listing 2.51.

Listing 2.51   The fmt.Sprint Function

```
$ go doc fmt.Sprint

package fmt // import "fmt"
```

```
func Sprint(a ...any) string
    Sprint formats using the default formats for its operands and returns
    ➥the resulting string. Spaces are added between operands when neither
    ➥is a string.
```

Go Version: go1.19

Print Functions

Functions starting with `Print`, such as `fmt.Print`, all print the formatted string to the standard output, Listing 2.52.

Listing 2.52 The `fmt.Print` Function

```
$ go doc fmt.Print

package fmt // import "fmt"

func Print(a ...any) (n int, err error)
    Print formats using the default formats for its operands and writes to
    ➥standard output. Spaces are added between operands when neither is
    ➥a string. It returns the number of bytes written and any write
    ➥error encountered.
```

Go Version: go1.19

Fprint Functions

Functions starting with `Fprint`, such as `fmt.Fprint`, all print the formatted string to the provided `io.Writer`.[23] Listing 2.53 shows an example of `Fprint`.

Listing 2.53 The `fmt.Fprint` Function

```
$ go doc fmt.Fprint

package fmt // import "fmt"

func Fprint(w io.Writer, a ...any) (n int, err error)
    Fprint formats using the default formats for its operands and writes
    ➥to w. Spaces are added between operands when neither is a string.
    ➥It returns the number of bytes written and any write error encountered.
```

Go Version: go1.19

---

23. https://pkg.go.dev/io#Writer

New Lines

Most printing, and sprinting, functions in the `fmt` package do *not* add a new line to the end of the string.

In Listing 2.54, you can see the output of the two `fmt.Print` functions is on the same line. To add a new line when using these functions, you can use the `\n` escape sequence to do so, or use the `fmt.Println`[24] method, as in Listing 2.55.

Listing 2.54 New Lines Are Not Automatically Added by Most Print Functions

```
package main

import "fmt"

func main() {
    fmt.Print("This statement is NOT printed with a line return at the end.")
    fmt.Print("Another statement without a line return.")
}
```

```
$ go run .

This statement is NOT printed with a line return at the end. Another statement
➥without a line return.
```

Go Version: go1.19

Listing 2.55 The `fmt.Println` Function Will Automatically Add a New Line to the End of the String

```
package main

import "fmt"

func main() {
    fmt.Println("This statement is printed with a line return at the end.")
    fmt.Print("Another statement with a line return.\n")
}
```

```
$ go run .

This statement is printed with a line return at the end.
Another statement with a line return.
```

Go Version: go1.19

---

24. https://pkg.go.dev/fmt#Println

Multiple Arguments with Println

When calling `fmt.Println`, Listing 2.56, multiple arguments are printed in the order they are passed, with a new line added to the end of each line.

Listing 2.56 `fmt.Println` Automatically Adds a New Line to the End of Each Argument to Be Printed

```go
package main

import "fmt"

func main() {

    a := 1

    fmt.Println("This will join all arguments and print them. a =", a)
    fmt.Println("Println will also automatically insert spaces between
    ➥arguments.", "foo", "bar")
    fmt.Println("So many arguments", "carrot", "onion", "potato", "tomato",
    ➥"celery", "spinach")
}
```

```
$ go run .

This will join all arguments and print them. a = 1
Println will also automatically insert spaces between arguments. foo bar
So many arguments carrot onion potato tomato celery spinach
```

```
Go Version: go1.19
```

Using Formatting Functions

All of the functions ending in `f`, such as `fmt.Sprintf`, allow for the use of formatting verbs. These verbs will create different styles of formatting. Verbs are usually proceeded by a `%` or `\` character.

Escape Sequences

Escape sequences, such as `\n` to create a new line and `\t` to create a tab, can be used to format the output, Listing 2.57.

Listing 2.57   Using Escape Sequences \n and \t

```go
package main

import (
    "fmt"

)

func main() {
    // use a '\n' to add a new line
    fmt.Printf("Hello, World!\n")

    // use a '\t' to add a tab
    fmt.Printf("\tHello, World!\n")
}
```

```
$ go run .

Hello, World!
        Hello, World!

Go Version: go1.19
```

Escaping Escape Characters

Formatting verbs begin with a % character. Escape sequences begin with a \ character. There may be times that you want to use those characters as themselves in the formatted string. To do this, each character needs to be escaped by repeating itself, Listing 2.58.

Listing 2.58   Escaping Escape Characters %s and \

```go
package main

import (
    "fmt"
)

func main() {
    // use a '\\' to produce a single backslash
    fmt.Printf("A '\\' is called a backslash\n")

    // use a '%%' to produce a single percent sign
    fmt.Printf("The '%%' symbol is called a percent sign\n")
}
```

```
$ go run .

A '\' is called a backslash
The '%' symbol is called a percent sign
```

```
Go Version: go1.19
```

Formatting Strings

When formatting a string, the two most common verbs are %s and %q. The %s verb prints the string as it is, whereas the %q verb prints the string as it is, with quotes around it, Listing 2.59.

Listing 2.59   Using %s and %q to Format Strings

```go
package main

import (
    "fmt"
)

func main() {

    s := "Hello, World!"

    // use '%s' to print a string
    fmt.Printf("%s\n", s)

    // use '%q' to print a string
    fmt.Printf("%q\n", s)
}
```

```
$ go run .

Hello, World!
"Hello, World!"
```

```
Go Version: go1.19
```

Formatting Integers

As discussed previously, Go has many integer-based types. Collectively, this group of types is known as "integers." All integers abide by the same formatting rules. Integers are printed with the %d verb, as shown in Listing 2.60.

Listing 2.60   Using %d to Format Integers

```go
package main

import (
    "fmt"
)

func main() {

    // use '%d' to print an integer
    fmt.Printf("%d\n", 12345)

    // use '%+d' to print an integer with sign
    fmt.Printf("%+d\n", 12345)
    fmt.Printf("%+d\n", -12345)
}
```

```
$ go run .

12345
+12345
-12345
```

```
Go Version: go1.19
```

Listing 2.60 also demonstrates that by adding a + to the verb, the integer is printed with its sign.

Padding Integers

The fmt package provides several ways to pad integers when formatting. The %d verb can be modified to add padding to the right or left of the integer. In either case, this padding is considered a *minimum* padding. If a number is larger than the minimum padding, the number is printed as it is.

Width of the padding is declared by using an integer in front of the d in the %d verb. For example, in Listing 2.61, the integer 5 is used to specify the width of the padding: %5d.

Listing 2.61   Padding Integers to the Left

```go
package main

import "fmt"

func main() {
```

```
    d := 123

    // use '%5d' to print an integer
    // padded on the left with spaces
    // to a minimum of 5 characters wide
    fmt.Printf("Padded: '%5d'\n", d)

    // use '%5d' to print an integer
    // padded on the left with zeros
    // to a minimum of 5 characters wide
    fmt.Printf("Padded: '%05d'\n", d)

    // a number larger than the padding
    // is printed as is
    fmt.Printf("Padded: '%5d'\n", 1234567890)
}
```

```
$ go run .

Padded: '  123'
Padded: '00123'
Padded: '1234567890'
```

```
Go Version: go1.19
```

By adding a 0 after the % character, you can specify that the padding should be done with zeros instead of spaces. For example, in Listing 2.61, the integer 5 is used to specify the width of the padding: %05d.

Integers can also be padded to the right using the - character after the % character. For example, in Listing 2.62, the integer 5 is used to specify the width of the padding: %-5d.

Listing 2.62   Padding Integers to the Right

```
package main

import "fmt"

func main() {

    d := 123

    // use '%-5d' to print an integer
    // padded on the right with spaces
```

(continued)

```
    // to a minimum of 5 characters wide
    fmt.Printf("Padded: '%-5d'\n", d)

    // a number larger than the padding
    // is printed as is
    fmt.Printf("Padded: '%-5d'\n", 1234567890)
}
```

```
$ go run .

Padded: '123  '
Padded: '1234567890'
```

Go Version: go1.19

Formatting Floats

Formatting floats is similar to formatting integers with the `%f` verb being used, as shown in Listing 2.63.

Listing 2.63   Using `%f` to Format Floats

```
package main

import (
    "fmt"
)

func main() {

    // use '%f' to print a float
    fmt.Printf("%f\n", 1.2345)

    // use '%.2f' to print a float
    // with 2 decimal places
    fmt.Printf("%.2f\n", 1.2345)
}
```

```
$ go run .

1.234500
1.23
```

Go Version: go1.19

Listing 2.63 also demonstrates formatting a float's decimal point to a specific number of places. For example, in Listing 2.63, the integer 2 is used to specify the number of decimal places: %.2f.

Printing a Value's Type

The %T verb prints the type of the value. For example, in Listing 2.64, the type of the variable u is printed using %T.

Listing 2.64   Using %T to Print a Value's Type

```
package main

import (
    "fmt"
)

type User struct {
    Name string
    Age  int
}

func main() {

    u := User{
        Name: "Kurt",
        Age:  27,
    }

    // use '%T' to print the type of a value
    fmt.Printf("%T\n", u)
}
```

```
$ go run .

main.User
```

```
Go Version: go1.19
```

Printing a Value

To print the value of a variable, you use the %v verb. For example, in Listing 2.65, the value of the variable u is printed using the %v formatting verb. The %v formatting verb prints the values of each of the struct's fields.

Listing 2.65   Using %v to Print a Value

```
package main

import (
    "fmt"
)

type User struct {
    Name string
    Age  int
}

func main() {

    u := User{
        Name: "Kurt",
        Age:  27,
    }

    // use '%v' to print a value
    fmt.Printf("%v\n", u)
}
```

```
$ go run .

{Kurt 27}
```

```
Go Version: go1.19
```

Printing a Value with More Detail

The %v verb can be extended with the + operator to print more information about the value, if possible. For example, in Listing 2.66, the %+v verb is used to print a struct's field names, as well as the values of the fields.

Listing 2.66   Using %+v to Print a Value

```
package main

import (
    "fmt"
)
```

```go
type User struct {
    Name string
    Age  int
}

func main() {

    u := User{
        Name: "Kurt",
        Age:  27,
    }

    // use '%+v' to print an extended
    // representation of a value, if possible
    fmt.Printf("%+v\n", u)
}
```

```
$ go run .

{Name:Kurt Age:27}

Go Version: go1.19
```

Printing a Value's Go-Syntax Representation

The %#v verb prints the value in a native Go-syntax format. For example, in Listing 2.67, the %#v verb is used to print a struct in its Go–syntax format.

Listing 2.67   Using %#v to Print the Go-Syntax Representation of a Value

```go
package main

import (
    "fmt"
)

type User struct {
    Name string
    Age  int
}

func main() {
```

(continued)

```
    u := User{
        Name: "Kurt",
        Age:  27,
    }

    // use '%#v' to print the
    // Go-syntax representation of a value
    fmt.Printf("%#v\n", u)
}
```

```
$ go run .

main.User{Name:"Kurt", Age:27}

Go Version: go1.19
```

Using Formatting Verbs Incorrectly

When you use a formatting verb incorrectly, such as trying to format a string with a %d verb, there will be no error to respond to. Instead, Go prints error information into the formatted string. Consider Listing 2.68, where several types are printed incorrectly.

Listing 2.68   Using Formatting Verbs Incorrectly

```
package main

import "fmt"

func main() {

    // print an integer with a the '%s' verb
    fmt.Printf("This is an int: %s\n", 42)

    // print a string with a the '%d' verb
    fmt.Printf("This is a string: %d\n", "hello")
}
```

```
$ go run .

This is an int: %!s(int=42)
This is a string: %!d(string=hello)

Go Version: go1.19
```

To avoid using the wrong verbs, and other issues, you should always run go vet on your code, Listing 2.69. Most editors or Go plugins have this feature already enabled.

Listing 2.69   Running go vet Catches Formatting Errors

```
$ go vet .

# demo
./main.go:8:2: fmt.Printf format %s has arg 42 of wrong type int
./main.go:11:2: fmt.Printf format %d has arg "hello" of wrong type string

Go Version: go1.19
```

Explicit Argument Indexes

The default behavior for these functions is for each formatting verb to format successive arguments passed into the call, as shown in Listing 2.70.

Listing 2.70   Using the Default Argument Indexing

```
package main

import "fmt"

func main() {
    fmt.Printf("in order: %s %s %s %s\n", "one", "two", "three", "four")
}
```

```
$ go run .

in order: one two three four

Go Version: go1.19
```

You can use [N] with the verb to indicate which argument to use. In Listing 2.71, we are able to reverse the order of the arguments using the [N] syntax.

Listing 2.71   Using Explicit Argument Indexes

```
package main

import "fmt"
```

(continued)

```
func main() {
    fmt.Printf("explicit: %[4]s %[3]s %[2]s %[1]s\n", "one", "two", "three",
    ➥ "four")
}
```

```
$ go run .

explicit: four three two one
```
Go Version: go1.19

Using the [N] syntax, as in Listing 2.72, you can use the same argument multiple times in the formatting string.

Listing 2.72   Using Explicit Argument Indexes to Reuse Arguments

```
package main

import "fmt"

func main() {

    name := "Janis"

    //use [1] to reuse the first argument in multiple places
    fmt.Printf("Value of name is %[1]q, type: %[1]T\n", name)
}
```

```
$ go run .

Value of name is "Janis", type: string
```
Go Version: go1.19

Converting Strings to and from Numbers

Unlike the fmt package, the strconv[25] package has functions to explicitly try to convert a single value or variable to a number and vice versa. The most commonly used functions

---

25. https://pkg.go.dev/strconv

are strconv.ParseInt,[26] strconv.ParseUint,[27] strconv.ParseFloat,[28] and strconv.Atoi.[29]

When trying to parse a number from a string, you need to tell Go what base you are using for the number and what bit size you are expecting. Listing 2.73 shows the documentation for the strconv.ParseInt[30] function. You can see that the function takes a string, a base, and a bit size.

Listing 2.73 Documentation for strconv.ParseInt

```
$ go doc strconv.ParseInt

package strconv // import "strconv"

func ParseInt(s string, base int, bitSize int) (i int64, err error)
    ParseInt interprets a string s in the given base (0, 2 to 36) and bit
    ➥size (0 to 64) and returns the corresponding value i.

    The string may begin with a leading sign: "+" or "-".

    If the base argument is 0, the true base is implied by the string's
    ➥prefix following the sign (if present): 2 for "0b", 8 for "0" or "0o", 16
    ➥for "0x", and 10 otherwise. Also, for argument base 0 only, underscore
    ➥characters are permitted as defined by the Go syntax for integer literals.

    The bitSize argument specifies the integer type that the result must fit
    ➥into. Bit sizes 0, 8, 16, 32, and 64 correspond to int, int8, int16,
    ➥int32, and int64. If bitSize is below 0 or above 64, an error
    ➥is returned.

    The errors that ParseInt returns have concrete type *NumError and include
    ➥err.Num = s. If s is empty or contains invalid digits, err.Err =
    ➥ErrSyntax and the returned value is 0; if the value corresponding to s
    ➥cannot be represented by a signed integer of the given size, err.Err =
    ➥ErrRange and the returned value is the maximum magnitude integer of the
    ➥appropriate bitSize and sign.

Go Version: go1.19
```

---

26. https://pkg.go.dev/strconv#ParseInt
27. https://pkg.go.dev/strconv#ParseUint
28. https://pkg.go.dev/strconv#ParseFloat
29. https://pkg.go.dev/strconv#Atoi
30. https://pkg.go.dev/strconv#ParseInt

For most use cases, including Listing 2.74, you can use the default values for the base and bit size, which are 0 and 64.

Listing 2.74   Converting to and from Strings and Numbers in Go

```go
package main

import (
    "fmt"
    "log"
    "strconv"
)

func main() {

    // parsing a string to a negative integer
    i, err := strconv.ParseInt("-42", 0, 64)
    if err != nil {
        log.Fatal(err)
    }

    fmt.Println("-42: ", i)

    // parsing a octal integer
    i, err = strconv.ParseInt("0x2A", 0, 64)
    if err != nil {
        log.Fatal(err)
    }

    fmt.Println("0x2A: ", i)

    // parsing an unsigned integer
    u, err := strconv.ParseUint("42", 0, 64)
    if err != nil {
        log.Fatal(err)
    }

    fmt.Println("42 (uint): ", u)

    // parsing a float
    f, err := strconv.ParseFloat("42.12345", 64)
    if err != nil {
        log.Fatal(err)
    }
```

```
    fmt.Println("42.12345: ", f)

    // converting a string to an integer
    a, err := strconv.Atoi("42")
    fmt.Printf("%[1]v [%[1]T]\n", a)

    if err != nil {
        log.Fatal(err)
    }

}
```

```
$ go run .

-42:  -42
0x2A:  42
42 (uint):  42
42.12345:  42.12345
42 [int]

Go Version: go1.19
```

Summary

In this chapter, we covered the basics of the Go language. We learned that Go is a statically typed, compiled, garbage-collected language. Next, we looked at a few of Go's built-in data types: numbers, strings, and booleans. Finally, we explored how variables, constants, and other identifiers are declared and initialized.

Arrays, Slices, and Iteration

In this chapter, we cover the built-in list types: `arrays` and `slices`. Next, we move on to discussing Go's `for` keyword for iteration. Finally, we cover using the `range` keyword to simplify iteration.

List Types: Arrays and Slices

Go has two built-in ordered list collection types: arrays and slices. Unlike other languages, there are no built-in complex list types such as linked lists[1] or trees.[2] Instead, Go uses the concept of composition[3] to allow for creating more complex data structures, an example of which can be found with the `list.List`[4] type. We cover composition in more detail as we progress through this book.

Arrays and slices are both ordered collections of values. The only difference between them is that arrays are fixed in size, whereas slices are not.

Arrays in Go are useful when planning for detailed layout of memory. Using arrays can sometimes help avoid allocation when you know exactly how much data you want to store. Arrays are also used as the building blocks of slices.

Slices wrap arrays in Go and provide a more general, powerful, and convenient way to work with ordered collections of values.

Differences between Arrays and Slices

Arrays and slices are both ordered collections of values. Both require that the values all be of the same type. Arrays, however, have a fixed length, whereas slices can grow as needed. Table 3.1 breaks down the differences between arrays and slices.

The capacity of an array is defined at creation time. Once an array has allocated its size, the size can no longer be changed. All of the memory needed to store the array is allocated at creation time. This means that the array is a fixed size, and once created, it cannot be resized. The array will be garbage collected once it's no longer in use.

---

1. https://en.wikipedia.org/wiki/Linked_list
2. https://en.wikipedia.org/wiki/Tree_%28data_structure%29
3. https://en.wikipedia.org/wiki/Object_composition
4. https://pkg.go.dev/container/list#List

Table 3.1 Comparing Arrays and Slices

	Arrays	**Slices**
Fixed length	X	—
Fixed type	X	X
Zero based	X	X

In Listing 3.1, we create an array of four strings. The array is allocated at creation time, and once created, it cannot be resized.

Listing 3.1 An Array of Four Strings

```
func main() {
    names := [4]string{"Kurt", "Janis", "Jimi", "Amy"}
    fmt.Println(names)
}
```

```
$ go run .

[Kurt Janis Jimi Amy]
```

```
Go Version: go1.19
```

Arrays are very useful when you know exactly how much data you need to store. Often, though, you don't know the size you will need at creation time; in this case, you need to use slices.

Slices are a more flexible way to store data. They are not fixed in size and can grow as needed. Because of their flexibility, slices are more often used in daily situations instead of arrays.

In Listing 3.2, we create a slice of four strings. The slice is not allocated at creation time and can grow as needed.

Listing 3.2 A Slice of Four Strings

```
func main() {
    names := []string{"Kurt", "Janis", "Jimi", "Amy"}
    fmt.Println(names)
}
```

```
$ go run .

[Kurt Janis Jimi Amy]
```

```
Go Version: go1.19
```

Spotting the Difference

Once created, arrays and slices behave nearly identically. The only place to see the difference is in the way they are created. Arrays require that you specify the size of the array at creation time. Slices do not require that you specify the size of the array at creation time.

In Listing 3.3, the `namesArray` variable is an array of four strings. The `namesSlice` variable is a slice that currently has four strings.

Listing 3.3 Creating an Array versus a Slice

```
func main() {
    namesArray := [4]string{"Kurt", "Janis", "Jimi", "Amy"}
    namesSlice := []string{"Kurt", "Janis", "Jimi", "Amy"}

    fmt.Println(namesArray)
    fmt.Println(namesSlice)
}
```

```
$ go run .

[Kurt Janis Jimi Amy]
[Kurt Janis Jimi Amy]
```

```
Go Version: go1.19
```

Initializing Arrays and Slices

With simple data types, such as strings, numbers, and booleans, you can use them with no special initialization. With more complex data types, values may need to be initialized before they can be used. At this initialization time, you have the option of filling the type with values or leaving the type empty.

When initializing a type, you must use a pair of curly braces to indicate that the type is being initialized: `<type>{<optional: values>}`.

Arrays and slices don't need to be initialized before they are used. As with strings and numbers, they can be used without being initialized. However, initializing an array or slice gives you the ability to fill the array or slice with values immediately. In Listing 3.4, for

example, we declare and initialize different slices and arrays. For example, variable a is
declared and initialized to an array that holds five int values. Variable e declares the same
array but is automatically initialized to an array of five int values.

Listing 3.4   Initializing Arrays and Slices

```go
func main() {
    // initialize array without values:
    a := [5]int{}

    // initialize slice without values:
    b := []int{}

    // initialize array with values:
    c := [3]int{1, 2, 3}

    // initialize slice with values:
    d := []int{1, 2, 3}

    // declare an array variable:
    var e [5]int

    // declare slice variable:
    var f []int

    fmt.Println(a)
    fmt.Println(b)
    fmt.Println(c)
    fmt.Println(d)
    fmt.Println(e)
    fmt.Println(f)
}
```

```
$ go run .

[0 0 0 0 0]
[]
[1 2 3]
[1 2 3]
[0 0 0 0 0]
[]


Go Version: go1.19
```

Array and Slice Zero Values

The zero value of each element in an array or slice is the zero value for the type of elements in the array or slice. For example, if an array of strings is created, each element in the array will be a string with a zero value of " ".

In Listing 3.5, we print several different arrays using the %#v formatting verb. The %#v verb prints the Go syntax representation of the value. For an array, this shows the type, the length, and the values, which are all zero values in this case.

Listing 3.5 Array and Slice Zero Values

```
func main() {
    var a [5]int
    var b [4]string
    var c [3]bool

    fmt.Printf("%#v\n", a)
    fmt.Printf("%#v\n", b)
    fmt.Printf("%#v\n", c)
}
```

```
$ go run .

[5]int{0, 0, 0, 0, 0}
[4]string{"", "", "", ""}
[3]bool{false, false, false}

Go Version: go1.19
```

Indexing Arrays and Slices

When attempting to access an array with a hard-coded index, the Go compiler checks to see if the index is out of bounds. If the index being accessed is out of bounds, the compiler errors, Listing 3.6.

Listing 3.6 Indexing an Array out of Bounds

```
func main() {
    names := [4]string{"Kurt", "Janis", "Jimi", "Amy"}
    fmt.Println(names[5])
}
```

(continued)

```
$ go build .

# demo
./main.go:8:20: invalid argument: array index 5 out of bounds [0:4]
```

```
Go Version: go1.19
```

If, however, the index is a variable or the type is a slice instead of an array, the compiler does not check for out-of-bounds errors. Instead, the Go runtime raises a panic and possibly crashes the program, as shown in Listing 3.7.

Listing 3.7   Indexing an Array out of Bounds with a Variable

```go
func main() {
    names := [4]string{"Kurt", "Janis", "Jimi", "Amy"}

    i := 5
    fmt.Println(names[i])
}
```

```
$ go run .

panic: runtime error: index out of range [5] with length 4

goroutine 1 [running]:
main.main()
    ./main.go:10 +0x28
exit status 2
```

```
Go Version: go1.19
```

We discuss panicking in Chapter 9 when we discuss errors; however, it is worth understanding that a panic *will* crash your application if you're not careful.

Array and Slice Types

It's important to remember that arrays and slices can only hold values of the type they were declared to hold. For example, if you declare an array of strings, you can only store strings in the array. Attempting a different type results in either a compile-time error or a runtime panic. In Listing 3.8, several attempts are made to mix different types within slices and arrays. For example, the `ints` variable is a slice of an `int` value. If we try to set index 0 of the `ints` variable with a `string` type, we get a compilation error telling us we can't do this.

Listing 3.8 Mixing Types within an Array or Slice Is Not Allowed

```go
func main() {
    strings := [4]string{"one", "two", "three", "four"}
    strings[0] = 5 // can't put an int in a string array

    ints := []int{1, 2, 3, 4}
    ints[0] = "five" // can't put a string in an int slice

    // can't mix types during initialization
    mixed := []string{"one", 2, "three", "four"}
}
```

```
$ go run .

# demo
./main.go:6:15: cannot use 5 (untyped int constant) as string value in
➥assignment
./main.go:9:12: cannot use "five" (untyped string constant) as int value in
➥assignment
./main.go:12:2: mixed declared but not used
./main.go:12:27: cannot use 2 (untyped int constant) as string value in
➥array or slice literal
```

```
Go Version: go1.19
```

Array and Slice Type Definitions

When you have variables that been assigned to arrays and slices, those variables have a type associated with them. This type is called the type definition.

Because arrays are of fixed length, the type definition for an array is comprised of both the declared length of the array and the type it will store. For example, in Listing 3.9, the type for the array, [2]string{"one", "two"}, is [2]string.

Listing 3.9 Length of the Array Is Part of Its Type Definition

```go
func main() {
    a1 := [2]string{"one", "two"} // type: [2]string
    var a2 [2]string              // type: [2]string
    a3 := [3]string{}             // type: [3]string
```

(continued)

```
    a2 = a1
    fmt.Println(a2)

    // this can't be done, as it is not of the same type:
    a3 = a2
}
```

```
$ go run .

# demo
./main.go:16:7: cannot use a2 (variable of type [2]string) as type [3]string
↪in assignment
```

Go Version: go1.19

Slices are not fixed length, so a slice's type is comprised of just the type it will store. For example, in Listing 3.10, the type for slice []string{"one", "two"} is []string.

Listing 3.10 Length Is Not a Part of a Slice's Type Definition

```
func main() {
    s1 := []string{"one", "two"} // Type: []string
    var s2 []string
    s3 := []int{}

    s2 = s1

    fmt.Println(s2)

    // this can't be done, as it is not of the same type
    s3 = s2
}
```

```
$ go run .

# demo
./main.go:16:7: cannot use s2 (variable of type []string) as type []int
↪in assignment
```

Go Version: go1.19

Setting Array and Slice Values

If you create two like arrays and then set the value of one array to the other, they still continue to have their own memory space. In Listing 3.11, when a1 is assigned to a2, the a2 array receives copies of the values in a1. Changing what value is in a1[0] does not affect the previous value that was there, so a2[0] is still able to access the "one" string.

Listing 3.11 Arrays and Slices Have Separate Memory Spaces but Can Share the Same Values

```go
func main() {
    a1 := [2]string{"one", "two"}
    a2 := [2]string{}

    a2 = a1

    fmt.Println("a1:", a1)
    fmt.Println("a2:", a2)

    a1[0] = "three"

    fmt.Println("a1:", a1)
    fmt.Println("a2:", a2)
}
```

```
$ go run .

a1: [one two]
a2: [one two]
a1: [three two]
a2: [one two]


Go Version: go1.19
```

Appending to Slices

Unlike object-oriented languages, slices and arrays don't have functions on them to allow you to append, remove, index, or otherwise manipulate the values in the array or slice. Instead, it is expected that those functions can be implemented by the end user. With the introduction of generics in Go 1.18, there is much more flexibility in how these functions can be implemented.

You can use the append[5] function, Listing 3.12, to append values to a slice. Although appending only works with slices, we discuss later in "Converting an Array to a Slice" how an array can be coerced into a slice.

Listing 3.12   The append Function

```
$ go doc builtin.append

package builtin // import "builtin"

func append(slice []Type, elems ...Type) []Type
    The append built-in function appends elements to the end of a slice.
    ➥If it has sufficient capacity, the destination is resliced to
    ➥accommodate the new elements. If it does not, a new underlying array will
    ➥be allocated. Append returns the updated slice. It is therefore
    ➥necessary to store the result of append, often in the variable holding
    ➥the slice itself:

        slice = append(slice, elem1, elem2)
        slice = append(slice, anotherSlice...)

    As a special case, it is legal to append a string to a byte slice, like
    this:

        slice = append([]byte("hello"), "world"...)
```

Go Version: go1.19

The append function takes a slice and zero or more values to append to the slice. The return value is a new slice with the values appended to the original slice. All values being appended must be of the same type as the slice being appended to. In Listing 3.13, we start with the names variable, which is an empty slice of string values. Then we use the append function to append the string Kris to the slice. The result of the append function is assigned back to the names variable. The append function is used again to add multiple names, Janis and Jimi, to the names slice. Again, the result of this operation is assigned back to the names variable.

Listing 3.13   Appending to a Slice

```
func main() {
    // create a slice of strings
    var names []string
```

---

5. https://pkg.go.dev/builtin#append

```
    // append a name to the slice
    names = append(names, "Kris")

    fmt.Println(names)

    // append multiple names to the slice
    names = append(names, "Janis", "Jimi")

    fmt.Println(names)
}
```

```
$ go run .

[Kris]
[Kris Janis Jimi]

Go Version: go1.19
```

Appending Slices to Slices

The append function, as previously mentioned, can take zero or more values to append to a slice. All values being appended must be of the same type as the slice being appended to. This means that we cannot use a slice as the second argument to append.

Consider Listing 3.14. When trying to pass a second slice to the append function, we get a compilation error or a runtime panic.

Listing 3.14   Error Attempting to Append Two Slices Together

```
func main() {
    // create a slice of strings
    var names []string

    // append a name to the slice
    names = append(names, "Kris")

    fmt.Println(names)

    // create another slice of strings
    more := []string{"Janis", "Jimi"}

    // append multiple names to the slice
    names = append(names, more)
```

(continued)

```
    fmt.Println(names)
}
```

```
$ go run .

# demo
./main.go:19:24: cannot use more (variable of type []string) as type string
➥in argument to append

Go Version: go1.19
```

The reason for this error is that the `append` function expects values to be of the same type as the slice being appended to. In short, the type `[]string` is not the same type as `string`.

To append the second slice to the first, we need to pass the individual values of the second slice to the `append` function. One way to do this would be to use a loop to iterate over the values in the second slice and append them to the first slice, as shown in Listing 3.15. We discuss iteration later in Chapter 4, "Maps and Control Structures."

Listing 3.15 Appending Two Slices Using a `for` Loop

```go
func main() {
    // create a slice of strings
    var names []string

    // append a name to the slice
    names = append(names, "Kris")

    fmt.Println(names)

    // create another slice of strings
    more := []string{"Janis", "Jimi"}

    // loop through the additional names
    for _, name := range more {

        // append each name to the slice
        names = append(names, name)
    }

    fmt.Println(names)
}
```

```
$ go run .

[Kris]
[Kris Janis Jimi]
```

Go Version: go1.19

Although using a loop will work, it is not the most efficient way to append a slice to a slice. Functions in Go, as we discuss later in this book in Chapter 5, accept variadic arguments.[6] Variadic functions accept zero or more arguments of the same type through the use of the ... operator.

The append function, Listing 3.16, accepts a variadic argument and accepts any number of values of the same type as the slice being appended to.

Listing 3.16   The append Function with Variadic Arguments

```
$ go doc builtin.append

package builtin // import "builtin"

func append(slice []Type, elems ...Type) []Type
    The append built-in function appends elements to the end of a slice.
    ➥If it has sufficient capacity, the destination is resliced to
    ➥accommodate the new elements. If it does not, a new underlying array will
    ➥be allocated. Append returns the updated slice. It is therefore necessary
    ➥to store the result of append, often in the variable holding the slice
    ➥itself:

        slice = append(slice, elem1, elem2)
        slice = append(slice, anotherSlice...)

    As a special case, it is legal to append a string to a byte slice, like
    this:

        slice = append([]byte("hello"), "world"...)
```

Go Version: go1.19

Although you can use variadic arguments to accept multiple arguments of the same type, the reverse is also true. In Listing 3.17, the variadic operator (...) is used to take the more slice and append it to the names slice.

---

6. https://en.wikipedia.org/wiki/Variadic_function

Listing 3.17   Appending Two Slices Using the Variadic Operator

```go
func main() {
    // create a slice of strings
    var names []string

    // append a name to the slice
    names = append(names, "Kris")

    fmt.Println(names)

    // create another slice of strings
    more := []string{"Janis", "Jimi"}

    // use variadic operator to append more to names
    names = append(names, more...)

    // equivalent to:
    // names = append(names, "Janis", "Jimi")

    fmt.Println(names)
}
```

```
$ go run .

[Kris]
[Kris Janis Jimi]

Go Version: go1.19
```

How Slices Work

Although arrays are very straightforward to understand because they can hold a fixed number things, slices are a bit more complex. Slices can grow as needed to store as many values as needed.

To help understand how slices work, let's examine slices a bit further. Listing 3.18 shows that a slice has three parts: length, capacity, and a pointer to an underlying array:

- **Length:** How many values are in the slice.
- **Capacity:** How many values can be stored in the slice.
- **Pointer to the underlying array:** Where the values are actually stored.

Listing 3.18   Theoretical Representation of Slice Internals

```
type Slice struct {
    // N: the number of actual values in the array
    Length int
    // 10: the maximum number of values that can be stored in the array
    Capacity int
    // ["a", "b", "c"]: the actual values stored in the array
    Array [10]string
}
```

It's important to note that this definition of a slice is purely an academic representation of how slices are implemented in Go.

Length and Capacity

While writing programs, you often need to know how many values are in a collection type, such as an array or slice. Go provides a built-in function to do exactly this, called len,[7] the documentation for which can be found in Listing 3.19. The len function tells you how many elements the collection *actually* has.

Listing 3.19   The len Function

```
$ go doc builtin.len

package builtin // import "builtin"

func len(v Type) int
    The len built-in function returns the length of v, according to its type:

        Array: the number of elements in v.
        Pointer to array: the number of elements in *v (even if v is nil).
        Slice, or map: the number of elements in v; if v is nil, len(v) is zero.
        String: the number of bytes in v.
        Channel: the number of elements queued (unread) in the channel buffer;
              ↪if v is nil, len(v) is zero.

    For some arguments, such as a string literal or a simple array expression,
    the result can be a constant. See the Go language specification's "Length
    and capacity" section for details.

Go Version: go1.19
```

Occasionally, you may need to know how many elements the collection can hold. This is called capacity. The built-in cap[8] function, in Listing 3.20, tells you the capacity of the slice, or how many elements it *can* have.

Listing 3.20   The cap Function

```
$ go doc builtin.cap

package builtin // import "builtin"

func cap(v Type) int
    The cap built-in function returns the capacity of v, according to its type:

        Array: the number of elements in v (same as len(v)).
        Pointer to array: the number of elements in *v (same as len(v)).
        Slice: the maximum length the slice can reach when resliced;
        ➥if v is nil, cap(v) is zero.
        Channel: the channel buffer capacity, in units of elements;
        ➥if v is nil, cap(v) is zero.

    For some arguments, such as a simple array expression, the result can be
    a constant. See the Go language specification's "Length and capacity"
    section for details.
```

Go Version: go1.19

Growing a Slice

Because slices in Go are dynamically sized, the Go runtime increases the capacity of the underlying slice as necessary. Listing 3.21 shows the first few growth stages of a slice as new values are added.

Listing 3.21   Demonstrating the Basic Growth Rate of a Slice

```
func main() {
    names := []string{}
    fmt.Println("len:", len(names)) // 0
    fmt.Println("cap:", cap(names)) // 0

    names = append(names, "Kurt")
    fmt.Println("len:", len(names)) // 1
    fmt.Println("cap:", cap(names)) // 1
```

---

8. https://pkg.go.dev/builtin#cap

```
names = append(names, "Janis")
fmt.Println("len:", len(names)) // 2
fmt.Println("cap:", cap(names)) // 2

names = append(names, "Jimi")
fmt.Println("len:", len(names)) // 3
fmt.Println("cap:", cap(names)) // 4

names = append(names, "Amy")
fmt.Println("len:", len(names)) // 4
fmt.Println("cap:", cap(names)) // 4

names = append(names, "Brian")

fmt.Println("len:", len(names)) // 5
fmt.Println("cap:", cap(names)) // 8
}
```

The rate of growth can change with each Go release as the Go team fine-tunes the runtime. Growth rate can also be dependent of architecture and operating system.

Listing 3.22 demonstrates growth rate over a large number of iterations. As the capacity of the slice changes, it prints the previous capacity and the new capacity.

Listing 3.22 Printing Slice Capacity of One Million Iterations

```
func main() {
    var sl []int

    hat := cap(sl)
    for i := 0; i < 1_000_000; i++ {
        sl = append(sl, i)
        c := cap(sl)
        if c != hat {
            fmt.Println(hat, c)
        }
        hat = c
    }
}
```

```
$ go run .

0 1
1 2
```

(continued)

```
2  4
4  8
8  16
16  32
32  64
64  128
128  256
256  512
512  848
848  1280
1280  1792
1792  2560
2560  3408
3408  5120
5120  7168
7168  9216
9216  12288
12288  16384
16384  21504
21504  27648
27648  34816
34816  44032
44032  55296
55296  69632
69632  88064
88064  110592
110592  139264
139264  175104
175104  219136
219136  274432
274432  344064
344064  431104
431104  539648
539648  674816
674816  843776
843776  1055744
```

Go Version: go1.19

Making a Slice

Slices can be declared in several different ways, including using the built-in make[9] function. The documentation for the make function is in Listing 3.23.

Listing 3.23   The make Function

```
$ go doc builtin.make

package builtin // import "builtin"

func make(t Type, size ...IntegerType) Type
    The make built-in function allocates and initializes an object of type
    ➥slice, map, or chan (only). Like new, the first argument is a type,
    ➥not a value. Unlike new, make's return type is the same as the type of
    ➥its argument, not a pointer to it. The specification of the result
    ➥depends on the type:

        Slice: The size specifies the length. The capacity of the slice is
        ➥equal to its length. A second integer argument may be provided to
        ➥specify a different capacity; it must be no smaller than the
        ➥length. For example, make([]int, 0, 10) allocates an underlying
        ➥array of size 10 and returns a slice of length 0 and capacity 10
        ➥that is backed by this underlying array.
        Map: An empty map is allocated with enough space to hold the
        ➥specified number of elements. The size may be omitted, in which case
        ➥a small starting size is allocated.
        Channel: The channel's buffer is initialized with the specified
        ➥buffer capacity. If zero, or the size is omitted, the channel is
        ➥unbuffered.

Go Version: go1.19
```

In Listing 3.24, we are declaring new variables of type []string in several different ways. Functionally, each of these is equivalent. Each of these different ways to declare a slice has different advantages and disadvantages, and it is not uncommon to see these various declaration styles in code.

Listing 3.24   Declaring Slices in Several Different Ways

```
func main() {
    // declare and initialize a slice of strings
    // with a length of 0 and capacity of 0
    a := []string{}
```

(continued)

---

9. https://pkg.go.dev/builtin#make

```
    // declare a variable of type slice of strings
    // with a length of 0 and capacity of 0
    var b []string

    // declare and initialize a slice of strings
    // with a length of 0 and capacity of 0
    c := make([]string, 0)

    fmt.Println(a)
    fmt.Println(b)
    fmt.Println(c)
}
```

```
$ go run .

[]
[]
[]
```

```
Go Version: go1.19
```

Make with Length and Capacity

The `make` function enables you to define the starting "length" of the slice and, optionally, the starting "capacity" of the slice. In Listing 3.25, we use the `make` function to create a slice of `string` values that has a length of 1 and a capacity of 3. Using the `len` and `cap` functions, we are able to print the length and the capacity of the slice.

Listing 3.25   Using make to Define the Starting Length and Capacity of a Slice

```
func main() {
    a := make([]string, 1, 3)

    fmt.Println(a)      // []
    fmt.Println(len(a)) // 1
    fmt.Println(cap(a)) // 3
}
```

```
$ go run .

[]
1
3
```

Go Version: go1.19

It's important to remember that even though you "allocated" extra capacity, you can't access that capacity until you assign a value to it.

Make and Append

Be careful when using both `make` and `append` because you may inadvertently create `zero` values in your slice. In Listing 3.26, we use the `make` function to create a new slice of `string` values that has an initial length of 2. This slice is assigned the variable `a`. This `a` variable already has two empty `string` values when we append two new values, `foo` and `bar`. The result is the `a` slice now contains four `string` values. When we print the slice using the `%q` formatting verb, which quotes the `string` type, we can see the two empty `string` values at the start of the slice.

Listing 3.26   Using make and append Can Be Problematic

```
func main() {
    a := make([]string, 2)
    a = append(a, "foo", "bar")

    fmt.Printf("%q", a)
}
```

```
$ go run .

["" "" "foo" "bar"]
```

Go Version: go1.19

What Happens When a Slice Grows

Slices are composed of three parts: length, capacity, and a pointer to an underlying array. In Figure 3.1, you see a theoretical representation of the internals of the slice: `[]string{"A", "B", "C", "D"}`.

If you append the values E, F, and G, it forces the slice to expand because it currently has no capacity for the new values. Go creates a new underlying array, copies the original values into the new one, and adds the new values, as shown in Figure 3.2.

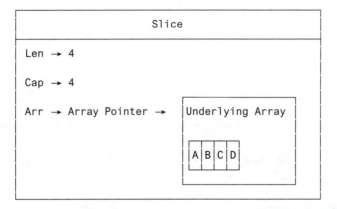

Figure 3.1   Theoretical representation of a slice

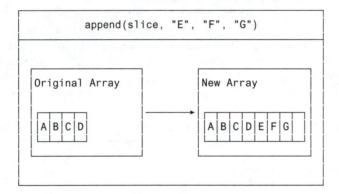

Figure 3.2   When full, a new array is created and values are copied over.

Figure 3.3 shows the final representation of the slice after the new values have been appended.

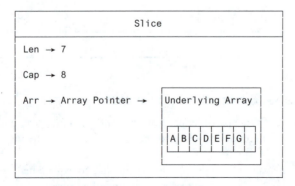

Figure 3.3   The final slice representation after appending

If the original underlying array is not reference by any other part of the program, it is marked for garbage collection.

Slice Subsets

Subsets of a slice (or a slice of a slice) allow you to work with just one section of a slice. To obtain a subset of a slice, you need to specify the starting index and ending index of the subset. In Listing 3.27, when we ask for `letters[2:5]`, we get a slice of the original slice, `letters`, containing elements from index 2 up to, but not including, index 5. In this case, the slice returned is `{"c", "d", "e"}`.

Listing 3.27 Obtaining Subsets of a Slice

```
func main() {
    letters := []string{"a", "b", "c", "d", "e", "f", "g"}

    fmt.Println(letters) // [a b c d e f g]

    // Get 3 elements starting with the third element
    fmt.Println(letters[2:5]) // [c d e]

    // functionally equivalent
    fmt.Println(letters[4:len(letters)]) // [e f g]
    fmt.Println(letters[4:])             // [e f g]

    // functionally equivalent
    fmt.Println(letters[0:4]) // [a b c d]
    fmt.Println(letters[:4])  // [a b c d]
}
```

```
$ go run .

[a b c d e f g]
[c d e]
[e f g]
[e f g]
[a b c d]
[a b c d]

Go Version: go1.19
```

When asking for a subset of a slice that starts at index 0, or that ends at the last index, you can omit the starting or ending index. In Listing 3.27, we ask for `letters[:4]`, which returns a slice of the original slice, `letters`, containing elements from index 0 up to, but not including, index 4. In this case, the slice returned is `{"a", "b", "c", "d"}`.

Mutating Slice Subsets

It is important to remember that when using a subset of a slice, you are just working with a reference to the original slice. Modifications to the subset will affect the original slice.

In Listing 3.28, you see that if we modify the subset but uppercase its values, the original slice also contains uppercase values.

Listing 3.28   Mutating Subsets of a Slice Affects the Original

```
func main() {
    names := []string{"Kurt", "Janis", "Jimi", "Amy"}

    // print the names slice
    fmt.Println(names)

    // get the first three elements of the 'names' slice
    subset := names[:3]

    // print out the subset slice
    fmt.Println(subset)

    // loop over the subset slice
    for i, g := range subset {
        // uppercase each string
        // and replace the value in
        // the subset slice
        subset[i] = strings.ToUpper(g)
    }

    // print out the subset slice, again
    fmt.Println(subset)

    // print out the original names slice
    fmt.Println(names)
}
```

```
$ go run .

[Kurt Janis Jimi Amy]
[Kurt Janis Jimi]
[KURT JANIS JIMI]
[KURT JANIS JIMI Amy]
```

```
Go Version: go1.19
```

Copying Slices

When a separate, independent copy of a slice is needed, you can use the built-in copy function, the documentation for which is in Listing 3.29.

Listing 3.29   The Built-In copy Function

```
$ go doc builtin.copy

package builtin // import "builtin"

func copy(dst, src []Type) int
    The copy built-in function copies elements from a source slice into a
    ➥destination slice. (As a special case, it also will copy bytes from a
    ➥string to a slice of bytes.) The source and destination may overlap.
    ➥Copy returns the number of elements copied, which will be the minimum
    ➥of len(src) and len(dst).
```

Go Version: go1.19

In Listing 3.30, we are using the copy[10] function instead of getting a subset of a slice. We are able to create a new slice that is independent of the original. The new slice can now be modified independently of the original.

Listing 3.30   Copying a Slice

```
func main() {
    names := []string{"Kurt", "Janis", "Jimi", "Amy"}

    // print the names slice
    fmt.Println(names)

    // make a new slice with
    // the correct length and
    // capacity to hold the subset
    subset := make([]string, 3)

    // copy the first three elements
    // of the names slice into the
    // subset slice
    copy(subset, names[:3])

    // print out the subset slice
    fmt.Println(subset)
```

(continued)

---

10. https://pkg.go.dev/builtin#copy

```go
    // loop over the subset slice
    for i, g := range subset {
        // uppercase each string
        // and replace the value in
        // the subset slice
        subset[i] = strings.ToUpper(g)
    }

    // print out the subset slice, again
    fmt.Println(subset)

    // print out the original names slice
    fmt.Println(names)
}
```

```
$ go run .

[Kurt Janis Jimi Amy]
[Kurt Janis Jimi]
[KURT JANIS JIMI]
[Kurt Janis Jimi Amy]

Go Version: go1.19
```

Converting an Array to a Slice

When writing functions or using most Go libraries, you will usually be working with slices because their flexibility often makes them easier to work with than arrays.

Consider the function defined in Listing 3.31. This function takes a slice of strings and prints out the values in the slice.

Listing 3.31 A Function That Accepts a Slice

```go
func slicesOnly(names []string) {
    for _, name := range names {
        fmt.Println(name)
    }
}
```

If we were to try and call the function with an array, we would get a compilation error, as shown in Listing 3.32.

Listing 3.32   Compilation Error Using an Array Instead of a Slice

```
func main() {
    // array of four strings
    names := [4]string{"Kurt", "Janis", "Jimi", "Amy"}

    // arrays can not be type cast to slices
    slicesOnly(names)
}
```

```
$ go run .

# demo
./main.go:11:13: cannot use names (variable of type [4]string) as type
➥[]string in argument to slicesOnly
```

```
Go Version: go1.19
```

We have demonstrated that Go can cast types like `int64` to `int`, but it is not possible to cast an array to a slice. If we were to try and cast an array to a slice, we would get a compilation error, as shown in Listing 3.33.

Listing 3.33   An Array Cannot Be Cast to a Slice

```
func main() {
    // array of four strings
    names := [4]string{"Kurt", "Janis", "Jimi", "Amy"}

    // try to cast array to slice
    slicesOnly([]string(names))
}
```

```
$ go run .

# demo
./main.go:11:22: cannot convert names (variable of type [4]string) to type
➥[]string
```

```
Go Version: go1.19
```

We can convert our array to a slice by asking for a subset of the array. Like slices, subsets of arrays can be created with the `[low:high]` syntax. For example, `names[0:2]` would create a slice of the first two elements of the array.

In Listing 3.34, we use the `[:]` syntax. This returns a slice of the entire array. With this new slice, we can now properly call our function.

Listing 3.34   Using a Slice of the Entire Array

```go
func main() {
    // array of four strings
    names := [4]string{"Kurt", "Janis", "Jimi", "Amy"}

    // convert to slice of strings
    // using the 'array[:]' syntax
    slicesOnly(names[:])
}
```

```
$ go run .

Kurt
Janis
Jimi
Amy
```

Go Version: go1.19

Iteration

In this section, we start to review how iteration works in Go. We look at the for and
range keywords and how to control loops using break and continue. We also explain how
to iterate over slices and arrays. As we progress through this book, we reveal more about
how iteration works with specific types and workflows.

The for Loop

In Go, there is only *one* looping construct: the for loop. The for loop is very versatile
and can be used to implement patterns such as for, while, do while, and do until.
Listing 3.35 gives an example of a for loop in Go. This example may seem familiar to you
if you have previous programming experience. It is very similar to how many languages
format their for loops.

A for loop can consist of three parts, with the parts being separated by a semicolon (;).
The first part is the precondition. In this example, the precondition is i := 0, which
creates a new variable, i, that is "untyped" and initialized to value of 0. The i variable
only exists within the scope of the for loop. The precondition is executed only once.

The second part of a for loop is the conditional, which is responsible for returning a
bool that indicates whether the loop should continue, true, or stop, false. In Listing
3.35, the conditional is i < len(names). This returns true as long as the variable i is less
than the length of the slice, names.

The last part of a for loop is the postcondition, which runs after each iteration of the
loop and before the next execution of the conditional. In this example, the postcondition

is i++, which increments the i variable by 1 after each iteration of the loop. When the i variable reaches the 4, the loop breaks as the condition of i being less than the length of the names slice is now `false`.

Listing 3.35   A for Loop in Go

```
for i := 0; i < N; i++ {
  // do work until i equals N
}
```

Iterating over Arrays and Slices

Iterating over arrays, slices, and maps is done using the for loop. In Listing 3.36, the len[11] function is used to return the length of the array, 4, so the for loop stops when i reaches 4.

Listing 3.36   Iterating over an Array

```
func main() {
    names := [4]string{"Kurt", "Janis", "Jimi", "Amy"}

    // iterate over the array using a for loop
    for i := 0; i < len(names); i++ {
        fmt.Println(names[i])
    }
}
```

```
$ go run .

Kurt
Janis
Jimi
Amy
```

```
Go Version: go1.19
```

The range Keyword

Previously, we used a "classic" for loop for iteration. Looping over collection types is so common in Go that the language offers the range keyword to simplify this code, as shown in Listing 3.37.

---

11. https://pkg.go.dev/builtin#len

Listing 3.37   Using the range Keyword to Iterate over an Array

```
names := [4]string{"Kurt", "Janis", "Jimi", "Amy"}

for i, n := range names {
    fmt.Printf("%d %s\n", i, n)
}
```

```
$ go run .

0 Kurt
1 Janis
2 Jimi
3 Amy

Go Version: go1.19
```

Range returns the index and the value of each item in the array or slice. If only the index of the loop is needed, as shown in Listing 3.38, and not the value, using only a single variable in the for loop with range returns the index of each loop.

Listing 3.38   Using the range Keyword to Iterate over an Array, Only Returning the Index

```
func main() {
    names := [4]string{"Kurt", "Janis", "Jimi", "Amy"}

    for i := range names {

        fmt.Printf("%d %s\n", i, names[i])
    }
}
```

```
$ go run .

0 Kurt
1 Janis
2 Jimi
3 Amy

Go Version: go1.19
```

A lot of languages expose an interface, or similar mechanism, that can be implemented to allow for custom iterable types. Go does not provide any such interface. Only the built-in collection types, and a few other built-in types, such as structs, maps, and channels, are supported with the range keyword.

Controlling Loops

The `continue` keyword allows you to go back to the start of the loop and stop executing the rest of the code in the `for` block. For example, in Listing 3.39, if the variable `i` equals 3, the `continue` keyword tells the `for` loop to skip any further execution of that iteration. The `for` loop then moves on to the next iteration of the `for` loop.

Listing 3.39   Using the `continue` Keyword

```
if i == 3 {
    // go to the start of the loop
    continue
}
```

This does not stop the loop from executing but rather ends that particular run of the loop.

To stop execution of a loop, you can use the `break` keyword. In Listing 3.40, for example, if the variable `i` equals 10, then the `break` keyword is used to stop execution of the loop.

Listing 3.40   Using the `break` Keyword

```
if i == 10 {
    // stops the loop
    break
}
```

With the `continue` and `break` keywords, you can control a `for` loop's execution to deliver the results you want.

In Listing 3.41, we have an infinite `for` loop, which is a loop that runs forever. In Go, an infinite `for` loop is one that has no precondition, condition, or postcondition.

We are controlling the execution of this infinite loop using the `continue` and `break` keywords. If `i` equals 3, we use the `continue` keyword to skip ahead to the next execution. If `i` equals 10, we use the `break` keyword to stop further execution of the loop.

Reviewing the output of the command, in Listing 3.41, we can see that the third iteration of the loop was skipped and the loop stopped when `i` became equal to 10.

Listing 3.41   Using the `continue` and `break` Keywords

```
func main() {

    // create a variable to act as an index
    var i int
```

(continued)

```go
    // create an infinite loop
    for {
        // increment the index
        i++

        if i == 3 {
            // go to the start of the loop
            continue
        }

        if i == 10 {
            // stops the loop
            break
        }

        fmt.Println(i)

    }

    fmt.Println("finished")
}
```

```
$ go run .

1
2
4
5
6
7
8
9
finished
```

```
Go Version: go1.19
```

Do While Loop

A do while loop is used in a situation where you want the loop to run at least 1 iteration, regardless of the condition.

A C/Java-style example would look something like Listing 3.42.

Listing 3.42 A C/Java-style do while Loop

```
do {

  // increment the index
  i++;

  // do the task
  task();

  // while the index is
  // less than N, continue
} while (i < N);
```

To create a do while style loop in Go, you can use a combination of an infinite loop and the break keyword, as shown in Listing 3.43.

Listing 3.43 A do while Loop in Go

```
// declare an index variable (0)
var i int

// use an infinite loop
// this ensures the first
// iteration is always executed
for {

    // increment the index
    i++

    // do the task
    task()

    // while the index is
    // less than N, continue
    if i < N {

        // index is N or greater
        // break the loop
        break
    }

}
```

Summary

In this chapter, we examined the differences between arrays and slices, the two basic list types in Go. We saw that slices are more flexible than arrays. Arrays are fixed length, and slices are dynamic. As a result, slices are used more often than arrays in Go.

We showed you how to use built-in functions, such as `append`, `len`, and `cap`, to manipulate arrays and slices. We also explained how to use the `make` function to create slices with specific capacities and lengths for efficiency.

Finally, in this chapter, we covered iteration in Go using the `for` keyword. We discussed how to use the `range` keyword to simplify iteration.

4

Maps and Control Structures

This chapter covers the basics of maps and control structures. We explain how maps are a powerful tool for storing key-value pairs. This chapter also covers control structures such as `if` and `switch` statements.

Maps

Maps are a powerful built-in data structure that associates keys and values. A map is an *unordered* set of values indexed by a unique key. Map keys and values can be set and retrieved using the [] syntax. In Listing 4.1, we create a new map, `map[string]string{}`, and assign it to the `users` variable. To assign a value, we can access the key using the `users[<key>]` syntax. In this case, we are accessing the key, `Janis`, for assignment. To retrieve the `Janis` key from the map, we can reverse the process. If we move the `users[<key>]` syntax to the right of the assignment operator, we are now accessing the value of the key for reading.

Listing 4.1 Setting and Retrieving Map Values

```
func main() {
    // create a map of strings to strings
    users := map[string]string{}

    // add a new key/value pair
    users["Janis"] = "janis@example.com"

    // ask for a value using the key
    email := users["Janis"]

    // print the value
    fmt.Println(email)
}
```

(continued)

```
$ go run .

janis@example.com
```

```
Go Version: go1.19
```

Length and Capacity

You can use built-in len[1] function to find the length (the number of keys) of a map. In Listing 4.2, we assigning 4 values into the users map. We then use the len function to retrieve the number of keys in the map. As shown in the output in Listing 4.2, the len function is correctly reporting the length of the users map as 4.

Listing 4.2   Using the len Function to Find the Length of a Map

```
func main() {
    users := map[string]string{}

    users["Kurt"] = "kurt@example.com"
    users["Janis"] = "janis@example.com"
    users["Jimi"] = "jimi@example.com"
    users["Amy"] = "Amy@example.com"

    fmt.Println("Map length:", len(users))
}
```

```
$ go run .

Map length: 4
```

```
Go Version: go1.19
```

Theoretically, maps are able to hold an infinite number of keys. Because maps have unlimited capacity, the built-in cap function cannot be used to find the capacity of a map. Listing 4.3 shows that trying to call the cap function with a map results in a compilation error informing us that a map is an invalid argument for the cap function.

Listing 4.3   Maps Have an "Unlimited" Capacity

```
func main() {
    users := map[string]string{}

    users["Kurt"] = "kurt@example.com"
    users["Janis"] = "janis@example.com"
```

---

1. https://pkg.go.dev/builtin#len

```
    users["Jimi"] = "jimi@example.com"
    users["Amy"] = "Amy@example.com"

    fmt.Println("Map capacity:", cap(users))
}
```

```
$ go run .

# demo
./main.go:14:35: invalid argument: users (variable of type
➥map[string]string) for cap
```

```
Go Version: go1.19
```

Initializing Maps

You can initialize maps in a couple of ways. The first, and *recommended*, way is to initialize the map at the same time as declaring the variable, as in Listing 4.4. This also allows for initializing the map with an initial set of keys and values.

Listing 4.4   Initializing a Map with a Short Syntax

```
users := map[string]string{
    "kurt@example.com":  "Kurt",
    "janis@example.com": "Janis",
    "jimi@example.com":  "Jimi",
}
```

You also can use the make[2] function to create new maps, as in Listing 4.5. Unlike slices and arrays, maps cannot be initialized with a length and capacity. Older code may use the make function; however, it is considered nonidiomatic in most circumstances to use the make function for map initialization.

Listing 4.5   Initializing a Map with the make Function

```
var users map[string]string
users = make(map[string]string)
users["kurt@example.com"] = "Kurt"
users["janis@example.com"] = "Janis"
users["jimi@example.com"] = "Jimi"
```

---

2. https://pkg.go.dev/builtin#make

Uninitialized Maps

If you don't initialize a map and try to access the values, you will receive a runtime `panic`, as shown in Listing 4.6.

Listing 4.6   Accessing an Uninitialized Map

```
var users map[string]string
users["kurt@example.com"] = "Kurt"
```

```
$ go run .

map[janis@example.com:Janis jimi@example.com:Jimi
↪kurt@example.com:Kurt]
map[janis@example.com:Janis jimi@example.com:Jimi
↪kurt@example.com:Kurt]

panic: assignment to entry in nil map

goroutine 1 [running]:
main.bad()
        ./main.go:41 +0x38
main.main()
        ./main.go:8 +0x28
exit status 2

Go Version: go1.19
```

Map Keys

Map keys must be comparable, which means the Go runtime can check the equality of the key in the map with the key being given. In Go, not all types are comparable. Basic data types, such as `string`, `[]byte`, and `int`, are the most-used key types. All are comparable and provide enough type variation to handle most use cases.

Complex and noncomparable types—such as functions (Listing 4.7), maps, or slices—cannot be used as key types in maps. Use of noncomparable types causes a compile time error.

Listing 4.7   Using a Noncomparable Type as a Map Key

```
m := map[func()]string{}
fmt.Println(m)
```

```
$ go build .

# demo
```

```
./main.go:8:15: invalid map key type func()
```

```
Go Version: go1.19
```

Structs as Keys

A struct whose fields are all simple comparable types can be used as a key type for a map. This can be useful for creating tuple-style keys. In Listing 4.8, because the `Simple` struct is composed of two fields, `ID` and `Name`, both of which are comparable types, the `Simple` struct can be used as the key type for a map.

Listing 4.8   Using a Struct with Simple Fields as a Map Key

```go
// Simple contains only comparable fields
// and can be used as a key type for a map.
type Simple struct {
    ID   int
    Name string
}

func main() {

    // create a map of Simple keys
    // to string values
    simple := map[Simple]string{}

    // create a new Simple key
    sk := Simple{ID: 1, Name: "Kurt"}
    // add a new key/value pair
    simple[sk] = "kurt@example.com"

    // print the simple map
    fmt.Println(simple)
}
```

```
$ go run .

map[{1 Kurt}:kurt@example.com]
```

```
Go Version: go1.19
```

Structs that contain noncomparable fields, however, *cannot* be used as the key type for a map. Trying to do so causes a compilation error. In Listing 4.9, the `Complex` struct type is composed of two fields: Data and Fn. Both of these fields are complex noncomparable types. The Fn field, for example, is a function, and functions cannot be compared.

Listing 4.9   Using a Struct with Noncomparable Fields as a Map Key

```
// Complex contains non-comparable fields
// and cannot be used as a key type for a map.
type Complex struct {
    Data map[string]string
    Fn   func() error
}


func main() {

    // create a map of Complex keys
    // to string values
    complex := map[Complex]string{}

    // print the complex map
    fmt.Println(complex)
}
```

```
$ go run .

# demo
./main.go:19:17: invalid map key type Complex
```

```
Go Version: go1.19
```

Iterating Maps

Maps can be iterated over using the range keyword, in much the same way that arrays and slices can. The range keyword, in the case of maps, returns the key and the value for each entry in the map. In Listing 4.10, using the range keyword to iterate over the users map, we are given a single key/value pair, which are assigned to the key and value variables.

Listing 4.10   Iterating over a Map

```
func main() {
    users := map[string]string{
        "Kurt":  "kurt@example.com",
        "Janis": "janis@example.com",
        "Jimi":  "jimi@example.com",
        "Amy":   "Amy@example.com",
    }
```

```
    // iterate over the map using a for loop
    // retrieve the key and value as variables
    for key, value := range users {
        fmt.Printf("%s <%s>\n", key, value)
    }
}
```

```
$ go run .

Kurt <kurt@example.com>
Janis <janis@example.com>
Jimi <jimi@example.com>
Amy <Amy@example.com>

Go Version: go1.19
```

When iterating over a map with a range loop, the iteration order is not specified and is not guaranteed to be the same from one iteration to the next.

Range returns the key and the value of each item in the map. If only the key for each loop is needed, and not the value, using only a single variable in the for loop with range returns only the key in the map. In Listing 4.11, instead of asking for both the key and value for each iteration of the map, we just ask for the key. We can then use that key to access the value from the map users[key].

Listing 4.11 Iterating over a Map with Only the Key

```
func main() {
    users := map[string]string{
        "Kurt":  "kurt@example.com",
        "Janis": "janis@example.com",
        "Jimi":  "jimi@example.com",
        "Amy":   "Amy@example.com",
    }

    // iterate over the map using a for loop
    // retrieve the key as a variable
    for key := range users {

        // retrieve the value from the map
        // using the key
        fmt.Printf("%s <%s>\n", key, users[key])
```

(continued)

```
    }
}
```

```
$ go run .

Kurt <kurt@example.com>
Janis <janis@example.com>
Jimi <jimi@example.com>
Amy <Amy@example.com>
```

Go Version: go1.19

Deleting Keys from a Map

You can use the built-in `delete`[3] function, Listing 4.12, to remove a key, and its value, from a map.

Listing 4.12   The `delete` Function

```
$ go doc builtin.delete

package builtin // import "builtin"

func delete(m map[Type]Type1, key Type)
    The delete built-in function deletes the element with the specified
    ➥key (m[key]) from the map. If m is nil or there is no such
    ➥element, delete is a no-op.
```

Go Version: go1.19

Only one key at a time can be deleted from a map. In Listing 4.13, we call the `delete` function passing in the `users` map and the key `Kurt`. The result, when printed, is a map that no longer contains the `Kurt` key.

Listing 4.13   Deleting a Key from a Map

```
func main() {
    users := map[string]string{
        "Kurt":   "kurt@example.com",
        "Janis":  "janis@example.com",
        "Jimi":   "jimi@example.com",
        "Amy":    "Amy@example.com",
    }
```

---

3. https://pkg.go.dev/builtin#delete

```
    // delete the "Kurt" entry
    delete(users, "Kurt")

    // print the map
    fmt.Println(users)
}
```

```
$ go run .

map[Amy:Amy@example.com Janis:janis@example.com
➥Jimi:jimi@example.com]

Go Version: go1.19
```

If the key is not present in the map, the delete function is a no-op, and the map will not be modified. In Listing 4.14, trying to delete a nonexistent key, Unknown, from the users map neither returns an error nor raises a panic. There is no indication as to the success or failure of calling the delete function.

Listing 4.14   Deleting a Key from a Map That Is Not Present

```go
func main() {
    users := map[string]string{
        "Kurt":  "kurt@example.com",
        "Janis": "janis@example.com",
        "Jimi":  "jimi@example.com",
        "Amy":   "Amy@example.com",
    }

    // delete the "Unknown" entry
    delete(users, "Unknown")

    // print the map
    fmt.Println(users)
}
```

```
$ go run .

map[Amy:Amy@example.com Janis:janis@example.com
➥Jimi:jimi@example.com Kurt:kurt@example.com]

Go Version: go1.19
```

Nonexistent Map Keys

When asking for a key from a map that doesn't exist, Go returns the zero of the map's value type. This can often lead to bugs in code.

In Listing 4.15, you see that even if you don't get an error, you still have a bug because you didn't check for the existence of the value.

Listing 4.15   Getting a Nonexistent Map Key

```go
func main() {
    data := map[int]string{}
    data[1] = "Hello, World"

    value := data[10]

    // Because of the way Zero values in Go work,
    // we still get an 'zero' value representation of the struct
    // which is certainly a bug in production
    fmt.Printf("%q", value)
}
```

```
$ go run .

""
```

Go Version: go1.19

Checking Map Key Existence

Maps in Go return an optional second boolean argument that tells you if the key exists in the map. Checking for the existence of the key in your code can help you avoid bugs caused by nonexistent keys.

In Listing 4.16, we ask for the optional second boolean argument when retrieving a value from a map. We then use that boolean, ok, to handle the case where the key is not present in the map.

Listing 4.16   Checking for the Existence of a Key in a Map

```go
func main() {
    users := map[string]string{
        "Kurt":  "kurt@example.com",
        "Janis": "janis@example.com",
        "Jimi":  "jimi@example.com",
        "Amy":   "Amy@example.com",
    }
```

```
    key := "Kurt"

    email, ok := users[key]
    if !ok {
        fmt.Printf("Key not found: %q\n", key)
        os.Exit(1)
    }

    fmt.Printf("Found key %q: %q", key, email)

}
```

```
$ go run .

Found key "Kurt": "kurt@example.com"
```

```
Go Version: go1.19
```

Exploiting Zero Value

There may be times when the zero value is OK. Consider Listing 4.17 and the task of counting the occurrences of words in a string. To store the count of each word, you can use a map with the key type `string` and the value type `int`.

When asking this map for a key that doesn't exist, the zero value of the map's value type is returned. The zero value of an `int` is 0, which is a valid starting point for counting a word's occurrences.

Listing 4.17 Counting the Occurrences of Words in a String

```
func main() {
    counts := map[string]int{}

    sentence := "The quick brown fox jumps over the lazy dog"

    words := strings.Fields(strings.ToLower(sentence))

    for _, w := range words {
        // if the word is already in the map, increment it
        // otherwise, set it to 1 and add it to the map
        counts[w] = counts[w] + 1
    }
```

(continued)

```
        fmt.Println(counts)
}
```

```
$ go run .

map[brown:1 dog:1 fox:1 jumps:1 lazy:1 over:1 quick:1 the:2]

Go Version: go1.19
```

Integers in Go can be incremented and decremented in place, using the ++ or --
operators, respectively. This means our code could be simplified because the act of
incrementing the zero value of a missing map key causes the key/value pair to be added to
the map. For example, in Listing 4.18, we are incrementing a map key's value in-place
using the ++ operator.

Listing 4.18   Using ++ to Increment a Map Value in Place

```
for _, w := range words {
    // if the word is already in the map, increment it
    // otherwise, set it to 1 and add it to the map
    counts[w]++
}
```

Testing Presence Only

When retrieving a value from a map, you can use the second, optional, boolean argument
to test whether the key exists in the map. To do this, however, you must also capture the
value. There may be times when the value is not needed. In this case, you can use the
_ to discard the value. For example, in Listing 4.19, when asking for the key foo from the
map, we can discard the value by using the underscore (_) operator and only retain the
second boolean value to the exists variable.

Listing 4.19   Testing the Presence of a Key in a Map

```
func main() {
    words := map[string]int{
        "brown": 1,
        "dog":   1,
        "fox":   1,
        "jumps": 1,
        "lazy":  1,
        "over":  1,
```

```
        "quick": 1,
        "the":   2,
    }

    // discard the value using '_'
    // keep only the existence boolean
    _, exists := words["foo"]

    fmt.Println(exists)
}
```

```
$ go run .

false
```

Go Version: go1.19

Maps and Complex Values

Storing complex values, such as a struct, in a map is a very common practice. However, updating those complex values is not as straightforward as updating a simple value, like an int.

It may seem intuitive to simply assign a new value to a struct via a map lookup, like we did with an int in Listing 4.17. However, this is not the case. In Listing 4.20, you see that trying to update a struct in place causes a compilation error.

Listing 4.20 Compilation Error Trying to Update a Struct in a Map

```
type User struct {
    ID   int
    Name string
}

func main() {

    // create a map of users
    data := map[int]User{}

    // create a new user
    user := User{ID: 1, Name: "Kurt"}

    // add the user to the map
    data[1] = user
```

(continued)

```
    // update the user in the map
    data[1].Name = "Janis"

    fmt.Printf("%+v", data)
}
```

```
$ go run .

# demo
./main.go:23:2: cannot assign to struct field data[1].Name in map
```

Go Version: go1.19

Copy on Insert

When inserting a value into a map, the value is copied, Listing 4.21. This means that changes made to the original value *after* insertion aren't reflected in the value stored in the map.

Listing 4.21 Values Inserted into a Map Are Copied

```
type User struct {
    ID   int
    Name string
}

func main() {

    // create a map of users
    data := map[int]User{}

    // create a new user
    user := User{ID: 1, Name: "Kurt"}

    // add the user to the map
    data[1] = user

    // update the user
    user.Name = "Janis"

    fmt.Printf("User: %+v\n", user)
    fmt.Printf("Map:  %+v\n", data)
}
```

```
$ go run .

User: {ID:1 Name:Janis}
Map:  map[1:{ID:1 Name:Kurt}]
```

Go Version: go1.19

Updating Complex Map Values

When updating a complex value in a map, Listing 4.22, that value must first be retrieved from the map. Once retrieved, the value can be updated. After the changes have been made, the value needs to be reinserted into the map for the changes to take effect.

Listing 4.22 Updating Complex Values in a Map

```go
type User struct {
    ID   int
    Name string

}

func main() {

    // create a map of users
    data := map[int]User{}

    // create a new user
    user1 := User{ID: 1, Name: "Kurt"}

    // add the user to the map
    data[1] = user1

    // retrieve the user from the map
    user2 := data[1]

    // update the user
    user2.Name = "Janis"

    // re-insert the user into the map
    data[1] = user2

    fmt.Printf("%+v", data)
}
```

(continued)

```
$ go run .

map[1:{ID:1 Name:Janis}]

Go Version: go1.19
```

Listing Keys in a Map

Go does not provide a way to get just a list of keys or values from a map. To build a list of keys or values, Listing 4.23, you must iterate over the map and save the keys or values to a slice or array.

Listing 4.23   Listing Keys from a Map

```go
func main() {

    // create a map of months
    months := map[int]string{
        1:  "January",
        2:  "February",
        3:  "March",
        4:  "April",
        5:  "May",
        6:  "June",
        7:  "July",
        8:  "August",
        9:  "September",
        10: "October",
        11: "November",
        12: "December",
    }

    // create a slice to hold the keys
    // set its length to 0 to start with
    // and its capacity to the length
    // of the map
    keys := make([]int, 0, len(months))

    // loop through the map
    for k := range months {

        // append the key to the slice
        keys = append(keys, k)
    }
```

```
    fmt.Printf("keys: %+v\n", keys)
}
```

```
$ go run .

keys: [2 3 4 6 7 8 10 1 5 9 11 12]

Go Version: go1.19
```

In Go, maps are not ordered and there are no built-in methods for sorting maps. When iterating over a map, like in Listing 4.23, the order of the keys is not guaranteed.

Sorting Keys

To sort a map, you must first get the keys from the map, sort the keys, and then use the sorted keys to retrieve the values from the map. The sort[4] package, Listing 4.24, provides a number of functions and interfaces for sorting collection types.

Listing 4.24   The sort Package

```
$ go doc sort

package sort // import "sort"

Package sort provides primitives for sorting slices and
➥user-defined collections.

func Float64s(x []float64)
func Float64sAreSorted(x []float64) bool
func Ints(x []int)
func IntsAreSorted(x []int) bool
func IsSorted(data Interface) bool
func Search(n int, f func(int) bool) int
func SearchFloat64s(a []float64, x float64) int
func SearchInts(a []int, x int) int
func SearchStrings(a []string, x string) int
func Slice(x any, less func(i, j int) bool)
func SliceIsSorted(x any, less func(i, j int) bool) bool
func SliceStable(x any, less func(i, j int) bool)
func Sort(data Interface)
func Stable(data Interface)
func Strings(x []string)
```

(continued)

---

4. https://pkg.go.dev/sort

```
func StringsAreSorted(x []string) bool
type Float64Slice []float64
type IntSlice []int
type Interface interface{ ... }
    func Reverse(data Interface) Interface
type StringSlice []string
```

Go Version: go1.19

In Listing 4.25, after iterating over the map and building a slice of keys, we can sort those keys in place using the sort.Ints[5] function. With a sorted list of keys, we can then iterate over the keys and retrieve the values from the map. The result, as shown in Listing 4.25, is a sorted list of values.

Listing 4.25   Sorting Keys and Retrieving Values from a Map

```
func main() {

    // create a map of months
    months := map[int]string{
        1:  "January",
        2:  "February",
        3:  "March",
        4:  "April",
        5:  "May",
        6:  "June",
        7:  "July",
        8:  "August",
        9:  "September",
        10: "October",
        11: "November",
        12: "December",
    }

    // create a slice to hold the keys
    // set its length to 0 to start with
    // and its capacity to the length
    // of the map
    keys := make([]int, 0, len(months))

    // loop through the map
    for k := range months {
```

5. https://pkg.go.dev/sort#Ints

```go
        // append the key to the slice
        keys = append(keys, k)
    }

    // sort the keys
    sort.Ints(keys)

    // loop through the keys
    // and print the key/value pairs
    for _, k := range keys {
        fmt.Printf("%02d: %s\n", k, months[k])
    }
}
```

```
$ go run .

01: January
02: February
03: March
04: April
05: May
06: June
07: July
08: August
09: September
10: October
11: November
12: December

Go Version: go1.19
```

If Statements

If statements are the core way that most programming languages use to make logic decisions. The if statement in Go is like most other languages, with a few extra syntax options.

In Listing 4.26, we use an equality comparison, the == operator, to determine whether the greet variable is equal to true. If it is, we print the hello string.

Listing 4.26 A Basic Boolean Logic Check

```go
func main() {
    greet := true
```

(continued)

```
    if greet == true {
        fmt.Println("Hello")
    }
}
```

```
$ go run .

Hello

Go Version: go1.19
```

Due to the way that Go interprets the expression, you can use anything that evaluates to true. Listing 4.26 can be rewritten to remove the comparison against true. Listing 4.27 functions identically to Listing 4.26, but it does so by just using the single variable greet that evaluates to true or false.

Listing 4.27   A Basic if Statement

```
func main() {
    greet := true

    if greet {
        fmt.Println("Hello")
    }
}
```

```
$ go run .

Hello

Go Version: go1.19
```

The else **Statement**

We can also make use of the else statement, Listing 4.28. This allows us to program for both the true and false state of our expression.

Listing 4.28   An if Statement with an else Statement

```
func main() {
    greet := true

    if greet {
        fmt.Println("Hello")
```

```
    } else {
        fmt.Println("Goodbye")
    }
}
```

```
$ go run .

Hello

Go Version: go1.19
```

Although Listing 4.28 is valid code, in Go, it is considered best practice to avoid using the else statement whenever possible. A common use case is to use what is referred to as an "early return." Listing 4.29 is functionally equivalent to Listing 4.28, but it uses an early return to avoid using the else keyword. The typical result is clearer code.

Listing 4.29   An if Statement with an Early Return

```
func main() {
    greet := true

    if greet {
        fmt.Println("Hello")
        return
    }

    fmt.Println("Goodbye")
}
```

```
$ go run .

Hello

Go Version: go1.19
```

The else if Statement

When necessary, you can make use of the else if syntax, Listing 4.30. This allows you to evaluate several different expressions in one if statement.

Listing 4.30   An `if` Statement with an `else if` Statement

```
func main() {
    greet := true
    name := "Janis"

    if greet && name != "" {
        fmt.Println("Hello", name)
    } else if greet {
        fmt.Println("Hello")
    } else {
        fmt.Println("Goodbye")
    }
}
```

```
$ go run .

Hello Janis

Go Version: go1.19
```

Listing 4.30 could also be written with early returns as well as nested `if` statements. This would result in simpler code that is both more readable and less likely to introduce bugs later on in refactoring.

Assignment Scope

A common operation in Go is to look up a value in a `map`. When doing this, it is important to check that the item was found in the map. You do this by asking for the second optional boolean value.

In Listing 4.31, the name is looked up, and then an `if` statement is used to validate that the name was found.

Although doing the lookup and the logic test in two lines of code is fine, it does have one disadvantage, which is that the scope of the `age` and `ok` variables are available throughout the entire `main` function. From a code quality standpoint, any time you can reduce variable scope, you are likely reducing future bugs in your code.

Listing 4.31   Scoping Variables to an `if` Statement

```
func main() {
    users := map[string]int{
        "Kurt":  27,
        "Janis": 15,
        "Jimi":  40,
    }
```

```
    name := "Amy"

    age, ok := users[name]
    if ok {
        fmt.Printf("%s is %d years old\n", name, age)
        return
    }

    fmt.Printf("Couldn't find %s in the users map\n", name)
}
```

```
$ go run .

Couldn't find Amy in the users map

Go Version: go1.19
```

As such, Go also allows you to create a simple statement before the expression is evaluated. You can use this approach when performing map lookups, as in Listing 4.31, or for other operations that require setting a local variable only for use in the logic expression of the if statement.

To make use of this syntax, you can first write the assignment statement and then use the semicolon followed by the logic expression.

One of the primary advantages of creating the assignment as part of the if statement is that it scopes those variables to the if statement. In Listing 4.32, the age and ok variables are no longer available in the entire scope of the main function but only available within the scope of the if statement. Any time you can reduce the scope of where a variable is used, it results in better code quality because you are less likely to introduce a bug.

Listing 4.32 Scoping Variables to an if Statement

```
func main() {
    users := map[string]int{
        "Kurt":  27,
        "Janis": 15,
        "Jimi":  40,
    }

    name := "Amy"
```

(continued)

```
if age, ok := users[name]; ok {
    fmt.Printf("%s is %d years old\n", name, age)
    return
}

fmt.Printf("Couldn't find %s in the users map\n", name)
}
```

```
$ go run .

Couldn't find Amy in the users map
```

```
Go Version: go1.19
```

Logic and Math Operators

When dealing with logic control statements such as the `if` statement, understanding how logic operators work can help simplify your code.

While there are several operators, we can break them down into four categories: boolean, mathematical, logical, and bitwise. Tables 4.1 through 4.4 outline these categories.

Table 4.1   Boolean Operators

Operator	Description
&&	Conditional AND
||	Conditional OR
!	NOT

Table 4.2   Mathematical Operators

Operator	Description
+	Sum
-	Difference
*	Product
/	Quotient
%	Remainder (modulus)

Table 4.3 Logic Comparison

Operator	Description
==	Equals
!=	Not equal
<	Less than
<=	Less than or equal
>	Greater than
>=	Greater than or equal

Table 4.4 Bitwise Operators

Operator	Description
&	Bitwise AND
|	Bitwise OR
^	Bitwise XOR
&^	Bit clear (AND NOT)
«	Left shift
»	Right shift

Switch **Statements**

Switch statements allow for the same type of logic decisions as if statements but tend to be easier to read.

Consider Listing 4.33. The large amount of if/else if statements make it difficult to read and maintain.

Listing 4.33 A Complex Set of if/else if Statements

```
func main() {
    month := 3

    if month == 1 {
        fmt.Println("January")
    } else if month == 2 {
        fmt.Println("February")
```

(continued)

```
    } else if month == 3 {
        fmt.Println("March")
    } else if month == 4 {
        fmt.Println("April")
    } else if month == 5 {
        fmt.Println("May")
    } else if month == 6 {
        fmt.Println("June")
    } else if month == 7 {
        fmt.Println("July")
    } else if month == 8 {
        fmt.Println("August")
    } else if month == 9 {
        fmt.Println("September")
    } else if month == 10 {
        fmt.Println("October")
    } else if month == 11 {
        fmt.Println("November")
    } else if month == 12 {
        fmt.Println("December")
    }
}
```

```
$ go run .

March
```

```
Go Version: go1.19
```

The switch statement is a more compact way to write the same logic. In Listing 4.34, we are able to replace the if/else if statements with a switch statement and use the case keyword to evaluate the expression. Each case statement is evaluated in order, and the first one that evaluates to true is used.

Listing 4.34   A Long Version of a switch Statement

```
func main() {
    month := 3

    switch {
    case month == 1:
        fmt.Println("January")
    case month == 2:
```

```
        fmt.Println("February")
    case month == 3:
        fmt.Println("March")
    case month == 4:
        fmt.Println("April")
    case month == 5:
        fmt.Println("May")
    case month == 6:
        fmt.Println("June")
    case month == 7:
        fmt.Println("July")
    case month == 8:
        fmt.Println("August")
    case month == 9:
        fmt.Println("September")
    case month == 10:
        fmt.Println("October")
    case month == 11:
        fmt.Println("November")
    case month == 12:
        fmt.Println("December")
    }
}
```

```
$ go run .

March
```

```
Go Version: go1.19
```

In Listing 4.34, there is no expression provided to the switch statement. However, the switch statement allows for the use of an expression on the initial line. This removes the need to repeat the month == part of the statement on each line. In Listing 4.35, we use the switch statement to evaluate the month variable. Each case statement can then be simplified to case N, where N is the number of the month.

Listing 4.35 The switch Statement with a Variable

```
func main() {
    month := 3

    switch month {
```

(continued)

```
    case 1:
        fmt.Println("January")
    case 2:
        fmt.Println("February")
    case 3:
        fmt.Println("March")
    case 4:
        fmt.Println("April")
    case 5:
        fmt.Println("May")
    case 6:
        fmt.Println("June")
    case 7:
        fmt.Println("July")
    case 8:
        fmt.Println("August")
    case 9:
        fmt.Println("September")
    case 10:
        fmt.Println("October")
    case 11:
        fmt.Println("November")
    case 12:
        fmt.Println("December")
    }
}
```

Default

When using a switch statement, if none of the cases are matched, a default block can be used, as in Listing 4.36.

Listing 4.36 Using a default Case with a switch Statement

```
func main() {
    month := 13

    switch month {
    case 1:
        fmt.Println("January")
    case 2:
        fmt.Println("February")
    case 3:
        fmt.Println("March")
```

```
    case 4:
        fmt.Println("April")
    case 5:
        fmt.Println("May")
    case 6:
        fmt.Println("June")
    case 7:
        fmt.Println("July")
    case 8:
        fmt.Println("August")
    case 9:
        fmt.Println("September")
    case 10:
        fmt.Println("October")
    case 11:
        fmt.Println("November")
    case 12:
        fmt.Println("December")
    default:
        fmt.Println("Invalid Month")
    }
}
```

```
$ go run .

Invalid Month
```

```
Go Version: go1.19
```

Fallthrough

When there is a need to match more than one condition, you can use `fallthrough` to allow more than one case to be matched. (See Listing 4.37.)

Listing 4.37   Using `fallthrough` with a `switch` Statement

```
func RecommendActivity(temp int) {

    fmt.Printf("It is %d degrees out. You could", temp)

    switch {
    case temp <= 32:
        fmt.Print(" go ice skating,")
        fallthrough
```

(continued)

```go
        case temp >= 45 && temp < 90:
            fmt.Print(" go jogging,")
            fallthrough
        case temp >= 80:
            fmt.Print(" go swimming,")
            fallthrough
        default:
            fmt.Print(" or just stay home.\n")
        }
}
```

```go
func main() {
    RecommendActivity(19)
    RecommendActivity(45)
    RecommendActivity(90)
}
```

```
$ go run .

It is 19 degrees out. You could go ice skating, go jogging,
➥go swimming, or just stay home.
It is 45 degrees out. You could go jogging, go swimming, or
➥just stay home.
It is 90 degrees out. You could go swimming, or just stay home.

Go Version: go1.19
```

Summary

In this chapter, we explored maps in Go. We explained how to declare and use maps and how to use control structures such as if and switch statements. We discussed that maps need to be initialized before they can be used. We showed you how to check for key existence, how to delete a key, and how to iterate over a map.

With this chapter, we have now covered most of the basic data types, operators, keywords, functions, and control structures in Go. With this knowledge, you can now begin to delve into more interesting, and fun, topics. If at any point in the rest of this book you start to feel lost, the answers are most likely in Chapters 1 through 4.

5

Functions

In this chapter, we discuss a core part of any language: functions. In Go, functions are first-class citizens that can be used in many ways. First, we show you how to create functions using the `func` keyword. Then we explain how to handle inbound arguments and return values. Finally, we cover advance function topics, such as variadic arguments, deferring functions, and the `init` function.

Function Definitions

Functions in Go resemble functions from most other programming languages. Listing 5.1 shows the definition of two functions: `main` and `sayHello`. It also shows two different function calls: `sayHello()` and `fmt.Println("Hello")`.

Listing 5.1 A Program That Prints `Hello`

```
func main() {
    sayHello()
}

func sayHello() {
    fmt.Println("Hello")
}
```

```
$ go run .

Hello
```

```
Go Version: go1.19
```

Arguments

Functions can take N number of arguments, including other functions. Function arguments are declared as (`name type`). Because Go is a typed language, you must define the types of the arguments in the function definition. The type of the argument follows the name of the argument.

In Listing 5.2, the function, sayHello, accepts one argument named greeting of type string.

Listing 5.2 Using Function Arguments

```
func main() {
    sayHello("Hello")
}

func sayHello(greeting string) {
    fmt.Println(greeting)
}
```

```
$ go run .

Hello
```

```
Go Version: go1.19
```

Arguments of the Same Type

When declaring multiple arguments of the same type, the type only needs to be declared at the end of the argument list. In Listing 5.3, both examples are functionally identical. The more explicit (longer) version is preferred for clarity.

Listing 5.3 Declaring Multiple Arguments of the Same Type

```
func main() {
    sayHello("Hello", "Kurt")
    sayHello2("Hello", "Janis")
}

func sayHello(greeting, name string) {
    fmt.Printf("%s, %s\n", greeting, name)
}

func sayHello2(greeting string, name string) {
    fmt.Printf("%s, %s\n", greeting, name)
}
```

```
$ go run .

Hello, Kurt
Hello, Janis
```

```
Go Version: go1.19
```

When declaring the type only once at the end of the argument list, if you need to insert an argument between the two and you don't declare the type for the first argument, it inherits the type from the newly inserted argument. In Listing 5.4, the type of `greeting` was `string` and now is of type `int`.

Listing 5.4   Possible Bug Caused by Not Declaring *All* Argument Types

```go
func sayHello3(greeting, i int, name string) {
    fmt.Printf("%s, %s\n", greeting, name)
}
```

By always declaring the type for each argument, you make your code more readable, maintainable, and bug resistant.

Return Arguments

Functions can return `0` to `N` numbers of values, though it is considered best practice to not return more than two or three.

The type of the return value(s) is declared after the function definition (Listing 5.5).

Listing 5.5   Returning Values

```go
package main

import "fmt"

func main() {
    fmt.Println(sayHello())
}

func sayHello() string {
    return "Hello"
}
```

When returning an `error`, which is covered in Chapter 9, it is considered best practice to return that value as the last value. In Listing 5.6, we see three examples of functions that return values. The functions `two` and `three` both return multiple values, with an `error` as the last value.

Listing 5.6   Returning an error

```
func one() string
func two() (string, error)
func three() (int, string, error)
```

Multiple Return Arguments

Multiple return arguments need to be placed inside of a set of (). In Listing 5.7, the function two returns three values: `string`, `int`, and `int`.

Listing 5.7   Multiple Return Arguments Need to Be Placed Inside of ()

```
// info returns the Go-syntax representation
// of the slice and its length and capacity
func info(s []string) (string, int, int) {
    gs := fmt.Sprintf("%#v", s)
    l := len(s)
    c := cap(s)
    return gs, l, c
}
```

When multiple return arguments are used, then *all* return arguments must be used. For example, in Listing 5.8, the `info` function returns three values. Each of these values must be captured. In this case, the values returned from the `info` function are assigned to the variables gs, `length`, and `capacity`.

Listing 5.8   Using Multiple Return Arguments

```
func main() {
    names := []string{"Kurt", "Janis", "Jimi", "Amy"}

    // call info with names slice
    // assign the return values
    // to the variables gs, l, and c
    gs, length, capacity := info(names)

    // print the Go-syntax representation
    fmt.Println(gs)
```

```
    // print the length and capacity
    fmt.Println("len: ", length)
    fmt.Println("cap: ", capacity)
}
```

```
$ go run .

[]string{"Kurt", "Janis", "Jimi", "Amy"}
len:  4
cap:  4
```

```
Go Version: go1.19
```

Unwanted return arguments can be ignored by using the _ placeholder. In Listing 5.9, for example, we are only interested in capturing the second return value from the info function. Using the _, operator, we can discard the values we don't want.

Listing 5.9 Ignoring Unwanted Return Arguments

```
names := []string{"Kurt", "Janis", "Jimi", "Amy"}

// capture only the second return value
// to the length variable and
// discard other returned values
_,length, _ := info(names)

fmt.Println(length)
```

```
$ go run .

4
```

```
Go Version: go1.19
```

Named Returns

You can give the return argument of a Go function a name and use it just like another variable declaration within the function. In Listing 5.10, the IsValid function has a named returned, valid, of type bool. Inside of the IsValid function, the valid variable is already initialized and ready for use. The following are rules for named returns:

- Variables are automatically initialized to their zero values within the function scope.
- Executing a return with no value returns the value of the named return.
- Names are not mandatory.

Listing 5.10   Named Returns

```
func IsValid() (valid bool) {
    valid = true
    return
}
```

It is best practice to *not use named returns*, unless they are needed for documentation.

Given the coordinates function in Listing 5.11 that returns latitude and longitude, it would be hard to remember which parameter is meant for which value.

Listing 5.11   A Function Returning Two Unnamed Arguments

```
func coordinates() (int, int)
```

In Listing 5.12, using named returns for the coordinates function helps to clarify the intentions of the returned values. Using named returns should only be used for documentation purposes. Even then, it could be argued that they still should be avoided.

Listing 5.12   A Function Returning Two Named Arguments

```
func coordinates() (lat int, lng int)
```

When Named Returns Go Bad

Listing 5.13 is an example of the confusion, and bugs, that can occur when using a named return. For example, what does the following return? Can you tell by looking at the code? Before running the code, what is your expectation of the outcome?

Listing 5.13   Named Returns Confusion

```
// MeaningOfLife returns the meaning of life
func MeaningOfLife() (meaning int) {

    // defer a function print the meaning of life
    // then set the meaning to 0
    defer func() {
        fmt.Println("defer", meaning)
        meaning = 0
```

```
    }()

    // return the value 42
    return 42
}
```

```
$ go run .

defer 42
0
```

Go Version: go1.19

When using a named return, that return is automatically assigned to the value returned by the function. In Listing 5.13, when `return 42` is executed, the value of the named return variable `meaning` is assigned the value of 42. However, a defer statement is executed when the function finishes but not before it returns. This gives the deferred function a chance to change the value of `meaning` *before* the function returns.

First-Class Functions

In Go, functions are first-class citizens. That means you can treat functions as you do any other types. Function signatures are a `type`. Everything you've learned so far about the Go type system applies to functions as well. Functions can be arguments and return values to/from other functions, just as any other Go type can.

Functions as Variables

Like other types you have seen, such as slices and maps, a function definition can also be assigned to a variable for use later. In Listing 5.14, for example, we define and initialize a new variable, `f`, to a function definition, `fun()`, which neither accepts nor returns any values. Later, the `f` variable can be called just like any other function call.

Listing 5.14 Functions as Variables

```
func main() {

    // create a new function and
    // assign it to a variable
    f := func() {

        // print Hello when called
        fmt.Println("Hello")
    }
```

(continued)

```
    // call the function
    f() // Hello
}
```

```
$ go run .

Hello
```

```
Go Version: go1.19
```

Functions as Arguments

In Go, functions behave as any other type we've discussed so far. Because functions in Go are types, you can pass them as arguments to another function. Declaring arguments for functions requires a name for the variable and the type of the variable: (s string). To define an argument that is a function, you have to include the full method signature as the type for the argument.

In Listing 5.15, the name of the argument/variable is fn, and its type is func() string. The signature of the function being passed in *must* match the function signature of the argument in the callee function.

Listing 5.15 Functions as Arguments

```
func sayHello(fn func() string) {

    // call the function
    // and print the result
    fmt.Println(fn())
}
```

In Listing 5.16, we are declaring a new variable, f, and assigning it to a function that matches the required signature of the sayHello function. Then we can pass the variable f to the sayHello function. As you see from the output, the sayHello function executed the f variable we had created.

Listing 5.16 Calling a Function with a Function as an Argument

```
func main() {

    // create a new function and
    // assign it to a variable
    f := func() string {
        return "Hello"
```

```
    }

    // pass the function to the sayHello
    sayHello(f)
}
```

```
$ go run .

Hello

Go Version: go1.19
```

Closures

Functions close over their environment when they are defined. This means that a function has access to arguments declared before its declaration. Consider Listing 5.17. First, we declare and initialize a new variable name with the value Janis. Next, we assign a function definition to the f variable. This time, however, we use the name variable when the function is executed. Finally, the f variable is passed to the sayHello function as an argument and executed.

The output of Listing 5.17 demonstrates that the name variable declared in the main function was properly closed over and made available when the f variable is executed later.

Listing 5.17 Closing over a Variable

```
func main() {
    name := "Janis"

    // create a new function and
    // assign it to a variable
    f := func() {

        // name is available here
        // because it is in the scope of
        // of the closure
        fmt.Printf("Hello %s", name)
    }

    // pass the function to sayHello
    sayHello(f)
}
```

(continued)

```
func sayHello(fn func()) {

    // call the function
    fn()
}
```

```
$ go run .

Hello Janis

Go Version: go1.19
```

Anonymous Functions

Anonymous functions are functions that aren't assigned to a variable or that don't have a "name" associated with them.

This is a very common pattern in Go, and one you should get comfortable seeing and using in Go code. Using anonymous functions is very common when working with the net/http[1] package, creating your own iterators, or allowing others to extend your application's functionality. In Listing 5.18, for example, we are calling the sayHello function with a brand new function we are defining inline.

Listing 5.18 Anonymous Functions

```
func main() {
    name := "Janis"

    // call sayHello with
    // an anonymous function
    sayHello(func() {
        fmt.Printf("Hello %s", name)
    })
}
```

```
$ go run .

Hello Janis

Go Version: go1.19
```

---

1. https://pkg.go.dev/net/http

Functions Accepting Arguments from Functions

Functions can accept the return arguments of one function as its input arguments. This is only possible as long as the return types and number of return arguments are identical to the input arguments and number of input arguments. In Listing 5.19, the returnTwo() function returns two strings. The takeTwo function accepts two strings as arguments. Because the return types and number of return arguments are identical to the input arguments and number of input arguments, the takeTwo function can accept the return arguments of returnTwo() as its input arguments.

Listing 5.19 Results from One Function Being Passed Directly to Another Function

```go
func main() {
    takeTwo(returnTwo())
}

func returnTwo() (string, string) {
    return "hello", "world"
}

func takeTwo(a string, b string) {
    fmt.Println(a, b)
}
```

```
$ go run .

hello world

Go Version: go1.19
```

Variadic Arguments

Functions can take variadic arguments, meaning 0 to N arguments of the same type. This is done by pre-pending the type of the argument with .... In Listing 5.20, the sayHello function accepts a variadic argument of type string.

Listing 5.20 Accepting Variadic Arguments

```go
func sayHello(names ...string) {

    // iterate over the names
    for _, n := range names {
```

(continued)

```
                // print the name
                fmt.Printf("Hello %s\n", n)
        }
}
```

In Listing 5.21, we call the now variadic function sayHello three different ways. The first is with many different names. Next, we call the function with only one value. Finally, the function is called with no values passed. The result of this last call produces no output because no arguments were passed to the sayHello function to print.

Listing 5.21 Calling Variadic Functions

```
func main() {

    // call sayHello with a lot of names
    sayHello("Kurt", "Janis", "Jimi", "Amy")

    // call sayHello with only one name
    sayHello("Brian")

    // call sayHello with no names
    sayHello()
}
```

```
$ go run .

Hello Kurt
Hello Janis
Hello Jimi
Hello Amy
Hello Brian

Go Version: go1.19
```

Variadic Argument Position

Variadic arguments *must* be the last argument of the function. In Listing 5.22, the sayHello function is defined with a variadic argument as the first of two arguments. The result is a compilation error indicating that the variadic argument must be the last argument.

Listing 5.22   Variadic Arguments Must Be the Last Argument

```
func sayHello(names ...string, group string) {
    for _, n := range names {
        fmt.Printf("Hello %s\n", n)
    }
}
```

```
$ go run .

# demo
./main.go:9:21: can only use ... with final parameter in list
```

```
Go Version: go1.19
```

Expanding Slices

Slices cannot be passed directly to functions using variadic arguments. In Listing 5.23, when trying to pass a slice directly to the sayHello function, the result is a compilation error indicating that slices cannot be used as variadic arguments.

Listing 5.23   Slices Cannot Be Used as Variadic Arguments

```
func main() {

    // create a slice of users
    users := []string{"Kurt", "Janis", "Jimi", "Amy"}

    // call sayHello with a slice
    sayHello(users)

}
```

```
$ go run .

# demo
./main.go:12:11: cannot use users (variable of type []string)
➥as type string in argument to sayHello
```

```
Go Version: go1.19
```

Slices can be "expanded" using a trailing variadic operator, . . . , to send them as individual arguments to a function. In Listing 5.24, we expand the users slice, using the variadic operator, to be passed as individual values to the sayHello function.

Listing 5.24   Expanding Slices Using the Variadic Operator

```
func main() {

    // create a slice of strings
    users := []string{"Kurt", "Janis", "Jimi", "Amy"}

    // use ... to pass the slice as variadic arguments
    sayHello(users...)
}
```

```
$ go run .

Hello Kurt
Hello Janis
Hello Jimi
Hello Amy


Go Version: go1.19
```

When to Use a Variadic Argument

While using a variadic argument is not the common use case, it certainly can make your code look nicer and be easier to read and use. The most common reason to use a variadic is when your function is commonly called with zero, one, or many arguments.

Consider the `LookupUsers` function in Listing 5.25. It accepts a `[]int` as an argument, and returns a `[]User`.

Listing 5.25   LookupUsers Function Definition Before Variadic Arguments

```
func LookupUsers(ids []int) []User {

    var users []User

    // iterate over the ids
    for _, id := range ids {
        // do work
        fmt.Printf("looking up id: %d\n", id)
    }

    return users
}
```

You may have one or many users to look up. Without using a variadic signature, calling this function can be messy and hard to read. Consider Listing 5.26. When calling LookupUsers with a single id, a new []int is created and passed to the function.

Listing 5.26 LookupUsers Function Call Before Variadic Arguments

```
id1 := 1
id2 := 2
id3 := 3
ids := []int{id1, id2, id3}

LookupUsers([]int{id1})
LookupUsers([]int{id1, id2, id3})
LookupUsers(ids)
```

In Listing 5.27, the LookupUsers function has a variadic signature and can be called with a single id or a list of ids.

Listing 5.27 LookupUsers Function Definition After Variadic Arguments

```
func LookupUsers(ids ...int) []User {

    var users []User

    // iterate over the ids
    for _, id := range ids {
        // do work
        fmt.Printf("looking up id: %d\n", id)
    }

    return users
}
```

With a variadic function signature, the LookupUsers function can now be called with a single id or a list of ids. The result, as shown in Listing 5.28, is cleaner, more efficient, and easier to read.

Listing 5.28 LookupUsers Function Call After Variadic Arguments

```
id1 := 1
id2 := 2
id3 := 3
ids := []int{id1, id2, id3}
```

(continued)

```
LookupUsers(id1)
LookupUsers(id1, id2, id3)
LookupUsers(ids...)
```

Deferring Function Calls

The `defer` keyword in Go allows you to defer the execution of a function call until the
return of the parent function. Listing 5.29 shows an example of deferring a function call.
When executed, `hello` is first printed, and then, when the function exits, `goodbye` is
printed.

Listing 5.29   Deferring a Function Call

```
func main() {

    // defer execution until
    // the main function returns
    defer fmt.Println("goodbye")

    fmt.Println("hello")
}
```

```
$ go run .

hello
goodbye
```

```
Go Version: go1.19
```

Deferring with Multiple Returns

The `defer` keyword is useful for ensuring functions get called regardless of which path
your code takes. When working with various types of IO in Go, it is very common to use
`defer` to ensure the appropriate resources are cleaned up when the function exits.

In Listing 5.30, for example, once we open a file, using `os.Open`, we immediately defer
a call to the `Close` method on the file. This ensures that regardless of how the
rest of the program exits, the `Close` method will be called, and the underlying file will
be properly closed. This prevents the leaking of file descriptors and a potential crash of
the application.

Listing 5.30   Deferring Cleanup of Resources on Function Exit

```
func ReadFile(name string) ([]byte, error) {

    // open the file
    f, err := os.Open(name)
```

```
    if err != nil {
        return nil, err
    }

    // ensure the file is closed when
    // ReadFile returns, regardless of exit point
    defer f.Close()

    // read the entire file
    // (not normally recommended)
    b, err := ioutil.ReadAll(f)
    if err != nil {

        // return the error
        // the file will still be closed
        return nil, err
    }

    // return the bytes and nil for error
    // the file will be closed
    return b, nil
}
```

Defer Call Order

The order of execution for deferred function calls is LIFO (last in, first out). In Listing 5.31, you see the output of the function is printed in reverse order of the defer statements.

Listing 5.31   Deferred Function Calls Are Executed in LIFO Order

```
func main() {
    defer fmt.Println("one")
    defer fmt.Println("two")
    defer fmt.Println("three")
}
```

```
$ go run .

three
two
one

Go Version: go1.19
```

Deferred Calls and Panic

If one or many deferred function calls panics, the panic is caught. The rest of the deferred calls are still executed and then the panic is reraised. Panics, and recovering from them using the `recover`[2] function, are a very common use case to defer and are covered in Chapter 9.

In Listing 5.32, we have three function calls being deferred. The first and third function calls are simple print statements. The second deferred function call, however, calls the `panic` function, which raises an application panic that crashes the application. As you see from the output in Listing 5.32, the third function is called first, the first function is called second, and the panic is called last. As you see from this example, an application panic won't prevent deferred function calls, like closing a file, from happening.

Listing 5.32   Deferred Calls Are Executed Even if Another Deferred Call Panics

```go
func main() {
    defer fmt.Println("one")
    defer panic("two")
    defer fmt.Println("three")
}
```

```
$ go run .

three
one

panic: two

goroutine 1 [running]:
main.main.func2()
        ./main.go:8 +0x30
main.main()
        ./main.go:10 +0xec
exit status 2
```

Go Version: go1.19

Defers and Exit/Fatal

Deferred calls will *not* fire if the code explicitly calls `os.Exit`,[3] as in Listing 5.33, or if the code calls `log.Fatal`,[4] as in Listing 5.34.

---

2. https://pkg.go.dev/builtin#recover
3. https://pkg.go.dev/os#Exit
4. https://pkg.go.dev/log#Fatal

Listing 5.33   Deferred Calls Are Not Executed if the Code Exits

```
func main() {
    defer fmt.Println("one")
    os.Exit(1)
    defer fmt.Println("three")
}
```

```
$ go run .

exit status 1
```

Go Version: go1.19

Listing 5.34   Deferred Calls Are Not Executed if the Code Logs a Fatal Message

```
func main() {
    defer fmt.Println("one")
    log.Fatal("boom")
    defer fmt.Println("three")
}
```

```
$ go run .

2022/06/28 14:27:56 boom
exit status 1
```

Go Version: go1.19

Defer and Anonymous Functions

It is also common to combine cleanup tasks into a single defer using an anonymous function. In Listing 5.35, instead of deferring the Close function on each file directly, they are being wrapped in an anonymous function, along with logging. This anonymous function is then deferred and executed when the fileCopy function exits.

Listing 5.35   Deferring an Anonymous Function

```
func fileCopy(sourceName string, destName string) error {
    src, err := os.Open(sourceName)
    if err != nil {
        return err
    }
```

(continued)

```go
    defer func() {
        fmt.Println("closing", sourceName)
        src.Close()
    }()

    dst, err := os.Create(destName)
    if err != nil {
        return err
    }

    defer func() {
        fmt.Println("closing", destName)
        dst.Close()
    }()

    if _, err := io.Copy(dst, src); err != nil {
        return err
    }

    fmt.Println("file copied successfully")
    return nil
}
```

```
$ go run .

file copied successfully
closing readme-copy.txt
closing readme.txt

Go Version: go1.19
```

Defer and Scope

It is important to understand scope when using the defer keyword. What is your
expectation of the outcome for the program in Listing 5.36? It would be reasonable to
expect that time since program started should be at least 50ms.

Listing 5.36 Deferring a Function Call with No Scope

```go
func main() {

    // capture the current time
    now := time.Now()
```

```
    // defer a print statement
    // showing how long the main
    // function took to execute
    defer fmt.Printf("duration: %s\n", time.Since(now))

    fmt.Println("sleeping for 50ms...")

    // sleep for 50ms
    time.Sleep(50 * time.Millisecond)
}
```

```
$ go run .

sleeping for 50ms...
duration: 83ns
```

Go Version: go1.19

As shown by the program's output in Listing 5.36, the result of the time.Since[5] function, Listing 5.37, is far short of the expected value of 50ms.

Listing 5.37 The time.Since Function

```
$ go doc time.Since

package time // import "time"

func Since(t Time) Duration
    Since returns the time elapsed since t. It is shorthand for
    ↪time.Now().Sub(t).
```

Go Version: go1.19

The reason the output in Listing 5.36 is not as expected is because it is only the fmt.Printf[6] call that is being deferred. The arguments being sent to the fmt.Printf function are not being deferred and are being executed immediately. As a result, the time.Since function is being called almost immediately after the now variable has been initialized.

---

5. https://pkg.go.dev/time#Since
6. https://pkg.go.dev/fmt#Printf

To make sure your variables are evaluated when a deferred function executes and not when they are scheduled, you need to scope them via an anonymous function. In Listing 5.38, it is only when the deferred anonymous function executes that the time.Since function is called, producing the expected output.

Listing 5.38   Properly Scoping a Deferred Function Call

```
func main() {

    // capture the current time
    now := time.Now()

    // use an anonymous function
    // to scope variables to be
    // used in the defer
    defer func(now time.Time) {
        fmt.Printf("duration: %s\n", time.Since(now))
    }(now)

    fmt.Println("sleeping for 50ms...")

    // sleep for 50ms
    time.Sleep(50 * time.Millisecond)
}
```

```
$ go run .

sleeping for 50ms...
duration: 51.044542ms

Go Version: go1.19
```

Init

During initialization of a .go file, the compiler executes any init functions it finds in the file *before* the main function.

In Listing 5.39, we have an init function that prints the word *init*. The main function prints *main* but does not call the init function directly. As you see from the output, the init function is called before the main function.

Listing 5.39   A Basic Program with an init() Function

```
func init() {
    fmt.Println("init")
}
```

```go
func main() {
    fmt.Println("main")
}
```

```
$ go run .

init
main
```

Go Version: go1.19

Multiple Init Statements

Unlike all other functions that can only be declared once, the init() function can be declared multiple times throughout a package or file. However, multiple init()s can make it difficult to know which one has priority over the others.

When declaring multiple init functions within the same file, the init() functions execute in the order that you encounter them. In Listing 5.40, the four init functions are executed in the order that they are declared in the file.

Listing 5.40   Multiple init() Functions in the Same File

```go
package main

import "fmt"

func init() {
    fmt.Println("First init")
}

func init() {
    fmt.Println("Second init")
}

func init() {
    fmt.Println("Third init")
}

func init() {
    fmt.Println("Fourth init")
}

func main() {}
```

(continued)

```
$ go run .

First init
Second init
Third init
Fourth init

Go Version: go1.19
```

Init Order

If you have multiple init() declarations in a package in different files, the compiler runs them based on the order in which it loads files.

Given the directory structure in Listing 5.41, if you had an init() declaration in a.go and b.go, the first init() to run would be from a.go. However, if you renamed a.go to c.go, the init() from b.go would run first.

Care must be taken if any init() declarations have an order of precedence when running and exist in different files.

Listing 5.41   A Directory Structure with init() Declarations in Different Files

```
└── cmd
    ├─ a.go
    ├─ b.go
    └─ main.go
```

Using init Functions for Side Effects

In Go, it is sometimes required to import a package not for its content but for the side effects that occur upon importing the package. This often means that there is an init() statement in the imported code that executes before any of the other code, allowing for the developer to manipulate the state in which their program is starting. This technique is called importing for a *side effect*.

A common use case for importing for side effects is to *register* functionality in your code, which lets a package know what part of the code your program needs to use. In the image[7] package, for example, the image.Decode[8] function needs to know which format of the image it is trying to decode (jpg, png, gif, and so on) before it can execute. You can accomplish this by first importing a specific program that has an init() statement side effect.

Consider that you are trying to use image.Decode on a .png file with the function in Listing 5.42.

---

7. https://pkg.go.dev/image
8. https://pkg.go.dev/image#Decode

Listing 5.42   A Program That Uses image.Decode to Decode a .png File

```go
func decode(reader io.Reader) (image.Rectangle, error) {

    // decode the image reader
    m, _, err := image.Decode(reader)
    if err != nil {

        // return the error
        return image.Rectangle{}, err
    }
    return m.Bounds(), nil
}
```

A program with this code still compiles, but any time you try to decode a png image, you get an error, as shown in Listing 5.43.

Listing 5.43   Compilation Error Trying to Decode a png

```
$ go run .

image: unknown format

exit status 1
```

Go Version: go1.19

To fix this, you need to first register the .png image format for image.Decode to use. When imported, the image/png[9] package, which contains the init() statement in Listing 5.44, is called, and the package registers itself with the image package as an image format.

Listing 5.44   An init() Statement in the image.png Package Registering the .png Image Format

```go
func init() {
    image.RegisterFormat("png", pngHeader, Decode, DecodeConfig)
}
```

In Listing 5.45, we import image.png package into our application; then the image.RegisterFormat()[10] function in image/png runs before any of our code and registers the .png format before we try to use it.

---

9. https://pkg.go.dev/image/png
10. https://pkg.go.dev/image#RegisterFormat()

Listing 5.45 A Program That Uses `image.Decode` to Decode a `.png` File

```
import (
    "fmt"
    "image"
    _ "image/png"
    "io"
    "os"
)
```

```
$ go run .

decoded image bounds: (0,0)-(60,60)

Go Version: go1.19
```

While this use of `import` statements and `init` functions can be found in numerous places in the standard library, this is considered an anti-pattern in Go and should *never* be used. Always be *explicit* in your code.

Summary

In this chapter, we covered functions in Go. We explained how, in Go, functions are first-class citizens. We showed how you can create new types in the type system that are based on functions. We also discussed using variadic arguments to allow a function to accept an arbitrary number of arguments of one type. We also covered deferring functions, which allows you to defer a function call until a later time. We also explained how to use deferred functions to ensure that resources are cleaned up in the correct order and how to recover from panics. Finally, we showed you how to use the `init` function to initialize a package and explained the dangers of using it.

6

Structs, Methods, and Pointers

In this chapter, we look at structs in Go. We cover definition, initialization, and usage of structs. We also cover struct tags and their use for operations such as encoding and decoding. Next, we look at adding methods to types. Finally, we examine pointers and how you can use them to avoid copying data and how they enable you to allow others to mutate the underlying data.

Structs

A struct is a collection of fields, often called members (or attributes). A struct is often used to create custom complex types in Go. When trying to understand structs, it helps to think of them as a blueprint for what the new type will do. A struct definition does *not* contain any data.

Declaring New Types in Go

Before you can start working with structs, you need to first understand how to declare new types in Go. To declare a new type in Go, you use the `type` keyword. When declaring a new type, you also need to give it a name. Like all identifiers in Go, the type's name *must* be unique within the package and follow the naming conventions for Go identifiers. Finally, all new types *must* be based on an existing type.

In Listing 6.1, we declare three new types. The first, `MyInt`, is based on the `int` type. The second, `MyString`, is based on the `string` type. The third, `MyMap`, is based on the `map[string]string` type. These type definitions are read by the compiler and are made available at runtime. Because the types are defined at compile time, they are *unable* to hold data themselves, like traditional "class" types.

Listing 6.1   Declaring New Types in Go

```
type MyInt int
type MyString string
type MyMap map[string]string
```

In Listing 6.2, we use the three new types defined in Listing 6.1. When declaring and initializing the `MyInt` and `MyString` variables, we can simply cast the `int` and `string` values to the appropriate type. For the `MyMap`, we declare and initialize it as we would a regular map. Later in this chapter, we show you how to add methods, which are functions that have a type as a receiver, to the types we've defined.

Listing 6.2   Using the Custom Types from Listing 6.1

```go
func main() {

    // declare a variable of type MyInt
    i := MyInt(1)

    // declare a variable of type MyString
    s := MyString("foo")

    // declare a variable of type MyMap
    m := MyMap{"foo": "bar"}

    // print the type and value of i
    fmt.Printf("%[1]T:\t%[1]v\n", i)

    // print the type and value of s
    fmt.Printf("%[1]T:\t%[1]v\n", s)

    // print the type and value of m
    fmt.Printf("%[1]T:\t%[1]v\n", m)
}
```

```
$ go run .

main.MyInt:     1
main.MyString:  foo
main.MyMap:     map[foo:bar]
```

```
Go Version: go1.19
```

Defining a Struct

With an understanding of how to define new types in Go, let's look at structs. Structs provide you with a way to define complex types. Structs may have zero or more fields and zero or more methods. The struct type is essential to writing Go programs.

In Listing 6.3, we define a struct named `User` with two fields. The first field is `Name` and is of type `string`. The second field is `Age` and is of type `int`.

Listing 6.3 A User Struct with Two Fields

```
type User struct {
    Name  string
    Email string
}
```

Initializing a Struct

Struct initialization is nearly identical to that of map initialization. We use the {} syntax to initialize a struct. Optionally, like with maps, we can provide a value for each field. In Listing 6.4, we declare a new variable, u, and assign it a value of type User. We are not initializing the fields of u with values. To print the struct, we are using the %+v formatting verb. This will print the struct's field names, as well as their values.

Listing 6.4 Initializing a Struct with No Values

```
func main() {

    // initialize an empty user
    u := User{}

    fmt.Printf("%+v\n", u)
}
```

```
$ go run .

{Name: Age:0}

Go Version: go1.19
```

Fields on the struct can be set during initialization. You can set as many (or as few) of the field values on a struct at initialization time as you want. In Listing 6.5, we declare a new variable, u, and assign it a value of type User. We are initializing the fields of u with the values for the Name and Email fields.

Listing 6.5 Initializing a Struct with Values

```
func main() {

    // initialize a user
    // with values
    u := User{
```

(continued)

```
        Name: "Jimi",
        Age:  27,
    }

fmt.Printf("%+v\n", u)
}
```

```
$ go run .

{Name:Jimi Age:27}

Go Version: go1.19
```

Initialization without Field Names

In previous examples, such as Listing 6.5, when initializing a struct with values, we have always used the field names to specify the values. This is *required* when using multiline initialization. When initializing a struct on a single line, the use of field names is optional.

In Listing 6.6, we initialize the `User` struct with two fields, `Kurt` and `27`, without using their field names. Although this *is* valid Go, it is considered bad practice. There are many reasons why *not* using field names is a bad idea. The first is that it is hard to read. If you are unfamiliar with the code base, there is no reference as to what the values are being mapped to. Even more important, however, is that they inevitably need to be named.

Listing 6.6 Initializing a Struct without Field Names

```
func main() {

    // initialize a user
    // with values and no
    // field names
    u := User{"Kurt", 27}

    fmt.Printf("%+v\n", u)
}
```

```
$ go run .

{Name:Kurt Age:27}

Go Version: go1.19
```

When not using field names during initialization, *all* fields are *required* to be present. Failure to do so results in a compile-time error. In Listing 6.7, when initializing the `User`, we are only providing a value for the `Name` field. Because the `Age` field is not being set during initialization, we get a compile-time error.

Listing 6.7   Initializing a Struct without All Values

```go
func main() {

    // initialize a user
    // with missing values
    u := User{"Kurt"}

    fmt.Printf("%+v\n", u)
}
```

```
$ go run .

# demo
./main.go:18:18: too few values in struct literal

Go Version: go1.19
```

Finally, the order of the values *must* match how they are defined in the struct. If the order of the fields change in the struct, then the order of the values must also change. In Listing 6.8, we are initializing the `User` struct with values for the `Name` and `Age` fields. The order of the values does not match the order of the fields, so we get a compile-time error.

Listing 6.8   Initializing a Struct with Values in the Wrong Order

```go
func main() {

    // initialize a user
    // with values in
    // the wrong order
    u := User{27, "Kurt"}

    fmt.Printf("%+v\n", u)
}
```

```
$ go run .

# demo
./main.go:19:12: cannot use 27 (untyped int constant) as string
↪value in struct literal
```

(continued)

```
./main.go:19:16: cannot use "Kurt" (untyped string constant) as
→int value in struct literal
```

```
Go Version: go1.19
```

By being explicit and using field names right from the beginning, we can prevent these issues from happening.

Accessing Struct Fields

Fields can be referenced using dot notation (a followed by the field name). In Listing 6.9, the `printUser` function accesses the `Name` and `Age` fields of u and assigns them to the variables name and age. The `main` function, in Listing 6.9, sets the `Name` field of u to `Janis` with the line u.Name = "Janis".

Listing 6.9   Accessing a Struct's Fields

```go
func printUser(u User) {

    // access the user's name field
    // and assign it to a variable
    name := u.Name

    // access the user's age field
    // and assign it to a variable
    age := u.Age

    // print the user's name and age
    fmt.Printf("%s is %d years old\n", name, age)
}
```

```go
func main() {

    // initialize a user
    // with values
    u := User{Age: 27}

    // set the user's name
    u.Name = "Janis"

    // print the user's name and age
    printUser(u)
}
```

```
$ go run .

Janis is 27 years old

Go Version: go1.19
```

Struct Tags

Struct tags are small pieces of metadata attached to fields of a struct that provide instructions to other Go code that works with the struct. A struct tag is a string of the form <name>:"<value>". The <name> is the name of the tag, and the <value> is the value of the tag. In Listing 6.10, the Name field of the User struct has a tag of json:"name". The name of the tag is json and the value is name.

Listing 6.10   A Struct Tag

```
type User struct {
    Name string 'json:"name"'
}
```

Other Go code is then capable of examining these structs and extracting the values assigned to specific keys it requests. Struct tags have no effect on the operation of your code without some other code that examines them.

Struct Tags for Encoding

A common use for struct tags is for encoding the data of your struct to some type of other format. JSON[1] (Listing 6.11), XML,[2] and Protobuf[3] are all examples of encoding formats.

Listing 6.11   The json.Encoder Type

```
$ go doc encoding/json.Encoder

package json // import "encoding/json"

type Encoder struct {
        // Has unexported fields.
}
    An Encoder writes JSON values to an output stream.

func NewEncoder(w io.Writer) *Encoder
func (enc *Encoder) Encode(v any) error
```

(continued)

---

1. https://www.json.org/json-en.html
2. https://developer.mozilla.org/en-US/docs/Web/XML/XML_introduction
3. https://developers.google.com/protocol-buffers

```
func (enc *Encoder) SetEscapeHTML(on bool)
func (enc *Encoder) SetIndent(prefix, indent string)
```

Go Version: go1.19

In Listing 6.12, we use the encoding/json[4] package to encode the User struct. After creating a new json.Encoder,[5] Listing 6.11, we call the json.Encoder.Encode[6] method, passing the variable u as the argument. Because the User struct has no struct tags, the json.Encoder.Encode function uses the field's name as the JSON key.

Listing 6.12   Default JSON Encoding

```go
package main

import (
    "encoding/json"
    "log"
    "os"
)

type User struct {
    ID       int
    Name     string
    Phone    string
    Password string
}

func main() {
    u := User{
        ID:       1,
        Name:     "Amy",
        Password: "goIsAwesome",
    }

    // create a new JSON encoder
    // that will write to stdout
    enc := json.NewEncoder(os.Stdout)

    // encode the user
    if err := enc.Encode(u); err != nil {
```

---

4. https://pkg.go.dev/encoding/json
5. https://pkg.go.dev/encoding/json#Encoder
6. https://pkg.go.dev/encoding/json#Encoder.Encode

```
        // handle an error if one occurs
        log.Fatal(err)
    }
}
```

```
$ go run .

{"ID":1,"Name":"Amy","Phone":"","Password":"goIsAwesome"}

Go Version: go1.19
```

While the json.Encoder encodes the User properly to JSON, it has its issues. In Listing 6.12, the field names are not using the proper casing for JSON. Fields with zero values are being encoded and wasting bytes. Finally, sensitive data, like the Password field, is being encoded, which poses a security risk.

Using Struct Tags

To allow us to control the JSON encoding for the User struct, the encoding/json package makes use of the json struct tag. When present, this tag tells the json.Encoder what name to use for the field when encoding the struct and whether to encode the field.

In Listing 6.13, each of the fields on the User struct has been updated to use the json struct tag. The Name field is now using the json:"name" tag. This tells the json.Encoder to use name for the field, instead of Name.

Listing 6.13   Using the json Struct Tag to Control Encoding Output

```
type User struct {
    ID       int    'json:"id"'
    Name     string 'json:"name"'
    Phone    string 'json:"phone,omitempty"'
    Password string 'json:"-"'
}
```

```
$ go run .

{"id":1,"name":"Amy"}

Go Version: go1.19
```

The Phone field is now using the json:"phone,omitempty" tag. This tells the json.Encoder to use phone for the field instead of Phone. Because of the comma, the omitempty tag tells the json.Encoder to omit the field if it has a zero value.

Finally, the `Password` field now uses the `json:"-"` tag. This tells the `json.Encoder` not to encode the field. The - indication is often used within the standard library and other libraries to indicate that the field should not be encoded.

Each package that uses struct tags will have directions on how to specify tags for the proper behavior. For an in-depth look at options the `encoding/json` package uses for struct tags, you can refer to the `json.Marshal`[7] documentation for more detail.

Methods

Methods are syntactic sugar for declaring functions on types. Consider Listing 6.14 that adds a method, `String() string`, to the `User` struct. Before the name of the function, we are introducing a new set of (). This new set of () is there to allow us to define the receiver of the method. The receiver is the type of the value that is passed to the method. In this case, the receiver is `User`. The receiver is available inside the method as the variable u.

Listing 6.14   Declaring and Using a Method

```go
type User struct {
    Name string
    Age  int
}

func (u User) String() string {
    return fmt.Sprintf("%s is %d", u.Name, u.Age)
}
```

```go
func main() {

    u := User{
        Name: "Janis",
        Age:  27,
    }

    // call the String method
    // with 'u' as the receiver
    fmt.Println(u.String())
}
```

```
$ go run .

Janis is 27
```

```
Go Version: go1.19
```

---

7. https://pkg.go.dev/encoding/json#Marshal

Differences Between Methods and Functions

Methods conform to almost all of the rules that apply to functions, because that's what they essentially are. Methods can have any number of parameters, and they can return any number of values, just like functions.

Unlike functions, methods are bound to the type of the receiver. Methods cannot be called independently of the receiver. Later, in Chapter 10, when we look at generics, you find out that functions can use generics, but methods cannot.

Methods Expressions

Methods, as mentioned previously, are just syntactic sugar for functions that have a fixed first argument, the receiver. Consider Listing 6.15 and Listing 6.16. Both print the same result. In Listing 6.15, we are calling the String() method on the variable, u. Go automatically passes the value of u to the method. In Listing 6.16, we are calling the String(u User) method on the type, User. This is *actually* what happens when we call the method.

Listing 6.15 Normal Method Calling

```
func main() {

    u := User{
        Name: "Janis",
        Age:  27,
    }


    // call the String method
    // with 'u' as the receiver
    fmt.Println(u.String())
}
```

Listing 6.16 Syntactic Sugar for Methods

```
func main() {

    u := User{
        Name: "Janis",
        Age:  27,
    }


    // call the String method
    // with 'u' as the receiver
    fmt.Println(User.String(u))
}
```

(continued)

```
$ go run .

Janis is 27
```

```
Go Version: go1.19
```

Methods on Third-Party Types

In a lot of languages, it is possible to define methods on types that you did not define. In Listing 6.17, we are adding a greet method to all of the Integer types in that Ruby program.

Listing 6.17   Adding a Method to a Third-Party Type in Ruby

```ruby
# Integer is the base class for
# integers in Ruby. Any methods added
# here will be available to all integers
# while the application is running.
class Integer

    # add a greet method to every
    # integer in the application
    def greet
        puts "Hello, I am #{self}."
    end

end

# call the greet method on
# the integer 27
27.greet
```

```
$ ruby main.rb

Hello, I am 27.
```

In Go, you are not allowed to define methods on types you did not define. In Listing 6.18, we are trying to add a Greet() method to all of the int types in that Go program. This results in a compile-time error.

Listing 6.18   Adding a Method to a Third-Party Type in Go

```
package main

import "fmt"

func (i int) Greet() {
    fmt.Printf("Hello, I am %d\n", i)
}
```

```
$ go run .

# demo
./main.go:5:7: cannot define new methods on non-local type int

Go Version: go1.19
```

One solution to this problem is to create a new type based on `int`. In Listing 6.19, the `MyInt` type is based on `int`. We can then define the `Greet()` method on `MyInt`. To use the new type, we just need to cast an `int` to `MyInt`.

Listing 6.19   Defining a Custom Type for `int` to Add Methods On

```
package main

import "fmt"

type MyInt int

func (i MyInt) Greet() {
    fmt.Printf("Hello, I am %d\n", i)
}
func main() {
    i := MyInt(27)
    i.Greet()
}
```

```
$ go run .

Hello, I am 27

Go Version: go1.19
```

Functions as Types

Function signatures act as a defacto "type," but explicit types can also be created for a function signature.

The following are some benefits of function types:

- Argument declaration is cleaner and more maintainable.
- The new type can take full advantage of the Go type system.
- The new type can now easily be documented, providing valuable feedback in the future.

In Listing 6.20, a new type is created with the function signature, func() string. This new type is called greeter. The sayHello function accepts a greeter type as an argument. All of the previous rules for passing functions to other functions apply to the greeter type. In Listing 6.20, the sayHello function is called with an anonymous function as an argument.

Listing 6.20   Function Types

```
package main

import "fmt"

// greeter is any function that
// returns a string
// and has no arguments.
type greeter func() string

func sayHello(fn greeter) {

    // call the greeter function
    // and print the result
    fmt.Println(fn())
}

func main() {

    // call sayHello with an
    // anonymous function that
    // matches the signature of
    // the greeter type
    sayHello(func() string {
        return "Hello"
    })
}
```

```
$ go run .

Hello

Go Version: go1.19
```

Methods on Functions

By creating a new type for a function, we can treat that type like all types in Go, and it can act as a receiver for methods. A great example of this is `http.HandlerFunc`,[8] Listing 6.21, from the standard library. Methods will be discussed later in this book.

Listing 6.21 The `http.HandlerFunc` Type

```
$ go doc net/http.HandlerFunc

package http // import "net/http"

type HandlerFunc func(ResponseWriter, *Request)
    The HandlerFunc type is an adapter to allow the use of
    ➥ordinary functions as HTTP handlers. If f is a function with
    ➥the appropriate signature, HandlerFunc(f) is a Handler
    ➥that calls f.

func (f HandlerFunc) ServeHTTP(w ResponseWriter, r *Request)
```

```
Go Version: go1.19
```

No Inheritance

In Go, there is no inheritance. When basing a new type on an existing type, any methods that the existing type has are *not* available on the new type because there is no inheritance in Go. When defining a new type, any methods on the existing type are *not* carried over to the new type. If the existing type is a struct, its field definitions *will* be carried over to the new type.

In Listing 6.22, we are defining a `User` type and a `MyUser` type based on it. The `MyUser` type includes the same fields as the `User` type, but does *not* have its methods. In Listing 6.23, when trying to call the `String()` method on the `MyUser` type, we get a compile-time error.

---

8. https://pkg.go.dev/net/http#HandlerFunc

Listing 6.22   A User Type and a `MyUser` Type Based on It

```go
type User struct {
    Name string
    Age  int
}

func (u User) String() string {
    return fmt.Sprintf("%s is %d", u.Name, u.Age)
}

type MyUser User
```

Listing 6.23   New Types Do Not Inherit Methods from Their Base Types

```go
func main() {
    u := User{
        Name: "Janis",
        Age:  27,
    }

    fmt.Println(u.String())

    mu := MyUser{
        Name: "Janis",
        Age:  27,
    }

    fmt.Println(mu.String())
}
```

```
$ go run .

# demo
./main.go:33:17: mu.String undefined (type MyUser has no field or
↪method String)
```

Go Version: go1.19

Pointers

A pointer is a type that holds the address to the value of a variable. In this section, we explain the difference between "pass by value" and "pass by reference." We also discuss how to declare pointers and how to reference values as pointers. This section also covers performance and security and when to use pointers.

People are afraid of pointers. In other languages, you hear horror stories about pointer arithmetic, overriding memory by accident, and other terrible tales.

At their core, pointers in Go are fairly simple and straightforward.

Pass by Value

To understand pointers, you must first understand how Go passes data. When passing data from one function to another, Go first copies the data to be passed and then sends the copied data to the destination function. This is called "pass by value."

Figure 6.1 shows a simplified, graphical representation of how Go passes data between functions. A Go application has a global memory space, called a *heap*, that is available to all of the functions, types, and so on in the application. The heap is where global variables live, for example. Items in the heap are the most difficult, and slowest, to be removed by the garbage collector.

For each function call, a new memory space is created in the heap. This space is dedicated memory space for the running function. This space is called a "stack." The stack is where local variables in a function live. When a function exits, the entire stack can be cleaned up by the garbage collector. Because a function's memory can be collected at once (for example, all local variables), the garbage collector is able to work very efficiently.

In Figure 6.1, when the value u, inside of the func A stack, is passed to the func B stack, a new copy of the u value is created inside of the func B stack. In Figure 6.1, the u variable occupies the memory space 0x123 inside of the func A stack. In the func B stack, the u variable occupies a different memory space, 0x456.

In Listing 6.24, the changeName function is receiving a *copy* of the User value. Since the changeName function is receiving a copy of the User value, any changes made to the User within the context of this function will *not* affect the original User value.

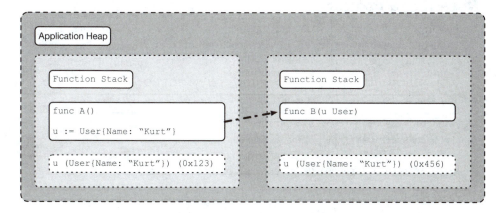

Figure 6.1   Pass by value

Listing 6.24   Pass by Value

```
func changeName(b User) {
    b.Name = "Janis"
    fmt.Println("new name:", b.Name)
}
```

```
type User struct {
    Name string
}

func main() {
    u := User{Name: "Kurt"}

    fmt.Println("before:", u.Name)

    changeName(u)

    fmt.Println("after:", u.Name)
}
```

```
$ go run .

before: Kurt
new name: Janis
after: Kurt
```

```
Go Version: go1.19
```

Receiving a Pointer

To indicate a function, or method, wants a pointer to a value, we use a * before the type. In Listing 6.25, we see two versions of the changeName function. The first takes a value of type User. The second takes a pointer to a value of type User.

Listing 6.25   Accepting a Pointer as an Argument

```
// value of type User (copy of User)
func changeName(b User) {}

// value of type pointer to User (copy of pointer to User)
func changeName(b *User) {}
```

Getting a Pointer

To get a pointer to a value, we use the & operator. In Listing 6.26, we are initializing a variable of type User, u, and then getting a pointer to that variable, &u.

Listing 6.26 *Getting a Pointer from a Variable*

```go
func main() {

    // initialize a user
    u := User{
        Name: "Jimi",
        Age:  27,
    }

    // get a pointer to the user
    ptr := &u

    // print the value of the pointer
    fmt.Printf("%+v\n", ptr)

    // print the pointer
    fmt.Printf("%p\n", ptr)
}
```

```
$ go run .

&{Name:Jimi Age:27}
0x1400000c030

Go Version: go1.19
```

In Listing 6.26, when printing the pointer using the %+v formatting verb, we see the same output as if we were printing a value of type User, but it is proceeded by a & to indicate that it is a pointer.

When you know that you need a pointer at initialization time, you don't have to first assign it to a variable. Instead, you can use the & operator to get a pointer to the newly initialized value. In Listing 6.27, we are getting a pointer to a new value of type User when we initialize it. The result is that the variable u is a pointer to a value of type User.

Listing 6.27 *Getting a Pointer Immediately at Initialization*

```go
func main() {

    // initialize a user
    // and immediately get
```

(continued)

```
        // a pointer to it
        u := &User{
            Name: "Jimi",
            Age:  27,
        }

        // print the value of the pointer
        fmt.Printf("%+v\n", u)

        // print the pointer
        fmt.Printf("%p\n", u)
}
```

```
$ go run .

&{Name:Jimi Age:27}
0x14000126018
```

```
Go Version: go1.19
```

Passing with Pointers

In Go, pointers are a small wrapper that holds the memory address of an underlying value. When we pass pointers as arguments from one function to another, as in Figure 6.2, Go creates a copy of the pointer and passes that to the receiving function. This behavior is *exactly* the same as you have already seen. The difference, however, is that even though the two pointers have different object IDs, they both still point to the same underlying data. The underlying data, however, no longer lives within the function stacks. Now that data has been moved to the application's heap, this is often referred to as "escaping the stack." For the garbage collector to safely remove the underlying data, it needs to first confirm that no other stack of value in the heap is still referencing that memory.

Since A and B in Figure 6.2 both have pointers to the same data, changes made to the data through either pointer mutate the data for *both* pointers.

Using Pointers

The example in Listing 6.24 can be rewritten using pointers to allow us to be able to modify the underlying value. In Listing 6.28, we are using a pointer to a value of type User to change the name of the user. The result is the name change is reflected in both references.

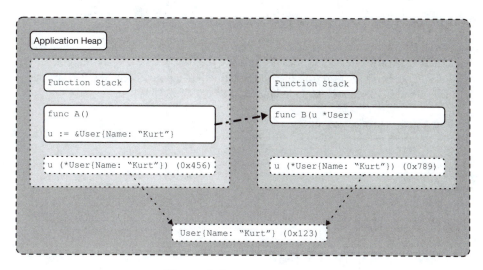

Figure 6.2   Pass by reference

Listing 6.28   Using a Pointer

```go
type User struct {
    Name string
}

func main() {
    u := User{Name: "Kurt"}

    fmt.Println("before:", u.Name)

    changeName(&u)

    fmt.Println("after:", u.Name)
}
```

```
$ go run .

before: Kurt
new name: Janis
after: Janis
```

```
Go Version: go1.19
```

Value versus Pointer Receivers

You can define a receiver for a method as either a value or a pointer receiver. They will behave differently. A value receiver cannot mutate the data, whereas a pointer receiver can.

In Listing 6.29, the `Titleize()` method is defined on a pointer receiver. This means that the method can mutate the underlying data.

Listing 6.29   Method Receivers

```go
type User struct {
    Name string
    Age  int
}

// Pointer Receiver
func (u *User) Titleize() {
    u.Name = strings.Title(u.Name)
}

// Value Receiver
func (u User) Reset() {
    u.Name = ""
    u.Age = 0
}

func main() {

    // initialize a user
    u := User{
        Name: "kurt",
        Age:  27,
    }

    // print the user
    fmt.Println("before title:\t", u)

    // call the titleize method
    u.Titleize()

    // print the user
    // after titleizing
    fmt.Println("after title:\t", u)

    // call the reset method
    u.Reset()
```

```
    // print the user
    // after resetting
    fmt.Println("after reset:\t", u)
}
```

```
$ go run .

before title:    {kurt 27}
after title:     {Kurt 27}
after reset:     {Kurt 27}
```

Go Version: go1.19

New

The built-in function new,[9] Listing 6.30, takes a type T, allocates storage for a variable of that type at run time and returns a value of type *T pointing to it. The variable is initialized with its zero value.

Listing 6.30   The new Function

```
$ go doc builtin.new

package builtin // import "builtin"

func new(Type) *Type
    The new built-in function allocates memory. The first argument
    ➥is a type, not a value, and the value returned is a pointer
    ➥to a newly allocated zero value of that type.
```

Go Version: go1.19

The use of new in code is very rare in Go in favor of using the & modifier: new(User) versus &User{}. Using the new function can be very beneficial with basic types such as string or int. Pointers to these types cannot be created using the & modifier: &"Hello". The new function allows for creating pointers to these types. Listing 6.31 shows a few examples of how to use new to get pointers to various types.

Listing 6.31   Using the new Function

```
func main() {

    // create a pointer to a string
    s := new(string)
```

(continued)

9. https://pkg.go.dev/builtin#new

```go
// dereference the pointer
// and assign a value to it
*s = "hello"

// create a pointer to an int
i := new(int)

// dereference the pointer
// and assign a value to it
*i = 42

// create a pointer to a user
u1 := new(User)

// functionally equivalent and idiomatic
u2 := &User{}

fmt.Printf("s: %v, *s: %q\n", s, *s)
fmt.Printf("i: %v, *i: %d\n", i, *i)
fmt.Printf("u1: %+v, *f: %+v\n", u1, *u1)
fmt.Printf("u2: %+v, *f1: %+v\n", u2, *u2)

}
```

```
$ go run .

s: 0x14000010230, *s: "hello"
i: 0x14000014098, *i: 42
u1: &{Name: Age:0}, *f: {Name: Age:0}
u2: &{Name: Age:0}, *f1: {Name: Age:0}

Go Version: go1.19
```

To get access to a pointer's underlying value, we use the * operator. In Listing 6.31, we create a new pointer to a string—the variable s. Then we dereference the pointer to get access to the underlying string to set it to "Hello". Next, we dereference the pointer again to get access to the underlying string and assign it to the s variable.

Performance

Pointers in Go can both help and hurt performance. In the case of a large chunk of memory (think an image file), passing a pointer around can reduce memory allocation and operational overhead.

However, pointers also indicate to the garbage collector, and the compiler, that the value in question might be used outside of its current stack, which may place the value on the heap instead. As mentioned previously, in Go, stacks are treated by the garbage collector as one chunk of memory that can be collected. Memory in the application stack, however, is much more difficult to clean up, and therefore slower to clean up. On the left, in Figure 6.3, is a graphical representation of how Go manages memory when passing a value between two functions. The right shows how Go manages memory when passing a pointer between two functions. When comparing these two images, you can see the extra load being put on the garbage collector when using pointers.

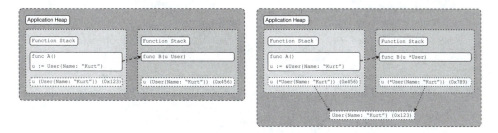

Figure 6.3   Pointers are automatically assigned to the heap.

While understanding how Go treats memory when working with pointers is important, using pointers in Go is prevalent. You should not worry, most of the time, about the allocation of the pointer's memory and its impact on the garbage collector.

Nil Receivers

Care must be taken when using pointer receivers. If the receiver itself is `nil`, you can still call methods that don't reference the receiver. But if you call a method that does reference a receiver, it raises a runtime panic.

In Listing 6.32, when trying to call the `String()` with a `nil` receiver, we get a runtime panic.

Listing 6.32   Nil Receivers

```
package main

import "fmt"

type User struct {
    Name string
    Age  int
}
```

(continued)

```go
func (u *User) String() string {
    return fmt.Sprintf("%s is %d", u.Name, u.Age)
}

func main() {

    // create a new pointer
    // to a user
    var u *User

    // call the String method
    // on the nil pointer
    fmt.Println(u.String())
}
```

```
$ go run .

panic: runtime error: invalid memory address or nil pointer
↪dereference [signal SIGSEGV: segmentation violation code=0x2
↪addr=0x0 pc=0x1043cd788]

goroutine 1 [running]:
main.(*User).String(...)
        ./main.go:11
main.main()
        ./main.go:22 +0x28
exit status 2
```

```
Go Version: go1.19
```

Nil Receivers Checks

You can check to see if the receiver is nil before referencing it. Although this may work in some scenarios, it may inadvertently end up as a Nop in your code and therefore fail silently, creating a very difficult bug to find later on.

You must decide how to handle these situations when they occur. In Listing 6.33, we are checking to see if the receiver is nil inside of the String() method before we call any fields on the receiver. If the receiver is nil, we return "<empty>". In situations where the method returns an error, then we can return an error if the receiver is nil.

Listing 6.33 Nil Receivers Check

```go
package main

import "fmt"

type User struct {
    Name string
    Age  int
}

func (u *User) String() string {
    if u == nil {
        return ""
    }

    return fmt.Sprintf("%s is %d", u.Name, u.Age)
}

func main() {

    // create a new pointer
    // to a user
    var u *User

    // call the String method
    // on the nil pointer
    fmt.Println(u.String())
}
```

```
$ go run .

<empty>
```

```
Go Version: go1.19
```

Summary

In this chapter, we covered structs, methods, and pointers. We also covered struct tags and their use for encoding and decoding. We also explained how to add methods to types. Finally, we discussed pointers, how they can be used to avoid copying data, and how they enable us to allow others to mutate the underlying data.

7

Testing

Testing in Go, as in any language, is a subject worthy of its own book. Unfortunately, covering all topics, such as benchmarking, example tests, and design patterns, is outside the scope of this book. In this chapter, we cover the fundamentals of testing in Go, including writing, running, and debugging tests. We also cover table driven tests, test helpers, and code coverage.

Testing Basics

Go ships with a powerful testing framework, and as such, there is a strong emphasis on testing in Go. Tests in Go are written in the Go language, so there is no need to learn another syntax. Because the language was designed with testing in mind, it tends to be easier to create and understand tests in Go than in some other languages.

As with any statically typed language, the compiler catches a lot of bugs for you. However, it cannot ensure your business logic is sound or bug free. In Go, there are several tools to ensure your code is bug free (such as tests), as well as tools to show you what part of your code has been tested and which has been not (code coverage).

We introduce some of the basic testing features now, and as we continue to introduce new topics later, we show the corresponding test features and approaches as they pertain to those topics and features.

Naming

Up until now, there has not been much convention to the naming or placement of files or functions in our Go code. However, with testing, naming of files and functions play an incredibly important part of how tests work.

Test File Naming

When creating the code for a test, that code has to be placed in a `test` file. Go identifies a file as being a test file with the test suffix. If a file has a `_test.go` suffix, Go knows to process that as a `test`.

A nice side effect of this naming convention is that all test files appear in the file list right next to the file they are usually testing, as in Listing 7.1.

This naming convention is a *required* naming convention. Even if you write test code in another file, if it does not have the `_test.go` suffix, the Go framework does not run the code as a test.

Listing 7.1   Test Files End in `_test.go` and Live Next to the File They're Testing

```
foo.go
foo_test.go
```

Test Function Signature

Aside from putting each test in a `_test.go` file, you also need to name your test functions properly. Without the proper naming and signature, Go does not run the function as a test.

Each test function *must* have the signature `Test<Name>(*testing.T)`.

In Listing 7.2, the function starts with the *uppercase* word `Test`. You can have other functions in your test files, but only the functions that start with the `Test` keyword run as a test. Additionally, each test *must* accept the `(t *testing.T)` argument.

Listing 7.2   A Simple Go Test

```
func TestSimple(t *testing.T) {
    if true {
        t.Fatal("expected false, got true")
    }
}
```

```
$ go test -v

=== RUN   TestSimple
    simple_test.go:8: expected false, got true
--- FAIL: TestSimple (0.00s)
FAIL
exit status 1
FAIL    demo    0.441s
```

```
Go Version: go1.19
```

The `*testing.T` Type

The `testing.T`[1] type, Listing 7.3, is used to validate and control the flow of a test. It has the following methods available to use to control the flow of a test. We cover most of the `testing.T` type, and its methods, in this chapter.

---

1. https://pkg.go.dev/testing#T

Listing 7.3   The testing.T Type

```
$ go doc testing.T

package testing // import "testing"

type T struct {
        // Has unexported fields.
}
    T is a type passed to Test functions to manage test state and
    ⇒support formatted test logs.

    A test ends when its Test function returns or calls any of
    ⇒the methods FailNow, Fatal, Fatalf, SkipNow, Skip, or Skipf.
    ⇒Those methods, as well as the Parallel method, must be called
    ⇒only from the goroutine running the Test function.

    The other reporting methods, such as the variations of Log and Error,
    ⇒may be called simultaneously from multiple goroutines.

func (c *T) Cleanup(f func())
func (t *T) Deadline() (deadline time.Time, ok bool)
func (c *T) Error(args ...any)
func (c *T) Errorf(format string, args ...any)
func (c *T) Fail()
func (c *T) FailNow()
func (c *T) Failed() bool
func (c *T) Fatal(args ...any)
func (c *T) Fatalf(format string, args ...any)
func (c *T) Helper()
func (c *T) Log(args ...any)
func (c *T) Logf(format string, args ...any)
func (c *T) Name() string
func (t *T) Parallel()
func (t *T) Run(name string, f func(t *T)) bool
func (t *T) Setenv(key, value string)
func (c *T) Skip(args ...any)
func (c *T) SkipNow()
func (c *T) Skipf(format string, args ...any)
func (c *T) Skipped() bool
func (c *T) TempDir() string
```

Go Version: go1.19

Marking Test Failures

Two of the most common calls to make while testing are `testing.T.Error`,[2] Listing 7.4, and `testing.T.Fatal`,[3] Listing 7.5. Both report a test failure, but `testing.T.Error` continues with execution of that test, whereas `testing.T.Fatal` ends that test.

Listing 7.4   The `testing.T.Error` Method

```
$ go doc testing.T.Error

package testing // import "testing"

func (c *T) Error(args ...any)
    Error is equivalent to Log followed by Fail.
```

Go Version: go1.19

Listing 7.5   The `testing.T.Fatal` Method

```
$ go doc testing.T.Fatal

package testing // import "testing"

func (c *T) Fatal(args ...any)
    Fatal is equivalent to Log followed by FailNow.
```

Go Version: go1.19

Using `t.Error`

In Listing 7.6, the `GetAlphabet` function returns a slice of letters for each country's alphabet. For example, if given the key `US`, the `GetAlphabet` function returns a slice of 26 characters, A-Z, and a `nil` to represent no error. If the requested key is not present in the map, then a `nil` is returned in place of the map, and the `fmt.Errorf` function is used to return an error.

Listing 7.6   A Function That May Return an Error

```
func GetAlphabet(key string) ([]string, error) {
    az := []string{"A", "B", "C", "D", "E", "F",
        "G", "H", "I", "J", "K", "L", "M", "N", "O",
        "P", "Q", "R", "S", "T", "U", "V", "W", "X",
        "Y", "Z"}
```

2. https://pkg.go.dev/testing#T.Error
3. https://pkg.go.dev/testing#T.Fatal

```
    m := map[string][]string{
        "US": az,
        "UK": az,
    }

    if v, ok := m[key]; ok {
        return v, nil
    }

    return nil, fmt.Errorf("no key found %s", key)
}
```

The test in Listing 7.7 for the GetAlphabet function marks test errors with the testing.T.Errorf[4] function. This tells Go that the test has failed; however, the test continues to run.

Listing 7.7   Using testing.T.Errorf to Indicate a Test Failure

```
func Test_GetAlphabet_Errorf(t *testing.T) {

    key := "CA"
    alpha, err := GetAlphabet(key)
    if err != nil {
        t.Errorf("could not find alphabet %s", key)
    }

    act := alpha[12]
    exp := "M"

    if act != exp {
        t.Errorf("expected %s, got %s", exp, act)
    }

}
```

```
$ go test -v

=== RUN    Test_GetAlphabet_Errorf
    alphabet_test.go:11: could not find alphabet CA
--- FAIL: Test_GetAlphabet_Errorf (0.00s)
```

(continued)

---

4. https://pkg.go.dev/testing#T.Errorf

```
panic: runtime error: index out of range [12] with length 0 [recovered]
        panic: runtime error: index out of range [12] with length 0

goroutine 34 [running]:
testing.tRunner.func1.2({0x104ea6940, 0x1400015c000})
        /usr/local/go/src/testing/testing.go:1389 +0x1c8
testing.tRunner.func1()
        /usr/local/go/src/testing/testing.go:1392 +0x384
panic({0x104ea6940, 0x1400015c000})
        /usr/local/go/src/runtime/panic.go:838 +0x204
demo.Test_GetAlphabet_Errorf(0x140001111e0)
        ./alphabet_test.go:14 +0x138
testing.tRunner(0x140001111e0, 0x104eb1538)
        /usr/local/go/src/testing/testing.go:1439 +0x110
created by testing.(*T).Run
        /usr/local/go/src/testing/testing.go:1486 +0x300
exit status 2
FAIL    demo    0.764s
```

Go Version: go1.19

In Listing 7.7, the key CA does not exist. The first error, could not find alphabet CA, is logged, and the test continues to run. The next check is to confirm that the thirteenth letter of the alphabet is the letter M. Because the alphabet was not found, the alpha slice is empty, so when the test tries to retrieve index 12, the test panics.

Using t.Fatal (Recommended)

Listing 7.8 uses testing.T.Fatalf[5] instead of testing.T.Errorf. This time, the test fails immediately at the first error, could not find alphabet CA. Since the test stops at that first error, the alpha[12] call is never executed, and the test doesn't panic.

Listing 7.8 Using testing.T.Fatalf to Indicate a Test Failure

```
func Test_GetAlphabet_Fatalf(t *testing.T) {

    key := "CA"
    alpha, err := GetAlphabet(key)
    if err != nil {
        t.Fatalf("could not find alphabet %s", key)
    }
```

5. https://pkg.go.dev/testing#T.Fatalf

```
    act := alpha[12]
    exp := "M"

    if act != exp {
        t.Fatalf("expected %s, got %s", exp, act)
    }
}
```

```
$ go test -v

=== RUN    Test_GetAlphabet_Fatalf
    alphabet_test.go:11: could not find alphabet CA
--- FAIL: Test_GetAlphabet_Fatalf (0.00s)
FAIL
exit status 1
FAIL    demo    0.594s
```

```
Go Version: go1.19
```

In summary, when trying to determine when to use `testing.T.Fatal` or `testing.T.Error`, it usually comes down to this: If the test continues but would result in more failures due to the current condition failing, you should prevent the test from continuing by using `testing.T.Fatal`. If the test could continue after failing a condition but still report other errors that are valid, then use `testing.T.Error`.

Crafting Good Test Failure Messages

When you decide that a test has failed, you need to make sure to craft a well-written failure message that informs the person running the test what the failure was and why. This failure message should also be resilient to change in the test later.

Consider the test in Listing 7.9. The test is designed to fail if the result of the `AddTen(int)` method does not return 11.

Listing 7.9 A Test That Fails

```
func Test_AddTen(t *testing.T) {
    v := AddTen(1)
    if v != 11 {
        t.Fatalf("expected %d, got %d", 11, v)
    }
}
```

While the error message in Listing 7.9 is very well-written, we have hard coded the expected value in two places. If we update one and forget to update the other, the resulting output would be very confusing. This is what we mean by all test messages should be "resilient to change" for future changes.

By using variables to hold data, Listing 7.10, like the expected value, we can easily update the code in one place and know that our error messages will be updated accordingly.

Listing 7.10 A Test That Fails but with a Better Error Message

```
func Test_AddTen(t *testing.T) {
    act := AddTen(1)
    exp := 11
    if act != exp {
        t.Fatalf("expected %d, got %d", exp, act)
    }
}
```

```
$ go test -v

=== RUN   Test_AddTen
    math_test.go:16: expected 11, got 12
--- FAIL: Test_AddTen (0.00s)
FAIL
exit status 1
FAIL    demo    0.115s

Go Version: go1.19
```

Now if the future expected value changes, only one variable needs to be changed, which reduces the chance that an invalid error message would be rendered.

Code Coverage

One of the most important parts of writing a solid application that is robust and maintainable is to ensure that the code is well tested. This is especially important when you are working with large code bases. In this section, we cover the basics of code coverage and how to use it to help you write better tests.

Basic Code Coverage

To write the best tests, you need to know which branches of the code are covered by tests. You can do this by generating code coverage reports.

Let's start by looking at code coverage for a package. When we run go test, Listing 7.11, the tests pass, but there is no code coverage information.

Listing 7.11   Running Tests with No Coverage Information

```
$ go test .

ok      demo     (cached)
```
Go Version: go1.19

In Listing 7.12, we run go test with the -cover flag. We get an overall code coverage printed for the package or packages being tested.

Listing 7.12   Running Tests with Coverage Information

```
$ go test -cover .

ok      demo     (cached)     coverage: 53.3% of statements
```
Go Version: go1.19

The -cover flag can be run both locally and in CI to help get a quick view into how well your packages are tested.

Generating a Coverage Profile

While the -cover flag gives you a quick view of how well your tests are covering your code, you can also generate a detailed coverage profile. This report gives you a breakdown of which lines of code are covered by tests and which lines are not.

In Listing 7.13, we pass the -coverprofile flag with a value of coverage.out to go test to generate a coverage profile. The tests run, and the coverage.out file is generated with the coverage information.

Listing 7.13   Generating a Coverage Profile

```
$ go test -coverprofile=coverage.out .

ok      demo     0.711s   coverage: 53.3% of statements
```
Go Version: go1.19

The file, coverage.out, as shown in Listing 7.14, generated by Listing 7.13, contains a list of all the lines of code that were covered by the tests.

Listing 7.14   Contents of the coverage.out File

```
mode: set
demo/errors.go:14.42,16.2 1 0
demo/store.go:25.39,26.12 1 1
```

(continued)

```
demo/store.go:30.2,30.12 1 1
demo/store.go:39.2,39.12 1 0
demo/store.go:26.12,28.3 1 0
demo/store.go:31.9,32.13 1 1
demo/store.go:33.9,34.37 1 0
demo/store.go:35.10,36.14 1 0
demo/store.go:47.48,51.15 2 1
demo/store.go:56.2,59.9 2 1
demo/store.go:67.2,67.18 1 0
demo/store.go:51.15,53.3 1 0
demo/store.go:59.9,64.3 1 1
```

The `go tool cover` Command

A coverage file, like the one in Listing 7.14, is not meant to be viewed directly. Instead, it's meant to be used with the cover.cmd command, Listing 7.15.

Listing 7.15 The go tool cover Command

```
$ go tool cover -h

Usage of 'go tool cover':
Given a coverage profile produced by 'go test':
        go test -coverprofile=c.out

Open a web browser displaying annotated source code:
        go tool cover -html=c.out

Write out an HTML file instead of launching a web browser:
        go tool cover -html=c.out -o coverage.html

Display coverage percentages to stdout for each function:
        go tool cover -func=c.out

Finally, to generate modified source code with coverage annotations
(what go test -cover does):
        go tool cover -mode=set -var=CoverageVariableName program.go

Flags:
  -V     print version and exit
  -func string
         output coverage profile information for each function
  -html string
         generate HTML representation of coverage profile
```

```
-mode string
      coverage mode: set, count, atomic
-o string
      file for output; default: stdout
-var string
      name of coverage variable to generate (default "GoCover")

Only one of -html, -func, or -mode may be set.
```

Go Version: go1.19

The go tool cover command can be used to transform the coverage profile generated by using the -coverprofile flag with go test. For example, in Listing 7.16, we use the go tool cover command to view the coverage profile generated by Listing 7.13 on a per-function basis.

Listing 7.16 Viewing the Coverage Profile on a Per-Function Basis

```
$ go tool cover -func=coverage.out

demo/errors.go:14:    Error         0.0%
demo/store.go:25:     Destroy       42.9%
demo/store.go:47:     All           71.4%
total:                (statements)  53.3%
```

Go Version: go1.19

Generating an HTML Coverage Report

Most often, you want to generate an HTML coverage report. This report gives you a nice visual breakdown of which lines of code are covered by tests and which lines are not. You can use the -html flag with a value of coverage.out, Listing 7.17, to generate an HTML coverage report from the coverage profile generated in Listing 7.13. The result opens in your
default browser.

In Listing 7.17, we are calling the go tool cover command with the -html flag and the name of the coverage file, coverage.out. When run locally, this opens the default OS browser and displays an HTML output of the code coverage, as shown in Figure 7.1.

Listing 7.17 Generating an HTML Coverage Report

```
$ go tool cover -html=coverage.out
```

Go Version: go1.19

You can use the -o flag, as shown in Listing 7.18, to specify an output file instead of opening the report in your default browser.

Listing 7.18 Generating an HTML Coverage Report with an Output File

```
$ go tool cover -html=coverage.out -o coverage.html
```

```
Go Version: go1.19
```

Figure 7.1 shows a copy of code coverage in a browser. The report highlights lines that are covered by the tests in green, and lines that are not covered in red. Gray lines are not tracked by coverage—for example, type definition and function declarations or comments.

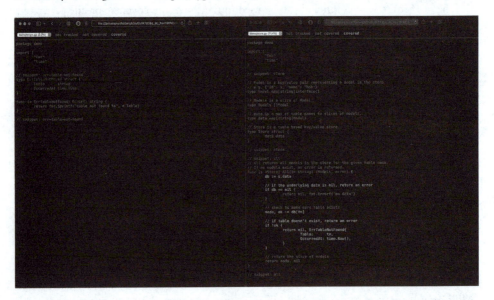

Figure 7.1   The HTML coverage report

Editor Support

A lot of editors, and their Go plugins, support code coverage. For example, the Go extension[6] for Visual Studio Code supports displaying code coverage directly in the editor, as shown in Figure 7.2.

Table Driven Testing

The code coverage demonstrated in Listing 7.19 shows that the A11 method has several code paths that are currently not covered by tests. Table driven tests can help us fix this.

---

6. https://code.visualstudio.com/docs/languages/go

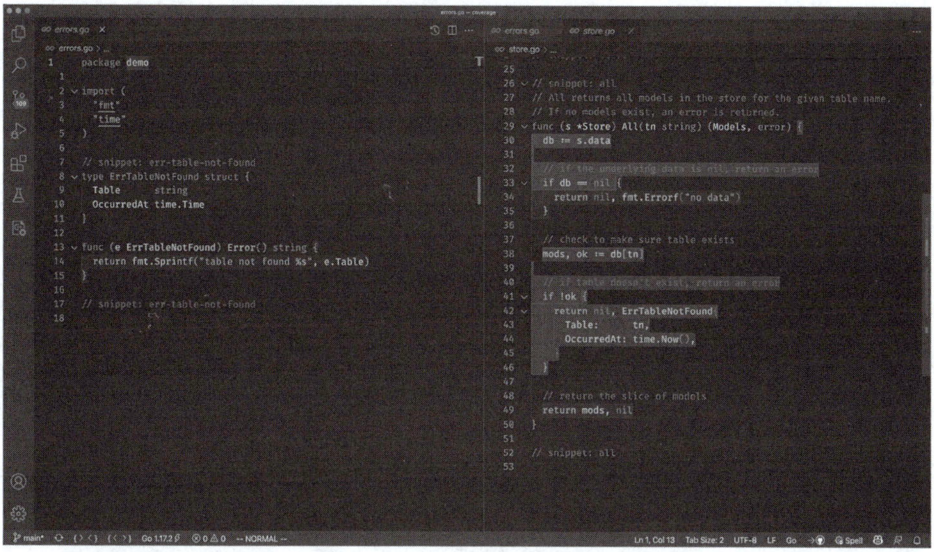

Figure 7.2 Highlighting code coverage directly in Visual Studio Code

Listing 7.19 Viewing the Coverage Profile on a Per-Function Basis

```
$ go tool cover -func=coverage.out

demo/errors.go:14:   Error        0.0%
demo/store.go:25:    Destroy      42.9%
demo/store.go:47:    All          71.4%
total:               (statements) 53.3%

Go Version: go1.19
```

You can use table driven tests to cover a lot of ground quickly while reusing common setup and comparison code. Table driven testing is not unique to Go; however, it is very popular in the Go community.

Anatomy of a Table Driven Test

Listing 7.20 is an example of the way a table driven test is structured. We use a slice of anonymous structs. The anonymous struct defines any fields needed for each test case; then we can fill that slice with the test cases we want to test. Finally, we loop through the slice of test cases and perform the tests.

Listing 7.20 Anatomy of a Table Driven Test

```go
func Test_TableDrivenTests_Anatomy(t *testing.T) {
    t.Parallel()

    // any setup code common to all
    // test cases goes here
    // create a slice of anonymous structs
    // initalize the slice with each of the
    // desired test cases and assign it to the
    // variable 'tcs'. tcs stands for "test cases"
    tcs := []struct {
        // fields needed for each test case
    }{
        // { tests cases go here },
        // { tests cases go here },
    }

    for _, tc := range tcs { // tc stands for "test case"
        // loop through each test case
        // and make the necessary assertions
        // for that test case
    }
}
```

Writing a Table Driven Test

Given the `All` method in Listing 7.21, we can use table driven tests to cover all of the error paths in the code.

Listing 7.21 The All Method

```go
// All returns all models in the store for the given table name.
// If no models exist, an error is returned.
func (s *Store) All(tn string) (Models, error) {
    db := s.data

    // if the underlying data is nil, return an error
    if db == nil {
        return nil, ErrNoData(tn)
    }

    // check to make sure table exists
    mods, ok := db[tn]
```

```
    // if table doesn't exist, return an error
    if !ok {
        return nil, ErrTableNotFound{
            Table:      tn,
            OccurredAt: time.Now(),
        }
    }


    // return the slice of models
    return mods, nil
}
```

In the test defined in Listing 7.22, we first set up our common test data. For example, we can define different implementations of the `Store` type that have various differences, such as whether their internal `data` field is initialized.

After that, we create a new slice of anonymous structs that hold the test cases we want to test. In this case, we need to be able to set the `Store` and the error we expect to see.

Finally, we loop through the slice of test cases and perform the tests.

Listing 7.22   Table Driven Tests with No Subtests

```
func Test_Store_All_Errors(t *testing.T) {
    t.Parallel()

    // the table name we will use
    tn := "users"

    // setup a few different Stores that
    // we can test against.
    noData := &Store{}
    withData := &Store{data: data{}}
    withUsers := &Store{data: data{"users": Models{}}}

    // create a slice of anonymous structs
    // with the fields for each case.
    tcs := []struct {
        store *Store
        exp   error
    }{
        // tests cases
        {store: noData, exp: ErrNoData(tn)},
        {store: withData, exp: ErrTableNotFound{}},
        {store: withUsers, exp: nil},
    }
```

(continued)

```go
    // loop through the table and test each case
    for _, tc := range tcs {
        _, err := tc.store.All(tn)

        ok := errors.Is(err, tc.exp)

        if !ok {
            t.Fatalf("expected error %T, got %T", tc.exp, err)
        }
    }
}
```

As you can see from the test output, Listing 7.23, our tests pass, but they are all in one test.

Listing 7.23 Output of the Table Driven Test

```
$ go test -v

=== RUN    Test_Store_All_Errors
=== PAUSE  Test_Store_All_Errors
=== CONT   Test_Store_All_Errors
--- PASS: Test_Store_All_Errors (0.00s)
PASS
ok      demo    0.542s

Go Version: go1.19
```

If one of the test cases fails, Listing 7.24, we don't know which one it is. We also don't have the ability to run just that one test. Using subtests solves both of these problems.

Listing 7.24 Uncertainty about Which Test Case Failed

```
$ go test -v

=== RUN    Test_Store_All_Errors
=== PAUSE  Test_Store_All_Errors
=== CONT   Test_Store_All_Errors
    store_test.go:39: expected error table not found , got no data
--- FAIL: Test_Store_All_Errors (0.00s)
FAIL
exit status 1
FAIL    demo    0.231s

Go Version: go1.19
```

Subtests

One of the problems with our tests as they are currently written is that they are not very descriptive, and if one of those test cases fails, we don't know which one, as we saw in Listing 7.24. This is where subtests come in. The testing.T.Run[7] method, Listing 7.25, allows us to create a whole new test for each test case we define. In Go, the name of the test is derived from the name of the test function. For example, if we have a test function called TestSomething, the name of the test is TestSomething. With subtests, we can create our own names for each test case to make them as useful and descriptive as we need.

Listing 7.25   The testing.T.Run Method

```
$ go doc testing.T.Run


package testing // import "testing"


func (t *T) Run(name string, f func(t *T)) bool
    Run runs f as a subtest of t called name. It runs f in a
    ⮕separate goroutine and blocks until f returns or calls t.
    ⮕Parallel to become a parallel test. Run reports whether f
    ⮕succeeded (or at least did not fail before calling
    ⮕t.Parallel).

    Run may be called simultaneously from multiple goroutines,
    ⮕but all such calls must return before the outer test
    ⮕function for t returns.


Go Version: go1.19
```

Anatomy of a Subtest

Using subtests is not much different than what we have been doing with table driven tests so far (refer to Listing 7.20). The biggest difference is in the for loop. In Listing 7.26, instead of making our assertions directly, we are, instead, calling the testing.T.Run method to create a new subtest. We give the testing.T.Run method the name of our test case and the function we want to run as a subtest.

Listing 7.26   Anatomy of a Subtest

```
func Test_Subtest_Anatomy(t *testing.T) {
    t.Parallel()

    // any setup code common to all
    // test cases goes here
```

(continued)

---

7. https://pkg.go.dev/testing#T.Run

```go
// create a slice of anonymous structs
// initalize the slice with each of the
// desired test cases and assign it to the
// variable 'tcs'.
tcs := []struct {

    // name of the test case
    name string
    // fields needed for each test case
}{
    // {name: "some test", tests cases go here },
    // {name: "some other test", tests cases go here },
}

for _, tc := range tcs {
    // create a subtest for each test case
    t.Run(tc.name, func(t *testing.T) {
        // loop through each test case
        // and make the necessary assertions
        // for that test case
    }
}
}
```

Writing Subtests

In Listing 7.27, we have added a call to the testing.T.Run method to create a subtest for each test case. When the tests are run, each test case is displayed as its own test. Should one of the subtests fail, it is easy to identify which one it is.

Listing 7.27   Subtests Displayed as Their Own Tests

```
$ go test -v

=== RUN    Test_Store_All_Errors_Sub
=== PAUSE Test_Store_All_Errors_Sub
=== CONT  Test_Store_All_Errors_Sub
=== RUN    Test_Store_All_Errors_Sub/no_data
=== RUN    Test_Store_All_Errors_Sub/with_data,_no_users
    store_test.go:41: expected error demo.ErrTableNotFound,
    ↪got demo.ErrNoData
=== RUN    Test_Store_All_Errors_Sub/with_users
--- FAIL: Test_Store_All_Errors_Sub (0.00s)
    --- PASS: Test_Store_All_Errors_Sub/no_data (0.00s)
    --- FAIL: Test_Store_All_Errors_Sub/with_data,_no_users (0.00s)
    --- PASS: Test_Store_All_Errors_Sub/with_users (0.00s)
```

```
FAIL
exit status 1
FAIL      demo      0.404s
```

Go Version: go1.19

Running Tests

Understanding the different options to run tests can greatly reduce the feedback cycle during development. In this section, we cover running specific tests, verbose output, failing fast, parallel options, and more.

Running Package Tests

You can run all of the tests in the current package (folder) using the `go test` command without specifying any test paths, as shown in Listing 7.28.

Listing 7.28   Running All the Tests in the Current Package

```
$ go test

PASS
ok        demo      1.500s
```

Go Version: go1.19

Running Tests with Subpackages

Often, Go projects consist of multiple packages. To run all of these packages, you can use the `./...`, Listing 7.29, identifier to tell Go to recurse through all subpackages as well as the current package.

Listing 7.29   Running All the Tests in the Current Package and Subpackages

```
$ go test ./...

ok        demo            (cached)
ok        demo/models     (cached)
ok        demo/web        (cached)
```

Go Version: go1.19

Optionally, as in Listing 7.30, you can specify the path of one or more packages to test.

Listing 7.30   Running All the Tests in the `models` Package

```
$ go test ./models


ok      demo/models (cached)
```

Go Version: go1.19

Verbose Test Output

It can be useful to output "verbose" information when running tests, such as when you're trying to debug a test. For example, as in Listing 7.31, you can see each test and subtest broken out individually. This allows you to see which tests were run and the status of that individual test. The `-v` flag turns on this verbose output.

Listing 7.31   Verbose Test Output

```
$ go test -v

=== RUN Test_Store
=== PAUSE Test_Store
=== RUN Test_Store_Order
=== PAUSE Test_Store_Order
=== RUN Test_Store_User_Order_History
=== PAUSE Test_Store_User_Order_History
=== RUN Test_Store_Address_Verification
=== PAUSE Test_Store_Address_Verification
=== CONT Test_Store
=== CONT Test_Store_Order
=== CONT Test_Store_User_Order_History
=== CONT Test_Store_Address_Verification
=== RUN Test_Store_Order/good_credit_card
=== RUN Test_Store_Order/bad_credit_card
--- PASS: Test_Store (0.02s)
--- PASS: Test_Store_User_Order_History (0.02s)
--- PASS: Test_Store_Address_Verification (0.04s)
=== RUN Test_Store_Order/user_not_logged_in
--- PASS: Test_Store_Order (0.11s)
    --- PASS: Test_Store_Order/good_credit_card (0.00s)
    --- PASS: Test_Store_Order/bad_credit_card (0.05s)
    --- PASS: Test_Store_Order/user_not_logged_in (0.06s)
PASS
ok      demo    0.394s
```

Go Version: go1.19

Logging in Tests

When using the -v flag, anything printed to the standard output is also displayed, regardless of whether the test was successful. This includes calls to fmt.Print and similar functions. You can use the testing.T.Log[8] and testing.T.Logf[9] methods to log information during tests. By default, any testing.T.Log and testing.T.Logf statements show up in test output only if the test fails. In Listing 7.32, you can see that when we run our test suite without the -v flag, there is no extra output.

Listing 7.32   Logging in Tests

```
$ go test .


ok      demo    (cached)

Go Version: go1.19
```

When tests are run with the -v flag, Listing 7.33, the output of testing.T.Log and testing.T.Logf statements is shown.

Listing 7.33   Enabling Logging in Tests with the -v Flag

```
$ go test -v .

=== RUN    Test_Store_All_Errors
=== PAUSE Test_Store_All_Errors
=== CONT   Test_Store_All_Errors
    store_test.go:13: using "users" for the table name
=== RUN    Test_Store_All_Errors/no_data
    store_test.go:31: running test: no data
=== RUN    Test_Store_All_Errors/with_data,_no_users
    store_test.go:31: running test: with data, no users
=== RUN    Test_Store_All_Errors/with_users
    store_test.go:31: running test: with users
--- PASS: Test_Store_All_Errors (0.00s)
    --- PASS: Test_Store_All_Errors/no_data (0.00s)
    --- PASS: Test_Store_All_Errors/with_data,_no_users (0.00s)
    --- PASS: Test_Store_All_Errors/with_users (0.00s)
PASS
ok      demo    (cached)

Go Version: go1.19
```

---

8. https://pkg.go.dev/testing#T.Log
9. https://pkg.go.dev/testing#T.Logf

Short Tests

Sometimes you have long running tests, or integration tests, that you might not want to run as part of your local development cycle. The testing.Short[10] function shown in Listing 7.34 can be used to mark a test as being "short."

Listing 7.34   The testing.Short Function

```
$ go doc testing.Short

package testing // import "testing"

func Short() bool
    Short reports whether the -test.short flag is set.
```

Go Version: go1.19

You can pass the -short argument to the test runner and check for that in your tests with the testing.Short function, as in Listing 7.35. This is useful also if your test has outside dependencies such as a database that you might not have available for local testing.

Listing 7.35   Using the -short Flag and testing.Short to Run Specific Tests

```
$ go doc testing.Short

package testing // import "testing"

func Short() bool
    Short reports whether the -test.short flag is set.
```

Go Version: go1.19

```
func Test_Example(t *testing.T) {
    if testing.Short() {
        t.Skip("skipping test in short mode.")
    }

    // ...
}
```

10. https://pkg.go.dev/testing#Short

```
$ go test -v -short .

=== RUN   Test_Example
    short_test.go:8: skipping test in short mode.
--- SKIP: Test_Example (0.00s)
PASS
ok      demo    (cached)
```

Go Version: go1.19

Running Package Tests in Parallel

By default, each package is run in parallel to make testing faster. This can be changed by setting the -parallel flag to 1, as in Listing 7.36. This is usually done to prevent packages that use transactions to a database or would otherwise cause contention between package tests.

Listing 7.36   Changing the Parallelism of the Test Runner

```
$ go test -parallel 1 ./...
```

Running Tests in Parallel

Although packages are run in different threads during testing, individual tests within those packages are not. They are run one test at a time. However, you can change this.

By using testing.t.Parallel,[11] Listing 7.37, you signal that this test is to be run in parallel with (and only with) other parallel tests.

Listing 7.37   The testing.T.Parallel Method

```
$ go doc testing.T.Parallel

package testing // import "testing"

func (t *T) Parallel()
    Parallel signals that this test is to be run in parallel with
    ➥(and only with) other parallel tests. When a test is run
    ➥multiple times due to use of -test.count or -test.cpu,
    ➥multiple instances of a single test never run in parallel
    ➥with each other.
```

Go Version: go1.19

---

11. https://pkg.go.dev/testing#t.Parallel

> It is *strongly* recommended that you use `testing.t.Parallel` in your tests. Not being able to run tests in parallel is usually a sign of poor architecture resulting from using a shared resource instead of passing in the resource to be used.

In Listing 7.38, the first thing we do inside of the `Test_Example` test function is to call the `t.Parallel` method to tell Go that this test is safe to be run concurrently with other tests.

Listing 7.38 Using `testing.t.Parallel` to Mark a Test as Parallel-Friendly

```
func Test_Example(t *testing.T) {
    // mark this test as safe
    // to be run in parallel
    // with other tests
    t.Parallel()

    // ...
}
```

Running Specific Tests

The `-run` flag allows for the passing of a regular expression to match the names of specific tests to run. For example, in Listing 7.39, we are passing the `-run` flag to the test runner to run only tests that contain the string `History`.

Listing 7.39 Running Only Tests That Have `History` in Their Name

```
$ go test -v -run History ./...

=== RUN   Test_Store_User_Order_History
=== PAUSE Test_Store_User_Order_History
=== CONT  Test_Store_User_Order_History
--- PASS: Test_Store_User_Order_History (0.09s)
PASS
ok      demo     (cached)
testing: warning: no tests to run
PASS
ok      demo/models (cached) [no tests to run]
testing: warning: no tests to run
PASS
ok      demo/web    (cached) [no tests to run]

Go Version: go1.19
```

In Listing 7.40, we are passing the -run flag to the test runner to run only tests that contain the string Address.

Listing 7.40   Subtests Are Also Run with the -run Flag

```
$ go test -v -run Address ./...

=== RUN    Test_Store_Address_Verification
=== PAUSE Test_Store_Address_Verification
=== CONT   Test_Store_Address_Verification
--- PASS: Test_Store_Address_Verification (0.07s)
PASS
ok      demo    (cached)
=== RUN    Test_Address
=== PAUSE Test_Address
=== CONT   Test_Address
--- PASS: Test_Address (0.01s)
PASS
ok      demo/models (cached)
=== RUN    Test_User_Update_Address
=== PAUSE Test_User_Update_Address
=== CONT   Test_User_Update_Address
--- PASS: Test_User_Update_Address (0.06s)
PASS
ok      demo/web    (cached)

Go Version: go1.19
```

Timing Out Tests

Eventually you will accidentally write an erroneous infinite for loop or other piece of code that will cause your tests to run forever. By using the -timeout flag, you can set a timeout for your tests to prevent these scenarios. In Listing 7.41, the tests stop and fail after fifty milliseconds.

Listing 7.41   Setting a Timeout for Tests with the -timeout Flag

```
$ go test -timeout 50ms ./...

panic: test timed out after 50ms

goroutine 33 [running]:
testing.(*M).startAlarm.func1()
        /usr/local/go/src/testing/testing.go:2029 +0x8c
```

(continued)

```
created by time.goFunc
        /usr/local/go/src/time/sleep.go:176 +0x3c

goroutine 1 [chan receive]:
testing.tRunner.func1()
        /usr/local/go/src/testing/testing.go:1405 +0x45c
testing.tRunner(0x14000138000, 0x1400010fcb8)
        /usr/local/go/src/testing/testing.go:1445 +0x14c
testing.runTests(0x1400001e1e0?, {0x102f3dea0, 0x1, 0x1},
➥{0x9000000000000000?, 0x102d69218?, 0x102f46640?)}
        /usr/local/go/src/testing/testing.go:1837 +0x3f0
testing.(*M).Run(0x1400001e1e0)
        /usr/local/go/src/testing/testing.go:1719 +0x500
main.main()
        _testmain.go:47 +0x1d0

goroutine 4 [sleep]:
time.Sleep(0x3b9aca00)
        /usr/local/go/src/runtime/time.go:194 +0x11c
demo.Test_Forever_(0x0?)
        ./timeout_test.go:11 +0x2c
testing.tRunner(0x140001381a0, 0x102e99298)
        /usr/local/go/src/testing/testing.go:1439 +0x110
created by testing.(*T).Run
        /usr/local/go/src/testing/testing.go:1486 +0x300
FAIL    demo 0.125s
FAIL
```

Go Version: go1.19

It is recommended to *always* provide a timeout when running tests. If/when your code deadlocks, it times out and provides a stack trace of the routines to assist in debugging.

Failing Fast

You can use the -failfast flag to stop your tests at the first test failure. This is specifically very useful when you're doing large refactors and you want tests to stop as soon as one test fails.

In Listing 7.42, we are running the tests without the -failfast flag. As we see from the output, all the tests are run before the failures are reported. In Listing 7.43, we are running the tests with the -failfast flag, and as you see from the output, once the first test fails, the rest of the tests are not run.

Listing 7.42 Setting the -failfast Flag

```
$ go test .

--- FAIL: Test_A (0.00s)
--- FAIL: Test_B (0.00s)
--- FAIL: Test_C (0.00s)
FAIL
FAIL    demo    0.327s
FAIL


Go Version: go1.19
```

Listing 7.43 Setting the -failfast Flag

```
$ go test -failfast .

--- FAIL: Test_A (0.00s)
FAIL
FAIL    demo    0.167s
FAIL


Go Version: go1.19
```

Disabling Test Caching

Go automatically caches any passing tests to make subsequent test runs faster. Go breaks this cache when either the test or the code it is testing changes. This means you almost never have to deal with test caches. Occasionally there are times when you might want to disable this behavior.

One reason you may want to disable caching is if you have tests that are integration tests and test packages or systems external to the package the tests are written in. Because it's likely the package didn't experience changes but the outside dependencies did, you would not want to cache your tests in this scenario.

To ensure your tests don't use any cached runs, use the -count flag, as shown in Listing 7.44, and force the tests to run at least once.

Listing 7.44 Disabling the Test Cache with the -count Flag

```
$ go test -count=1 ./...
```

Test Helpers

Just like when we're writing "real" code, our tests sometimes need helper functions. These helper functions are called "test helpers." Test helpers might set up, tear down, or provision resources for the test. They can be used to write assertions or to mock out external dependencies.

Defining Test Helpers

Test helper functions in Go are just like any other function. The difference is that they are only defined in your tests. While not required, it is recommended that you take the `testing.TB` interface, Listing 7.45, as the first argument to your test helper function. This interface is the common set of functions to both the `testing.T`[12] and `testing.B`,[13] used for benchmarking, types.

Listing 7.45   The `testing.TB`[14] Interface

```
$ go doc testing.TB

package testing // import "testing"

type TB interface {
        Cleanup(func())
        Error(args ...any)
        Errorf(format string, args ...any)
        Fail()
        FailNow()
        Failed() bool
        Fatal(args ...any)
        Fatalf(format string, args ...any)
        Helper()
        Log(args ...any)
        Logf(format string, args ...any)
        Name() string
        Setenv(key, value string)
        Skip(args ...any)
        SkipNow()
        Skipf(format string, args ...any)
        Skipped() bool
        TempDir() string
```

---

12. https://pkg.go.dev/testing#T
13. https://pkg.go.dev/testing#B
14. https://pkg.go.dev/testing#TB

```
        // Has unexported methods.
}
    TB is the interface common to T, B, and F.
```

Go Version: go1.19

Let's define some test helpers to help clean up tests in Listing 7.46. We create helpers to create the different `Store` implementations we need for the test.

Listing 7.46   The Test Function to Refactor with Helpers

```go
func Test_Store_All_Errors(t *testing.T) {
    t.Parallel()

    tn := "users"

    noData := &Store{}
    withData := &Store{data: data{}}
    withUsers := &Store{data: data{"users": Models{}}}

    // create a slice of anonymous structs
    // with the fields for each case.
    tcs := []struct {
        name   string
        store  *Store
        exp    error
    }{
        // tests cases
        {name: "no data", store: noData, exp: ErrNoData(tn)},
        {name: "with data, no users", store: withData, exp:
        ➥ErrTableNotFound{}},
        {name: "with users", store: withUsers, exp: nil},
    }

    // loop through the tcs and test each case
    for _, tc := range tcs {
        t.Run(tc.name, func(t *testing.T) {
            _, err := tc.store.All(tn)

            ok := errors.Is(err, tc.exp)
```

(continued)

```
        if !ok {
            t.Fatalf("expected error %v, got %v", tc.exp, err)
        }
    })
    }
}
```

First, in Listing 7.47, we create two helper functions. The first, `noData(testing.TB)`, returns a `&Store` that does not have any data. The second, `withData(testing.TB)`, returns a `&Store` that has its `data` field properly initialized.

Listing 7.47   Two Helper Functions for Initializing `Store` Values

```
func noData(t testing.TB) *Store {
    return &Store{}
}

func withData(t testing.TB) *Store {
    return &Store{
        data: data{},
    }
}
```

In Listing 7.48, we declare the `withUsers` helper function needed to clean up the tests. At the moment, however, we are unable to implement the `withUsers` test helper, so we can call the `testing.TB.Fatal`[15] method on the passed-in `testing.TB` to let Go know that we haven't implemented this helper yet.

Listing 7.48   An Unimplemented Helper Function

```
func withUsers(t testing.TB) *Store {
    // go test reports this line as failing:
    t.Fatal("not implemented")
    return nil
}
```

Finally, in Listing 7.49, we can update our tests to use the new test helpers, passing in the `testing.T` argument from the test to the helper function.

---

15. https://pkg.go.dev/testing#TB.Fatal

Listing 7.49   The Test Function with the New Helpers

```
func Test_Store_All_Errors(t *testing.T) {
    t.Parallel()

    tn := "users"

    tcs := []struct {
        name  string
        store *Store
        exp   error
    }{
        {name: "no data", store: noData(t), exp: ErrNoData(tn)},
        {name: "with data, no users", store: withData(t), exp:
        ➥ErrTableNotFound{}},
        {name: "with users", store: withUsers(t), exp: nil},
    }

    for _, tc := range tcs {
        t.Run(tc.name, func(t *testing.T) {
            _, err := tc.store.All(tn)

            ok := errors.Is(err, tc.exp)

            if !ok {
                t.Fatalf("expected error %v, got %v", tc.exp, err)
            }
        })
    }
}
```

As shown in Listing 7.50, because we have yet to implement the `withUsers` helper, our tests will fail.

Listing 7.50   The Stack Trace Prints the Line in the Helper That Failed

```
$ go test -v

=== RUN   Test_Store_All_Errors
=== PAUSE Test_Store_All_Errors
=== CONT  Test_Store_All_Errors
    store_test.go:24: not implemented
--- FAIL: Test_Store_All_Errors (0.00s)
```

(continued)

```
FAIL
exit status 1
FAIL    demo    0.687s
```

Go Version: go1.19

When the test fails, it reported the test failure as inside the `withUsers` helper, Listing 7.48, and not within the test itself. This can make it difficult to debug the test failure.

Marking a Function as a Helper

To get Go to report the correct line number, inside of the test and not the helper, we need to tell Go that the `withData` function is a test helper. To do that, we *must* use the `testing.TB.Helper`[16] method, Listing 7.51, inside of our test helpers.

Listing 7.51 The `testing.TB.Helper` Method

```
$ go doc testing.T.Helper

package testing // import "testing"
func (c *T) Helper()
    Helper marks the calling function as a test helper function.
    ↪When printing file and line information, that function will be
    ↪skipped. Helper may be called simultaneously from multiple
    ↪goroutines.
```

Go Version: go1.19

```
func withUsers(t testing.TB) *Store {
    t.Helper()
    t.Fatal("not implemented")
    return nil
}
```

Now, when the test fails, in Listing 7.52, the line number reported is the line number inside the test that failed, not the line number inside the helper.

---

16. https://pkg.go.dev/testing#TB.Helper

Listing 7.52 The Stack Track Now Points to the Text Line That Failed

```
$ go test -v

=== RUN    Test_Store_All_Errors
=== PAUSE Test_Store_All_Errors
=== CONT   Test_Store_All_Errors
    store_test.go:44: not implemented
--- FAIL: Test_Store_All_Errors (0.00s)
FAIL
exit status 1
FAIL    demo    0.490s
```

Go Version: go1.19

```go
table := []struct {
    name   string
    store  *Store
    exp    error
}{
    {name: "no data", store: noData(t), exp: ErrNoData(tn)},
    // go test now reports this line as the failure:
    {name: "with data, no users", store: withData(t), exp:
    ➥ErrTableNotFound{}},
    {name: "with users", store: withUsers(t), exp: nil},
}
```

Cleaning Up a Helper

It is very common that a test helper, or even a test itself, needs to clean up some resources when done. To do that, you need to use the `testing.TB.Cleanup`[17] method, Listing 7.53. With `testing.TB.Cleanup`, we can pass in a function that is called automatically when the test is done.

Listing 7.53 The `testing.TB.Cleanup` Method

```
$ go doc testing.T.Cleanup

package testing // import "testing"
```

(continued)

---

17. https://pkg.go.dev/testing#TB.Cleanup

```
func (c *T) Cleanup(f func())

    Cleanup registers a function to be called when the test
    ➥(or subtest) and all its subtests complete. Cleanup functions
    ➥will be called in last added, first called order.
```

Go Version: go1.19

In Listing 7.54, we implement the `withUsers` helper function. In it, we use the `testing.TB.Cleanup` method to clean up the users we created.

Listing 7.54 Using `testing.T.Cleanup` to Clean Up Helper Resources

```go
func withUsers(t testing.TB) *Store {
    t.Helper()

    users := Models{
        {"id": 1, "name": "John"},
        {"id": 2, "name": "Jane"},
    }

    t.Cleanup(func() {
        t.Log("cleaning up users", users)
    })

    return &Store{
        data: data{
            "users": users,
        },
    }

}
```

```
$ go test -v

=== RUN    Test_Store_All_Errors
=== PAUSE Test_Store_All_Errors
=== CONT  Test_Store_All_Errors
=== RUN    Test_Store_All_Errors/no_data
=== RUN    Test_Store_All_Errors/with_data,_no_users
=== RUN    Test_Store_All_Errors/with_users
=== CONT  Test_Store_All_Errors
    store_test.go:30: cleaning up users [map[id:1 name:John]
    ➥map[id:2 name:Jane]]
```

```
--- PASS: Test_Store_All_Errors (0.00s)
    --- PASS: Test_Store_All_Errors/no_data (0.00s)
    --- PASS: Test_Store_All_Errors/with_data,_no_users (0.00s)
    --- PASS: Test_Store_All_Errors/with_users (0.00s)
PASS
ok      demo    0.642s
```

```
Go Version: go1.19
```

Clarifying `Cleanup` **versus** `defer`

Although the `testing.TB.Cleanup` method might seem like a fancy `defer` statement, it is actually a different concept. When a function is deferred, that function is called when its parent function returns. In the case of `testing.TB.Cleanup`, the `testing.TB.Cleanup` function is called when the test is done.

Summary

In this chapter, we covered the basics of testing in Go. We covered how to write tests, how to run tests, how to write test helpers, and how to write table driven tests. We showed you how to generate code coverage reports and how to run tests in parallel. We also covered many of the important test flags, such as `-run`, `-v`, and `-timeout`. Finally, we explained how to write useful test helpers and how to properly clean up after them.

Interfaces

Interfaces in Go provide a way to specify the behavior of an object; "If something can do this, then it can be used here." In this chapter, we look at how to use interfaces to abstract behavior. Later in this chapter, we explain how generics can be used to further refine interfaces. Concepts such as the `Empty Interface`, satisfying multiple interfaces, value versus pointer receivers, and asserting for behavior also are covered in this chapter.

Concrete Types versus Interfaces

Interfaces allow you to specify behavior. They are about doing, not being. Interfaces also allow you to abstract code to make it more reusable, extensible, and testable.

To illustrate this, let's consider the concept of a performance venue. A performance venue should allow a variety of performers to perform at the venue.

An example of this as a function might look like Listing 8.1.

Listing 8.1 The PerformAtVenue Function

```
func PerformAtVenue(m Musician) {
    m.Perform()
}
```

The PerformAtVenue function takes a Musician, Listing 8.2, as an argument and calls the Perform method on the musician. The Musician type is a concrete type.

Listing 8.2 The Musician Type

```
type Musician struct {
    Name string
}

func (m Musician) Perform() {
    fmt.Println(m.Name, "is singing")
}
```

When we pass a `Musician` to the `PerformAtVenue` function in Listing 8.3, our code compiles, and we get the expected output.

Listing 8.3 A `PerformAtVenue` Being Called with a `Musician`

```
func main() {
    m := Musician{Name: "Kurt"}
    PerformAtVenue(m)
}
```

```
$ go run .

Kurt is singing
```

Go Version: go1.19

Because the `PerformAtVenue` function takes a `Musician`, which is a concrete type, as an argument, we are restricted as to who can perform at the venue. For example, if we were to try to pass a `Poet` to the `PerformAtVenue` function, we would get a compilation error, as shown in Listing 8.4.

Listing 8.4 Compilation Error When Using the Incorrect Type

```
type Poet struct {
    Name string
}

func (p Poet) Perform() {
    fmt.Println(p.Name, "is reading poetry")
}

func main() {
    m := Musician{Name: "Kurt"}
    PerformAtVenue(m)

    p := Poet{Name: "Janis"}
    PerformAtVenue(p)
}
```

```
$ go run .

# demo
./main.go:34:17: cannot use p (variable of type Poet) as type Musician in
➥argument to PerformAtVenue
```

Go Version: go1.19

Interfaces allow you to solve this problem by specifying a common set of methods that are required by the `PerformAtVenue` function.

In Listing 8.5, we introduce a `Performer` interface. This interface specifies that a `Perform` method is required to implement the `Performer` interface.

Listing 8.5   The `Performer` Interface

```
type Performer interface {
    Perform()
}
```

Both the `Musician` and `Poet` types have the `Perform` method. Therefore, we can implement the `Performer` interface on both of these types. By updating the `PerformAtVenue` function, in Listing 8.6, to take a `Performer` as an argument, as shown in Listing 8.6, we are now able to pass a `Musician` or a `Poet` to the `PerformAtVenue` function.

Listing 8.6   Both `Poet` and `Musician` Implement the `Performer` Interface

```
func PerformAtVenue(p Performer) {
    p.Perform()
}
```

```
$ go run .

Kurt is singing
Janis is reading poetry
```

```
Go Version: go1.19
```

By using an interface, instead of a concrete type, we are able to abstract the code and make it more flexible and expandable.

Explicit Interface Implementation

In a lot of object-oriented languages, such as C# and Java, you have to *explicitly* declare that your type is implementing a very specific interface.

In C#, Listing 8.7, for example, we declare that we are using the `Performer` interface by using the : operator after the class name and listing the interfaces we want to use.

Listing 8.7   Implementing the `Performer` Interface in C#

```
// C#
interface Performer {
    void Perform();
}
```

(continued)

```
// explicitly implements Performer
class Musician : Performer {
    public void Perform() {}
}
```

In Java, Listing 8.8, we use the `implements` keyword after the class name to tell the compiler that our type wants to implement the `Performer` interface.

Listing 8.8 Implementing the `Performer` Interface in Java

```
// Java
interface Performer {
    void Perform();
}

// explicitly implements Performer
class Musician implements Performer {
    void Perform() {}
}
```

Implicit Interface Implementation

In Go, interfaces are implemented *implicitly*. This means you don't have to indicate to Go that you are implementing an interface. Given a `Performer` interface, Listing 8.9, a type would need to implement the `Perform` method to be considered a performer.

Listing 8.9 The `Performer` Interface

```
type Performer interface {
    Perform()
}
```

By adding a `Perform` method that matches the signature of the `Performer` interface (Listing 8.10), the `Musician` type is now implicitly implementing the `Performer` interface.

Listing 8.10 The `Musician` Type Implicitly Implements the `Performer` Interface

```
type Musician struct {
    Name string
}
```

```
// Perform implicitly implements the Performer interface
func (m Musician) Perform() {
    fmt.Println(m.Name, "is singing")
}
```

Provided a type implements all behaviors specified in the interface, it can be said to implement that interface. The compiler checks to make sure a type is acceptable and reports an error if it does not. Sometimes this is called duck typing, but since it happens at compile-time in Go, it is called structural typing.

Structural typing has a handful of useful side effects:

- The concrete type does not need to know about your interface.

- You are able to write interfaces for concrete types that already exist.

- You can write interfaces for other people's types or types that appear in other packages.

Before Interfaces

Consider Listing 8.11. This function takes a pointer to os.File, along with a slice of bytes. The function then calls the os.File.Writer[1] function with the data passed in.

Listing 8.11 The WriteData Function

```
func WriteData(w *os.File, data []byte) {
    w.Write(data)
}
```

To call this function, we must have an os.File,[2] which is a concrete type in the system. To call this function, we either need to retrieve, or create, a file on the filesystem, or we can use os.Stdout,[3] which is an os.File, as we do Listing 8.12.

Listing 8.12 Using os.Stdout As os.File

```
func main() {
    WriteData(os.Stdout, []byte("Hello, World!"))
}
```

Testing this function involves significant setup. In Listing 8.13, we need to create a new file, call the WriteData function, close the file, reopen the file, read the file, and then compare the contents. We need to do all of this work to be able to call one function, Write, on os.File.

---

1. https://pkg.go.dev/os#File.Writer
2. https://pkg.go.dev/os#File
3. https://pkg.go.dev/os#Stdout

Listing 8.13   Testing the `WriteData` Function

```go
func Test_WriteData(t *testing.T) {
    t.Parallel()

    dir, err := ioutil.TempDir("", "example")
    if err != nil {
        t.Fatal(err)
    }

    fn := filepath.Join(dir, "hello.txt")

    f, err := os.Create(fn)

    if err != nil {
        t.Fatal(err)
    }

    data := []byte("Hello, World!")
    WriteData(f, data)

    f.Close()

    f, err = os.Open(fn)
    if err != nil {
        t.Fatal(err)
    }

    b, err := ioutil.ReadAll(f)
    if err != nil {
        t.Fatal(err)
    }

    act := string(b)
    exp := string(data)
    if act != exp {
        t.Fatalf("expected %q, got %q", exp, act)
    }

}
```

```
$ go test -v

=== RUN    Test_WriteData
=== PAUSE Test_WriteData
=== CONT  Test_WriteData
```

```
--- PASS: Test_WriteData (0.00s)
PASS
ok      demo    0.150s
```

Go Version: go1.19

The `WriteData` function is a prime candidate to be refactored using interfaces.

Using Interfaces

One of the most well-known interfaces in Go is the `io.Writer`[4] interface, Listing 8.14. The `io.Writer` interface requires the implementation of a `Write` method that matches the signature of `Write(p []byte) (n int, err error)`.

Listing 8.14   The `io.Writer` Interface

```
$ go doc io.Writer

package io // import "io"

type Writer interface {
        Write(p []byte) (n int, err error)
}
   Writer is the interface that wraps the basic Write method.

   Write writes len(p) bytes from p to the underlying data stream. It returns
  ➥the number of bytes written from p (0 <= n <= len(p)) and any error
  ➥encountered that caused the write to stop early. Write must return a
  ➥non-nil error if it returns n < len(p). Write must not modify the slice
  ➥data, even temporarily.

   Implementations must not retain p.

var Discard Writer = discard{}
func MultiWriter(writers ...Writer) Writer
```

Go Version: go1.19

Implementations of the `io.Writer` interface can be found all over the standard library, as well as in third-party packages. A few of the most common implementations of the `io.Writer` interface are `os.File`, `bytes.Buffer`,[5] and `strings.Builder`.[6]

---

4. https://pkg.go.dev/io#Writer
5. https://pkg.go.dev/bytes#Buffer
6. https://pkg.go.dev/strings#Builder

Knowing that the only portion of os.File we are using matches the io.Writer interface, we can modify the WriteData to use the io.Writer, Listing 8.15, and improve the compatibility and testability of the method.

Listing 8.15   The WriteData Function

```go
func WriteData(w io.Writer, data []byte) {
    w.Write(data)
}
```

The usage of the WriteData function does not change in Listing 8.16.

Listing 8.16   Using os.Stdout[7] As io.Writer

```go
func main() {
    WriteData(os.Stdout, []byte("Hello, World!"))
}
```

Testing the WriteData function, Listing 8.17, also becomes easier now that we can substitute the implementation with an easier-to-test implementation.

Listing 8.17   Testing the WriteData Function

```go
func Test_WriteData(t *testing.T) {
    t.Parallel()

    // create a buffer to write to
    bb := &bytes.Buffer{}

    data := []byte("Hello, World!")

    // write the data to the buffer
    WriteData(bb, data)

    // capture the data written to the buffer
    // to the act variable
    act := bb.String()

    exp := string(data)
    // compare the expected and actual values
    if act != exp     {
```

---

7. https://pkg.go.dev/os#Stdout

```
        t.Fatalf("expected %q, got %q", exp, act)
    }

}
```

```
$ go test -v

=== RUN    Test_WriteData
=== PAUSE Test_WriteData
=== CONT   Test_WriteData
--- PASS: Test_WriteData (0.00s)
PASS
ok        demo      0.197s

Go Version: go1.19
```

Implementing io.Writer

Now that WriteData uses the io.Writer, we cannot only use implementations from the standard library like os.File and bytes.Buffer, but we can create our own implementation of io.Writer.

In Listing 8.18, where we implement the Write function with the proper signature, we don't have to implicitly declare our type Scribe as an io.Writer. The compiler is able to determine whether the type being passed in implements the interface being requested.

Listing 8.18   The Scribe Type Implements io.Writer

```
type Scribe struct {
    data []byte
}

func (s Scribe) String() string {
    return string(s.data)
}

func (s *Scribe) Write(p []byte) (int, error) {
    s.data = p
    return len(p), nil
}
```

In Listing 8.19, we call the `WriteData` function with our implementation of the `io.Writer` interface, a pointer to the `Scribe` type.

Listing 8.19   The Scribe Type Implements `io.Writer`

```go
func main() {
    s := &Scribe{}
    WriteData(s, []byte("Hello, World!"))
}
```

```
$ go run .
```

```
Go Version: go1.19
```

The `*Scribe` type can also be used to test `WriteData` like we did with `bytes.Buffer`, Listing 8.20.

Listing 8.20   Testing the `WriteData` Function

```go
func Test_WriteData(t *testing.T) {
    t.Parallel()

    scribe := &Scribe{}
    data := []byte("Hello, World!")
    WriteData(scribe, data)

    act := scribe.String()
    exp := string(data)
    if act != exp {
        t.Fatalf("expected %q, got %q", exp, act)
    }

}
```

```
$ go test -v

=== RUN    Test_WriteData
=== PAUSE Test_WriteData
=== CONT  Test_WriteData
--- PASS: Test_WriteData (0.00s)
PASS
ok      demo    0.055s
```

```
Go Version: go1.19
```

Multiple Interfaces

Because interfaces are implemented implicitly, it means that types can implement many interfaces at once without explicit declaration. In addition to implementing io.Writer, the Scribe type also implements the fmt.Stringer[8] interface, Listing 8.21.

Listing 8.21   The fmt.Stringer Interface

```
$ go doc fmt.Stringer

package fmt // import "fmt"

type Stringer interface {
        String() string
}
    Stringer is implemented by any value that has a String method, which
    ➥defines the "native" format for that value. The String method is used
    ➥to print values passed as an operand to any format that accepts a string
    ➥or to an unformatted printer such as Print.
```

Go Version: go1.19

You use the fmt.Stringer interface to convert a value to a string. By implementing a String() string method on the Scribe type, the Scribe now implements both the fmt.Stringer and io.Writer interfaces, Listing 8.22.

Listing 8.22   The Scribe Type Implements Both fmt.Stringer and io.Writer

```
func (s Scribe) String() string {
    return string(s.data)
}
```

Asserting Interface Implementation

Often, especially while implementing an interface, it can be useful to assert that your type conforms to all of the interfaces you are trying to implement. One way to do this is to declare a new variable, whose type is the interface you are implementing, and try to assign your type to it, Listing 8.23. Using the _ character tells the compiler to do the assignment to the variable and then throw away the result. These assertions are usually done at the package level.

---

8. https://pkg.go.dev/fmt#Stringer

Listing 8.23   Asserting that the `Scribe` Type Implements the `io.Writer` and `fmt.Stringer` Interfaces

```
package main

var _ io.Writer = &Scribe{}
var _ fmt.Stringer = Scribe{}
```

The compiler keeps failing until the `Scribe` type implements both the `io.Writer` and `fmt.Stringer` interfaces.

The Empty Interface

All the interfaces you've seen so far have declared one or more methods. In Go, there is no *minimum* method count for an interface. That means it is possible to have what is called an empty interface, Listing 8.24. If you declare an interface with zero methods, then every type in the system is considered to have implemented it.

In Go, you use the empty interface to represent "anything."

Listing 8.24   The Empty Interface

```
// generic empty interface:
interface{} // aliased to "any"

// a named empty interface:
type foo interface{}
```

An `int`, for example, has no methods, and because of that, an `int` matches an interface with no methods.

The `any` Keyword

In `Go1.18`, generics[9] were added to the language. As part of this, a new keyword, `any`, was added to the language. This keyword is an alias for `interface{}`, Listing 8.25.

Using any rather than `interface{}` is a good idea because it is more explicit and it is easier to read.

Listing 8.25   Using any Instead of `interface{}`

```
// Go 1.x:
func foo(x interface{}) {
    // ...
}
```

---

9. https://go.dev/doc/tutorial/generics

```
// Go 1.18:
func foo(x any) {
    // ...
}
```

If you're using Go1.18 or greater, then you can use the any keyword instead of interface{}. Using any instead of interface{} is considered to be idiomatic.

The Problem with Empty Interfaces

"interface{} says nothing."

—Rob Pike

It is considered bad practice in Go to overuse the empty interface. You should always try to accept either a concrete type or a nonempty interface.

While there are valid reasons to use an empty interface, the downsides should be considered first:

- No type information.
- Runtime panics are *very* possible.
- Difficult code (to test, understand, document, and so on).

Using an Empty Interface

Consider we are writing a data store, similar to a database. We might have an Insert method that takes id and the value we want to store, Listing 8.26. This Insert method should be able to store our data models. These models might represent users, widgets, orders, and so on.

We can use the empty interface to accept all of our models and insert them into the data store.

Listing 8.26 The Insert Method

```
func (s *Store) Insert(id int, m any) error {
```

Unfortunately, this means that in addition to our data models, anybody may pass any type to our data store. This is clearly not our desire. We could try an set up an elaborate set of if/else or switch statements, but this becomes untenable and unmanageable over time. Interfaces allow us to filter out unwanted types and only allow through types that we want.

Defining Interfaces

You can create a new interface in the Go type system by using the type keyword, giving the new type a name, and then basing that new type on the interface type, Listing 8.27.

Listing 8.27   Defining an Interface

```
type MyInterface interface {}
```

Interfaces define behavior; therefore, they are only a collection of methods. Interfaces can have zero, one, or many methods.

"The larger the interface, the weaker the abstraction."

—Rob Pike

It is considered to be nonidiomatic to have large interfaces. Keep the number of methods per interface as small as possible, Listing 8.28. Small interfaces allow for easier interface implementations, especially when testing. Small interfaces also help you keep your functions and methods small in scope, making them more maintainable and testable.

Listing 8.28   Keep Interfaces Small with No More Than Two or Three Methods

```
type MyInterface interface {
    Method1()
    Method2() error
    Method3() (string, error)
}
```

It is important to note that interfaces are a collection of methods, not fields, Listing 8.29. In Go, only structs have fields; however, any type in the system can have methods. This is why interfaces are limited to methods only.

Listing 8.29   Interfaces Are Limited to Methods Only

```
// valid
type Writer interface {
    Write(p []byte) (int, error)
}

// invalid
type Emailer interface {
    Email string
}
```

Defining a Model Interface

Consider, again, the `Insert` method for our data store, Listing 8.30. The method takes two arguments. The first argument is the ID of the model to be stored.

Listing 8.30 The Insert Method

```
func (s *Store) Insert(id int, m any) error {
```

The second argument, in Listing 8.30, should be one of our data models. However, because we are using an empty interface, any type from `int` to `nil` may be passed in.

To prevent types, such as a function definition that isn't an expected data model, Listing 8.31, we can define an interface to solve this problem. Because the `Insert` function needs an ID for insertion, we can use that as the basis for an interface.

Listing 8.31 Passing a Function Type to the `Insert` Method

```
func Test_Store_Insert(t *testing.T) {
    t.Parallel()

    // create a store
    s := &Store{
        data: Data{},
    }

    exp := 1

    // insert a non-valid type
    err := s.Insert(exp, func() {})
    if err != nil {
        t.Fatal(err)
    }

    // retrieve the type
    act, err := s.Find(exp)
    if err != nil {
        t.Fatal(err)
    }

    // assert the returned value is a func()
    _, ok := act.(func())
    if !ok {
        t.Fatalf("unexpected type %T", act)
    }

}
```

(continued)

```
$ go test -v

=== RUN    Test_Store_Insert
=== PAUSE Test_Store_Insert
=== CONT  Test_Store_Insert
--- PASS: Test_Store_Insert (0.00s)
PASS
ok       demo     0.239s
```

```
Go Version: go1.19
```

To implement the Model interface, Listing 8.32, a type must have a ID() int method. We can clean up the Insert method's definition by accepting a single argument, the Model interface, Listing 8.33.

Listing 8.32   The Model Interface

```
type Model interface {
    ID() int
}
```

Listing 8.33   Changing the Insert Method to Accept a Model Interface

```
func (s *Store) Insert(m Model) error {
```

Now, the compiler and/or runtime rejects any type, such as string, []byte, and func(), that doesn't have a ID() int method, Listing 8.34.

Listing 8.34   Rejecting Types That Implement Model

```
func Test_Store_Insert(t *testing.T) {
    t.Parallel()

    // create a store
    s := &Store{}

    exp := 1

    // insert a non-valid type
    err := s.Insert(func() {})
```

```
    if err != nil {
        t.Fatal(err)
    }

    // retrieve the type
    act, err := s.Find(exp)
    if err != nil {
        t.Fatal(err)
    }

    // assert the returned value is a func()
    _, ok := act.(func())
    if !ok {
        t.Fatalf("unexpected type %T", act)
    }

}
```

```
$ go test -v

FAIL    demo [build failed]

# demo [demo.test]
./store_test.go:15:18: cannot use func() {} (value of type func()) as type
        ➥Model in argument to s.Insert: func() does not implement
        ➥Model (missing ID method)
./store_test.go:27:11: impossible type assertion: act.(func())
        ➥func() does not implement Model (missing ID method)

Go Version: go1.19
```

Implementing the Interface

Finally, let's create a new type, User, that implements the Model interface, Listing 8.35.

Listing 8.35   The User Type Implements the Model Interface

```
type User struct {
    UID int
}

func (u User) ID() int
```

When we update the tests, Listing 8.36, to use the User type, our tests now pass.

Listing 8.36 Using the User Type

```go
func Test_Store_Insert(t *testing.T) {
    t.Parallel()

    // create a store
    s := &Store{
        data: Data{},
    }

    // create a user
    exp := User{UID: 1}

    // insert the user
    err := s.Insert(exp)
    if err != nil {
        t.Fatal(err)
    }

    // retrieve the user
    act, err := s.Find(exp.UID)
    if err != nil {
        t.Fatal(err)
    }

    // assert the returned value is a user
    actu, ok := act.(User)
    if !ok {
        t.Fatalf("unexpected type %T", act)
    }

    // assert the returned user is the same as the inserted user
    if exp.UID != actu.UID {
        t.Fatalf("expected %v, got %v", exp, actu)
    }

}
```

```
$ go test -v

=== RUN    Test_Store_Insert
=== PAUSE Test_Store_Insert
=== CONT   Test_Store_Insert
--- PASS: Test_Store_Insert (0.00s)
```

```
PASS
ok        demo      0.101s
```

```
Go Version: go1.19
```

Embedding Interfaces

Interfaces in Go can be composed of other interfaces by embedding one or more interfaces in the new interface. This can be used to great effect to combine behaviors into more complex behaviors. The io[10] package defines many interfaces, including interfaces that are composed of other interfaces, such as io.ReadWriter[11] and io.ReadWriteCloser,[12] Listing 8.37.

Listing 8.37   The io.ReadWriteCloser Interface

```
$ go doc io.ReadWriteCloser

package io // import "io"

type ReadWriteCloser interface {
        Reader
        Writer
        Closer
}
    ReadWriteCloser is the interface that groups the basic Read, Write and
    ➥Close methods.
```

```
Go Version: go1.19
```

The alternative to embedding other interfaces is to redeclare those same methods in the combined interface, Listing 8.38.

Listing 8.38   A "Hardcoded" Representation of the io.ReadWriteCloser Interface

```
package io

// ReadWriteCloser is the interface that groups the basic Read, Write and
➥Close methods.
```

(continued)

---

10. https://pkg.go.dev/io
11. https://pkg.go.dev/io#ReadWriter
12. https://pkg.go.dev/io#ReadWriteCloser

```
type ReadWriteCloser interface {
  Read(p []byte) (n int, err error)
  Write(p []byte) (n int, err error)
  Close() error
}
```

This is, however, the wrong thing to do. If the intention is to implement the io.Read interface, as it is with io.ReadWriter, and the io.Read[13] interface changes, then it would no longer implement the correct interface. Embedding the desired interfaces allows us to keep our interfaces cleaner and more resilient.

Defining a Validatable Interface

Since the act of inserting a model is different than the act of updating a model, we can define an interface to ensure that only types that are *both* a Model and have a Validate() error method can be inserted, Listing 8.39.

Listing 8.39 The Validatable Interface

```
type Validatable interface {
    Model
    Validate() error
}
```

The Validatable interface, as shown in Listing 8.40, embeds the Model interface and introduces a new method, Validate() error, that must be implemented in addition to the method requirements of the Model interface. The Validate() error method allows the data model to validate itself before insertion.

Listing 8.40 The Insert Method Accepting a Validatable Interface

```
func (s *Store) Insert(m Validatable) error {
```

Type Assertion

With a concrete type, like an int or a struct, the Go compiler and/or runtime knows exactly what the capabilities of that type are. Interfaces, however, can be backed by any type that matches that interface. This means it is possible that the concrete type backing a particular interface provides additional functionality beyond the scope of the interface.

---

13. https://pkg.go.dev/io#Read

Go allows you to test an interface to see if its concrete implementation is of a certain type. In Go, this is called type assertion.

In Listing 8.41, we are asserting that variable i, of type any (empty interface), also implements the io.Writer[14] interface. The result of this assertion is assigned to the variable w. The variable w is of type io.Writer and can be used as such.

Listing 8.41   Asserting That any Is an io.Writer

```go
func WriteNow(i any) {
    w := i.(io.Writer)
    now := time.Now()
    w.Write([]byte(now.String()))
}
```

What happens, however, when someone passes a type, such as an int or nil, that does *not* implement io.Writer?

In Listing 8.42, when passing an int, instead of an io.Writer, the application panics. These panics can, and will, crash your applications and need to be protected against.

Listing 8.42   Asserting That any Is an io.Writer

```go
func main() {
    WriteNow(42)
}
```

```
$ go run .

panic: interface conversion: int is not io.Writer: missing method Write

goroutine 1 [running]:
main.WriteNow({0x1006c8680?, 0x1006bfd38})
        ./assert.go:10 +0x38
main.main()
        ./assert.go:19 +0x30
exit status 2
```

Go Version: go1.19

Asserting Assertion

To prevent a runtime panic when a type assertion fails, we can capture a second argument during the assertion, Listing 8.43. This second variable is of type bool and is true if the type assertion succeeded and false if it does not.

---

14. https://pkg.go.dev/io#Writer

Listing 8.43   Validating a Type Assertion Was Successful

```go
func WriteNow(i any) error {
    w, ok := i.(io.Writer)
    if !ok {
        return fmt.Errorf("expected io.Writer, got %T", i)
    }

    now := time.Now()
    w.Write([]byte(now.String()))

    return nil
}
```

You should *always* check this boolean to prevent panics and to help keep your applications from crashing.

Asserting Concrete Types

In addition to asserting that one interface implements another interface, you can use type assertion to get the concrete type underneath.

In Listing 8.44, we are trying to assert that variable w, of type io.Writer, to the type bytes.Buffer. If the assertion is successful, ok == true, then variable bb is of type bytes.Buffer, and we can now access any publicly exported fields and methods on bytes.Buffer.

Listing 8.44   Asserting that io.Writer Is a bytes.Buffer

```go
func WriteNow(w io.Writer) error {
    now := time.Now()

    if bb, ok := w.(*bytes.Buffer); ok {
        bb.WriteString(now.String())
        return nil
    }

    w.Write([]byte(now.String()))

    return nil
}
```

Assertions through Switch

When we want to assert an interface for a variety of different types, we can use the switch statement in lieu of a lot of if statements, Listing 8.45. Using switch statements when doing type assertions also prevents the type assertion panics we saw earlier with individual type assertions.

Listing 8.45   Using a `switch` Statement to Make Many Type Assertions

```
func WriteNow(i any) error {

    now := time.Now().String()

    switch i.(type) {
    case *bytes.Buffer:
        fmt.Println("type was a *bytes.Buffer", now)
    case io.StringWriter:
        fmt.Println("type was a io.StringWriter", now)
    case io.Writer:
        fmt.Println("type was a io.Writer", now)
    }

    return fmt.Errorf("cannot write to %T", i)
}
```

Capturing Switch Type

While just switching on a type can be useful, it is often much more useful to capture the result of the type assertion to a variable.

In Listing 8.46, the result of the type assertion in the switch is assigned to the variable `t := i.(type)`.

Listing 8.46   Capturing the Asserted Type to a Variable

```
func WriteNow(i any) error {

    now := time.Now().String()

    switch t := i.(type) {
    case *bytes.Buffer:
        t.WriteString(now)
    case io.StringWriter:
        t.WriteString(now)
    case io.Writer:
        t.Write([]byte(now))
    }

    return fmt.Errorf("cannot write to %T", i)
}
```

In the case of i being of type bytes.Buffer, then the variable t is also of type bytes.Buffer, and all publicly exported fields and methods of bytes.Buffer can now be used.

Beware of Case Order

The case clauses in a switch statement are checked in the order that they are listed. A poorly organized switch statement can lead to incorrect matches.

In Listing 8.47, because both bytes.Buffer and io.WriteStringer[15] implement io.Writer, the first case clause matches against io.Writer, which will match both of those types and prevent the correct clause from being run.

Listing 8.47   Incorrect switch Statement Layout

```
func WriteNow(i any) error {

    now := time.Now().String()

    switch t := i.(type) {
    case io.Writer:
        t.Write([]byte(now))
    case *bytes.Buffer:
        t.WriteString(now)
    case io.StringWriter:
        t.WriteString(now)
    }

    return fmt.Errorf("cannot write to %T", i)
}
```

The go-staticcheck[16] tool can be used to check switch statements for poor case clause organization, Listing 8.48.

Listing 8.48   Checking for Poor switch Statement Organization

```
$ staticcheck

assert.go:18:2: unreachable case clause: io.Writer will always match before
↪*bytes.Buffer (SA4020)
```

---

15. https://pkg.go.dev/io#WriteStringer
16. https://staticcheck.io/

Using Assertions

Assertion doesn't just work with empty interfaces. Any interface can be asserted against to see if it implements another interface. We can use this in our data store to add callback hooks: "before insert" and "after insert," Listing 8.49.

Listing 8.49   Inserting a Record into the Data Store

```go
func (s *Store) Insert(m Validatable) error {

    // TODO: before insert hook here

    // validate the model
    err := m.Validate()
    if err != nil {
        return err
    }

    // insert
    s.data[m.ID()] = m

    // TODO: after insert hook here

    return nil
}
```

Defining the Callback Interfaces

We can define two new interface types in our system to support before and after insert callbacks, Listing 8.50.

Listing 8.50   Defining the Callback Interfaces

```go
type BeforeInsertable interface {
    BeforeInsert() error
}

type AfterInsertable interface {
    AfterInsert() error
}
```

The Insert function can be updated, Listing 8.51, to check for these new interfaces at the appropriate time in the workflow.

Listing 8.51   Checking for the Callback Interfaces

```go
func (s *Store) Insert(m Validatable) error {

    // snippet: before
    if bi, ok := m.(BeforeInsertable); ok {
        if err := bi.BeforeInsert(); err != nil {
            return err
        }
    }
    // snippet: before

    // validate model
    err := m.Validate()
    if err != nil {
        return err
    }

    // insert
    s.data[m.ID()] = m

    // after insert

    // snippet: after
    if ai, ok := m.(AfterInsertable); ok {
        if err := ai.AfterInsert(); err != nil {
            return err
        }
    }
    // snippet: after

    return nil
}
```

These new interfaces allow a type that implements `Validatable` to opt-in to additional functionality.

Breaking It Down

Let's look at how we are using these interfaces in the `Insert` method.

In Listing 8.52, if the `m` variable, of type `Validatable` (interface), can be asserted to the `BeforeInsertable` interface, then the `bi` variable is of type `BeforeInsertable` and `ok` is true. The `BeforeInsert` method is called, the error it returns is checked, and the application continues or returns the error. If, however, `m` does not implement `BeforeInsertable` then, `ok` returns `false`, and the `BeforeInsert` method is never called.

Listing 8.52   Checking for the `BeforeInsert` Callback

```
if bi, ok := m.(BeforeInsertable); ok {
    if err := bi.BeforeInsert(); err != nil {
        return err
    }
}
```

We check the `AfterInsertable` interface in the same way, Listing 8.53.

Listing 8.53   Checking for the `AfterInsert` Callback

```
if ai, ok := m.(AfterInsertable); ok {
    if err := ai.AfterInsert(); err != nil {
        return err
    }
}
```

Summary

In this chapter, we discussed interfaces in Go. Interfaces are a collection of method definitions. We explained that if a type implements those methods, it is implicitly implementing that interface. We saw the dangers of using any or an empty interface. We showed you how to define interfaces, how to embed interfaces, and how to assert for behavior and types in code. Finally, we demonstrated that you can assert one interface for another interface, allowing you to accept a smaller interface and check for "optional" behavior.

## 9

Errors

This chapter covers the benefits of how Go's error model results in more reliable code. We cover how to handle basic errors and return errors as an interface that satisfies the error type. Additionally, we also discuss concepts such as custom error types, panics, recovering from panics, and sentinel errors.

Errors as Values

A lot of languages use the concept of exceptions.[1] When something goes wrong, an exception is thrown. This exception then needs to be caught. When catching an exception, you have the opportunity to log the exception and possibly move on with an alternate code path or reraise the exception to let the developer upstream deal with the problem.

Listing 9.1 shows an example of how to handle exceptions in Java.

Listing 9.1 Exceptions in Java

```
public static void main(String args[]) {
  try {
    // Open the file
    FileInputStream fstream = new FileInputStream("example.txt");

    // Get the object of DataInputStream
    DataInputStream in = new DataInputStream(fstream);
    BufferedReader br = new BufferedReader(new InputStreamReader(in));
    String strLine;

    // Read File Line By Line
    while ((strLine = br.readLine()) != null) {
```

(continued)

1. https://en.wikipedia.org/wiki/Exception_handling

```
    // Print the content on the console
    System.out.println(strLine);
    }

    // Close the input stream
    in.close();
  } catch (IOException e) {
    System.err.println("IO Error: " + e.getMessage());
  } catch (Exception e) {
    // Catch exception if any
    System.err.println("Error: " + e.getMessage());
  }
}
```

Go takes a different approach and treats errors as values. These values are returned and managed instead of throwing and capturing exceptions, Listing 9.2.

Listing 9.2 Errors in Go

```
func readFile() error {

    // open the file
    f, err := os.Open("example.txt")
    if err != nil {
        return err
    }

    // close the file when done
    defer f.Close()

    // open buffered scanner with file
    scanner := bufio.NewScanner(f)

    // scan through each line of the file
    for scanner.Scan() {

        // print line to the console
        fmt.Println(scanner.Text())
    }

    // if there was an error while scanning
    // return the error to the calling function
    if err := scanner.Err(); err != nil {
        return err
```

```
    }

    // everything was good, return nil
    return nil
}
```

The error Interface

In Go, errors are represented by the error[2] interface, as shown in Listing 9.3.

Listing 9.3   The error Interface

```
$ go doc builtin.error

package builtin // import "builtin"

type error interface {
        Error() string
}
    The error built-in interface type is the conventional interface for
    ↪representing an error condition, with the nil value representing
    ↪no error.
```

Go Version: go1.19

Creating Errors with errors.New

Go provides two quick ways to implement the error interface in your code.

The first is through the errors.New[3] function, Listing 9.4. This function takes a string and returns an implementation of error that uses the supplied string as the error message.

Listing 9.4   The errors.New Function

```
$ go doc errors.New

package errors // import "errors"

func New(text string) error
    New returns an error that formats as the given text. Each call to New
    ↪returns a distinct error value even if the text is identical.
```

Go Version: go1.19

---

2. https://pkg.go.dev/builtin#error
3. https://pkg.go.dev/errors#New

Creating Errors with `fmt.Errorf` **(Recommended)**

When creating errors, it is common to want to create a string that contains the error message and the values of variables that caused the error.

To clean up the pattern shown in Listing 9.5, the `fmt.Errorf`[4] method, Listing 9.6, can be used.

Listing 9.5   Creating Errors with `errors.New` and `fmt.Sprintf`[5]

```
err = errors.New(fmt.Sprintf("error at %s", time.Now()))
```

Listing 9.6   The `fmt.Errorf` Method

```
$ go doc fmt.Errorf

package fmt // import "fmt"

func Errorf(format string, a ...any) error
    Errorf formats according to a format specifier and returns the string
    ➥as a value that satisfies error.

    If the format specifier includes a %w verb with an error operand,
    ➥the returned error will implement an Unwrap method returning the
    ➥operand. It is invalid to include more than one %w verb or to supply it
    ➥with an operand that does not implement the error interface. The %w
    ➥verb is otherwise a synonym for %v.

Go Version: go1.19
```

In Listing 9.7, the code is now cleaner and more readable than in Listing 9.5.

Listing 9.7   Creating Errors with `fmt.Errorf`

```
err = fmt.Errorf("error at %s", time.Now())
```

Using `fmt.Errorf` handles *most* use cases for creating errors.

Handling Errors

With errors being a type in the Go type system, in this case an `interface` type, errors can be returned from, and accepted as, function arguments.

---

4. https://pkg.go.dev/fmt#Errorf
5. https://pkg.go.dev/fmt#Sprintf

In Go, if an error is returned from the function, it should *always* be returned as the last argument. While the Go compiler won't enforce this, it is the expected idiom in the Go ecosystem. In Listing 9.8, the functions one and two idiomatically return an error value as the last argument. The bad function, however, is nonidiomatic by returning an error value as its first argument.

Listing 9.8   Good and Bad Examples of Returning an `error`

```
// good
func one() error {}
func two() (int, error) {}


// bad
func bad() (error, int) {}
```

As with all interfaces in Go, the zero value of the error interface is nil. Error checking in Go is done by checking whether the returned error is nil, as shown in Listing 9.9.

Listing 9.9   Checking for Errors by Asserting Against nil

```
err := boom()
if err != nil {
  // the error was not nil
  // do something with the error
}
```

Using Errors

In Listing 9.10, if the key being requested in the map is found, its value is returned, and a nil is returned instead of an argument. If the key is not found in the map, an empty string and an error, created with fmt.Errorf, are returned.

Listing 9.10   A Function That Might Return an `error`

```
func Get(key string) (string, error) {
    m := map[string]string{
        "a": "A",
        "b": "B",
    }

    if v, ok := m[key]; ok {
        return v, nil
    }

    return "", fmt.Errorf("no key found %s", key)
}
```

A test for the Get function, Listing 9.11, demonstrates the error-checking pattern in action.

Listing 9.11   A Test for the Get Function

```go
func Test_Get(t *testing.T) {
    t.Parallel()

    act, err := Get("a")
    if err != nil {
        t.Fatalf("expect no error, got %s", err)
    }

    exp := "A"
    if act != exp {
        t.Fatalf("expected %s, got %s", exp, act)
    }

    _, err = Get("?")
    if err == nil {
        t.Fatalf("expected an error, got nil")
    }
}
```

Panic

Occasionally, your code does something that the Go runtime does not like. For example, in Listing 9.12, if we try to insert a value into an array or slice that is beyond the bounds of the array or slice, the runtime panics.

Listing 9.12   A Panic Caused by an Out-of-Bounds Index

```go
func main() {
    a := []string{}
    a[42] = "Bring a towel"
}
```

```
$ go run .

panic: runtime error: index out of range [42] with length 0

goroutine 1 [running]:
```

```
main.main()
        ./main.go:6 +0x28
exit status 2
```

Go Version: go1.19

Raising a Panic

A panic in Go can be raised using the built-in panic[6] function, Listing 9.13. The panic function takes any value as an argument.

Listing 9.13   The panic Function

```
$ go doc builtin.panic

package builtin // import "builtin"

func panic(v any)
    The panic built-in function stops normal execution of the current
    ↦goroutine. When a function F calls panic, normal execution of F stops
    ↦immediately. Any functions whose execution was deferred by F are run in
    ↦the usual way, and then F returns to its caller. To the caller G, the
    ↦invocation of F then behaves like a call to panic, terminating G's
    ↦execution and running any deferred functions. This continues until all
    ↦functions in the executing goroutine have stopped, in reverse order. At
    ↦that point, the program is terminated with a non-zero exit code. This
    ↦termination sequence is called panicking and can be controlled by the
    ↦built-in function recover.
```

Go Version: go1.19

Recovering from a Panic

With a combination of the defer keyword and the recover function, shown in Listing 9.14, you can recover from panics in your applications and gracefully handle them.

---

6. https://pkg.go.dev/builtin#panic

Listing 9.14   The recover[7] Function

```
$ go doc builtin.recover

package builtin // import "builtin"

func recover() any
    The recover built-in function allows a program to manage behavior of
    ➥a panicking goroutine. Executing a call to recover inside a deferred
    ➥function (but not any function called by it) stops the panicking
    ➥sequence by restoring normal execution and retrieves the error value
    ➥passed to the call of panic. If recover is called outside the deferred
    ➥function it will not stop a panicking sequence. In this case, or when
    ➥the goroutine is not panicking, or if the argument supplied to panic was
    ➥nil, recover returns nil. Thus the return value from recover reports
    ➥whether the goroutine is panicking.
```

Go Version: go1.19

In Listing 9.15, before we run the code that will panic, we use the `defer` keyword to execute an anonymous function that runs before the `main` function exits. Inside of the deferred function, we can call the `recover` function and check its return value for `nil`. A non-nil value is returned from the `recover` function if a panic occurred.

Now, when the panic occurs, it is caught by the deferred `recover` and can be handled gracefully.

Listing 9.15   Recovering from a Panic

```
func main() {
    defer func() {
        if i := recover(); i != nil {
            fmt.Println("oh no, a panic occurred:", i)
        }
    }()

    a := []string{}
    a[42] = "Bring a towel"
}
```

```
$ go run .

oh no, a panic occurred: runtime error: index out of range [42] with length 0
```

Go Version: go1.19

---

7. https://pkg.go.dev/builtin#recover

While this is not the common use case for using `recover`, it does show the mechanics of how it works. It is more common to use recover when your application calls a user-defined function that is passed in as an argument.

Listing 9.16 is an example of a function that takes a user-defined function to match a specific string. If the function passed in panics, it results in the `sanitize` function panicking as well.

Listing 9.16 A Function That Sanitizes a Given String

```go
type matcher func(rune) bool

func sanitize(m matcher, s string) (string, error) {
    var val string

    // iterate over the runes in the string
    for _, c := range s {

        // call the matcher function
        // with the rune as the argument
        if m(c) {
            // append '*' to the result
            val = val + "*"
            // continue to the next rune
            continue
        }

        // append the rune to the result
        val = val + string(c)
    }

    // return the sanitized string
    return val, nil
}
```

```go
func main() {

    // create a matcher function
    m := func(r rune) bool {
        // simulate doing something bad...
        panic("hahaha")

        // unreachable code
        return false
    }
```

(continued)

```
    // sanitize the string
    s, err := sanitize(m, "go is awesome")
    if err != nil {
        // handle the error
        log.Fatal(err)
    }

    // print the sanitized string
    fmt.Println(s)
}
```

```
$ go run .

panic: hahaha

goroutine 1 [running]:
main.main.func1(0x29e45b8?)
        ./main.go:14 +0x30
main.sanitize(0x1027b3f18, {0x10277bc12, 0xd})
        ./main.go:44 +0xa8
main.main()
        ./main.go:21 +0x34
exit status 2
```

```
Go Version: go1.19
```

However, if we use a `recover` in the `sanitize` function, we can gracefully handle any potential panic that the user-provided function may create. In Listing 9.17, we use the `recover` to handle panics in the `sanitize` function.

Listing 9.17 A Function That Sanitizes a Given String

```
func sanitize(m matcher, s string) (val string, err error) {
    // guard against an invalid matcher that could panic
    defer func() {
        if e := recover(); e != nil {
            err = fmt.Errorf("invalid matcher. panic occurred: %v", e)
        }
    }()

    for _, c := range s {
        if m(c) {
            val = val + "*"
            continue
```

```
        }
        val = val + string(c)
    }
    return
}
```

```
$ go run .

invalid matcher. panic occurred: hahaha
```

```
Go Version: go1.19
```

Now, if a user inadvertently raises a panic in the `matcher` function provided, the `sanitize` function handles it gracefully and returns an error instead of panicking as well.

Capturing and Returning Panic Values

When something panics in Go, you have three options for how to handle the panic:

- You can let the panic crash the application and deal with the fallout.
- You can recover from the panic, log it, and move on.
- You can properly capture the panicked value and return it as an error.

This last option gives you the most control over recovering from panics. However, it requires a number of steps, and functions, to make this happen.

Consider the function, `DoSomething(int)`, in Listing 9.18 that takes an integer and either returns `nil` or panics.

Listing 9.18 A Function That Returns `nil` or Panics

```
func DoSomething(input int) error {
    switch input {
    case 0:
        // input was 0, return no error (nil)
        return nil
    case 1:
        // input was 1, panic with the string "one"
        panic("one")
    }

    // no case was matched
    return nil
}
```

In Listing 9.19, we have a test for the `DoSomething(int)` function. When we call the `DoSomething(int)` function with the value 1, the test panics.

Listing 9.19 A Test for the DoSomething(1) Function in Listing 9.18

```
func Test_DoSomething(t *testing.T) {
    t.Parallel()

    err := DoSomething(0)
    if err != nil {
        t.Fatal(err)
    }

    err = DoSomething(1)

    if err != nil {
        t.Fatal("expected nil, got", err)
    }
}
```

```
$ go test -v

=== RUN    Test_DoSomething
=== PAUSE Test_DoSomething
=== CONT  Test_DoSomething
--- FAIL: Test_DoSomething (0.00s)
panic: one [recovered]
        panic: one

goroutine 4 [running]:
testing.tRunner.func1.2({0x1027f0e60, 0x1028116e0})
        /usr/local/go/src/testing/testing.go:1389 +0x1c8
testing.tRunner.func1()
        /usr/local/go/src/testing/testing.go:1392 +0x384
panic({0x1027f0e60, 0x1028116e0})
        /usr/local/go/src/runtime/panic.go:838 +0x204
demo.DoSomething(...)
        ./recover.go:11
demo.Test_DoSomething(0x0?)
        ./recover_test.go:16 +0x38
testing.tRunner(0x140001361a0, 0x102811298)
        /usr/local/go/src/testing/testing.go:1439 +0x110
created by testing.(*T).Run
        /usr/local/go/src/testing/testing.go:1486 +0x300
exit status 2
FAIL    demo    0.939s
```

Go Version: go1.19

To fix this problem, we need to properly recover from the panic being raised in the DoSomething(int) function. The following list outlines the steps required to properly recover from a panic:

1. Use a defer with a recover to catch the panic.

2. Use type assertion on the value returned from the panic to see if it was an error.

3. Use a named return to allow sending back the error from the deferred recover.

In Listing 9.20, we implement the steps we outlined to properly recover from the panic. As shown in Listing 9.20, we implemented the fix in the DoSomething(int) function and not in the test. This is because it is the responsibility of the function that panics to properly recover from it.

Listing 9.20   Properly Returning from a Panic

```
func DoSomething(input int) (err error) {
    // defer a function to recover from the panic
    defer func() {
        p := recover()
        if p == nil {
            // a nil was return, no panic was raised
            // return from the deferred function.
            return
        }

        // check if the recovered value is already an error
        if e, ok := p.(error); ok {
            // assign the recovered error to the err variable
            // outside of the anonymous function scope
            err = e
            return
        }

        // a non-error value was recovered
        // create a new error, 'ErrNonErrCaught', with
        // information about the recovered value
        msg := fmt.Sprintf("non-error panic type %T %s", p, p)
        err = ErrNonErrCaught(msg)
    }()

    switch input {
    case 0:
        // input was 0, return no error (nil)
        return nil
```

(continued)

```
    case 1:
        // input was 1, panic with the string "one"
        panic("one")
    }

    // no case was matched
    return nil
}


type ErrNonErrCaught string

func (e ErrNonErrCaught) Error() string {
    return string(e)
}
```

First, we have changed our function signature to use a named return for the error,[8] (err error). This enables us to set the error value inside the deferred function. Once inside the DoSomething(int) function, we use the defer keyword and an anonymous function to catch the panic. Inside of the anonymous function, we use the recover function to recover from the panic, and assign the value returned to the variable p.

As shown earlier in this chapter in Listing 9.14, the recover function returns any. This means that the value can be of any type, a string, int, an error, or nil. As a result, we must use type assertions to check the type of the value returned from the recover function. If the value is an error, we can use the named return to send the value back to the caller. If not, we create a new error with the value returned from the recover function.

As shown in Listing 9.21, the tests now are no longer panicking when run, and the test passes.

Listing 9.21 Tests Now Pass After Proper Panic Recovery

```
func Test_DoSomething(t *testing.T) {
    t.Parallel()

    err := DoSomething(0)
    if err != nil {
        t.Fatal(err)
    }

    err = DoSomething(1)

    if err != ErrNonErrCaught("non-error panic type string one") {
        t.Fatal("expected ErrNonErrCaught, got", err)
```

---

8. https://pkg.go.dev/builtin#error

```
    }
}
```

```
$ go test -v

=== RUN   Test_DoSomething
=== PAUSE Test_DoSomething
=== CONT  Test_DoSomething
--- PASS: Test_DoSomething (0.00s)
PASS
ok      demo    1.127s
```

Go Version: go1.19

Don't Panic

NEVER RAISE A PANIC IN YOUR CODE

Ok, maybe *never* is too strong of a stance. However, in general, it's considered nonidiomatic to panic instead of returning an error outside of specific conditions.

When a panic occurs, unless there is a recover in place, the program shuts down (usually not gracefully). It is usually a much better practice to return an error and let the code upstream handle the error.

The general rule is that if you are writing a package, you should not panic. The reason for this is that the caller should always have control of the program, and a package should not dictate control flow of a program.

On the other hand, if you are the caller (maybe you are in control of the `main` function in the program), then you already have total control of the program flow, and if needed, a panic may be appropriate. Many times this is manifested in the form of a `log.Fatal`, Listing 9.22, which exits the program with a nonzero exit code.

Listing 9.22 The `log.Fatal` Function

```
$ go doc log.Fatal

package log // import "log"

func Fatal(v ...any)
    Fatal is equivalent to Print() followed by a call to os.Exit(1).
```

Go Version: go1.19

Lastly, any code that panics may be more difficult to test. For all of these reasons, it is best to consider alternatives to a panicking. After all, most panics can be prevented by sensible code and well-designed tests.

Checking for Nil

The most common source of panics in Go are calls being made on `nil` values. Any type in Go that has a zero value of `nil` can be a source of these panics. Types such as interfaces, maps, pointers, channels, and functions all fall into this category. Checking whether these types are `nil` before using them can help you avoid these panics.

A common example of this is when a type has an embedded type that is a pointer. In Listing 9.23, `User` is embedded in `Admin` as a pointer. Because it's embedded, the methods are promoted. This means that the `Admin` type now has a `String` method. However, on the last line of code where `a.String()` is being called, the receiver to the method is actually the `User`. Because `User` is `nil`, it was never set, and the code panics when it tries to access the `String` method.

Listing 9.23   A Panic When Calling a Method on a `nil` Value

```go
package main

import "fmt"

type User struct {
    name string
}

func (u User) String() string {
    return u.name
}

type Admin struct {
    *User
    Perms map[string]bool
}

func main() {
    a := &Admin{}
    fmt.Println(a.String())
}
```

```
$ go run .

panic: runtime error: invalid memory address or nil pointer dereference
[signal SIGSEGV: segmentation violation code=0x2 addr=0x0 pc=0x102138020]

goroutine 1 [running]:
main.main()
```

```
        ./main.go:20 +0x20
exit status 2
```

Go Version: go1.19

In Listing 9.24, the `Admin` type is properly initialized with a `User`. Now, when the `String` method is called, the `User` is not `nil`, and the method properly executes.

Listing 9.24   Proper Initialization to Prevent Panicking

```go
package main

import "fmt"

type User struct {
    name string
}

func (u User) String() string {
    return u.name
}

type Admin struct {
    *User
    Perms map[string]bool
}

func main() {
    a := &Admin{
        User: &User{name: "Kurt"},
    }
    fmt.Println(a.String())
}
```

```
$ go run .

Kurt
```

Go Version: go1.19

Maps

When creating maps, you must `initialize` the memory space behind them. Consider Listing 9.25 as an example. We have created a map variable, but we have not initialized it. This causes a panic when we try to access the map.

Listing 9.25   A Panic When Creating a Map with a `nil` Value

```
package main

import "fmt"

func main() {

    // create a new map variable
    var m map[string]int

    // insert a key-value pair
    m["Amy"] = 27

    // print the map
    fmt.Printf("%+v\n", m)
}
```

```
$ go run .

panic: assignment to entry in nil map

goroutine 1 [running]:
main.main()
        ./main.go:11 +0x38
exit status 2
```

Go Version: go1.19

The easiest solution is to use the `:=` operator to initialize the map when the variable is declared. In Listing 9.26, we have initialized the map, and the code runs successfully.

Listing 9.26   Avoiding Panics When Creating Maps

```
package main

import "fmt"

func main() {

    // initialize a new map
    m := map[string]int{}

    // insert a key-value pair
    m["Amy"] = 27
```

```
    // print the map
    fmt.Printf("%+v\n", m)
}
```

```
$ go run .

map[Amy:27]

Go Version: go1.19
```

However, if a map is declared with long variable declaration and not initialized, later in the code, the map needs to be initialized or it panics when used. As shown in Listing 9.27, we check the m variable against nil before using it. If the variable has not been initialized, we can initialize a new map and assign it to the variable. This prevents panics from trying to access a nil map.

Listing 9.27   Checking a Map for nil before Accessing

```
package main

import "fmt"

func main() {

    // create a new map variable
    var m map[string]int

    if m == nil {
        // initialize the map
        m = map[string]int{}
    }

    // insert a key-value pair
    m["Amy"] = 27

    // print the map
    fmt.Printf("%+v\n", m)
}
```

```
$ go run .

map[Amy:27]

Go Version: go1.19
```

Finally, as in Listing 9.28, we can use the `make`[9] function to initialize the map. While this works, it is considered nonidiomatic to use `make` to initialize a map.

Listing 9.28   Using make to Initialize a Map

```
package main

import "fmt"

func main() {

    // initialize a new map
    m := make(map[string]int)

    // insert a key-value pair
    m["Amy"] = 27

    // print the map
    fmt.Printf("%+v\n", m)
}
```

```
$ go run .

map[Amy:27]

Go Version: go1.19
```

Pointers

Before a pointer can be used, it has to be initialized. In Listing 9.29, we define a new variable, `bb`, that is a pointer to a `bytes.Buffer`. If we try to use this variable before the pointer has been properly initialized, a runtime panic occurs.

In Listing 9.30, we declare and initialize the `bb` variable with a pointer to a `bytes.Buffer`. Because the `bb` variable has been properly initialized, the application no longer panics.

Listing 9.29   A Panic Caused by a `nil` Pointer

```
package main

import (
    "bytes"
    "fmt"
```

---

9. https://pkg.go.dev/builtin#make

```go
)

func main() {

    // create a new pointer
    // to a bytes.Buffer
    var bb *bytes.Buffer

    // use the pointer to
    // write data to the buffer
    bb.WriteString("Hello, world!")

    // print the buffer
    fmt.Println(bb.String())
}
```

```
$ go run .

panic: runtime error: invalid memory address or nil pointer dereference
[signal SIGSEGV: segmentation violation code=0x2 addr=0x20 pc=0x100a34e30]

goroutine 1 [running]:
bytes.(*Buffer).WriteString(0x1400005e768?, {0x100a59e9c?, 0x60?})
        /usr/local/go/src/bytes/buffer.go:182 +0x20
main.main()
        ./main.go:16 +0x30
exit status 2
```

```
Go Version: go1.19
```

Listing 9.30   Properly Initializing a Pointer before Use

```go
package main

import (
    "bytes"
    "fmt"
)

func main() {

    // create and initialize
    // a new pointer
```

(continued)

```
    // to a bytes.Buffer
    bb := &bytes.Buffer{}

    // use the pointer to
    // write data to the buffer
    bb.WriteString("Hello, world!")

    // print the buffer
    fmt.Println(bb.String())
}
```

```
$ go run .

Hello, world!
```

```
Go Version: go1.19
```

Interfaces

In Listing 9.31, we create a new variable, w, of type io.Writer. This variable has not been initialized with an implementation of the interface. This causes a panic when we try to use the variable.

Listing 9.31   A Panic Caused by a nil Interface

```
package main

import (
    "fmt"
    "io"
)

func main() {

    // create a new writer variable
    var w io.Writer

    // print to the writer
    fmt.Fprintln(w, "Hello, world!")
}
```

```
$ go run .

panic: runtime error: invalid memory address or nil pointer dereference
[signal SIGSEGV: segmentation violation code=0x2 addr=0x18 pc=0x1049e2bfc]
```

```
goroutine 1 [running]:
fmt.Fprintln({0x0, 0x0}, {0x14000098f58, 0x1, 0x1})
        /usr/local/go/src/fmt/print.go:265 +0x4c
main.main()
        ./main.go:14 +0x50
exit status 2
```

Go Version: go1.19

In Listing 9.32, we have initialized the w variable with an implementation of the interface, in this case io.Stdout.[10]

Listing 9.32   Initializing an Interface before Use

```
package main

import (
    "fmt"
    "os"
)

func main() {

    // create a new writer variable
    // with STDOUT as the
    // writer implementation
    w := os.Stdout

    // print to the writer
    fmt.Fprintln(w, "Hello, world!")
}
```

```
$ go run .

Hello, world!
```

Go Version: go1.19

More commonly, a panic occurs when an interface is embedded into a type and that interface was not backed by an instance.

In Listing 9.33, we are defining a Stream struct that embeds the io.Writer interface. By embedding the interface, the Stream type is now also an implementation io.Writer as the io.Writer.Write[11] method is promoted to the Stream type.

---

10. https://pkg.go.dev/io#Stdout
11. https://pkg.go.dev/io#Writer.Write

Listing 9.33 A Custom Type That Embeds an Interface

```
type Stream struct {
    io.Writer
}
```

However, if an instance of a writer is never assigned to the embedded io.Writer, as in Listing 9.34, the code panics when it tries to call the io.Writer.Write method because the receiver is nil.

Listing 9.34 A Panic Caused by a nil Interface

```
func main() {

    // initialize a stream
    // without a writer
    s := Stream{}

    fmt.Fprintf(s, "Hello Gophers!")
}
```

```
$ go run .

panic: runtime error: invalid memory address or nil pointer dereference
[signal SIGSEGV: segmentation violation code=0x2 addr=0x18 pc=0x100199230]

goroutine 1 [running]:
main.(*Stream).Write(0x1400011c820?, {0x14000134010?, 0xe?, 0x0?})
        <autogenerated>:1 +0x30
fmt.Fprintf({0x1001d41c8, 0x14000118210}, {0x10019ad19, 0xe}, {0x0, 0x0, 0x0})
        /usr/local/go/src/fmt/print.go:205 +0x88
main.main()
        ./main.go:22 +0x58
exit status 2
```

Go Version: go1.19

In Listing 9.35, we fix the code by properly assigning an implementation of an io.Writer interface—in this case, os.Stdout[12] to the embedded io.Writer in the Stream type.

---

12. https://pkg.go.dev/os#Stdout

Listing 9.35 Properly Assigning an Implementation of an Embedded `io.Writer`

```go
func main() {

    // initialize a stream
    // with STDOUT as the writer
    s := Stream{
        Writer: os.Stdout,
    }

    fmt.Fprintf(s, "Hello Gophers!")
}
```

```
$ go run .

Hello Gophers!

Go Version: go1.19
```

Functions

A function's zero value is `nil`. As such, a function needs to be assigned before using it. In Listing 9.36, we have created a function variable, `fn`, that is not backed by an actual function. This causes a panic when we try to call the function.

Listing 9.36 Using an Uninitialized Function Variable

```go
func main() {

    // create a new function
    // type variable
    var fn func() string

    // print the results
    // of the function
    fmt.Println(fn())
}
```

```
$ go run .

panic: runtime error: invalid memory address or nil pointer dereference
[signal SIGSEGV: segmentation violation code=0x2 addr=0x0 pc=0x100b60020]
```

(continued)

```
goroutine 1 [running]:
main.main()
        ./main.go:16 +0x20
exit status 2
```

Go Version: go1.19

In Listing 9.37, we have assigned a function to the fn variable and the application runs successfully.

Listing 9.37   Assigning a Function Definition to the fn Variable

```go
func main() {

    // create a new function
    // type variable
    var fn func() string

    // back the fn variable
    // with a function
    fn = func() string {
        return "Hello, World!"
    }

    // print the results
    // of the function
    fmt.Println(fn())
}
```

```
$ go run .

Hello, World!
```

Go Version: go1.19

Type Assertions

When type asserting in Go, if the assertion fails, Go panics.

Consider the WriteToFile(io.Writer, []byte) function defined in Listing 9.38. This function takes an io.Writer as an argument, along with a []byte slice of data to write. Inside of the function, the io.Writer argument, w, is being type asserted to the concrete type os.File. In Listing 9.39, we are calling this function with a bytes.Buffer as the first argument, which is not an instance of os.File. This causes a panic.

Listing 9.38 Type Assertion without Safety Checking

```go
func WriteToFile(w io.Writer, data []byte) error {

    // assert that w is a file
    f := w.(*os.File)

    // defer closing the file
    defer f.Close()

    // log the file name
    fmt.Printf("writing to file %s\n", f.Name())

    // write the data
    _, err := f.Write(data)
    if err != nil {
        return err
    }

    return nil
}
```

Listing 9.39 Panic Caused by a Failed Type Assertion

```go
func main() {

    // create a buffer
    // to write to
    bb := &bytes.Buffer{}

    // data to be written
    data := []byte("Hello, world!")

    // call WriteToFile
    // passing the buffer
    // and the data
    err := WriteToFile(bb, data)

    // check for errors
    if err != nil {
        fmt.Println(err)
        os.Exit(1)
    }
}
```

(continued)

```
$ go run .

panic: interface conversion: io.Writer is *bytes.Buffer, not *os.File

goroutine 1 [running]:
main.WriteToFile({0x102ab43e8?, 0x14000106f40?}, {0x14000106f23?,
    ↪0x1400008e000?, 0x0?})
    ./main.go:38 +0x154
main.main()
    ./main.go:23 +0x6c
exit status 2
```

Go Version: go1.19

If asked, Go returns a second argument, a boolean, during the assertion. That boolean is true if the assertion was successful and false if it wasn't. Checking this second argument, as shown in Listing 9.40, prevents panics on type assertion failures and keeps your application up and running.

Listing 9.40 Proper Type Assertion Checking Prevents Panics

```go
func WriteToFile(w io.Writer, data []byte) error {

    // assert that w is a file
    f, ok := w.(*os.File)

    // check the assertion was successful
    if !ok {
        return fmt.Errorf("expected *os.File, got %T", w)
    }

    // defer closing the file
    defer f.Close()

    // log the file name
    fmt.Printf("writing to file %s\n", f.Name())

    // write the data
    _, err := f.Write(data)
    if err != nil {
        return err
    }

    return nil
}
```

```
$ go run .

expected *os.File, got *bytes.Buffer

exit status 1
```

```
Go Version: go1.19
```

It is very important that you don't avoid a type check. In virtually all cases, avoiding a type check leads to a future bug in your code.

Array/Slice Indexes

When accessing indexes on slices and arrays if the index is greater than the length of the slice/array, Go panics.

Consider the function defined in Listing 9.41. This function attempts to access the given index of the given slice. If the index is greater than the length of the slice, Go panics, Listing 9.42.

Listing 9.41   A Function for Retrieving the Index of a Slice

```
func find(names []string, index int) (string, error) {

    // find the name at the index
    s := names[index]

    // return an error if the value is empty
    if len(s) == 0 {
        return s, fmt.Errorf("index %d empty", index)
    }

    // return the name
    return s, nil
}
```

Listing 9.42   An Out-of-Bounds Panic

```
func main() {

    // create a slice
    names := []string{"Kurt", "Janis", "Jimi", "Amy"}

    // find index 42
    s, err := find(names, 42)
```

(continued)

```
// check for errors
if err != nil {
    fmt.Println(err)
    os.Exit(1)
}

// print the result
fmt.Println("found: ", s)
}
```

```
$ go run .

panic: runtime error: index out of range [42] with length 4

goroutine 1 [running]:
main.find(...)
        ./main.go:33
main.main()
        ./main.go:15 +0x28
exit status 2
```

Go Version: go1.19

To avoid this panic, check the length of slice/array to ensure the requested index can safely be retrieved. In Listing 9.43, the index is checked against the length of the slice/array before being accessed. If the index is greater than the length of the slice/array, the function returns an error[13] instead of panicking.

Listing 9.43 Proper Type Assertion Checking Prevents Panics

```
func find(names []string, index int) (string, error) {

    // check for out of bounds index
    if index >= len(names) {
        return "", fmt.Errorf("out of bounds index %d [%d]", index, len(names))
    }

    // find the name at the index
    s := names[index]

    // return an error if the value is empty
    if len(s) == 0 {
        return s, fmt.Errorf("index %d empty", index)
    }
```

---

13. https://pkg.go.dev/builtin#error

```
      // return the name
      return s, nil
}
```

```
$ go run .

out of bounds index 42 [4]

exit status 1
```

Go Version: go1.19

Custom Errors

Errors in Go are implemented via the error interface, Listing 9.44. This means you can create your own custom error implementations. Custom errors allow you to manage workflow and provide detailed information about an error beyond the scope of the error interface.

Listing 9.44 The error Interface

```
$ go doc builtin.error

package builtin // import "builtin"

type error interface {
        Error() string
}
    The error built-in interface type is the conventional interface for
    ➥representing an error condition, with the nil value representing
    ➥no error.
```

Go Version: go1.19

Standard Errors

Consider Listing 9.45. A couple of types are being defined. The first, Model, is based on map[string]any. For example, {"age": 27, "name": "jimi"}. Next, a Store struct type is defined with a data field of type map[string][]Model. This data field is a map of table names to their models.

Listing 9.45 Type Definitions

```
// Model is a key/value pair representing a model in the store.
// e.g. {"id": 1, "name": "bob"}
type Model map[string]any

// Store is a table based key/value store.
type Store struct {
    data map[string][]Model
}
```

The Store has a method, All(string), shown in Listing 9.46, that returns all of the models in the store for the given table. If the table doesn't exist, an error is returned. This error is created using the fmt.Errorf function.

Listing 9.46 The Store.All Method

```
// All returns all models in the store for the given table name.
// If no models exist, an error is returned.
func (s *Store) All(tn string) ([]Model, error) {
    db := s.data

    // if the underlying data is nil, return an error
    if db == nil {
        return nil, fmt.Errorf("no data")
    }

    // check to make sure table exists
    mods, ok := db[tn]

    // if table doesn't exist, return an error
    if !ok {
        return nil, fmt.Errorf("table %s not found", tn)
    }

    // return the slice of models
    return mods, nil
}
```

Listing 9.47 is a test that asserts whether a given table exists in the store. This test, however, is lacking. Yes, it asserts that an error was returned, but we don't know which error was returned. Did the All method return an error because the table didn't exist or because the underlying data map was nil?

Listing 9.47 A Test for the `Store.All` Method

```go
func Test_Store_All_NoTable(t *testing.T) {
    t.Parallel()

    s := &Store{
        data: map[string][]Model{},
    }

    _, err := s.All("users")
    if err == nil {
        t.Fatal("expected error, got nil")
    }

    exp := "table users not found"
    act := err.Error()
    if act != exp {
        t.Fatalf("expected %q, got %q", exp, act)
    }
}
```

```
$ go test -v

=== RUN    Test_Store_All_NoTable
=== PAUSE  Test_Store_All_NoTable
=== CONT   Test_Store_All_NoTable
--- PASS:  Test_Store_All_NoTable (0.00s)
PASS
ok      demo     1.082s

Go Version: go1.19
```

As in Listing 9.47, it might be tempting to assert against an error's message, but that is considered nonidiomatic and should never be used. The reason for this is simple: Error messages change. If the error message changes, the following test fails. We consider this to be a "brittle" test.

Defining Custom Errors

You can define custom errors that can help distinguish one error from another, as well as add more context about the error.

In Listing 9.48, we define a new `struct` type, `ErrTableNotFound`, that implements the error interface. This type contains information such as what table was missing and what time the error occurred.

Listing 9.48   The ErrTableNotFound Struct

```
type ErrTableNotFound struct {
    Table      string
    OccurredAt time.Time
}


func (e ErrTableNotFound) Error() string {
    return fmt.Sprintf("[%s] table not found %s", e.OccurredAt, e.Table)
}
```

Listing 9.49 updates the Store.All(string) method to return an ErrTableNotFound error if the table doesn't exist. We also set the table name and the time the error occurred.

Listing 9.49   The Store.All Method with Custom Errors

```
// All returns all models in the store for the given table name.
// If no models exist, an error is returned.
func (s *Store) All(tn string) ([]Model, error) {
    db := s.data

    // if the underlying data is nil, return an error
    if db == nil {
        return nil, fmt.Errorf("no data")
    }

    // check to make sure table exists
    mods, ok := db[tn]

    // if table doesn't exist, return an error
    if !ok {
        return nil, ErrTableNotFound{
            Table:      tn,
            OccurredAt: time.Now(),
        }
    }

    // return the slice of models
    return mods, nil
}
```

The test can now be updated, Listing 9.50, to assert that the error is an ErrTableNotFound error. The test passes, and we can see the table name and the time the error occurred.

Listing 9.50 A Test for the `Store.All` Method with Custom Errors

```go
func Test_Store_All_NoTable(t *testing.T) {
    t.Parallel()

    s := &Store{
        data: map[string][]Model{},
    }

    _, err := s.All("users")
    if err == nil {
        t.Fatal("expected error, got nil")
    }

    exp := "users"
    e, ok := err.(ErrTableNotFound)
    if !ok {
        t.Fatalf("expected ErrTableNotFound, got %T", err)
    }

    act := e.Table
    if act != exp {
        t.Fatalf("expected %q, got %q", exp, act)
    }

    if e.OccurredAt.IsZero() {
        t.Fatal("expected non-zero time")
    }
}
```

```
$ go test -v

=== RUN    Test_Store_All_NoTable
=== PAUSE  Test_Store_All_NoTable
=== CONT   Test_Store_All_NoTable
--- PASS: Test_Store_All_NoTable (0.00s)
PASS
ok      demo      1.171s

Go Version: go1.19
```

Wrapping and Unwrapping Errors

Consider the method defined in Listing 9.51. If an error occurs, a custom `error` implementation, `ErrTableNotFound`, is initialized with the appropriate information. Before being returned, however, `error` is then wrapped with `fmt.Errorf` to a message that includes the type and method that caused the error. To wrap an error using `fmt.Errorf`, we can use the `%w` formatting verb, meant for errors.

Listing 9.51 The `Store.All` Method

```
// All returns all models in the store for the given table name.
// If no models exist, an error is returned.
func (s *Store) All(tn string) ([]Model, error) {
    db := s.data

    // if the underlying data is nil, return an error
    if db == nil {
        return nil, fmt.Errorf("no data")
    }

    // check to make sure table exists
    mods, ok := db[tn]

    // if table doesn't exist, return an error
    if !ok {
        err := ErrTableNotFound{
            Table:      tn,
            OccurredAt: time.Now(),
        }
        return nil, fmt.Errorf("[Store.All] %w", err)
    }

    // return the slice of models
    return mods, nil
}
```

Listing 9.52 shows a test for the method in Listing 9.51. This test tries to assert the returned error is of type `ErrTableNotFound`. When an error is wrapped with `fmt.Errorf`, the resulting type is that of the general `error` interface. As such, by wrapping the `ErrTableNotFound` error with `fmt.Errorf`, we have changed the resulting type of the error. This also results in the tests failing as the error is no longer an `ErrTableNotFound`, but a different type.

Listing 9.52   A Wrapped Error Can No Longer Be Asserted against Correctly

```go
func Test_Store_All_NoTable(t *testing.T) {
    t.Parallel()

    s := &Store{
        data: map[string][]Model{},
    }

    _, err := s.All("users")
    if err == nil {
        t.Fatal("expected error, got nil")
    }

    exp := "users"
    e, ok := err.(ErrTableNotFound)
    if !ok {
        t.Fatalf("expected ErrTableNotFound, got %T", err)
    }

    act := e.Table
    if act != exp {
        t.Fatalf("expected %q, got %q", exp, act)
    }

    if e.OccurredAt.IsZero() {
        t.Fatal("expected non-zero time")
    }
}
```

```
$ go test -v

=== RUN    Test_Store_All_NoTable
=== PAUSE  Test_Store_All_NoTable
=== CONT   Test_Store_All_NoTable
    store_test.go:21: expected ErrTableNotFound, got *fmt.wrapError
--- FAIL: Test_Store_All_NoTable (0.00s)
FAIL
exit status 1
FAIL    demo    0.987s

Go Version: go1.19
```

Wrapping Errors

To get to the original error, we need to unwrap the errors until we reach the original error. This is similar to peeling an onion, where each error is a layer of wrapping.

Let's take a simplified look at how wrapping and unwrapping errors works in Go. Consider the error types defined in Listing 9.53. Each one contains an err field that holds the error that is wrapping.

Listing 9.53   The Three Error Types

```go
type ErrorA struct {
    err error
}

func (e ErrorA) Error() string {
    return fmt.Sprintf("[ErrorA] %s", e.err)
}

type ErrorB struct {
    err error
}

func (e ErrorB) Error() string {
    return fmt.Sprintf("[ErrorB] %s", e.err)
}

type ErrorC struct {
    err error
}

func (e ErrorC) Error() string {
    return fmt.Sprintf("[ErrorC] %s", e.err)
}
```

In Listing 9.54, the Wrapper function takes an error and the proceeds to wrap it in each of the three error types.

Listing 9.54   The Wrapper Function

```go
// Wrapper wraps an error with a bunch of
// other errors.
// ex. Wrapper(original) #=> ErrorC -> ErrorB -> ErrorA -> original
func Wrapper(original error) error {
    original = ErrorA{original}
```

```
    original = ErrorB{original}
    original = ErrorC{original}
    return original
}
```

Another way to do this same wrapping is to use multiline initialization and fill each error type with the next error type, as shown in Listing 9.55. Both of these are valid implementations of the same wrapping.

Listing 9.55 The Wrapper Function

```
// WrapperLong wraps an error with a bunch of
// other errors.
// ex. WrapperLong(original) #=> ErrorC -> ErrorB -> ErrorA -> original
func WrapperLong(original error) error {
    return ErrorC{
        err: ErrorB{
            err: ErrorA{
                err: original,
            },
        },
    }
}
```

Unwrapping Errors

You can use the errors.Unwrap[14] function, Listing 9.56, to unwrap an error until it reaches the original error. This will continue to peel the wrapped layers until it, hopefully, reaches the original error.

Listing 9.56 The errors.Unwrap Function

```
$ go doc errors.Unwrap

package errors // import "errors"

func Unwrap(err error) error
    Unwrap returns the result of calling the Unwrap method on err, if err's
    ↪type contains an Unwrap method returning error. Otherwise, Unwrap
    ↪returns nil.

Go Version: go1.19
```

---

14. https://pkg.go.dev/errors#Unwrap

In Listing 9.57, the test has been updated to use the `errors.Unwrap` function to unwrap the error until it reaches the original error. Unfortunately, however, the test fails because the result of `errors.Unwrap` is `nil`.

Listing 9.57   Using `errors.Unwrap` to Get the Original Error

```go
func Test_Unwrap(t *testing.T) {
    t.Parallel()

    original := errors.New("original error")
    wrapped := Wrapper(original)

    unwrapped := errors.Unwrap(wrapped)
    if unwrapped != original {
        t.Fatalf("expected %v, got %v", original, unwrapped)
    }

}
```

```
$ go test -v

=== RUN    Test_Wrapper
=== PAUSE Test_Wrapper
=== RUN    Test_Unwrap
=== PAUSE Test_Unwrap
=== CONT  Test_Wrapper
--- PASS: Test_Wrapper (0.00s)
=== CONT  Test_Unwrap
    errors_test.go:32: expected original error, got <nil>
--- FAIL: Test_Unwrap (0.00s)
FAIL
exit status 1
FAIL    demo    1.005s
```

```
Go Version: go1.19
```

Unwrapping Custom Errors

As the documentation states (refer to Listing 9.56), `errors.Unwrap` returns the result of calling the `Unwrap` method on an error if the error's type contains an `Unwrap` method returning `error`. Otherwise, `errors.Unwrap` returns `nil`.

What the documentation is trying to say is that your custom error types need to implement the interface shown in Listing 9.58. Unfortunately, the Go standard library does not define this interface for you outside of the documentation.

Listing 9.58 The Missing Unwrapper Interface

```
type Unwrapper interface {
    Unwrap() error
}
```

Let's update the error types defined in Listing 9.53 to implement the Unwrapper interface. Although Listing 9.59 only shows one implementation, all of our types need to be made to implement the Unwrapper interface. The implementation of this interface needs to make sure to call errors.Unwrap on the error it is wrapping.

Listing 9.59 Implementing the Unwrapper Interface

```
func (e ErrorA) Unwrap() error {
    return errors.Unwrap(e.err)
}
```

```
$ go test -v

=== RUN    Test_Wrapper
=== PAUSE Test_Wrapper
=== RUN    Test_Unwrap
=== PAUSE Test_Unwrap
=== CONT  Test_Wrapper
--- PASS: Test_Wrapper (0.00s)
=== CONT  Test_Unwrap
    errors_test.go:32: expected original error, got <nil>
--- FAIL: Test_Unwrap (0.00s)
FAIL
exit status 1
FAIL    demo    0.585s

Go Version: go1.19
```

The tests in Listing 9.59, however, are still failing. If the error we are wrapping does not contain an Unwrap method, the errors.Unwrap function returns nil, and we can't get access to the original error.

To fix this, we need to check the error we are wrapping for the Unwrapper interface, as shown Listing 9.60. If it does, we can call errors.Unwrap with the error. If it does not exist, we can return the error as is.

Listing 9.60 Properly Implementing the Unwrap Method

```go
func (e ErrorA) Unwrap() error {
    if _, ok := e.err.(Unwrapper); ok {
        return errors.Unwrap(e.err)
    }

    return e.err
}
```

```
$ go test -v

=== RUN    Test_Wrapper
=== PAUSE Test_Wrapper
=== RUN    Test_Unwrap
=== PAUSE Test_Unwrap
=== CONT   Test_Wrapper
--- PASS: Test_Wrapper (0.00s)
=== CONT   Test_Unwrap
--- PASS: Test_Unwrap (0.00s)
PASS
ok      demo      1.267s
```

Go Version: go1.19

With an understanding of errors.Unwrap, we can fix the test in Listing 9.61 to get the original error.

Listing 9.61 The WrappedError Type

```go
func Test_Store_All_NoTable(t *testing.T) {
    t.Parallel()

    s := &Store{
        data: map[string][]Model{},
    }

    _, err := s.All("users")
    if err == nil {
        t.Fatal("expected error, got nil")
    }

    // unwrap the error
    err = errors.Unwrap(err)
```

```go
        exp := "users"
        e, ok := err.(ErrTableNotFound)
        if !ok {
            t.Fatalf("expected ErrTableNotFound, got %T", err)
        }

        act := e.Table
        if act != exp {
            t.Fatalf("expected %q, got %q", exp, act)
        }

        if e.OccurredAt.IsZero() {
            t.Fatal("expected non-zero time")
        }
    }
}
```

```
$ go test -v

=== RUN    Test_Store_All_NoTable
=== PAUSE Test_Store_All_NoTable
=== CONT  Test_Store_All_NoTable
--- PASS: Test_Store_All_NoTable (0.00s)
PASS
ok      demo    1.034s

Go Version: go1.19
```

To Wrap or Not To Wrap

You've seen that you can use the fmt.Errorf with the %w verb to wrap an error. This allows for the unwrapping of an error later, either from the caller of your function/method or in a test.

While the normal rule is always to wrap the errors with the %w, there are exceptions. If you don't want some internal information or package-specific information not to be wrapped, then it is acceptable to use the %s verb to hide any implementation details. Keep in mind that this is normally the exception and not the rule.

If in doubt, it is usually safer to wrap the error so that other code that calls your package can check for specific errors later.

Errors As/Is

While unwrapping an error allows us to get to the original, underlying error, it does not allow us to get access to any of the other errors that it might have been wrapped with.

Consider Listing 9.62. When we unwrap the error returned from the `Wrapper` function, we can get access to the original error passed in, but how do we check whether the wrapped error has `ErrorB` in its stack and how do we get access to the `ErrorA` error? The errors package provides two functions—`errors.Is`[15] and `errors.As`[16]—that will help us with these questions.

Listing 9.62   A Function That Nests One Error in Many Errors

```
// Wrapper wraps an error with a bunch of
// other errors.
// ex. Wrapper(original) #=> ErrorC -> ErrorB -> ErrorA -> original
func Wrapper(original error) error {
    original = ErrorA{original}
    original = ErrorB{original}
    original = ErrorC{original}
    return original
}
```

As

When working with errors, we often don't care about the underlying error. There are times, however, when we do care about the underlying error, and we want to get access to it. The `errors.As`, Listing 9.63, function is designed to do this. It takes an `error` and a type to match against. If the error matches the type, it returns the underlying error. If the error does not match the type, it returns `nil`.

Listing 9.63   The `errors.As` Function

```
$ go doc errors.As

package errors // import "errors"

func As(err error, target any) bool
    As finds the first error in err's chain that matches target, and if one
    ↪is found, sets target to that error value and returns true. Otherwise,
    ↪it returns false.

    The chain consists of err itself followed by the sequence of errors
    ↪obtained by repeatedly calling Unwrap.

    An error matches target if the error's concrete value is assignable to
    ↪the value pointed to by target, or if the error has a method
```

---

15. https://pkg.go.dev/errors#Is
16. https://pkg.go.dev/errors#As

➥As(interface{}) bool such that As(target) returns true. In the latter
➥case, the As method is responsible for setting target.

An error type might provide an As method so it can be treated as if it
➥were a different error type.

As panics if target is not a non-nil pointer to either a type that
➥implements error, or to any interface type.

Go Version: go1.19

Like the errors.Unwrap function, errors.As *also* has a documented, but unpublished, interface, Listing 9.64, that can be implemented on custom errors.

Listing 9.64 The AsError Interface

```
type AsError interface {
    As(target any) bool
}
```

For the errors.As function to work properly, we need to implement an As method on our error types. In Listing 9.65, you can see an implementation of this function for the ErrorA type. This method is called when errors.As is called on our error. The As method should return true if the error matches the target and false otherwise. If false, we need to call errors.As on our error's underlying error. If true, we can return true and set the target to the current error.

Listing 9.65 Implementing the AsError Interface

```
func (e ErrorA) As(target any) bool {
    ex, ok := target.(*ErrorA)
    if !ok {
        // if the target is not an ErrorA,
        // pass the underlying error up the chain
        // by calling errors.As with the underlying error
        // and the target error
        return errors.As(e.err, target)
    }

    // set the target to the current error
    (*ex) = e
    return true
}
```

It is important to note that to set the target to the current error, we must first dereference the target pointer. This is because the As method is responsible for setting the target to the current error. If we don't dereference the target pointer, any changes we make would be lost when the As method returns.

As we can see from the test in Listing 9.66, we are able to take the wrapped error and extract the ErrorA type from the error stack. The As method sets the value of act to the error in the stack, and we are able to then access the ErrorA type directly.

Listing 9.66   Testing the AsError Implementation

```go
func Test_As(t *testing.T) {
    t.Parallel()

    original := errors.New("original error")
    wrapped := Wrapper(original)

    act := ErrorA{}

    ok := errors.As(wrapped, &act)
    if !ok {
        t.Fatalf("expected %v to act as %v", wrapped, act)
    }

    if act.err == nil {
        t.Fatalf("expected non-nil, got nil")
    }

}
```

```
$ go test -v

=== RUN    Test_As
=== PAUSE Test_As
=== CONT   Test_As
--- PASS: Test_As (0.00s)
PASS
ok        demo      0.848s
```

```
Go Version: go1.19
```

Is

While the errors.As function, Listing 9.63, is used to check for the type of an error, the errors.Is function, Listing 9.67, is used to check if an error in the error chain matches a specific error type. This provides a quick true/false check for an error type.

Listing 9.67 The errors.Is Function

```
$ go doc errors.Is

package errors // import "errors"

func Is(err, target error) bool
    Is reports whether any error in err's chain matches target.

    The chain consists of err itself followed by the sequence of errors
    ↪obtained by repeatedly calling Unwrap.

    An error is considered to match a target if it is equal to that target
    ↪or if it implements a method Is(error) bool such that Is(target)
    ↪returns true.

    An error type might provide an Is method so it can be treated as
    ↪equivalent to an existing error. For example, if MyError defines

        func (m MyError) Is(target error) bool { return target == fs.ErrExist }

    then Is(MyError{}, fs.ErrExist) returns true. See syscall.Errno.Is for an
    ↪example in the standard library. An Is method should only shallowly
    ↪compare err and the target and not call Unwrap on either.
```

Go Version: go1.19

The errors.Is documentation, like errors.As and errors.Unwrap, has a documented but unpublished interface. This interface is defined in Listing 9.68.

Listing 9.68 The IsError Interface

```
type IsError interface {
    Is(target error) bool
}
```

Like with errors.As, we have to implement the Is method for our custom error types, Listing 9.69. If our error type is the same type as the target error, then we can return true. If the target error is not a match, we then need to call errors.Is with our underlying error and the target error so that error can be checked as well.

Listing 9.69   Implementing the `IsError` Interface

```
func (e ErrorA) Is(target error) bool {
    if _, ok := target.(ErrorA); ok {
        // return true if target is ErrorA
        return true
    }

    // if not, pass the underlying error up the chain
    // by calling errors.Is with the underlying error
    // and the target error
    return errors.Is(e.err, target)
}
```

Finally, in Listing 9.70, we can write a test to assert that our `Is` method works as expected.

Listing 9.70   Testing the `IsError` Implementation

```
func Test_Is(t *testing.T) {
    t.Parallel()

    original := errors.New("original error")
    wrapped := Wrapper(original)

    exp := ErrorB{}

    ok := errors.Is(wrapped, exp)
    if !ok {
        t.Fatalf("expected %v to be %v", wrapped, exp)
    }

}
```

```
$ go test -v

=== RUN    Test_Is
=== PAUSE  Test_Is
=== CONT   Test_Is
--- PASS: Test_Is (0.00s)
PASS
ok      demo    1.222s
```

```
Go Version: go1.19
```

Stack Traces

Using a stack trace to debug your code can be very helpful at times. A stack trace shows where you are in the code and how you got there by printing a list of all calling functions.

The runtime/debug[17] package provides a couple of functions that you can use to get, or print, a stack trace. The debug.Stack[18] function, Listing 9.71, returns a slice of bytes that represent the stack trace.

Listing 9.71   The debug.Stack Function

```
$ go doc runtime/debug.Stack

package debug // import "runtime/debug"

func Stack() []byte
    Stack returns a formatted stack trace of the goroutine that calls it.
    ➥It calls runtime.Stack with a large enough buffer to capture the
    ➥entire trace.
```

Go Version: go1.19

The debug.PrintStack[19] function, Listing 9.72, prints the stack trace to the standard output.

Listing 9.72   The debug.PrintStack Function

```
$ go doc runtime/debug.PrintStack

package debug // import "runtime/debug"

func PrintStack()
    PrintStack prints to standard error the stack trace returned by
    ➥runtime.Stack.
```

Go Version: go1.19

In Listing 9.73, we print the stack trace of a program to standard output using debug.PrintStack.

---

17. https://pkg.go.dev/runtime/debug
18. https://pkg.go.dev/runtime/debug#Stack
19. https://pkg.go.dev/runtime/debug#PrintStack

Listing 9.73 Printing a Stack Trace

```
package main

import "runtime/debug"

func main() {
    First()
}

func First() {
    Second()
}

func Second() {
    Third()
}

func Third() {
    debug.PrintStack()
}
```

```
$ go run .

goroutine 1 [running]:
runtime/debug.Stack()
        /usr/local/go/src/runtime/debug/stack.go:24 +0x68
runtime/debug.PrintStack()
        /usr/local/go/src/runtime/debug/stack.go:16 +0x20
main.Third(...)
        ./main.go:18
main.Second(...)
        ./main.go:14
main.First(...)
        ./main.go:10
main.main()
        ./main.go:6 +0x2c

Go Version: go1.19
```

Summary

In this chapter, we discussed Go's error handling in depth. We covered error handling, and creation, in our code. We showed you how to create custom implementations of `error` interface. Next, we demonstrated how a panic can crash an application, and we discussed various ways to recover from panics. We showed you that you can use `errors.Unwrap` to try to get the original error from a wrapped error. We also explained how to use `errors.As` to try to assert an error has a certain type in its chain, and if so, it binds the error to a variable to be used in the rest of the function. Finally, we discussed how to use `errors.Is` to check whether an error in the chain is of a certain type.

10

Generics

Generics[1] were first introduced to Go with the release of Go 1.18[2] in March 2022, as we were writing this book. We, like the Go team, have tried our best to present the current idioms and thoughts on the how, what, when, where, and why questions about generics in Go.

What Are Generics?

Generic programming is a programming paradigm that allows you to stub out the implementation of a function with a type that will be provided later. This has benefits for both writing and using generic functions. With generics, you can write functions that can work with multiple types directly without having to write the same function multiple times, once for each type. When using generic functions, you can continue to use your types as concrete types instead of interface representations.

The Problem with Interfaces

Interfaces in Go are a powerful concept that allows developers to create flexible and reusable code. Interfaces allow you to define a set of methods that describe the behavior of a type. Any type that implements those methods and behaviors is considered to implement that interface.

We have already discussed the benefits and drawbacks of interfaces earlier in this book, so we don't have to reiterate their benefits, but let's discuss some problems with interfaces. For example, consider the function defined in Listing 10.1 and the problem of how to write a function that returns the keys for a given map.

Listing 10.1   A Function That Returns the Keys of a Map

```
func Keys(m map[any]any) []any {

    // make a slice of the keys
    keys := make([]any, 0, len(m))
```

1. https://en.wikipedia.org/wiki/Generic_programming
2. https://go.dev/blog/intro-generics

```
    // iterate over the map
    for k := range m {

        // add the key to the slice
        keys = append(keys, k)
    }

    // return the keys
    return keys
}
```

Go is a statically typed language, so you have to specify the type of the map that you want to get the keys from. A map needs to have both its key and value types specified. You also need to specify the type of slice this function will be returning. For this function to support all map types, you need to use the any, or empty interface, type, which will match any type.

Although this means you can write a function that you return a list of keys from a map, it also means that this function is difficult to use. Consider a test, Listing 10.2, that tries to use a map that isn't of type map[any]any. This code fails to compile because the type of map in the test is not compatible with the type of map required by the function.

Listing 10.2   Compilation Error Caused by a Type Mismatch

```
func Test_Keys(t *testing.T) {
    t.Parallel()

    // create a map with some values
    m := map[int]string{
        1: "one",
        2: "two",
        3: "three",
    }

    // get the keys
    act := Keys(m)

    // sort the returned keys for comparison
    sort.Slice(act, func(i, j int) bool {
        return act[i] < act[j]
    })

    // set the expected values
    exp := []int{1, 2, 3}
```

```
    // assert the length of the actual and expected values
    al := len(act)
    el := len(exp)
    if al != el {
        t.Fatalf("expected %d, but got %d", el, al)
    }

    // loop through the expected values and
    // assert they are in the actual values
    for i, v := range exp {
        if v != act[i] {
            t.Fatalf("expected %d, but got %d", v, act[i])
        }
    }

}
```

```
$ go test -v

FAIL    demo [build failed]

# demo [demo.test]
./keys_test.go:20:14: cannot use m (variable of type map[int]string) as type
➥map[any]any in argument to Keys
./keys_test.go:24:10: invalid operation: act[i] < act[j] (operator < not
➥defined on interface)

Go Version: go1.19
```

Listing 10.3 is an attempt to solve this problem. First, we need to create a new, interstitial map of the correct type and copy all of the keys from the original map into the new map. The same is true of trying to handle the results. We need to loop through the returned slice of keys, assert the keys are of the correct type, and then copy those values into a new slice of the correct type.

Listing 10.3 Copying Maps to Satisfy a Type Constraint

```
func Test_Keys(t *testing.T) {
    t.Parallel()

    // create a map with some values
    m := map[int]string{
```

(continued)

```go
    1: "one",
    2: "two",
    3: "three",
}

// create an interstitial map to pass to the function
im := map[any]any{}

// copy the map into the interstitial map
for k, v := range m {
    im[k] = v
}

// get the keys
keys := Keys(im)

// create a slice to hold the keys as
// integers for comparison
act := make([]int, 0, len(keys))

// copy the keys into the integer slice
for _, k := range keys {
    // assert that the key is an int
    i, ok := k.(int)
    if !ok {
        t.Fatalf("expected type int, got %T", k)
    }

    act = append(act, i)
}

// sort the returned keys for comparison
sort.Slice(act, func(i, j int) bool {
    return act[i] < act[j]
})

// set the expected values
exp := []int{1, 2, 3}

// assert the length of the actual and expected values
al := len(act)
el := len(exp)
```

```go
    if al != el {
        t.Fatalf("expected %d, but got %d", el, al)
    }

    // loop through the expected values and
    // assert they are in the actual values
    for i, v := range exp {
        if v != act[i] {
            t.Fatalf("expected %d, but got %d", v, act[i])
        }
    }

}
```

```
$ go test -v

=== RUN    Test_Keys
=== PAUSE  Test_Keys
=== CONT   Test_Keys
--- PASS: Test_Keys (0.00s)
PASS
ok      demo    0.167s

Go Version: go1.19
```

Although Listing 10.3 fixes the tests, it is a very cumbersome way to work with a function such as this. Generics were designed to help solve exactly this sort of problem.

Type Constraints

Generics in Go introduced a new concept to the language—type constraints. Type constraints allow you to specify that a type fits within a certain set of constraints. This is useful when you want to write a function that can work with multiple types, but you want to be able to specify that the function can only work with a specific type.

For example, so far, we have been using an int for the key type in a map and string for the value type. This is fine, but we can use generics to make this more flexible. We may want to use an int32 or a float64 for the key type and any value for the value type.

Generics allows you to specify those types as constraints when defining a function or a type. Constraints are added with [] after the name of the function or type, but before any parameters. Listing 10.4 lays out the anatomy of a generic function.

Listing 10.4 Anatomy of a Generic Function

```
func Name[constraints](parameters) (returns) {
    // ...
}
```

For example, in Listing 10.5, we define a Slicer function that defines a constraint, type T, which can be of any type. That new T type can then be used in the function signature. In Listing 10.5, the Slicer function returns a slice of T values.

Listing 10.5 A Generic Function That Returns a Slice of Values

```
func Slicer[T any](input T) []T {
    return []T{input}
}
```

When calling the Slicer function, as shown in Listing 10.6, we can pass any type, and it returns a slice of that same type back.

Listing 10.6 Calling a Generic Function

```
func Test_Slicer(t *testing.T) {
    t.Parallel()

    // create input string
    input := "Hello World"

    // capture output []string
    act := Slicer(input)

    exp := []string{input}

    if len(act) != len(exp) {
        t.Fatalf("expected %v, got %v", exp, act)
    }

    for i, v := range exp {
        if act[i] != v {
            t.Fatalf("expected %v, got %v", exp, act)
        }
    }

}
```

```
$ go test -v

=== RUN    Test_Slicer
=== PAUSE  Test_Slicer
=== CONT   Test_Slicer
--- PASS: Test_Slicer (0.00s)
PASS
ok      demo    0.194s
```

Go Version: go1.19

In our tests, we passed a `string` type to the `Slicer` function. At compile time, Go sees that we are calling the `Slicer` function with a `string` type and then inserts a function with the appropriate typed signature. For example, by passing a `string` type to the `Slicer` function, the compiler generates a function that looks like Listing 10.7.

Listing 10.7   A Static Function That Returns a Slice of Strings

```go
func Slicer(input string) []string {
    return []string{input}
}
```

Multiple Generic Types

Now that you have an understanding of the basics of generics, it's time to revisit the `Keys` function in Listing 10.8 and update it to support generics.

Listing 10.8   The Keys Function before Generics

```go
// snippet: def
func Keys(m map[any]any) []any {
    // snippet: def

    // make a slice of the keys
    keys := make([]any, 0, len(m))

    // iterate over the map
    for k := range m {

        // add the key to the slice
        keys = append(keys, k)
    }
```

(continued)

```
    // return the keys
    return keys
}
```

A map has both a key and a value type. We can use generics to specify which types are allowed to be used for both. In Listing 10.9, we can specify that the key type, K, must be of a type int, but the value type, V, can be of any type.

Listing 10.9 The Keys Function after Generics

```
// snippet: def
func Keys[K int, V any](m map[K]V) []K {
    // snippet: def

    // make a slice of the keys
    keys := make([]K, 0, len(m))

    // iterate over the map
    for k := range m {

        // add the key to the slice
        keys = append(keys, k)
    }

    // return the keys
    return keys
}
```

With the changes in Listing 10.9, we can pass a map of key type int and a value type of string to the Keys function, and it returns a slice of int values, as shown in Listing 10.10.

Listing 10.10 Tests Now Passing after Using Generics in Listing 10.9

```
func Test_Keys(t *testing.T) {
    t.Parallel()

    // create a map with some values
    m := map[int]string{
        1: "one",
        2: "two",
        3: "three",
    }
```

```go
    // get the keys
    act := Keys(m)

    // sort the returned keys for comparison
    sort.Slice(act, func(i, j int) bool {
        return act[i] < act[j]
    })

    // set the expected values
    exp := []int{1, 2, 3}

    // assert the length of the actual and expected values
    if len(exp) != len(act) {
        t.Fatalf("expected len(%d), but got len(%d)", len(exp), len(act))
    }

    // assert the types of the actual and expected values
    at := fmt.Sprintf("%T", act)
    et := fmt.Sprintf("%T", exp)

    if at != et {
        t.Fatalf("expected type %s, but got type %s", et, at)
    }

    // loop through the expected values and
    // assert they are in the actual values
    for i, v := range exp {
        if v != act[i] {
            t.Fatalf("expected %d, but got %d", v, act[i])
        }
    }

}
```

```
$ go test -v

=== RUN    Test_Keys
=== PAUSE Test_Keys
=== CONT  Test_Keys
--- PASS: Test_Keys (0.00s)
PASS
ok      demo    0.244s

Go Version: go1.19
```

As Listing 10.10 shows, this doesn't work if we want to use a map key of type `string` or `float64`. To do this, we need to specify a bigger set of constraints for the key type.

Instantiating Generic Functions

When calling a generic function or creating a new value of a generic type, the Go compiler needs to know which types are being provided for the generic parameters. So far, we have been letting the Go compiler infer the types of the generic parameters based on the types of the values passed in. In Listing 10.11, a variable, `fn`, is being declared and initialized with the Keys function from Listing 10.9. When the `fn` variable is called, the compiler is unable to infer the types of the generic parameters. The result is a compilation error.

Listing 10.11   The Keys Function before Instantiation

```
// create a function variable pointing
// to the Keys function
fn := Keys

// get the keys
act := fn(m)
```

```
$ go test -v

FAIL    demo [build failed]

# demo [demo.test]
./keys_test.go:22:8: cannot use generic function Keys without instantiation

Go Version: go1.19
```

In these situations, you need to provide the compiler with the types of the generic parameters. In Listing 10.12, the types `int` and `string` are being provided when grabbing a reference to the Keys function for the variable `fn`.

Listing 10.12   The Keys Function after Instantiation

```
// create a function variable pointing
// to the Keys function
fn := Keys[int, string]

// get the keys
act := fn(m)
```

```
$ go test -v

=== RUN    Test_Keys
=== PAUSE Test_Keys
=== CONT   Test_Keys
--- PASS: Test_Keys (0.00s)
PASS
ok      demo    0.213s
```

Go Version: go1.19

Defining Constraints

So far, we have been using pretty simple types, such as int and any for the key and value types. But what if we want to use more types than just these? To specify which types can be used for a generic parameter, we can use constraints. Constraints are defined in a similar way to interfaces, but instead of specifying a set of methods, we specify a set of types.

As a start, we can define a constraint, Listing 10.13, that requires the type to be an int.

Listing 10.13 A Constraint That Requires the Type to Be an int

```
// MapKey is a set of a constraints
// on types that can be used as map keys.
type MapKey interface {
    int
}
```

With the MapKey constraint defined in Listing 10.13, we can update the Keys function to use it instead of int in Listing 10.14.

Listing 10.14 The Keys Function Using the MapKey Constraint

```
func Keys[K MapKey, V any](m map[K]V) []K {

    // make a slice of the keys
    keys := make([]K, 0, len(m))

    // iterate over the map
    for k := range m {

        // add the key to the slice
        keys = append(keys, k)
    }
```

(continued)

```
    // return the keys
    return keys
}
```

Multiple Type Constraints

Currently, the MapKey constraint only allows an int to be used for the key. In
Listing 10.15, we try to use the Keys function with a map using a key type of
float64. The result is a compilation error.

Listing 10.15   The Keys Function with a float64 Key

```
// create a map with some values
m := map[float64]string{
    1.1: "one",
    2.2: "two",
    3.3: "three",
}

// get the keys
act := Keys(m)

// sort the returned keys for comparison
sort.Slice(act, func(i, j int) bool {
    return act[i] < act[j]
})

// set the expected values
exp := []float64{1.1, 2.2, 3.3}

// assert the length of the actual and expected values
if len(exp) != len(act) {
    t.Fatalf("expected len(%d), but got len(%d)", len(exp), len(act))
}

// assert the types of the actual and expected values
at := fmt.Sprintf("%T", act)
et := fmt.Sprintf("%T", exp)

if at != et {
    t.Fatalf("expected type %s, but got type %s", et, at)
}
```

```
// loop through the expected values and
// assert they are in the actual values
for i, v := range exp {
    if v != act[i] {
        t.Fatalf("expected %d, but got %d", v, act[i])
    }
}
```

```
$ go test -v

FAIL    demo [build failed]

# demo [demo.test]
./keys_test.go:21:13: float64 does not implement MapKey

Go Version: go1.19
```

When defining constraints, you can use the | operator to create an intersection of constraints. For example, in Listing 10.16, we define a constraint that requires the key type to be either int or float64.

Listing 10.16   A Constraint That Requires the Key Type to Be Either int or float64

```
// MapKey is a set of a constraints
// on types that can be used as map keys.
type MapKey interface {
    int | float64
}
```

With the change to the MapKey constraint in Listing 10.16, we can use the Keys function with a map using a key type of float64. The tests in Listing 10.17 now pass.

Listing 10.17   Tests Now Passing with the MapKey Constraint

```
$ go test -v

=== RUN    Test_Keys
=== PAUSE Test_Keys
=== CONT    Test_Keys
--- PASS: Test_Keys (0.00s)
PASS
ok      demo    0.214s

Go Version: go1.19
```

Underlying Type Constraints

In Go, you are allowed to create new types based on other types. For example, in Listing 10.18, we can create a new type, MyInt, that is based on the int type.

Listing 10.18   A New Type Based on the int Type

```
type MyInt int
```

However, in Listing 10.19, when we try to use the Keys function with a map using a key type of MyInt, we get a compile error.

Listing 10.19   The MyInt Type Does Not Meet the int Constraint

```
func Test_Keys(t *testing.T) {
    t.Parallel()

    // create a map with some values
    m := map[MyInt]string{
        1: "one",
        2: "two",
        3: "three",
    }

    // get the keys
    act := Keys(m)

    // sort the returned keys for comparison
    sort.Slice(act, func(i, j int) bool {
        return act[i] < act[j]
    })

    // set the expected values
    exp := []MyInt{1, 2, 3}

    // assert the length of the actual and expected values
    if len(exp) != len(act) {
        t.Fatalf("expected len(%d), but got len(%d)", len(exp), len(act))
    }

    // assert the types of the actual and expected values
    at := fmt.Sprintf("%T", act)
    et := fmt.Sprintf("%T", exp)
```

```
    if at != et {
        t.Fatalf("expected type %s, but got type %s", et, at)
    }

    // loop through the expected values and
    // assert they are in the actual values
    for i, v := range exp {
        if v != act[i] {
            t.Fatalf("expected %d, but got %d", v, act[i])
        }
    }
}
```

```
$ go test -v

FAIL    demo [build failed]

# demo [demo.test]
./keys_test.go:21:13: MyInt does not implement MapKey (possibly missing ~ for
➡int in constraint MapKey)

Go Version: go1.19
```

The reason for the compilation error in Listing 10.19 is that the type `MyInt`, while based on `int`, does not satisfy the `MapKey` constraint because it is *not* an `int` itself. When writing constraints, we usually are interested in the underlying type, not the type that is wrapped by the type. To express this when defining a constraint, we can use the ~ operator, as shown in Listing 10.20.

Listing 10.20   Using the ~ Operator to Allow for Supertypes

```
// MapKey is a set of a constraints
// on types that can be used as map keys.
type MapKey interface {
    ~int
}
```

By updating the constraint to use the ~ operator, the `Keys` function accepts any type based on `int`. Because `MyInt` is based on `int`, we can now use the `Keys` function with a map using a key type of `MyInt`. As shown in Listing 10.21, the tests now pass.

Listing 10.21   Tests Passing with the ~ Constraint Operator

```
$ go test -v

=== RUN    Test_Keys
=== PAUSE Test_Keys
=== CONT  Test_Keys
--- PASS: Test_Keys (0.00s)
PASS
ok      demo     0.174s
```

Go Version: go1.19

The Constraints Package

When generics were released in Go 1.18, the Go team decided to be cautious and not update the standard library immediately to use them. The team wanted to see how generics were being used before updating the standard library. As a result, the Go team has created a series of packages in the `golang.org/x/exp`[3] namespace to experiment with generics. One of these packages is the `golang.org/x/exp/constraints`[4] package, Listing 10.22. The `golang.org/x/exp/constraints` package defines a set of constraints for all of the numerical and comparable types in the language.

Listing 10.22   The `golang.org/x/exp/constraints` Package

```
$ go doc golang.org/x/exp/constraints

package constraints // import "golang.org/x/exp/constraints"

Package constraints defines a set of useful constraints to be used with type
parameters.

type Complex interface{ ... }
type Float interface{ ... }
type Integer interface{ ... }
type Ordered interface{ ... }
type Signed interface{ ... }
type Unsigned interface{ ... }
```

Go Version: go1.19

---

3. https://pkg.go.dev/golang.org/x/exp
4. https://pkg.go.dev/golang.org/x/exp/constraints

For example, consider the `constraints.Signed`[5] constraint, Listing 10.23. This constraint requires that the type be any of the signed integer types, +/-, defined in the Go language, such as `int` and `int64`, and any types based on those types.

Listing 10.23   The `constraints.Signed` Constraint

```
$ go doc golang.org/x/exp/constraints.Signed

package constraints // import "golang.org/x/exp/constraints"

type Signed interface {
        ~int | ~int8 | ~int16 | ~int32 | ~int64
}

    Signed is a constraint that permits any signed integer type. If future
    releases of Go add new predeclared signed integer types, this constraint
    will be modified to include them.
```

Go Version: go1.19

The `constraints.Integer`[6] constraint, Listing 10.24, requires the type to be based on *any* integer type, signed or unsigned, such as `int`, `int64`, `uint`, `uint64`, and so on.

Listing 10.24   The `constraints.Integer` Constraint

```
$ go doc golang.org/x/exp/constraints.Integer

package constraints // import "golang.org/x/exp/constraints"

type Integer interface {
        Signed | Unsigned
}

    Integer is a constraint that permits any integer type. If future releases
    ↳of Go add new predeclared integer types, this constraint will be
    ↳modified to include them.
```

Go Version: go1.19

The Ordered Constraint

One of the most useful constraints defined in the `golang.org/x/exp/constraints` package is the `constraints.Ordered` constraint, Listing 10.25. This constraint lists all of

---

5. https://pkg.go.dev/golang.org/x/exp/constraints#Signed
6. https://pkg.go.dev/golang.org/x/exp/constraints#Integer

the comparable types in the language and any types based on those types. The
constraints.Ordered[7] constraint covers all numerical types and strings.

Listing 10.25   The constraints.Ordered Constraint

```
$ go doc golang.org/x/exp/constraints.Ordered


package constraints // import "golang.org/x/exp/constraints"


type Ordered interface {
        Integer | Float | ~string
}
    Ordered is a constraint that permits any ordered type: any type that
    ⮕supports the operators < <= >= >. If future releases of Go add new
    ⮕ordered types, this constraint will be modified to include them.
```

Go Version: go1.19

The constraints.Ordered constraint is perfect for map keys because all of the types
defined in the constraint are comparable. In Listing 10.26, the Keys function has been
updated to use the constraints.Ordered constraint. We can now use the Keys function
with a map using a key type of string or any other type that is comparable.

Listing 10.26   The Keys Function Definition

```
func Keys[K constraints.Ordered, V any](m map[K]V) []K {

    // make a slice of the keys
    keys := make([]K, 0, len(m))

    // iterate over the map
    for k := range m {

        // add the key to the slice
        keys = append(keys, k)
    }

    // return the keys
    return keys
}
```

---

7. https://pkg.go.dev/golang.org/x/exp/constraints#Ordered

Type Assertions

When using constraints that are based on types and not on methods like interfaces, type assertions are not allowed. For example, in Listing 10.27, the `Keys` function tries to print each map key out to the console but only if it implements the `fmt.Stringer`[8] interface.

Listing 10.27   The Keys Function with Type Assertions

```go
func Keys[K constraints.Ordered, V any](m map[K]V) []K {

    // make a slice of the keys
    keys := make([]K, 0, len(m))

    // iterate over the map
    for k := range m {

        // if k implements fmt.Stringer,
        // print the string representation
        if st, ok := k.(fmt.Stringer); ok {
            fmt.Println(st.String())
        }

        // add the key to the slice
        keys = append(keys, k)
    }

    // return the keys
    return keys
}
```

With method-based interfaces, this is possible, but with constraints, we can't make this sort of assertion, Listing 10.28.

Listing 10.28   Compilation Error Making Assertions on a Constraint

```
$ go test -v

FAIL    demo [build failed]

# demo [demo.test]
./keys.go:19:16: invalid operation: cannot use type assertion on type
➥parameter value k (variable of type K constrained by constraints.Ordered)

Go Version: go1.19
```

---

8. https://pkg.go.dev/fmt#Stringer

As mentioned previously, at compile time, generic function calls are replaced with their concrete types. The result is a `Keys` function that takes a map of `string` to `int` and returns a `[]string`, Listing 10.29.

Listing 10.29   The Compiled Output of a Generic Function

```
func Keys(m map[string]int) []string {

    // make a slice of the keys
    keys := make([]string, 0, len(m))

    // iterate over the map
    for k := range m {

        // if k implements fmt.Stringer,
        // print the string representation
        if st, ok := k.(fmt.Stringer); ok {
            fmt.Println(st.String())
        }

        // add the key to the slice
        keys = append(keys, k)
    }

    // return the keys
    return keys
}
```

When looking at the compilation error in Listing 10.30, for "concrete" representation of the `Keys` function, the error is a little more clear.

Listing 10.30   Compilation Error Type Asserting on a Concrete Type

```
$ go test -v

FAIL    demo [build failed]

# demo [demo.test]
./keys.go:17:16: invalid operation: k (variable of type string)
➥is not an interface

Go Version: go1.19
```

In Go, type assertions against concrete types, such as those in Listing 10.29, are not allowed. There is no reason to assert if `string` or `User` or another type implements the interface because the compiler automatically performs this assertion.

Mixing Method and Type Constraints

When defining constraints, we have to choose between type-based constraints and method-based constraints. For example, in Listing 10.31, we can't define a constraint that is either `constraints.Ordered` or `fmt.Stringer`.

Listing 10.31 Compilation Error Mixing Method and Type Constraints

```go
type MapKey interface {
    constraints.Ordered | fmt.Stringer
}
```

```go
func Keys[K MapKey, V any](m map[K]V) []K {

    // make a slice of the keys
    keys := make([]K, 0, len(m))

    // iterate over the map
    for k := range m {

        // add the key to the slice
        keys = append(keys, k)
    }

    // return the keys
    return keys
}
```

```
$ go test -v

FAIL    demo [build failed]

# demo [demo.test]
./keys.go:10:24: cannot use fmt.Stringer in union (fmt.Stringer contains
➥methods)
./keys.go:13:34: invalid map key type K (missing comparable constraint)

Go Version: go1.19
```

Generic Types

Types can be generic just as functions can. If you consider building a data store, you might define a generic type to represent a "model." In Listing 10.32, we define a `Model` interface that defines a constraint that all implementations of the `Model` interface must satisfy. The `Model` interface has a type constraint, `[T constraints.Ordered]`. This constraint is now available for use on the interface's methods.

Listing 10.32   The `Model` Interface with Generics

```
type Model[T constraints.Ordered] interface {
    ID() T
}
```

Now, to implement the `Model` interface in Listing 10.32, a type needs an `ID()` method that returns a type listed in the `constraints.Ordered` constraint. In Listing 10.33, the `Use` type implements the `Model` interface by having an `ID` method that returns a `string`, which is part of the `constraints.Ordered` constraint.

Listing 10.33   A User Type That Implements Listing 10.32

```
type User struct {
    Email string
}

func (u User) ID() string
```

In Listing 10.34, we define a `Store` struct type that has two type constraints: `[K constraints.Ordered]` and `[M Model[K]]`. In this example, we are using the `K` constraint defined on the `Store` type to define the constraint on the `Model` type.

Listing 10.34   The `Store` Type with Generics

```
// Store is a map of models where the map key is any
// comparable type and the map value is any type that
// implements the Model constraint.
type Store[K constraints.Ordered, M Model[K]] struct {
    data map[K]M
}

func (s Store[K, M]) Find(id K) (M, error)
func (s *Store[K, M]) Insert(m M) error
```

When defining methods on types that use generics, the receiver of the method needs to be instantiated with the appropriate concrete type or types. Consider the `Find` method on the `Store` type in Listing 10.35.

Listing 10.35 The `Find` Method on the `Store` Type

```go
func (s Store[K, M]) Find(id K) (M, error) {
    m, ok := s.data[id]
    if !ok {
        return m, fmt.Errorf("key not found %v", id)
    }

    return m, nil
}
```

The receiver, `(s Store[K, M])`, is instantiated with the concrete types that the `Store` type was instantiated with. Those types can also be used to define arguments and return values for these methods. In Listing 10.36, we initialize a new `Store` type with the constraints of `string` and `User`. In the tests, we are able to work with the original concrete types instead of interfaces backed by unknown types.

Listing 10.36 Testing a `Store` Type with Constraints

```go
func Test_Store_Insert(t *testing.T) {
    t.Parallel()

    // create a store
    s := &Store[string, User]{
        data: map[string]User{},
    }

    // create a user
    exp := User{Email: "kurt@exampl.com"}

    // insert the user
    err := s.Insert(exp)
    if err != nil {
        t.Fatal(err)
    }

    // retreive the user
    act, err := s.Find(exp.Email)
    if err != nil {
        t.Fatal(err)
```

```
    }

    // assert the returned user is the same as the inserted user
    if exp.Email != act.Email {
        t.Fatalf("expected %v, got %v", exp, act)
    }

}
```

```
$ go test -v

=== RUN    Test_Store_Insert
=== PAUSE Test_Store_Insert
=== CONT   Test_Store_Insert
--- PASS: Test_Store_Insert (0.00s)
PASS
ok        demo      0.174s

Go Version: go1.19
```

Summary

In this chapter, we covered the basics of generics in Go. We showed you how to define constraints, how to use constraints on types, and how to use constraints on methods. Generics are still new to Go, but they are a powerful tool that can be used to make your code more expressive and maintainable.

11

Channels

In this chapter, we start exploring concurrency in Go. We begin by discussing the difference between concurrency and parallelism. We cover goroutines—what they are and how they behave. Finally, we discuss channels and how they can be used to communicate between goroutines as well as control them.

Before we get too far into concurrency and channels, there are some quotes about them that may help guide you in their usage:

> "I can't tell you how many times I start with channels, and by the time I'm done, I've completely optimized them out."
>
> — Cory LaNou

> "When I first learned about channels, I wanted to use them everywhere. Now, I rarely use them at all."
>
> — Mat Ryer

The preceding quotes are not intended to steer you away from using channels, but more to encourage you to think about whether you in fact need a channel. It is common for developers new to Go to overuse channels, which leads to unnecessary code complexity with no benefit to program performance.

Concurrency and Parallelism

According to Rob Pike, "concurrency[1] is the composition of independently executing computations, and concurrency is not parallelism: concurrency is about dealing with lots of things at once but parallelism is about doing lots of things at once. Concurrency is about structure, parallelism is about execution, concurrency provides a way to structure a solution to solve a problem that may (but not necessarily) be parallelizable."

---

1. https://bit.ly/3GwX4V6

Concurrency Is Not Parallelism

Concurrency is not parallelism, although it enables parallelism. The following statements explain the difference between concurrency and parallelism:

- Concurrency is about *dealing with* a lot of things at once.
- Parallelism is about *doing* a lot of things at once.

If you have only one processor, your program can still be concurrent, but it cannot be parallel.

If you have a single resource and multiple tasks, you can share your time across those tasks, thus working on all tasks concurrently. However, to work on all tasks in parallel, you need need more than one resource.

Understanding Concurrency

Consider the task of feeding a dog, as shown in Figure 11.1. The dog is hungry and needs to be fed, and the treats are in a box. To feed the dog, you need to open the box, take a treat out of the box, carry the treat in your hand, and then feed the dog the treat.

Figure 11.1   Feeding one dog, one treat, with one hand (Images: box courtesy of valdis torms/Shutterstock; hand courtesy of croisy/123RF; dog bone courtesy of doomu/123RF; puppy courtesy of Mhm Amin1/Shutterstock)

Adding Dogs

In Figure 11.2, a second dog also needs to be fed a treat. However, there is a resource constraint of just one hand. With one hand, you can only carry one treat at a time, and thus feed only one dog at a time.

To feed both dogs, you have to feed a treat to one dog and then take another treat from the box in your hand to feed a treat to the other dog. It's important to note that because you can only feed one dog at a time, the other dog is waiting.

This is a *concurrent* operation.

Concurrency takes advantage of tasks in a "waiting" state. Instead of waiting for the first dog to finish the treat before going to the second dog and feeding it a treat, we immediately started the second dog on the task of eating a treat while the first dog was busy.

Figure 11.2   Feeding two dogs, one treat, with one hand

More Hands

The one-hand resource constraint can be lifted by using your other hand, as shown in Figure 11.3. With two hands, you can carry two treats at a time, and thus feed two dogs at a time. However, only one hand at a time can be placed into the box to retrieve a treat. This is a *serial* operation and requires the scheduling of one hand at a time to retrieve a treat.

Feeding the dogs is a *concurrent*, not *parallel*, operation. Even though there are enough hands to feed both dogs, only one hand can retrieve a treat at a time.

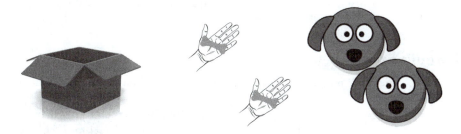

Figure 11.3   Feeding two dogs, two treats, with two hands

More Scenarios

If more treat boxes and dogs are added, as shown in Figure 11.4, there are still only two hands. Although this may allow for a faster concurrent operation (less waiting to get the treats because there is less contention with scheduling), there is always at least one dog waiting for a treat. This is one of many common design challenges that software engineers need to solve for when creating concurrent solutions.

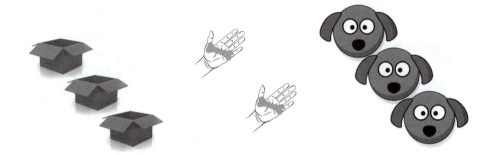

Figure 11.4   Feeding multiple dogs, from multiple boxes, with two hands

Go's Concurrency Model

In a lot of languages, concurrency is achieved through the use of creating heavyweight system processes,[2] kernel threads, third-party libraries, or other means. There are mechanics for joining threads, managing threads, implementing thread interfaces, and more.

In Go, concurrency is built directly into the language without the need for third-party libraries, system processes, or kernel threads.

Goroutines

Go uses the coroutine[3] model to achieve concurrency. In Go, these coroutine functions are called "goroutines."

Simply put, a goroutine is an independent function launched by a go statement and capable of being run concurrently with other goroutines. See Listing 11.1 for examples of creating goroutines.

Listing 11.1   Examples of Launching Goroutines

```
go someFunction()

go func() {
  // do something
}()
```

A goroutine is *NOT* a system thread or process. It is a lightweight thread of execution that is managed by the Go runtime scheduler.

---

2. https://bit.ly/3Cu5NVB
3. https://en.wikipedia.org/wiki/Coroutine

But if it helps you to think of a goroutine as a very cheap thread, you won't be far off.

Goroutine Memory

Goroutines have their own memory call stack that starts with a small amount of memory and grows as needed. The amount of memory each goroutine starts with can change with releases based on changes to the Go runtime, garbage collector, and language.

> Go does not allow developers to control the amount of memory allocated to a goroutine.

Because goroutines are cheap and easy to use, it is not uncommon to have hundreds, thousands, or even millions of goroutines running at once.

The Go Scheduler

The scheduler in Go is responsible for distributing the runnable goroutines over multiple OS threads that run on one or more processors.

> Go does not allow developers to control the scheduling of goroutines.

Goroutines are created in code and are then scheduled by the Go runtime scheduler (see Figure 11.5). The scheduler is then responsible for managing those goroutines across multiple OS threads.

Work Sharing and Stealing

Go uses a dual model of "work sharing" and "work stealing"[4] to manage goroutines.

Work Sharing

With work sharing, the scheduler tries to distribute the work to the available processes, which makes better use of the available CPUs.

Listing 11.2 has an uneven distribution of goroutines across the CPUs. Work sharing makes sure that the goroutines are distributed evenly across the available CPUs, Listing 11.3.

Listing 11.2   CPU Load Before Work Sharing

```
CPU1: A  B  C  D  E  F  G
CPU2: H  I
CPU3: J  K
CPU4:
```

---

4. https://en.wikipedia.org/wiki/Work_stealing

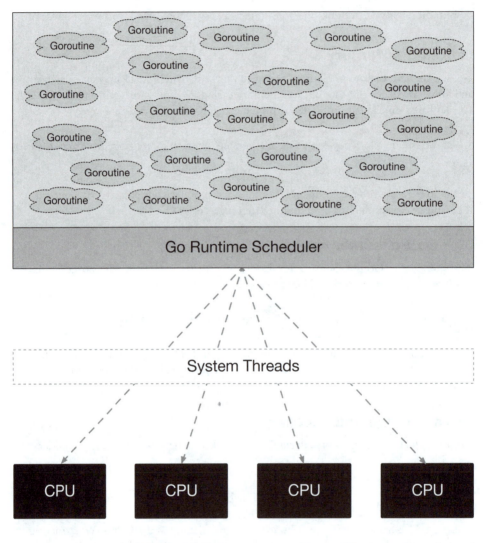

Figure 11.5   The Go runtime scheduler

Listing 11.3   CPU Load after Work Sharing

```
CPU1: A  B  C
CPU2: D  E  F
CPU3: G  H  I
CPU4: J  K
```

Work Stealing

Unlike work sharing, work stealing works from the other side of the scheduler. An underutilized process in the scheduler attempts to steal work from another process.

Listing 11.4 shows an uneven distribution of goroutines across the CPUs. Work stealing in Listing 11.5 steals work from the other CPUs to make the distribution even.

Listing 11.4 CPU Load before Work Stealing

```
CPU1: A   B   C   D   E   F   G
CPU2: H   I
CPU3: J   K
CPU4:
```

Listing 11.5 CPU Load after Work Stealing

```
CPU1: A   C   D   E   F   G
CPU2: H   I
CPU3: J   K
CPU4: B
```

Don't Worry about the Scheduler

Go offers little to developers in the way of managing, controlling, or tuning the scheduler. Each release of Go makes subtle, sometimes large, and sometimes unobvious changes to the scheduler and garbage collector. Because of this, there is little point to worrying about the inner workings of the scheduler on a daily basis.

The runtime[5] package provides a number of functions that can be used to query and make small changes to the Go runtime. One of the most useful functions is runtime.GOMAXPROCS,[6] Listing 11.6, which allows you to set the number of OS threads that the Go runtime will use.

Listing 11.6 The runtime.GOMAXPROCS Function

```
$ go doc runtime.GOMAXPROCS

package runtime // import "runtime"
```

(continued)

---

5. https://pkg.go.dev/runtime
6. https://pkg.go.dev/runtime#GOMAXPROCS

```
func GOMAXPROCS(n int) int
    GOMAXPROCS sets the maximum number of CPUs that can be executing
    ↪simultaneously and returns the previous setting. It defaults to the
    ↪value of runtime.NumCPU. If n < 1, it does not change the current
    ↪setting. This call will go away when the scheduler improves.
```

Go Version: go1.19

Goroutine Example

Consider the program in Listing 11.7. This program should be familiar to you; it is a basic "Hello, World" program. The difference is that it uses a goroutine to print the message.

Listing 11.7   Using a Goroutine to Print `Hello, World!`

```
package main

import "fmt"

func main() {
    go fmt.Println("Hello, World!")
}
```

When this code is run, Listing 11.8, no message is printed out. The reason is that before the scheduler has a chance to run the goroutine, the program has exited. Later in Chapter 13, we explain how to prevent premature exiting from a program before the scheduler has a chance to run its goroutines. We also discuss how to let your running goroutines know when it is time for them to stop.

Listing 11.8   The Goroutine Was Never Run

```
$ go run .
```

Go Version: go1.19

Communicating with Channels

Channels are used in Go as a conduit to communicate between goroutines. This section covers basic channel usage along with the corresponding patterns for each. We explain the difference between a buffered and unbuffered channel and when to use them. We also discuss how to use channels for signaling for concepts such as graceful application shutdown. Finally, we demonstrate how to spot common concurrency pitfalls and how to properly structure your concurrent code to avoid them.

What Are Channels?

Channels are a typed conduit through which you can send and receive values. All channels have the following characteristics:

- They are typed. You can only send and receive values of the same type. For example, you can't send a string and an int over the same channel.

- The values are transmitted/received in a synchronous manner. The sender and receiver must wait for the other to finish before sending or receiving.

- The values are transmitted/received in a FIFO (first in, first out) manner. The first value sent is the first value received.

- They are either unbuffered or buffered. A buffered channel holds a limited number of values. When the channel is full, the sender blocks until a value is received. When the channel is empty, the receiver blocks until a value is sent.

- They are directional. Channels can either be bidirectional or unidirectional. You can use a bidirectional channel to send and receive values. You can use a unidirectional channel only to send or receive values.

Understanding Channel Blocking/Unblocking

To understand channels, you need to understand when they block and when they unblock. Consider the idea of making a phone call. When you call someone, you are blocked until they answer the call. Once connected, you are unblocked and can start bidirectional communication—in this case, audio can now be exchanged back and forth between you and the person you are calling. The channel type would be `audio`, and you would not be able to pass each other a `fruit` over the phone line.

Figure 11.6 shows the caller is blocked until the receiver picks up the call. Once the receiver picks up the phone, the call is unblocked, and bidirectional communication can start. In this scenario, a phone call is a bidirectional and unbuffered channel. The caller and receiver are both blocked until the other unblocks them. Finally, the channel would have a type of `audio`. To reiterate, a phone call has the following characteristics:

- A bidirectional channel
- An unbuffered channel
- Type of `audio`

Creating Channels

Channels are indicated by the `chan` keyword followed by the type of the channel. For example, `chan string` indicates a channel of strings, `chan int` indicates a channel of integers, and so on.

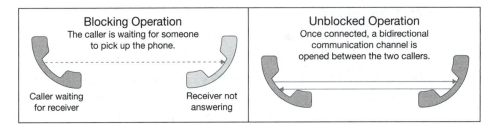

Figure 11.6   Blocking and unblocking for a telephone call

New channels are created with the built-in make function, Listing 11.9. For example, make(chan string) creates a channel of strings.

Listing 11.9   The make Function

```
$ go doc builtin.make

package builtin // import "builtin"

func make(t Type, size ...IntegerType) Type
    The make built-in function allocates and initializes an object of type
    ↪slice, map, or chan (only). Like new, the first argument is a type,
    ↪not a value. Unlike new, make's return type is the same as the type of
    ↪its argument, not a pointer to it. The specification of the result
    ↪depends on the type:

        Slice: The size specifies the length. The capacity of the slice is
        ↪equal to its length. A second integer argument may be provided to
        ↪specify a different capacity; it must be no smaller than the
        ↪length. For example, make([]int, 0, 10) allocates an underlying
        ↪array of size 10 and returns a slice of length 0 and capacity 10
        ↪that is backed by this underlying array.
        Map: An empty map is allocated with enough space to hold the
        ↪specified number of elements. The size may be omitted, in which case
        ↪a small starting size is allocated.
        Channel: The channel's buffer is initialized with the specified
        ↪buffer capacity. If zero, or the size is omitted, the channel is
        ↪unbuffered.

Go Version: go1.19
```

Sending and Receiving Values

In Go, the <- operator is used to indicate sending or receiving information on a channel. At first, it can be difficult to remember where the arrow goes and what the arrow indicates.

When working with channels, the arrow (as shown in Listing 11.10) points in the direction in which the data is traveling in regard to the channel.

Listing 11.10 Arrows Indicating Sending and Receiving Data

```
ch <- // data is going into the channel
<- ch // data is coming out of the channel
```

Consider the code in Listing 11.11. The first line blocks trying to send `Hello, Janis!` to the phone channel: `phone <- "Hello, Janis!"`. This line only unblocks when someone else is ready to receive the message. Once the message is sent and received, the application is unblocked and may continue to run.

The second line blocks trying to receive a message from the `phone` channel: `msg :=` `<-phone`. This line only unblocks when someone else is ready to send the message. Once the message is sent and received, the application is unblocked and may continue to run.

Listing 11.11 A Simple Example of Blocking and Unblocking

```
// This line blocks until there is a line of code ready to
// read from the channel.
phone <- "Hello, Janis!"

// This line blocks until there is a line of code ready to
// send a message down the channel.
msg := <-phone
```

A Simple Channel Example

Consider the example in Listing 11.12. In this example, the `Janis` function is running as a goroutine. Because it is in a goroutine, it can be blocked waiting to send/receive messages on a channel and without impacting the `main` function.

Listing 11.12 A Simple Example of a Channel

```
package main

import "fmt"

func Janis(ch chan string) {
    // This line blocks until a message is sent to the channel
    msg := <-ch
```

(continued)

```
    fmt.Println("Jimi said:", msg)

    // This line blocks until the channel is read from
    ch <- "Hello, Jimi!"
}

func main() {

    // make a new channel of type string
    // and assign it to the phone variable
    phone := make(chan string)

    // Close the channel to signal that no more messages
    // will be sent/received.
    defer close(phone)

    // Launch the Janis function as a goroutine.
    // This will run concurrently with the main function.
    go Janis(phone)

    // This line blocks until there is a line of code ready to
    // read from the channel.
    phone <- "Hello, Janis!"

    // This line blocks until there is a line of code ready to
    // send a message down the channel.
    msg := <-phone

    fmt.Println("Janis said:", msg)

}
```

```
$ go run .

Jimi said: Hello, Janis!
Janis said: Hello, Jimi!

Go Version: go1.19
```

If we stop using a goroutine for the Janis function and instead run the function serially in the main function, as in Listing 11.13, the application would deadlock and crash. This is because the Janis function is blocking waiting for a message on the phone channel, but the main function is unable to send a message on the phone channel because Janis is blocked.

Listing 11.13   Deadlock Caused by a Channel That Can't Be Unblocked

```go
func main() {

    // make a new channel of type string
    // and assign it to the phone variable
    phone := make(chan string)

    // Close the channel to signal that no more messages
    // will be sent/received.
    defer close(phone)

    // Run the Amy serially instead of concurrently with a goroutine.
    Amy(phone)

    // This line blocks until Amy is ready to read from the channel.
    phone <- "Hello, Amy!"

    // This line blocks until Amy sends a message back down the channel.
    msg := <-phone

    fmt.Println("Amy said:", msg)

}
```

```
$ go run .

fatal error: all goroutines are asleep - deadlock!

goroutine 1 [chan receive]:
main.Amy(0x14000084f28?)
        ./main.go:7 +0x2c
main.main()
        ./main.go:28 +0x60
exit status 2
```

Go Version: go1.19

Ranging over a Channel

Often you will want to keep listening for messages on a channel until the channel is closed. You can do this with an infinite loop, but the more appropriate way is to use a `for range` loop, Listing 11.14. When the channel is closed, the `range` loop stops iterating, and the `listener` function returns. We discuss closing channels in more detail shortly.

Listing 11.14   A Simple Example of a `range` Loop

```
func listener(ch chan int) {
    for i := range ch {
        fmt.Println(i)
    }

    fmt.Println("listener exit")
}
```

Listening to Channels with `select`

When writing concurrent applications, it is often useful to listen to multiple channels at the same time. For example, an employee might need to listen to multiple channels at the same time, such as to receive work from their boss or be told that it is time to stop. The `select` statement lets a goroutine wait on multiple channels and respond to the first channel that is ready.

Consider the old telephone, such as the one in Figure 11.7. The telephone operator waits for incoming calls into the switchboard. When a call comes in, the operator answers the call and redirects the call to the appropriate destination. The operator then goes back to waiting for the next incoming call and so on.

Figure 11.7   A telephone switchboard (Photo courtesy of Everett Collection/Shutterstock)

Using `select` **Statements**

The `select` statement lets a goroutine wait on multiple channels and respond to the first channel that is ready. The `select` statement blocks until one of the channels is ready. Once it is ready, the `select` statement executes the corresponding `case`, and the `select` statement exits. Because the `select` can be run only once, it is often wrapped inside of an infinite `for` loop to rerun the `select` statement after every `case` is executed.

Consider Listing 11.15. The `operator` function takes three different channels as arguments. The `select` statement listens to each channel and responds to the first channel that is ready.

Listing 11.15 An Example of a `select` Statement

```
func operator(line1 chan string, line2 chan string, quit chan struct{}) {

    // Use an infinite loop to keep listening for new messages after
    // handling a previous one.
    for {

        // select blocks until one of the cases can be executed.
        select {
        case msg := <-line1:
            // listen for incoming messages on line1 and assign to msg variable
            fmt.Printf("Line 1: %s\n", msg)
        case msg := <-line2:
            // listen for incoming messages on line2 and assign to msg variable
            fmt.Printf("Line 2: %s\n", msg)
        case <-quit:
            // listen for the quit channel to be closed and exit the function
            fmt.Println("Quit")
            return
        }

    }
}
```

Channels Are Not Message Queues

Only one goroutine receives a message sent down a channel. If multiple goroutines are listening to a channel, only one receives that message.

It is also possible, and likely, that one goroutine receives more messages than another goroutine. For example, in Listing 11.16, the goroutine with the ID of 0 is receiving half of the total messages being sent.

Listing 11.16 Messages Are Pulled off a Channel by the First Goroutine to Read from It

```go
func main() {
    const N = 5

    // make a new channel
    // of type int
    ch := make(chan int)

    for i := 0; i < N; i++ {

        // create a goroutine to listen to the channel
        go func(i int) {

            // listen for new messages
            for m := range ch {
                fmt.Printf("routine %d received %d\n", i, m)
            }

        }(i)
    }

    // print messages to the channel
    for i := 0; i < N*2; i++ {
        ch <- i
    }

    // close the channel
    // this will break the 'range'
    // statement in the goroutine
    close(ch)

    // wait for the goroutines to finish
    time.Sleep(50 * time.Millisecond)
}
```

```
$ go run .

routine 0 received 0
routine 0 received 5
routine 4 received 1
routine 0 received 6
routine 0 received 8
routine 3 received 4
routine 4 received 7
routine 2 received 3
routine 1 received 2
routine 0 received 9
```

Go Version: go1.19

Unidirectional Channels

By default, channels are bidirectional, meaning you can both send and receive data from the channel.

A common use for unidirectional channels is when you are passing a channel as an argument or receiving a channel as a return value. This allows for control of the channel for the function/method and prevents outside callers from polluting the channel.

The standard library does this in the time package with methods like time.Ticker, Listing 11.17.

Listing 11.17   The time.Ticker Function

```
$ go doc time.Ticker

package time // import "time"

type Ticker struct {
    C <-chan Time // The channel on which the ticks are delivered.
    // Has unexported fields.
}
    A Ticker holds a channel that delivers "ticks" of a clock at intervals.

func NewTicker(d Duration) *Ticker
func (t *Ticker) Reset(d Duration)
func (t *Ticker) Stop()
```

Go Version: go1.19

Understanding Unidirectional Channels

Consider Listing 11.18. The `Newspaper` contains a bidirectional channel, `headlines chan string`, as a field. It also exposes two methods: `TopHeadlines` and `ReportStory`.

Listing 11.18   The Newspaper Type

```
type Newspaper struct {
    headlines chan string
    quit      chan struct{}
}


// TopHeadlines returns a read-only channel of strings
// that represent the top headlines of the newspaper.
// This channel is consumed by newspaper readers.
func (n Newspaper) TopHeadlines() <-chan string {
    return n.headlines
}



// ReportStory returns a write-only channel of strings
// that a reporter can use to report a story.
func (n Newspaper) ReportStory() chan<- string {
    return n.headlines
}
```

The `TopHeadlines` method returns a read-only version of the `headlines` channel that can be consumed by newspaper readers.

The `ReportStory` method returns a write-only version of the `headlines` channel that can be used by newspaper reporters to report their stories to the newspaper.

In both cases, Go casts the bidirectional channel, `headlines`, to the appropriate unidirectional channel returned by the method.

Closing Channels

As we have previously mentioned, when a message is sent to a channel, only one receiver can pull that message off the channel. Channels do not provide a "fan-out" type of functionality where many receivers can pull the same message off of a channel.

The exception to this rule is when a channel is closed. When a channel is closed, *all* receivers are notified that the channel is closed. This can be exploited to signal to many listeners (goroutines) that it is time to stop what they're doing.

Consider Listing 11.19. The `listener` function takes a `<-chan struct{}` as the last argument, `quit`. The function listens for a signal on the `quit` channel, which is a blocking operation. When the `quit` channel is closed elsewhere, the `listener` function exits.

Listing 11.19 The Listener Function

```go
func listener(i int, quit <-chan struct{}) {
    fmt.Printf("listener %d is waiting\n", i)

    // this will block until the channel is closed
    <-quit

    fmt.Printf("listener %d is exiting\n", i)
}
```

In Listing 11.20, we create a chan struct{} named quit. Then we create a handful of goroutines for the listener function passing it the loop index and the quit channel.

Listing 11.20 The main Function

```go
func main() {
    // create a channel to signal listeners to exit
    quit := make(chan struct{})

    // create 5 listeners
    for i := 0; i < 5; i++ {
        // launch listener in a goroutine
        go listener(i, quit)
    }

    // allow the listeners to start
    time.Sleep(10 * time.Millisecond)

    fmt.Println("closing the quit channel")

    // close the channel to signal listeners to exit
    close(quit)

    // allow the listeners to exit
    time.Sleep(50 * time.Millisecond)
}
```

```
$ go run .

listener 0 is waiting
listener 2 is waiting
listener 3 is waiting
listener 1 is waiting
listener 4 is waiting
```

(continued)

```
closing the quit channel
listener 0 is exiting
listener 4 is exiting
listener 1 is exiting
listener 3 is exiting
listener 2 is exiting
```

```
Go Version: go1.19
```

We sleep shortly to allow the `listener` goroutines to start and listen to the `quit` channel. Then we close the `quit` channel: `close(quit)`. Finally, we sleep again to allow the `listener` goroutines to exit.

Detecting Closed Channels on Read

When listening to a channel, it can often be useful to know if the channel is closed or not. Like we've seen with type assertions and map key assertions, we can use the magic ok value to check whether a channel is closed.

In Listing 11.21, we ask for not just the incoming message from the channel but also the second boolean argument ok, which is `true` if the channel is open and `false` if it is closed.

Listing 11.21   Reading from a Closed Channel

```go
func listener(ch <-chan int) {

    // infinite loop to keep listening
    // for messages on the channel
    for {

        // store the message from the channel to variable i
        // capture if the channel is closed or not to variable ok
        i, ok := <-ch

        // if the channel is closed, return from the function
        if !ok {
            fmt.Println("closed channel")
            return
        }

        // print the message
        fmt.Printf("read %d from channel\n", i)
    }

}
```

```
$ go run .

read 0 from channel
read 1 from channel
read 2 from channel
read 3 from channel
read 4 from channel
closed channel
```
```
Go Version: go1.19
```

Zero Value on Closed Read

When reading from a channel that has been closed, we get the zero value of the channel's type returned, Listing 11.22. This is similar to when we ask for a map key that doesn't exist, and we get back the zero value of the map's value type.

Listing 11.22   Returning a Zero Value When Reading a Closed Channel

```go
func main() {
    // make a channel of type User
    ch := make(chan User)

    // launch a goroutine to send a User down the channel
    go func() {

        // send a User down the channel
        ch <- User{ID: 1, Name: "Amy"}
    }()

    // read the User from the channel
    user := <-ch
    fmt.Printf("read successful: %+v\n", user)

    // close the channel
    close(ch)

    // try to read from the channel again
    user = <-ch
    fmt.Println("attempted read of closed channel")
    fmt.Printf("received zero value %s\n", user)

}
```

(continued)

```
$ go run .

read successful: <User: id:"1" name:"Amy">
attempted read of closed channel
received zero value <User: id:"0" name:"">
```

```
Go Version: go1.19
```

In Listing 11.23, by checking whether the channel is closed, we can avoid the zero value and take appropriate action.

Listing 11.23   No Zero Value Returned When Reading a Closed Channel

```go
func main() {

    // make a channel of type User
    ch := make(chan User)

    // launch a goroutine to send a User down the channel
    go func() {

        // send a User down the channel
        ch <- User{ID: 1, Name: "Amy"}
    }()

    // read the User from the channel
    user := <-ch
    fmt.Printf("read successful: %+v\n", user)

    // close the channel
    close(ch)

    // try to read from the channel again
    user, ok := <-ch

    // check if the channel is closed
    if !ok {
        fmt.Println("attempted read of closed channel")
        fmt.Printf("received zero value %s\n", user)
        return
    }
```

```
    // the channel is still open, so print the user.
    fmt.Printf("read successful: %+v\n", user)
}
```

```
$ go run .

read successful: <User: id:"1" name:"Amy">
attempted read of closed channel
received zero value <User: id:"0" name:"">
```

Go Version: go1.19

Closing an Already-Closed Channel

Care must be taken when closing a channel. If the channel has already been closed, a panic is raised, and the application crashes, as in Listing 11.24.

Listing 11.24 Panicking When Closing an Already-Closed Channel

```
func main() {

    // make a new channel
    ch := make(chan struct{})

    // close the channel
    close(ch)

    // try to close the channel again
    // this will panic
    close(ch)

}
```

```
$ go run .

panic: close of closed channel

goroutine 1 [running]:
main.main()
        ./main.go:14 +0x3c
exit status 2
```

Go Version: go1.19

Later in Chapter 13, we discuss different synchronization primitives that can be used to help prevent this sort of situation.

Writing to a Closed Channel

If you attempt to write to a closed channel, as in Listing 11.25, a panic is raised, and the application crashes. Unfortunately, there is no way to check whether the channel is closed before writing. With proper synchronization, good architecture, and solid tests, you can prevent this situation.

Listing 11.25   Panicking When Writing to a Closed Channel

```go
func main() {

    // make a new channel
    ch := make(chan int)

    // close the channel
    close(ch)

    // try to write to the closed channel
    // this will panic
    ch <- 1

}
```

```
$ go run .

panic: send on closed channel

goroutine 1 [running]:
main.main()
        ./main.go:14 +0x44
exit status 2

Go Version: go1.19
```

Buffered Channels

By default, channels are unbuffered. Someone trying to send a message down a channel blocks until someone else is ready to receive the message. A buffered channel, however, is a channel that can hold N messages before writing to the channel blocks.

Consider a phone call that results in a voicemail, as in Figure 11.8. It's a buffered operation. The caller isn't blocked waiting for the recipient to pick up the phone. The caller can leave a voicemail message, and the recipient can retrieve the message later. The size of the buffer is dependent on the number of messages that can be held in memory.

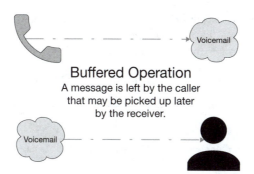

Buffered Operation
A message is left by the caller
that may be picked up later
by the receiver.

Figure 11.8   Leaving a voicemail is a buffered operation.

Basic Buffered Channel Example

With slices, you have seen that you can use the make function to create a slice of a particular length. make([]int, 10) creates a slice of 10 integers.

To create a buffered channel, you use the make function with a second argument, just as with slices. In Listing 11.26, we are creating a buffered channel of strings: make(chan string, 2).

Listing 11.26   A Buffered Channel Example

```go
func main() {

    // adding a second argument to the make function creates a
    // buffered channel
    messages := make(chan string, 2)

    // the program is no longer blocked on writing to a channel,
    // as it has capacity to write 2 messages to the channel
    // before blocking.
    messages <- "hello!"
    messages <- "hello again!"

    // reads are no longer blocked as there is already something to read from
    fmt.Println(<-messages)
    fmt.Println(<-messages)
}
```

```
$ go run .

hello!
hello again!
```

Go Version: go1.19

If we were to try to write a third message into the channel before it has had a chance to be read, the program would block. In the case of Listing 11.26, because it is impossible for someone to read the message, the application crashes with a deadlock, as in Listing 11.27.

Listing 11.27   A Deadlock Caused by Trying to Write to a Channel When No One Can Read from It

```go
func main() {

    // adding a second argument to the make function creates a
    // buffered channel
    messages := make(chan string, 2)

    // the program is no longer blocked on writing to a channel,
    // as it has capacity to write 2 messages to the channel
    // before blocking.
    messages <- "hello!"
    messages <- "hello again!"

    // this line will block until someone is ready to read from the channel
    // this application will deadlock and crash here.
    messages <- "hello once more"

    // reads are no longer blocked as there is already something to read from
    fmt.Println(<-messages)
    fmt.Println(<-messages)
}
```

```
$ go run .

fatal error: all goroutines are asleep - deadlock!

goroutine 1 [chan send]:
main.main()
        ./main.go:19 +0x5c
exit status 2
```

```
Go Version: go1.19
```

Buffered Channel and Delivery

Use buffered channels cautiously. They do not guarantee delivery of the message. It is your responsibility to ensure a channel is drained before exiting a routine.

Consider Listing 11.28. The goroutine is able to write two messages into the queue before blocking. The `main` function blocks and waits for the first message in the channel and then exits. The second message is never read. In fact, the goroutine has had the opportunity to write one more message into the channel before the program exits.

Listing 11.28   A Failure to Drain a Buffered Channel

```go
func main() {

    // make a buffered channel of type strings
    // with a buffer size of 2
    messages := make(chan string, 2)

    // launch a goroutine to send messages
    // to the channel
    go func() {

        // try to send 10 messages down the channel
        for i := 0; i < 10; i++ {
            msg := fmt.Sprintf("message %d", i+1)

            // send the message down the channel
            // if the channel is full, this will block
            // if not, the message will be buffered
            // in the channel
            messages <- msg

            // log the message was sent down the channel
            fmt.Printf("sent: %s\n", msg)
        }

    }()

    // listen for the first message in the channel
    m := <-messages

    // log the message received
    fmt.Printf("received: %s\n", m)

    // exit the program
}
```

(continued)

```
$ go run .

sent: message 1
sent: message 2
sent: message 3
received: message 1
```

```
Go Version: go1.19
```

Reading from Closed Buffered Channels

If a buffered channel is closed but still has messages in it, those messages can still be read from the channel until it is empty, as in Listing 11.29. You can't, however, continue to write to the closed channel.

Listing 11.29   Reading from a Closed Buffered Channel

```go
func main() {
    // make a buffered channel of ints
    // that can hold 5 values before blocking
    ch := make(chan int, 5)

    // write messages to the channel
    for i := 0; i < 5; i++ {
        ch <- i
    }

    // close the channel
    close(ch)

    // we can continue to read messages
    // from the closed channel until it is empty.
    // when it is empty the for loop will exit.
    for i := range ch {
        fmt.Println(i)
    }

    // trying to write to the closed channel
    // will cause a panic and the program will crash.
    ch <- 42
}
```

```
$ go run .

0
1
2
3
4

panic: send on closed channel

goroutine 1 [running]:
main.main()
        ./main.go:30 +0xd0
exit status 2
```

Go Version: go1.19

Capturing System Signals with Channels

All programs should attempt a graceful shutdown. This means that instead of crashing or exiting an application before resources are released, the application should instead wait for the resources to be released. The following list covers the rules for graceful shutdown:

- Detecting that the program was requested to shut down

- Shutting down all internal processes, including long-running goroutines

- Having a reasonable timeout in the event that internal processes are taking too long to shut down or are deadlocked

- Responding to an actual user request for immediate hard shutdown

- Recording the result of the shutdown (success, timeout, user intervention)

The `os/signals` Package

Using channels and the `os/signal`[7] package, you can capture system signals and respond accordingly. The `signal.Notify`[8] function in Listing 11.30 allows you to register a channel to receive notifications of `os.Signal`,[9] Listing 11.31.

---

7. https://pkg.go.dev/os/signal
8. https://pkg.go.dev/os/signal#Notify
9. https://pkg.go.dev/os#Signal

Listing 11.30   The `signal.Notify` Function

```
$ go doc os/signal.Notify

package signal // import "os/signal"

func Notify(c chan<- os.Signal, sig ...os.Signal)
    Notify causes package signal to relay incoming signals to c. If no
    ↪signals are provided, all incoming signals will be relayed to c.
    ↪Otherwise, just the provided signals will.

    Package signal will not block sending to c: the caller must ensure that
    ↪c has sufficient buffer space to keep up with the expected signal rate.
    ↪For a channel used for notification of just one signal value, a buffer
    ↪of size 1 is sufficient.

    It is allowed to call Notify multiple times with the same channel: each
    ↪call expands the set of signals sent to that channel. The only way to
    ↪remove signals from the set is to call Stop.

    It is allowed to call Notify multiple times with different channels
    ↪and the same signals: each channel receives copies of incoming signals
    ↪independently.
```

Go Version: go1.19

Listing 11.31   The `os.Signal` Type

```
$ go doc os.Signal

package os // import "os"

type Signal interface {
        String() string
        Signal() // to distinguish from other Stringers
}
    A Signal represents an operating system signal. The usual underlying
    ↪implementation is operating system-dependent: on Unix it is
    ↪syscall.Signal.

var Interrupt Signal = syscall.SIGINT ...
```

Go Version: go1.19

In Listing 11.32, we register a channel, ch, to listen for os.Interrupt[10] with signal.Notify.

Listing 11.32 Listening for os.Interrupt

```go
func main() {

    // set up channel on which to send signal notifications.
    // we must use a buffered channel or risk missing the signal
    // if we're not ready to receive when the signal is sent.
    ch := make(chan os.Signal, 1)

    // wire up the channel to an 'os.Signal'
    // this tells the signal package to send
    // the specified signals to our channel
    // this is not a blocking operation
    signal.Notify(ch, os.Interrupt)

    fmt.Println("awaiting signal...")

    // block until a signal is received.
    s := <-ch

    fmt.Println("Got signal:", s)

    // perform final shutdown operations
    // then exit the program
}
```

Implementing Graceful Shutdown

Consider Listing 11.33. It creates a new Monitor and starts the monitor in a goroutine, giving it a quit channel to listen for shutdown. The application runs for a bit and then closes the quit channel.

Listing 11.33 An Application without Graceful Shutdown

```go
func main() {
    // create a new quit channel
    quit := make(chan struct{})

    // create a new monitor
    mon := Monitor{}
```

(continued)

---

10. https://pkg.go.dev/os#Interrupt

```go
// launch the monitor in a goroutine
go mon.Start(quit)

// sleep for a while to let the monitor run
time.Sleep(50 * time.Millisecond)

// close the quit channel to stop the monitor
// and exit the program
close(quit)
}
```

In Listing 11.34, the Monitor listens to both the quit channel and a ticker channel that sends the time down the channel at the set interval. If a tick is received, a message is printed, and the for loop and select statement go back to listen to the two channels. If the quit channel is closed, the function returns.

Listing 11.34   Listening to Multiple Channels with a Select Statement

```go
type Monitor struct{}

func (m Monitor) Start(quit chan struct{}) {

    // create a new ticker channel to listen to
    tick := time.NewTicker(10 * time.Millisecond)
    defer tick.Stop()

    // use an infinite loop to continue to listen
    // to new messages after the select statement
    // has been executed
    for {

        select {
        case <-quit: // shut down if the quit channel is closed
            fmt.Println("shutting down monitor")
            return
        case <-tick.C: // listen to the ticker channel
            fmt.Println("monitor check")
        }

    }

}
```

If we were to interrupt the program in Listing 11.33, then in Listing 11.35, you would see that the Monitor was never shut down properly.

Listing 11.35 Output from Interrupting Listing 11.34

```
monitor check
monitor check
monitor check
monitor check
monitor check
monitor check
^Csignal: interrupt
```

Listening for System Signals

The first step in implementing graceful shutdown is to listen for system signals. In Listing 11.36, update the main function to listen for the Interrupt signal on a new channel, sig. Finally, instead of the application sleeping for a while, we can listen for the Interrupt signal on the sig channel and respond accordingly.

Listing 11.36 Listening for os.Interrupt

```go
func main() {

    // create a new channel to listen to
    // system signals
    sig := make(chan os.Signal, 1)

    // register the channel to be notified
    // on os.Interrupt signals
    signal.Notify(sig, os.Interrupt)

    // create a new quit channel
    quit := make(chan struct{})

    // create a new monitor
    mon := Monitor{}

    // launch the monitor in a goroutine
    go mon.Start(quit)

    // block until the os.Interrupt signal is
    // is received (ctrl-c)
    <-sig
```

(continued)

```
    // close the quit channel to stop the monitor
    // and exit the program
    close(quit)
}
```

From the output in Listing 11.37, you can see that the Monitor was still not properly shut down.

Listing 11.37   Output from Interrupting Listing 11.36

```
monitor check
monitor check
monitor check
monitor check
^Cmonitor check
```

The reason that the monitor was not shut down properly is because we didn't give the Monitor goroutine enough time to shut down gracefully.

Listening for Shutdown Confirmation

To ensure that the Monitor was shut down properly, the Monitor has to provide the main function with a way of receiving confirmation that the Monitor was shut down.

You can update the Monitor to have an internal done chan struct{} channel, as in Listing 11.38. The Monitor also exposes a Done method that returns a read-only channel that closes when the Monitor has properly shut down.

Listing 11.38   The Monitor with the done Channel

```
type Monitor struct {
    done chan struct{}
}

func (m Monitor) Done() <-chan struct{} {
    return m.done
}
```

In the main function in Listing 11.39, after we close the quit channel, close(quit), we can block and wait for the <-mon.Done() channel to be closed. This happens when the Monitor has properly shut down.

Listing 11.39 Listening for Shutdown Confirmation

```go
func main() {

    // create a new channel to listen to
    // system signals
    sig := make(chan os.Signal, 1)

    // register the channel to be notified
    // on os.Interrupt signals
    signal.Notify(sig, os.Interrupt)

    // create a new quit channel
    quit := make(chan struct{})

    // create a new monitor
    mon := Monitor{
        done: make(chan struct{}),
    }

    // launch the monitor in a goroutine
    go mon.Start(quit)

    // block until the os.Interrupt signal is
    // is received (ctrl-c)
    <-sig

    // close the quit channel to stop the monitor
    // and exit the program
    close(quit)

    // wait for the monitor to shut down
    <-mon.Done()

}
```

Now, when you look at the output in Listing 11.40, you can see that the Monitor was shut down properly, and the application shut down gracefully.

Listing 11.40 Output from Interrupting Listing 11.39

```
monitor check
monitor check
```

(continued)

```
monitor check
monitor check
^Cshutting down monitor
```

Timing Out a Nonresponsive Shutdown

Occasionally, the resources you are waiting on to shut down properly fail to respond and cause the application to hang indefinitely. The user is then required to manually force the application to stop. To prevent this from happening, you can use a timeout.

In Listing 11.41, we update the `main` function to no longer wait for the `<-mon.Done()` channel to be closed before exiting. Now, the `main` uses a `select` statement to listen for the `<-mon.Done()` channel and a `<-time.After(timeout)` channel. If the `<-mon.Done()` channel is closed before the timeout, the application gracefully shuts down.

Listing 11.41   Listening for Shutdown Confirmation

```go
func main() {

    // create a new channel to listen to
    // system signals
    sig := make(chan os.Signal, 1)

    // register the channel to be notified
    // on os.Interrupt signals
    signal.Notify(sig, os.Interrupt)

    // create a new quit channel
    quit := make(chan struct{})

    // create a new monitor
    mon := Monitor{
        done: make(chan struct{}),
    }

    // launch the monitor in a goroutine
    go mon.Start(quit)

    // block until the os.Interrupt signal is
    // is received (ctrl-c)
    <-sig

    // close the quit channel to stop the monitor
    // and exit the program
    close(quit)
```

```
    select {
    case <-mon.Done(): // wait for the monitor to shut down
        // success shutdown
        os.Exit(0)
    case <-time.After(500 * time.Millisecond): // timeout after 500ms
        fmt.Println("timed out while trying to shut down the monitor")

        // non-successful shutdown
        os.Exit(1)
    }
}
```

As you can see from the output in Listing 11.42, if the `Monitor` does not shut down within the specified timeout period, the application exits with an error.

Listing 11.42 Output from Interrupting Listing 11.41

```
monitor check
monitor check
monitor check
monitor check
monitor check
^Cshutting down monitor
timed out while trying to shut down the monitor
exit status 1
```

Summary

In this chapter, we started to explore concurrency in Go with channels. We explained the differences between parallelism and concurrency and how to use goroutines and channels to achieve concurrency. We discussed channels and how they can be used to communicate between, and control, goroutines. We pointed out the differences between buffered and unbuffered channels and when each one blocks and unblocks. Finally, we showed you how you can use channels to listen for system signals so you can gracefully shut down your applications.

## 12

Context

The context[1] package was introduced in Go 1.7 to provide a cleaner way than using channels to manage cancellation and timeouts across goroutines.

While the scope and API footprint of the package is pretty small, it was a welcome addition to the language when introduced.

The context package in Listing 12.1 defines the context.Context[2] type, which carries deadlines, cancellation signals, and other request-scoped values across API boundaries and between processes.

Listing 12.1 The context Package

```
$ go doc -short context

var Canceled = errors.New("context canceled")
var DeadlineExceeded error = deadlineExceededError{}
func WithCancel(parent Context) (ctx Context, cancel CancelFunc)
func WithDeadline(parent Context, d time.Time) (Context, CancelFunc)
func WithTimeout(parent Context, timeout time.Duration) (Context, CancelFunc)
type CancelFunc func()
type Context interface{ ... }
    func Background() Context
    func TODO() Context
    func WithValue(parent Context, key, val any) Context
```

Go Version: go1.19

Context is, mostly, used for controlling concurrent subsystems in your application. In this chapter, we cover the different kinds of behavior with contexts, including canceling, timeouts, and values. We also explain how you can clean up a lot of code involving channels by using contexts.

---

1. https://pkg.go.dev/context
2. https://pkg.go.dev/context#Context

The Context Interface

The context.Context interface, Listing 12.2, consists of four methods. These methods provide the ability to listen for cancellation and timeout events and retrieve values from the context hierarchy. They also provide a way to check what error, if any, caused the context to be canceled.

Listing 12.2   The context.Context Interface

```
type Context interface {
  Deadline() (deadline time.Time, ok bool)
  Done() <-chan struct{}
  Err() error
  Value(key interface{}) interface{}
}
```

In Listing 12.2, you can see that the context.Context interface implements several of the channel patterns we talk about in Chapter 11, such as having a Done channel that can be listened to for cancellation.

We cover each of these methods in more detail later. For now, let's briefly look at each one of them.

Context#Deadline

You can use the context.Context.Deadline[3] method, Listing 12.3, to check whether a context has a cancellation deadline set and, if so, what that deadline is.

Listing 12.3   The context.Context.Deadline Method

```
$ go doc context.Context.Deadline

package context // import "context"

type Context interface { .
    // Deadline returns the time when work done on behalf of this context
    // should be canceled. Deadline returns ok==false when no deadline is
    // set. Successive calls to Deadline return the same results.
    Deadline() (deadline time.Time, ok bool)
}

Go Version: go1.19
```

---

3. https://pkg.go.dev/context#Context.Deadline

Context#Done

You can use the context.Context.Done[4] method, Listing 12.4, to listen for cancellation events. This is similar to how you can listen for a channel being closed, but it is more flexible.

Listing 12.4 The context.Context.Done Method

```
$ go doc context.Context.Done

package context // import "context"

type Context interface {

    // Done returns a channel that's closed when work done on behalf of this
    // context should be canceled. Done may return nil if this context can
    // never be canceled. Successive calls to Done return the same value.
    // The close of the Done channel may happen asynchronously,
    // after the cancel function returns.
    //
    // WithCancel arranges for Done to be closed when cancel is called;
    // WithDeadline arranges for Done to be closed when the deadline
    // expires; WithTimeout arranges for Done to be closed when the timeout
    // elapses.
    //
    // Done is provided for use in select statements:
    //
    //   // Stream generates values with DoSomething and sends them to out
    //   // until DoSomething returns an error or ctx.Done is closed.
    //   func Stream(ctx context.Context, out chan<- Value) error {
    //       for {
    //               v, err := DoSomething(ctx)
    //               if err != nil {
    //                       return err
    //               }
    //               select {
    //               case <-ctx.Done():
    //                       return ctx.Err()
    //               case out <- v:
    //               }
    //       }
    //   }
    //
```

(continued)

4. https://pkg.go.dev/context#Context.Done

```
    // See https://blog.golang.org/pipelines for more examples of how to use
    // a Done channel for cancellation.
    Done() <-chan struct{}
}
```

Go Version: go1.19

Context#Err

You can use the context.Context.Err[5] method, Listing 12.5, to check whether a context has been canceled.

Listing 12.5 The context.Context.Err Method

```
$ go doc context.Context.Err

package context // import "context"

type Context interface {

    // If Done is not yet closed, Err returns nil.
    // If Done is closed, Err returns a non-nil error explaining why:
    // Canceled if the context was canceled
    // or DeadlineExceeded if the context's deadline passed.
    // After Err returns a non-nil error, successive calls to Err return the
    ↪same error.
    Err() error

}
```

Go Version: go1.19

Context#Value

You can use the context.Context.Value[6] method, Listing 12.6, to retrieve values from the context hierarchy.

Listing 12.6 The context.Context.Value Method

```
$ go doc context.Context.Value

package context // import "context"

type Context interface {
```

5. https://pkg.go.dev/context#Context.Err
6. https://pkg.go.dev/context#Context.Value

```
// Value returns the value associated with this context for key, or nil
// if no value is associated with key. Successive calls to Value with
// the same key returns the same result.
//
// Use context values only for request-scoped data that transits
// processes and API boundaries, not for passing optional parameters to
// functions.
//
// A key identifies a specific value in a Context. Functions that wish
// to store values in Context typically allocate a key in a global
// variable then use that key as the argument to context.WithValue and
// Context.Value. A key can be any type that supports equality;
// packages should define keys as an unexported type to avoid
// collisions.
//
// Packages that define a Context key should provide type-safe accessors
// for the values stored using that key:
//
//        // Package user defines a User type that's stored in Contexts.
//        package user
//
//        import "context"
//
//        // User is the type of value stored in the Contexts.
//        type User struct {...}
//
//        // key is an unexported type for keys defined in this package.
//        // This prevents collisions with keys defined in other packages.
//        type key int
//
//        // userKey is the key for user.User values in Contexts. It is
//        // unexported; clients use user.NewContext and user.FromContext
//        // instead of using this key directly.
//        var userKey key
//
//        // NewContext returns a new Context that carries value u.
//        func NewContext(ctx context.Context, u *User) context.Context {
//                return context.WithValue(ctx, userKey, u)
//        }
//
//        // FromContext returns the User value stored in ctx, if any.
//        func FromContext(ctx context.Context) (*User, bool) {
//                u, ok := ctx.Value(userKey).(*User)
//                return u, ok
```

(continued)

```
    //      }
    Value(key any) any
}
```

Go Version: go1.19

Helper Functions

The context package, Listing 12.7, provides a number of useful helper functions for wrapping a context.Context, making the need for custom implementations of the context.Context interface less common.

Listing 12.7   The context Package

```
$ go doc -short context ,

var Canceled = errors.New("context canceled")
var DeadlineExceeded error = deadlineExceededError{}
func WithCancel(parent Context) (ctx Context, cancel CancelFunc)
func WithDeadline(parent Context, d time.Time) (Context, CancelFunc)
func WithTimeout(parent Context, timeout time.Duration) (Context, CancelFunc)
type CancelFunc func()
type Context interface{ ... }
    func Background() Context
    func TODO() Context
    func WithValue(parent Context, key, val any) Context
```

Go Version: go1.19

The Background Context

Although often you might be given a context.Context, you might also be the one to start a context.Context. The most common way to provide a quick and easy way to start a context.Context is to use the context.Background[7] function, Listing 12.8.

Listing 12.8   The context.Background Function

```
$ go doc context.Background

package context // import "context"
```

---

7. https://pkg.go.dev/context#Background

```
func Background() Context
    Background returns a non-nil, empty Context. It is never canceled, has no
    ➥values, and has no deadline. It is typically used by the main function,
    ➥initialization, and tests, and as the top-level Context for incoming
    ➥requests.
```

Go Version: go1.19

In Listing 12.9, we print the context.Context returned by context.Background. As you can see from the output, the context is empty.

Listing 12.9   The context.Background Function

```
func main() {
    ctx := context.Background()

    // print the current value
    // of the context
    fmt.Printf("%v\n", ctx)

    // print Go-syntax representation of the value
    fmt.Printf("\t%#v\n", ctx)
}
```

```
$ go run main.go

context.Background
        (*context.emptyCtx)(0x14000122000)
```

Go Version: go1.19

Default Implementations

Although the context.Background interface is empty, it does provide default implementations of the context.Context interface, Listing 12.10. Because of this, the context.Background context is almost always used as the base of a new context.Context hierarchy.

Listing 12.10   The context.Background Function Provides Default Implementation of the context.Context Interface

```
func main() {
    ctx := context.Background()
```

(continued)

```
    // print the current value
    // of the context
    fmt.Printf("%v\n", ctx)

    // print Go-syntax representation of the value
    fmt.Printf("\t%#v\n", ctx)

    // print the value of the Done channel
    // does not block because we are not
    // trying to read/write to the channel
    fmt.Printf("\tDone:\t%#v\n", ctx.Done())

    // print the value of the Err
    fmt.Printf("\tErr:\t%#v\n", ctx.Err())

    // print the value of "KEY"
    fmt.Printf("\tValue:\t%#v\n", ctx.Value("KEY"))

    // print the deadline time
    // and true/false if there is no deadline
    deadline, ok := ctx.Deadline()
    fmt.Printf("\tDeadline:\t%s (%t)\n", deadline, ok)
}
```

```
$ go run main.go

context.Background
        (*context.emptyCtx)(0x1400018e000)
        Done:    (<-chan struct {})(nil)
        Err:     <nil>
        Value:   <nil>
        Deadline:        0001-01-01 00:00:00 +0000 UTC (false)
```

```
Go Version: go1.19
```

Context Rules

According to the context documentation, the following rules must be adhered to when using the context package:

- Programs that use contexts should follow these rules to keep interfaces consistent across packages and enable static analysis tools to check context propagation.
- Do not store contexts inside a struct type; instead, pass a context explicitly to each function that needs it. The context should be the first parameter, typically named ctx.

- Do not pass a `nil` context, even if a function permits it. Pass `context.TODO` if you are unsure about which context to use.

- Use context values only for request-scoped data that transits processes and APIs, not for passing optional parameters to functions.

- The same context may be passed to functions running in different goroutines; contexts are safe for simultaneous use by multiple goroutines.

Context Nodal Hierarchy

As the `context` documentation states, a `context.Context` is not meant to be stored and held onto but should be passed at runtime.

Consider an HTTP request. An HTTP request is a *runtime* value that gets passed along through the application until eventually the response is returned. You would not want to store, or hold on to, the request for future use because it would be of no benefit once the response is returned.

Using `context.Context` in your code behaves like the HTTP request. You pass a `context.Context` through the application where it can be listened to for cancellation, or for other purposes, at runtime.

As a `context.Context` is passed through the application, a receiving method may wrap the context with its cancellation functionality or with `context.WithValue` to add a value, such as a request ID, before passing the `context.Context` along to any functions or methods that it may call.

The result is a nodal hierarchy of `context.Context` values that starts at the beginning of the request or the start of the application and spiders out throughout the application.

Understanding the Nodal Hierarchy

Consider Listing 12.11. We start with a `context.Background` context and pass it the A and B functions. Each function wraps the given `context.Context`, prints that new `context.Context` with a new one, and then either passes it along to the next function or returns.

Listing 12.11 Wrapping Context Creates Nodal Hierarchies

```
func main() {
    // create a background context
    bg := context.Background()

    // pass the background context to the A function
    A(bg)

    // pass the background context to the B function
    B(bg)
}
```

Wrapping with Context Values

To wrap the context.Context with a new one, we use context.WithValue. The context.WithValue function takes a context.Context and a key and value, and it returns a new context.Context with the given key and value that wraps the original context.Context. We discuss more about context.WithValue later in this chapter.

Following the Context Nodes

In Listing 12.12, we define the functions used in Listing 12.11. Each of these functions takes a context.Context as an argument. They then wrap the context.Context with a new one, print the new context.Context with a new one, and pass it along to the next function.

Listing 12.12   The Example Application

```
func A(ctx context.Context) {
    // wrap ctx with a new context
    // with the ID set to "A"
    A := context.WithValue(ctx, ID, "A")
    print("A", A)

    // pass the A context to the A1 function
    A1(A)
}

func A1(ctx context.Context) {
    A1 := context.WithValue(ctx, ID, "A1")
    print("A1", A1)
}

func B(ctx context.Context) {
    // wrap ctx with a new context
    // with the ID set to "B"
    B := context.WithValue(ctx, ID, "B")
    print("B", B)

    // pass the B context to the B1 function
    B1(B)
}

func B1(ctx context.Context) {
    // wrap ctx with a new context
    // with the ID set to "B1"
    B1 := context.WithValue(ctx, ID, "B1")
    print("B1", B1)
```

```
    // pass the B1 context to the B1a function
    B1a(B1)
}

func B1a(ctx context.Context) {
    // wrap ctx with a new context
    // with the ID set to "B1a"
    B1a := context.WithValue(ctx, ID, "B1a")
    print("B1a", B1a)
}
```

When you look at the output of the program, Listing 12.13, you can see that when we print out any given context.Context, we see that it is at the bottom of the node tree, and the context.Background context is at the top of the node tree hierarchy.

Listing 12.13   Printing the Node Tree

```
$ go run main.go

A.WithValue(key: ctx_id, value: A)
      --> Background

A1.WithValue(key: ctx_id, value: A1)
      --> WithValue(key: ctx_id, value: A)
              --> Background

B.WithValue(key: ctx_id, value: B)
      --> Background

B1.WithValue(key: ctx_id, value: B1)
      --> WithValue(key: ctx_id, value: B)
              --> Background

B1a.WithValue(key: ctx_id, value: B1a)
        --> WithValue(key: ctx_id, value: B1)
                --> WithValue(key: ctx_id, value: B)
                        --> Background

Go Version: go1.19
```

In Figure 12.1, you see that the B1a context.Context is a child of the B1 context.Context, the B1 context.Context is a child of the B context.Context, and the B context.Context is a child of the original background context.Context.

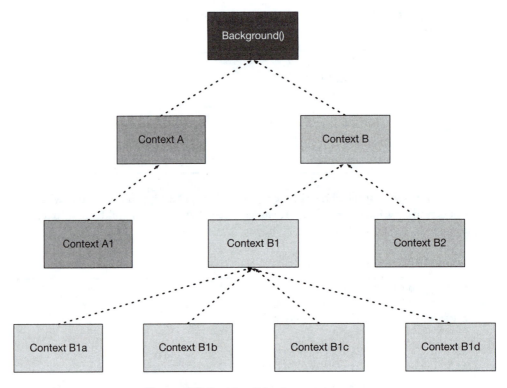

Figure 12.1   Visualizing the node tree

Context Values

As we have seen, one feature of the `context` package is that it allows you to pass request specific values to the next function in the chain.

This provide a lot of useful benefits, such as passing request or session specific values, such as the request id, user id of the requestor, etc. to the next function in the chain.

Using values, however, has its disadvantages, as we will see shortly.

Understanding Context Values

You can use the `context.WithValue`[8] function to wrap a given `context.Context` with a new `context.Context` that contains the given key/value pair (see Listing 12.14).

---

8. https://pkg.go.dev/context#WithValue

Listing 12.14 The context.WithValue Function

```
$ go doc context.WithValue

package context // import "context"

func WithValue(parent Context, key, val any) Context
    WithValue returns a copy of parent in which the value associated with
    ➥key is val.

    Use context Values only for request-scoped data that transits processes
    ➥and APIs, not for passing optional parameters to functions.

    The provided key must be comparable and should not be of type string or
    ➥any other built-in type to avoid collisions between packages using
    ➥context. Users of WithValue should define their own types for keys.
    ➥To avoid allocating when assigning to an interface{}, context keys often
    ➥have concrete type struct{}. Alternatively, exported context key
    ➥variables' static type should be a pointer or interface.
```

Go Version: go1.19

The context.WithValue function takes a context.Context as its first argument and a key and a value as its second and third arguments.

Both the key and value are any values. Although this may seem like you can use any type for the key, this is not the case. Like maps, keys must be comparable, so complex types like maps or functions are not allowed. In Listing 12.15, for example, when trying to use a map as a key for the context, the application crashes with a panic.

Listing 12.15 A Compilation Panic because of a Noncomparable Key Type in a Map

```
ctx := context.Background()

// strings shouldn't be used as keys
// because they can easily collide
// with other functions, libraries, etc.
// that set that same key.
// instead strings should wrapped in their
// own type.
ctx = context.WithValue(ctx, "key", "value")

// keys must be comparable.
// maps, and other complex types,
// are not comparable and can't be used
// used as keys.
ctx = context.WithValue(ctx, map[string]int{}, "another value")
```

(continued)

```
$ go run main.go

panic: key is not comparable

goroutine 1 [running]:
context.WithValue({0x1004968c0, 0x1400007c060}, {0x10048e980?, 0x1400007c090},
➥{0x10048d040?, 0x100496718})
        /usr/local/go/src/context/context.go:531 +0x140
main.main()
        ./main.go:24 +0x84
exit status 2
```

Go Version: go1.19

Key Resolution

When you ask for a key through the context.Context.Value function, the
context.Context first checks whether the key is present in the current context.Context.
If the key is present, the value is returned. If the key is not present, the context.Context
then checks whether the key is present in the parent context.Context. If the key is
present, the value is returned. If the key is not present, the context.Context then checks
whether the key is present in the context.Context's parent's parent, and so on.

Consider the example in Listing 12.16. We wrap a context.Context multiple times
with different key/values.

Listing 12.16   Nesting and Printing Different Contextual Nodes

```
func main() {

    // create a new background context
    ctx := context.Background()

    // wrap the context with a new context
    // that has the key "A" and the value "a",
    ctx = context.WithValue(ctx, CtxKey("A"), "a")

    // wrap the context with a new context
    // that has the key "B" and the value "b",
    ctx = context.WithValue(ctx, CtxKey("B"), "b")

    // wrap the context with a new context
    // that has the key "C" and the value "c",
    ctx = context.WithValue(ctx, CtxKey("C"), "c")
```

```
// print the final context
print("ctx", ctx)

// retrieve and print the value
// for the key "A"
a := ctx.Value(CtxKey("A"))
fmt.Println("A:", a)

// retrieve and print the value
// for the key "B"
b := ctx.Value(CtxKey("B"))
fmt.Println("B:", b)

// retrieve and print the value
// for the key "C"
c := ctx.Value(CtxKey("C"))
fmt.Println("C:", c)

}
```

From the output in Listing 12.17, you can see that the final context.Context has a parentage that includes all of the values added with context.WithValue. You can also see that we are able to find all of the keys, including the very first one that we set.

Listing 12.17   Output Demonstrating Context Nodal Ancestry

```
$ go run main.go

ctx.WithValue(key: C, value: c)
        --> WithValue(key: B, value: b)
              --> WithValue(key: A, value: a)
                      --> Background

A: a
B: b
C: c

Go Version: go1.19
```

Problems with String Keys

As is mentioned in the context documentation, shown in Listing 12.18, using string keys is not recommended. As you just saw when `context.Context.Value` tries to resolve a key, it finds the first, if any, `context.Context` that contains the key and returns that value.

Listing 12.18   Using Strings as Context Keys Is Not Recommended per the Documentation

```
$ go doc context.WithValue

package context // import "context"

func WithValue(parent Context, key, val any) Context
    WithValue returns a copy of parent in which the value associated with key
    ➥is val.

    Use context Values only for request-scoped data that transits processes
    ➥and APIs, not for passing optional parameters to functions.

    The provided key must be comparable and should not be of type string or
    ➥any other built-in type to avoid collisions between packages using
    ➥context. Users of WithValue should define their own types for keys.
    ➥To avoid allocating when assigning to an interface{}, context keys
    ➥often have concrete type struct{}. Alternatively, exported context
    ➥key variables' static type should be a pointer or interface.

Go Version: go1.19
```

When you use the `context.Context.Value` function, you get the last value that was set for the given key. Each time you use `context.WithValue` to wrap a `context.Context` with a new `context.Context`, the new `context.Context` essentially will have replaced the previous value for the given key. For example, in Figure 12.2, Context B is setting the key `request_id` with the value B-123. Context B1 also sets a value, B1-abc, using the `request_id` key. Now, any child nodes of Context B1, such as Context B1a, will have a different `request_id` from other direct descendants of Context B1.

Key Collisions

Consider the example in Listing 12.19. We wrap a `context.Context` multiple times, each time with a different value but the same key, `request_id`, which is of type `string`.

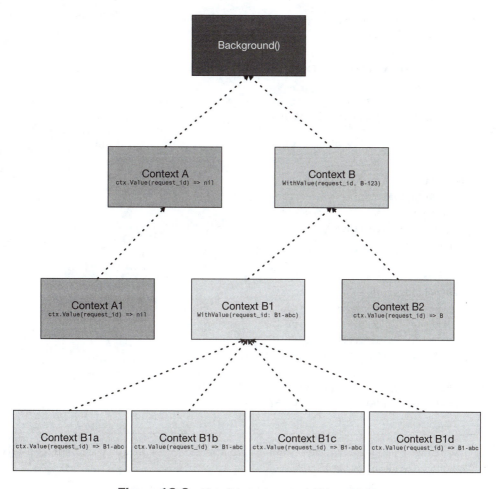

Figure 12.2 Visualizing context nodal hierarchies

Listing 12.19 Overwriting Context Values by Using Identical Keys

```go
func main() {
    // create a new background context
    ctx := context.Background()

    // call the A function
    // passing in the background context
    A(ctx)
}
```

(continued)

```go
func A(ctx context.Context) {
    // wrap the context with a request_id
    // to represent this specific A request
    ctx = context.WithValue(ctx, "request_id", "123")

    // call the B function
    // passing in the wrapped context
    B(ctx)
}

func B(ctx context.Context) {
    // wrap the context with a request_id
    // to represent this specific B request
    ctx = context.WithValue(ctx, "request_id", "456")
    Logger(ctx)
}

// Logger logs the webs request_id
// as well as the request_id from the B
func Logger(ctx context.Context) {
    a := ctx.Value("request_id")
    fmt.Println("A\t", "request_id:", a)

    b := ctx.Value("request_id")
    fmt.Println("B\t", "request_id:", b)
}
```

When we try to log the request_id for both A and B, we see that they are both set to the same value (as in Listing 12.20).

Listing 12.20   The Value Set in Function A Is Overridden by Function B

```
$ go run main.go

A          request_id: 456
B          request_id: 456
```

Go Version: go1.19

One way to solve this problem is to try to "namespace" your string keys, myapp.request_id. Although you may never get into a collision scenario, the possibility of someone else using the same key does exist.

Custom String Key Types

Because Go is a typed language, you can leverage the type system to solve the problem of key collisions. You can create a new type based on string that you can use as the key, as in Listing 12.21.

Listing 12.21 Using Different Types for Keys Can Prevent Collisions

```
// CtxKeyA is used to wrap keys
// associated with a A request
//      CtxKeyA("request_id")
//      CtxKeyA("user_id")
type CtxKeyA string
// CtxKeyB is used to wrap keys
// associated with a B request
//      CtxKeyB("request_id")
//      CtxKeyB("user_id")
type CtxKeyB string
```

```
func A(ctx context.Context) {
    // wrap the context with a request_id
    // to represent this specific A request
    key := CtxKeyA("request_id")
    ctx = context.WithValue(ctx, key, "123")

    // call B with the wrapped context
    B(ctx)
}
```

```
func B(ctx context.Context) {
    // wrap the context with a request_id
    // to represent this specific B request
    key := CtxKeyB("request_id")
    ctx = context.WithValue(ctx, key, "456")

    Logger(ctx)
}
```

```
// Logger logs the webs request_id
// as well as the request_id from the B
func Logger(ctx context.Context) {
    // retrieve the request_id from the A request
    aKey := CtxKeyA("request_id")
    aVal := ctx.Value(aKey)

    // print the request_id from the A request
    print("A", aKey, aVal)

    // retrieve the request_id from the B request
    bKey := CtxKeyB("request_id")
    bVal := ctx.Value(bKey)
```

(continued)

```
        // print the request_id from the B request
        print("B", bKey, bVal)
}
```

The Logger is now properly able to retrieve the two different request_id values because they are no longer of the same type (see Listing 12.22).

Listing 12.22   The Value Set in Function A Is No Longer Overridden by Function B

```
$ go run main.go

A: main.CtxKeyA(request_id): 123
B: main.CtxKeyB(request_id): 456


Go Version: go1.19
```

This code can be further cleaned up by using constants for the keys that our package, or application, uses. This allows for cleaner code and makes it easier to document the potential keys that may be in a context.Context. For example, in Listing 12.23, new constants, such as A_RequestID, are defined and exported by the package along with documentation for the constants' usage. These constants can now be safely used to set and retrieve context values.

Listing 12.23   Using Constants Can Make Working with Context Values Easier

```
const (
    // A_RequestID can be used to
    // retrieve the request_id for
    // the A request
    A_RequestID CtxKeyA = "request_id"
    //  A_SESSION_ID CtxKeyA = "session_id"
    //  A_SERVER_ID CtxKeyA = "server_id"
    //  other keys...

    // B_RequestID can be used to
    // retrieve the request_id for
    // the B request
    B_RequestID CtxKeyB = "request_id"
)
```

```
// Logger logs the webs request_id
// as well as the request_id from the B
func Logger(ctx context.Context) {
    // retrieve the request_id from the A request
    aKey := A_RequestID
    aVal := ctx.Value(aKey)
```

```
// print the request_id from the A request
print("A", aKey, aVal)
// retrieve the request_id from the B request
bKey := B_RequestID
bVal := ctx.Value(bKey)

// print the request_id from the B request
print("B", bKey, bVal)
}
```

Securing Context Keys and Values

If we export or make public the types and names of the context.Context keys our package or application uses, we run the risk of a malicious agent stealing or modifying our values. For example, in a web request, we might set a request_id at the beginning of the request, but a piece of middleware later in the chain might modify that value to something else. In Listing 12.24, the WithBar function is replacing the value set in the WithFoo function by using the exported foo.RequestID key.

Listing 12.24 Exporting Context Keys Can Lead to Malicious Use

```
type CtxKey string

const (
    RequestID CtxKey = "request_id"
)
```

```
func WithBar(ctx context.Context) context.Context {
    // wrap the context with a request_id
    // to represent this specific bar request
    ctx = context.WithValue(ctx, RequestID, "456")

    // maliciously replace the request_id
    // set by foo
    ctx = context.WithValue(ctx, foo.RequestID, "???")

    // return the wrapped context
    return ctx
}
```

```
func main() {
    // create a background context
    ctx := context.Background()
```

(continued)

```
    // wrap the context with foo
    ctx = foo.WithFoo(ctx)

    // wrap the context with bar
    ctx = bar.WithBar(ctx)

    // retrieve the foo.RequestID
    // value from the context
    id := ctx.Value(foo.RequestID)

    // print the value
    fmt.Println("foo.RequestID: ", id)
}
```

```
func WithFoo(ctx context.Context) context.Context {
    // wrap the context with a request_id
    // to represent this specific foo request
    ctx = context.WithValue(ctx, RequestID, "123")

    // return the wrapped context
    return ctx
}
```

```
$ go run main.go

foo.RequestID:  ???
```

```
Go Version: go1.19
```

Securing by Not Exporting

The best way to ensure that your key/value pairs aren't maliciously overwritten or accessed is by not exporting the types, and any constants, used for keys. In Listing 12.25, the constant requestID is not exported and can only be used within its defining package.

Listing 12.25   Unexported Context Keys with Custom Types Provide the Best Security

```
type ctxKey string

const (
    requestID ctxKey = "request_id"
)
```

Now you are in control of what values from the context you want to make public. For example, you can add a helper function to allow others to get access to the request_id value.

Because the return value from context.Context.Value is an empty interface, interface{}, you can use these helper functions to not just retrieve access to the value but also type assert the value to the type you want or return an error if it doesn't. In Listing 12.26, the RequestIDFrom function takes a given context.Context and tries to extract a value using the nonexported custom type context key. In addition to hiding details about the key, it also hides details of how the value is stored. In the future, if the value is no longer stored as a string but rather as a struct, this function prevents external API breakage.

Listing 12.26 Future-Proofing Implementation Details with a Helper Function

```
func RequestIDFrom(ctx context.Context) (string, error) {
    // get the request_id from the context
    s, ok := ctx.Value(requestID).(string)
    if !ok {
        return "", fmt.Errorf("request_id not found in context")
    }
    return s, nil
}
```

Our application can be updated to use the new helper function to print the request_id or exit if there was a problem getting the value (see Listing 12.27).

Listing 12.27 Using the RequestIDFrom Function to Properly Retrieve a Context Value

```
func main() {
    // create a background context
    ctx := context.Background()

    // wrap the context with foo
    ctx = foo.WithFoo(ctx)

    // wrap the context with bar
    ctx = bar.WithBar(ctx)

    // retrieve the foo.RequestID
    // value from the context
    id, err := foo.RequestIDFrom(ctx)
    if err != nil {
        log.Fatal(err)
    }
```

(continued)

```
    // print the value
    fmt.Println("foo.RequestID: ", id)
}
```

The malicious `bar` package can no longer set or retrieve the `request_id` value set
by the `foo` package (Listing 12.28). The `bar` package does not have the ability to create a
new type of value `foo.ctxKey` because the type is unexported and cannot be accessed
outside of the `foo` package.

Listing 12.28   The `WithBar` Function Can No Longer Maliciously Access Values Set
by `WithFoo`

```
func WithBar(ctx context.Context) context.Context {
    // wrap the context with a request_id
    // to represent this specific bar request
    ctx = context.WithValue(ctx, requestID, "456")

    // no longer able to set the foo request id
    // it does not have access to the foo.ctxKey type
    // as it is not exported, so bar cannot create
    // a new key of that type.
    // ctx = context.WithValue(ctx, foo.ctxKey("request_id"), "???")

    // return the wrapped context
    return ctx
}
```

As a result of securing our `context.Context` values, the application now correctly
retrieves the `request_id` value set by the `foo` package (see Listing 12.29).

Listing 12.29   The Request ID Set by `WithFoo` Is Now Safe-Guarded

```
$ go run main.go

foo.RequestID:   123

Go Version: go1.19
```

Cancellation Propagation with Contexts

Although having the ability to pass contextual information via a `context.Context` is
useful, the real benefit, and design of the `context` package, is that it can be used to
propagate cancellation events to those listening to the context. When a parent
`context.Context` is canceled, all its children are also canceled.

Creating a Cancelable Context

To cancel a `context.Context`, you must have a way of cancelling it. The `context.WithCancel` function, Listing 12.30, wraps a given `context.Context` with a `context.Context` that can be canceled.

Listing 12.30 The `context.WithCancel` Function

```
$ go doc context.WithCancel

package context // import "context"

func WithCancel(parent Context) (ctx Context, cancel CancelFunc)
    WithCancel returns a copy of parent with a new Done channel. The returned
    ➥context's Done channel is closed when the returned cancel function is
    ➥called or when the parent context's Done channel is closed, whichever
    ➥happens first.

    Canceling this context releases resources associated with it, so code
    ➥should call cancel as soon as the operations running in this Context
    ➥complete.
```

Go Version: go1.19

The `context.WithCancel`[9] function returns a second argument—that of a `context.CancelFunc`[10] function, which can be used to cancel the `context.Context`.

The Cancel Function

There a few things that need to be noted about the `context.CancelFunc` function, Listing 12.31. So let's examine each in more detail.

Listing 12.31 The `context.CancelFunc` Function

```
$ go doc context.CancelFunc

package context // import "context"

type CancelFunc func()
    A CancelFunc tells an operation to abandon its work. A CancelFunc does
    ➥not wait for the work to stop. A CancelFunc may be called by multiple
    ➥goroutines simultaneously. After the first call, subsequent calls to a
    ➥CancelFunc do nothing.
```

Go Version: go1.19

---

9. https://pkg.go.dev/context#WithCancel
10. https://pkg.go.dev/context#CancelFunc

Idempotent Behavior

> "After the first call, subsequent calls to a CancelFunc do nothing."
>
> —context.CancelFunc documentation

According to the context.CancelFunc documentation, the context.CancelFunc function is idempotent, Listing 12.32. That is, calling it multiple times has no effect beyond the first call.

Listing 12.32   The Idempotent Behavior of the context.CancelFunc Function

```
ctx, cancel := context.WithCancel(context.Background())
cancel() // cancels the context
cancel() // has no effect
cancel() // has no effect
```

Leaking Resources

> "Canceling this context releases resources associated with it, so code should call cancel as soon as the operations running in this Context complete."
>
> —context.WithCancel documentation

Often you will want to defer execution of the context.CancelFunc function, as in Listing 12.33, until the function or application exits. This ensures proper shutdown of the context.Context and prevents the context.Context from leaking resources.

Listing 12.33   Prevent Leaking Goroutines by Calling the context.CancelFunc

```
ctx, cancel := context.WithCancel(context.Background())
// ensure the cancel function is called at least once
// to avoid leaking resources
defer cancel()
```

Always call the context.CancelFunc function when you no longer need the context.Context. Failure to do so may cause your program to leak resources.

Canceling a Context

Consider Listing 12.34. The listener function takes a context.Context as its first argument and an int representing the goroutine id as its second argument.

The listener function blocks until the context.Context is canceled, which closes the channel behind context.Context.Done method. This unblocks the listener function and allows it to exit.

Listing 12.34   Blocking on context.Context.Done

```
func listener(ctx context.Context, i int) {
    fmt.Printf("listener %d is waiting\n", i)
```

```
    // this will block until the context
    // given context is canceled
    <-ctx.Done()

    fmt.Printf("listener %d is exiting\n", i)
}
```

The application creates a context.Background context and then wraps it with a cancellable context.Context. The context.CancelFunc returned is immediately deferred to ensure the application doesn't leak any resources.

In Listing 12.35, we create several goroutines that listen for the context.Context to be canceled.

Listing 12.35 Using Context Cancellation

```
func main() {

    // create a background context
    ctx := context.Background()

    // wrap the context with the ability
    // to cancel it
    ctx, cancel := context.WithCancel(ctx)

    // defer cancellation of the context
    // to ensure that any resources are
    // cleaned up regardless of how the
    // function exits
    defer cancel()

    // create 5 listeners
    for i := 0; i < 5; i++ {

        // launch listener in a goroutine
        go listener(ctx, i)

    }

    // allow the listeners to start
    time.Sleep(time.Millisecond * 500)

    fmt.Println("canceling the context")
```

(continued)

```
    // cancel the context and tell the
    // listeners to exit
    cancel()

    // allow the listeners to exit
    time.Sleep(time.Millisecond * 500)
}
```

As you can see from the output in Listing 12.36, the listener function unblocks and exits when the context.CancelFunc is called, cancel().

Listing 12.36   The Output of the Application

```
$ go run main.go

listener 0 is waiting
listener 1 is waiting
listener 2 is waiting
listener 4 is waiting
listener 3 is waiting
canceling the context
listener 0 is exiting
listener 2 is exiting
listener 1 is exiting
listener 3 is exiting
listener 4 is exiting

Go Version: go1.19
```

Only Child Nodes of the Context Are Canceled

Figure 12.3 shows that by canceling a node in the hierarchy, all its child nodes are also canceled. Other notes in the hierarchy, such as parent and sibling nodes, are unaffected.

Listening for Cancellation Confirmation

Previously, we have used time.Sleep[11] to block the execution of the program. This is not a good practice because it can lead to deadlocks and other problems. Instead, the application should receive a context.Context cancellation confirmation.

---

11. https://pkg.go.dev/time#Sleep

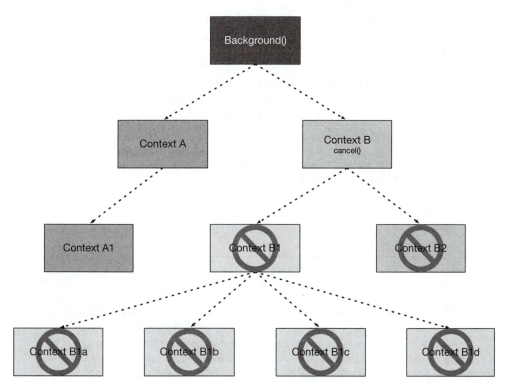

Figure 12.3   Cancellation propagation

Starting a Concurrent Monitor

Consider Listing 12.37. To start a Monitor, we must use the Start method, giving it a context.Context. In return, the Start method returns a context.Context that can be listened to by the application to confirm the shutdown of the Monitor later on.

Listing 12.37   Accepting a context.Context and Returning a New One

```go
type Monitor struct {
    cancel context.CancelFunc
}

func (m *Monitor) Start(ctx context.Context) context.Context {

    // start the monitor with the given context
    go m.listen(ctx)
```

(continued)

```
    // create a new context that will be canceled
    // when the monitor is shut down
    ctx, cancel := context.WithCancel(context.Background())

    // hold on to the cancellation function
    // when context that started the manager is canceled
    // this cancellation function will be called.
    m.cancel = cancel

    // return the new, cancellable, context.
    // clients can listen to this context
    // for cancellation to ensure the
    // monitor is properly shut down.
    return ctx
}
```

To prevent the application from blocking, we launch the listen method in a goroutine with the given context.Context. Unless this context.Context is canceled, the listen method never stops and continues to leak resources until the application exits.

The context.CancelFunc is held onto by the Manager so when the Manager is told to cancel by the client, it also cancels the Monitor context. This tells the client that the Monitor has been shut down, confirming the cancellation of the Monitor.

Monitor Checking

The listen method blocks until the context.Context, given by the application, is canceled, Listing 12.38. We first make sure to defer the context.CancelFunc in the Monitor to ensure that if the listen method exits for any reason, clients will be notified that the Monitor has been shut down.

Listing 12.38 The Monitor Calls Its context.CancelFunc if External context.Context Is Canceled

```
func (m *Monitor) listen(ctx context.Context) {
    defer m.cancel()

    // create a new ticker channel to listen to
    tick := time.NewTicker(time.Millisecond * 10)
    defer tick.Stop()

    // use an infinite loop to continue to listen
    // to new messages after the select statement
    // has been executed
    for {
```

```
    select {
    case <-ctx.Done(): // listen for context cancellation
        // shut down if the context is canceled
        fmt.Println("shutting down monitor")

        // if the monitor was told to shut down
        // then it should call its cancel function
        // so the client will know that the monitor
        // has properly shut down.
        m.cancel()

        // return from the function
        return
    case <-tick.C: // listen to the ticker channel
        // and print a message every time it ticks
        fmt.Println("monitor check")
    }
  }

}
```

Using the Cancellation Confirmation

In Listing 12.39, the application starts with a context.Background context and then wraps that with a cancellable context.Context. The context.CancelFunc returned is immediately deferred to ensure the application doesn't leak any resources. After a short while, in a goroutine, the cancel function is called, and the context.Context is canceled.

The Monitor is then started with our cancellable context.Context. The context.Context returned by the Start method is listened to by the application. When the Monitor is canceled, the application is unblocked and can exit. Alternatively, if the application is still running after a couple of seconds, the application is forcibly terminated.

Listing 12.39 Using the Cancellation Confirmation

```
func main() {

    // create a new background context
    ctx := context.Background()

    // wrap the background context with a
    // cancellable context.
    // this context can be listened to by any
    // children of this context for notification
```

(continued)

```go
    // of application shutdown/cancellation.
    ctx, cancel := context.WithCancel(ctx)

    // ensure the cancel function is called
    // to shut down the monitor when the program
    // exits
    defer cancel()

    // launch a goroutine to cancel the application
    // context after a short while.
    go func() {
        time.Sleep(time.Millisecond * 50)

        // cancel the application context
        // this will shut the monitor down
        cancel()
    }()

    // create a new monitor
    mon := Monitor{}

    // start the monitor with the application context
    // this will return a context that can be listened to
    // for cancellation signaling the monitor has shut down.
    ctx = mon.Start(ctx)

    // block the application until either the context
    // is canceled or the application times out
    select {
    case <-ctx.Done(): // listen for context cancellation
        // success shutdown
        os.Exit(0)
    case <-time.After(time.Second * 2): // timeout after 2 second
        fmt.Println("timed out while trying to shut down the monitor")

        // check if there was an error from the
        // monitor's context
        if err := ctx.Err(); err != nil {
            fmt.Printf("error: %s\n", err)
        }

        // non-successful shutdown
        os.Exit(1)
    }
}
```

As you can see from the output in Listing 12.40, the application waits for the `Monitor` to properly shut down before exiting. We were also able to remove the use of `time.Sleep` to allow the monitor to finish.

Listing 12.40   The Output of the Application

```
$ go run main.go

monitor check
monitor check
monitor check
monitor check
monitor check
shutting down monitor

Go Version: go1.19
```

Timeouts and Deadlines

In addition to enabling you to manually cancel a `context.Context`, the context package also provides mechanisms for creating a `context.Context` that self-cancels after or at a given time. Using these mechanics allows you to control how long to run some before you give up and assume that the operation has failed.

Canceling at a Specific Time

The context package provides two functions for creating a time-based self-canceling `context.Context`: `context.WithTimeout`[12] and `context.WithDeadline`.[13]

When using `context.WithDeadline`, Listing 12.41, we need to provide an *absolute* time at which the `context.Context` should be canceled. That means we need an exact date/time we want this `context.Context` to be canceled—for example, `March 14, 2029 3:45pm`.

Listing 12.41   The `context.WithDeadline` Function

```
$ go doc context.WithDeadline

package context // import "context"

func WithDeadline(parent Context, d time.Time) (Context, CancelFunc)
    ➥WithDeadline returns a copy of the parent context with the deadline
```

(continued)

---

12. https://pkg.go.dev/context#WithTimeout
13. https://pkg.go.dev/context#WithDeadline

➥adjusted to be no later than d. If the parent's deadline is already
➥earlier than d, WithDeadline(parent, d) is semantically equivalent to
➥parent. The returned context's Done channel is closed when the deadline
➥expires, when the returned cancel function is called, or when the parent
➥context's Done channel is closed, whichever happens first.

Canceling this context releases resources associated with it, so code
➥should call cancel as soon as the operations running in this Context
➥complete.

Go Version: go1.19

Consider Listing 12.42. In it, we create a new time.Time[14] for January 1, 2030 00:00:00 and use it to create a context.Context that self-cancels at that date and time.

Listing 12.42   Using context.WithDeadline

```go
func main() {

    // create a background context
    ctx := context.Background()

    // create an absolute date/time (January 1, 2030)
    deadline := time.Date(2030, 1, 1, 0, 0, 0, 0, time.UTC)
    fmt.Println("deadline:", deadline.Format(time.RFC3339))

    // create a new context with a deadline
    // that will cancel at January 1, 2030 00:00:00.
    ctx, cancel := context.WithDeadline(ctx, deadline)
    defer cancel()

    print(ctx)
}
```

```
$ go run .

deadline: 2030-01-01T00:00:00Z
WithTimeout(deadline: {wall:0 ext:64029052800 loc:<nil>})
        --> Background
```

Go Version: go1.19

---

14. https://pkg.go.dev/time#Time

Canceling after a Duration

Although being able to cancel a context.Context at a particular time is useful, more often than not you want to cancel a context.Context after a certain amount of time has passed.

When using context.WithTimeout, Listing 12.43, we need to provide a *relative* time.Duration[15] at which the context.Context should be canceled.

Listing 12.43   The context.WithTimeout Function

```
$ go doc context.WithTimeout

package context // import "context"

func WithTimeout(parent Context, timeout time.Duration) (Context, CancelFunc)
    WithTimeout returns WithDeadline(parent, time.Now().Add(timeout)).

    Canceling this context releases resources associated with it, so code
    ➥should call cancel as soon as the operations running in this
    ➥Context complete:

        func slowOperationWithTimeout(ctx context.Context) (Result, error) {
                ➥ctx, cancel := context.WithTimeout(ctx, 100*time.
                ➥Millisecond) defer cancel()   // releases resources if
                ➥slowOperation completes before timeout elapses return
                ➥slowOperation(ctx)
        }
```

Go Version: go1.19

Consider Listing 12.44. In it, we create a new self-canceling context.Context that uses context.WithTimeout to self-cancel after 10 milliseconds.

Listing 12.44   Using context.WithTimeout

```
func main() {

    // create a background context
    ctx := context.Background()

    // create a new context with a timeout
    // that will cancel the context after 10ms
    // equivalent to:
    //          context.WithDeadline(ctx,
    //          time.Now().Add(10 *time.Millisecond))
```

(continued)

---

15. https://pkg.go.dev/time#Duration

```
    ctx, cancel := context.WithTimeout(ctx, 10*time.Millisecond)
    defer cancel()

    print(ctx)
}
```

```
$ go run .

WithTimeout(deadline: {13882047106188520224 ext:10199834 loc:0x100ea06a0})
        --> Background
```

Go Version: go1.19

Functionally, we could have used context.WithDeadline instead, but
context.WithTimeout is more convenient when we want to cancel a context.Context
after a certain amount of time has passed.

Context Errors

In a complex system, or even in a small one, when a context.Context is canceled, you
need a way to know what caused the cancellation. It is possible that context.Context was
canceled by a context.CancelFunc successfully, was canceled because it timed out, or
was canceled for some other reason.

The context.Context.Err method in Listing 12.45 returns the error that caused the
context to be canceled.

Listing 12.45 The context.Context.Err Method

```
$ go doc context.Context.Err

package context // import "context"

type Context interface {

        // If Done is not yet closed, Err returns nil.
        // If Done is closed, Err returns a non-nil error explaining why:
        // Canceled if the context was canceled
        // or DeadlineExceeded if the context's deadline passed.
        // After Err returns a non-nil error, successive calls to Err return
        // the same error.
        Err() error

}
```

Go Version: go1.19

Context Canceled Error

The `context` package defines two different error variables that can be used to check an error that was returned from `context.Context.Err` method.

The first is `context.Canceled`, Listing 12.46, which is returned when the context is canceled through the use of a `context.CancelFunc` function. This `error` is considered to indicate a "successful" cancellation.

Listing 12.46   The `context.Canceled` Error

```
$ go doc context.Canceled

package context // import "context"

var Canceled = errors.New("context canceled")
    Canceled is the error returned by Context.Err when the context is canceled.
```

Go Version: go1.19

Consider Listing 12.47. When we first check the `context.Context.Err` method, it returns `nil`. After we call the `context.CancelFunc` function provided by `context.WithCancel`, the `context.Context.Err` method returns a `context.Canceled` error.

Listing 12.47   Checking for Cancellation Errors

```
func main() {

    // create a background context
    ctx := context.Background()

    // wrap the context with a
    // cancellable context
    ctx, cancel := context.WithCancel(ctx)

    // check the error:
    //
    fmt.Println("ctx.Err()", ctx.Err())

    // cancel the context
    cancel()

    // check the error:
    // context.Canceled
    fmt.Println("ctx.Err()", ctx.Err())
```

(continued)

```
    // check the error again:
    //  context.Canceled
    fmt.Println("ctx.Err()", ctx.Err())
}
```

```
$ go run .

ctx.Err() <nil>
ctx.Err() context canceled
ctx.Err() context canceled
```

Go Version: go1.19

As you can see from the output in Listing 12.47, repeated calls to the context.Context.Err method return the same context.Canceled error.

Context Deadline Exceeded Error

When a context.Context is canceled due to a deadline or timeout being exceeded, the context.Context.Err method returns a context.DeadlineExceeded[16] error, as in Listing 12.48.

Listing 12.48   The context.DeadlineExceeded Error

```
$ go doc context.DeadlineExceeded

package context // import "context"

var DeadlineExceeded error = deadlineExceededError{}
    DeadlineExceeded is the error returned by Context.Err when the context's
    ↪deadline passes.
```

Go Version: go1.19

Consider Listing 12.49. We create a context.Context that self-cancels after 1 second. When we check the context.Context.Err method before the context.Context times out, it returns nil.

Listing 12.49   Checking for Deadline Exceeded Errors

```
func main() {

    // create a background context
    ctx := context.Background()
```

---

16. https://pkg.go.dev/context#DeadlineExceeded

```
        // wrap the context that will
        // self cancel after 10 milliseconds
        ctx, cancel := context.WithTimeout(ctx, 10*time.Millisecond)
        defer cancel()

        // check the error:
        //
        fmt.Println("ctx.Err()", ctx.Err())

        // wait for the context to self-cancel
        <-ctx.Done()

        // check the error:
        //   context.Canceled
        fmt.Println("ctx.Err()", ctx.Err())

        // check the error again:
        //   context.DeadlineExceeded
        fmt.Println("ctx.Err()", ctx.Err())
}
```

```
$ go run .

ctx.Err() <nil>
ctx.Err() context deadline exceeded
ctx.Err() context deadline exceeded

Go Version: go1.19
```

As you can see from the output, the `context.Context` times out after the specified time, and the `context.Context.Err` method returns a `context.DeadlineExceeded` error.

Listening for System Signals with Context

Previously, when we discussed channels in Chapter 11, we showed you how to capture system signals, such as `ctrl-c`, using `signal.Notify`.[17] The `signal.NotifyContext`[18] function, Listing 12.50, is a variant of `signal.Notify` that takes a `context.Context` as an argument. In return, we are given a `context.Context` that will be canceled when the signal is received.

---

17. https://pkg.go.dev/os/signal#Notify
18. https://pkg.go.dev/os/signal#NotifyContext

Listing 12.50   The `signal.NotifyContext` Function

```
$ go doc os/signal.NotifyContext

package signal // import "os/signal"

func NotifyContext(parent context.Context, signals ...os.Signal)
    ➥(ctx context.Context, stop context.CancelFunc) NotifyContext returns a
    ➥copy of the parent context that is marked done (its Done channel is
    ➥closed) when one of the listed signals arrives, when the returned stop
    ➥function is called, or when the parent context's Done channel is closed,
    ➥whichever happens first.

    The stop function unregisters the signal behavior, which, like
    ➥signal.Reset, may restore the default behavior for a given signal.
    ➥For example, the default behavior of a Go program receiving os.Interrupt
    ➥is to exit. Calling NotifyContext(parent, os.Interrupt) will change the
    ➥behavior to cancel the returned context. Future interrupts received will
    ➥not trigger the default (exit) behavior until the returned stop function
    ➥is called.

    The stop function releases resources associated with it, so code should
    ➥call stop as soon as the operations running in this Context complete
    ➥and signals no longer need to be diverted to the context.
```

Go Version: go1.19

Consider Listing 12.51. We use `signal.NotifyContext` to listen for `ctrl-c`. This function returns a wrapped `context.Context` that will cancel when the signal is received. It also returns a `context.CancelFunc` that can be used to cancel `context.Context` when needed.

Listing 12.51   Listening for System Signals

```go
func main() {

    // create a background context
    ctx := context.Background()

    // wrap the context with a timeout
    // of 50 milliseconds to ensure the application
    // will eventually exit
    ctx, cancel := context.WithTimeout(ctx, 50*time.Millisecond)
    defer cancel()
```

```go
// wrap the context with a context
// that will be canceled when an
// interrupt signal is received (ctrl-c)
ctx, cancel = signal.NotifyContext(ctx, os.Interrupt)
defer cancel()

// launch a goroutine that will
// trigger an interrupt signal
// after 10 milliseconds (ctrl-c)
go func() {
    time.Sleep(10 * time.Millisecond)

    fmt.Println("sending ctrl-c")

    // send the interrupt signal
    // to the current process
    syscall.Kill(syscall.Getpid(), syscall.SIGINT)
}()

fmt.Println("waiting for context to finish")

// wait for the context to finish
<-ctx.Done()

fmt.Printf("context finished: %v\n", ctx.Err())

}
```

Testing Signals

Testing system signals is tricky, and you must take care not to accidentally exit your running tests. Unfortunately, the syscall[19] package does not provide a "test" signal or a way to implement a test signal.

You can use syscall.SIGUSR1[20] or syscall.SIGUSR2[21] in your tests because these are allocated to the developer to use for their own purposes.

When you are testing signals, you are testing a *global* signal that will be caught by anyone else who is listening to that signal. We want to make that when testing signals, we aren't running the tests in parallel and that you don't have other tests also listening to the same signal.

---

19. https://pkg.go.dev/syscall
20. https://pkg.go.dev/syscall#SIGUSR1
21. https://pkg.go.dev/syscall#SIGUSR2

Consider Listing 12.52. How do we test that the `Listener` function will respond properly to a signal? We don't want to make that the responsibility of the `Listener` function; it already has a `context.Context` that it can listen to for cancellation. The `Listener` function doesn't care why it was told to stop listening; it just needs to stop listening. This could be because we receive an interrupt signal because a deadline has passed or because the application no longer needs the `Listener` function to keep running.

Listing 12.52   The `Listener` Function

```
func Listener(ctx context.Context, t testing.TB) {
    t.Log("waiting for context to finish")

    // wait for the context to finish
    <-ctx.Done()


}
```

In Listing 12.53, before we call the `Listener` function, we first create a `context.Context` that self-cancels after 5 seconds if nothing else happens. We then wrap that `context.Context` with one received from the `signal.NotifyContext` function that self-cancels when the system receives a `TEST_SIGNAL` signal.

Our test blocks with a `select` waiting for either `context.Context` to be canceled and then respond accordingly.

Listing 12.53   Testing the `Listener` Function

```
// use syscall.SIGUSR2 to test
const TEST_SIGNAL = syscall.SIGUSR2

func Test_Signals(t *testing.T) {

    // create a background context
    ctx := context.Background()

    // wrap the context with a context
    // that will self cancel after 5 seconds
    // if the context is not finished
    ctx, cancel := context.WithTimeout(ctx, 5*time.Second)
    defer cancel()

    // wrap the context with a context
    // that will self cancel if the system
    // receives a TEST_SIGNAL
    sigCtx, cancel := signal.NotifyContext(ctx, TEST_SIGNAL)
    defer cancel()
```

```go
    print(t, sigCtx)

    // launch a goroutine to wait for the context
    // to finish
    go Listener(sigCtx, t)

    // launch a goroutine to send a TEST_SIGNAL
    // to the system after 1 second
    go func() {
        time.Sleep(time.Second)

        t.Log("sending test signal")

        // send the TEST_SIGNAL to the system
        syscall.Kill(syscall.Getpid(), TEST_SIGNAL)
    }()

    // wait for the context to finish
    select {
    case <-ctx.Done():
        t.Log("context finished")
    case <-sigCtx.Done():
        t.Log("signal received")
        t.Log("successfully completed")
        return
    }

    err := ctx.Err()
    if err == nil {
        return
    }

    // if we receive a DeadlineExceeded error then
    // the context timed out and the signal was never
    // received.
    if err == context.DeadlineExceeded {
        t.Fatal("unexpected error", err)
    }

}
```

Inside the test, in a goroutine, we can trigger the `TEST_SIGNAL` signal by sending it to the current process, `syscall.Getpid`,[22] with the `syscall.Kill`[23] function, as shown in Listing 12.54. We can also see in Listing 12.54 the test successfully exits after 1s.

Listing 12.54   Sending a TEST_SIGNAL Signal

```go
// launch a goroutine to send a TEST_SIGNAL
// to the system after 1 second
go func() {
    time.Sleep(time.Second)

    t.Log("sending test signal")

    // send the TEST_SIGNAL to the system
    syscall.Kill(syscall.Getpid(), TEST_SIGNAL)
}()
```

```
$ go test -v

=== RUN    Test_Signals
    signals_test.go:46: SignalCtx([]os.Signal{31})
                --> WithCancel
                    --> WithTimeout(deadline:{wall:13882047112088836168
            ⮥ext:5001109709 loc:0x104dde700})
                        --> Background
    signals_test.go:15: waiting for context to finish
    signals_test.go:58: sending test signal
    signals_test.go:70: signal received
    signals_test.go:71: successfully completed
--- PASS: Test_Signals (1.00s)
PASS
ok      demo    1.674s
```

```
Go Version: go1.19
```

Summary

In this chapter, we explored the concept of contexts in Go. We explained that contexts are a way to manage cancellation, timeouts, and other request-scoped values across API boundaries and between processes. We also discussed how to use contexts to clean up a lot

---

22. https://pkg.go.dev/syscall#Getpid
23. https://pkg.go.dev/syscall#Kill

of code involving channels, such as listening for system signals. We discussed the nodal hierarchy of how the `context` package wraps a new `context.Context` around a parent `context.Context`. We explained the difference was to cancel a `context.Context` and how to use multiple `context.Context`s to confirm shutdown behavior. The `context` package, while small, is a very powerful tool for managing concurrency in your application.

## 13

Synchronization

In Chapter 11, we explained how to use channels for passing data between goroutines. Then in Chapter 12, we discussed how to use the `context`[1] package to manage the cancellation of goroutines. In this chapter, we cover the final part of concurrent programming: synchronization.

We show you how to wait for a number of goroutines to finish. We explain race conditions,[2] how to find them using Go's `-race`[3] flag, and how to fix them with `sync.Mutex`[4] and `sync.RWMutex`.[5]

Finally, we discuss how to use `sync.Once` to ensure a function is only executed one time.

Waiting for Goroutines with a WaitGroup

Often, you might want to wait for a number of goroutines to finish before you continue your program. For example, you might want to spawn a number of goroutines to create a number of thumbnails of different sizes and wait for them all to complete before you continue.

The Problem

Consider Listing 13.1. We launch 5 new goroutines, each of which creates a thumbnail of a different size. We then wait for all of them to complete.

Listing 13.1 Launching Multiple Goroutines to Complete One Task

```
func Test_ThumbnailGenerator(t *testing.T) {
    t.Parallel()

    // image that we need thumbnails for
    const image = "foo.png"
```

(continued)

---

1. https://pkg.go.dev/context
2. https://en.wikipedia.org/wiki/Race_condition
3. https://golang.org/doc/articles/race_detector
4. https://pkg.go.dev/sync#Mutex
5. https://pkg.go.dev/sync#RWMutex

```
    // start 5 goroutines to generate thumbnails
    for i := 0; i < 5; i++ {

        // start a new goroutine for each thumbnail
        go generateThumbnail(image, i+1)

    }

    fmt.Println("Waiting for thumbnails to be generated")
}
```

The generateThumbnail function, Listing 13.2, generates a thumbnail of the specified size. In this example, we sleep one millisecond per "size" of thumbnail to simulate the time it takes to generate the thumbnail. For example, if we call generateThumbnail("foo.png", 200), we sleep 200 milliseconds before returning.

Listing 13.2 A Test Exiting before All Goroutines Have Finished

```
func generateThumbnail(image string, size int) {

    // thumbnail to be generated
    thumb := fmt.Sprintf("%s@%dx.png", image, size)

    fmt.Println("Generating thumbnail:", thumb)

    // wait for the thumbnail to be ready
    time.Sleep(time.Millisecond * time.Duration(size))

    fmt.Println("Finished generating thumbnail:", thumb)
}
```

```
$ go test -v

=== RUN    Test_ThumbnailGenerator
=== PAUSE Test_ThumbnailGenerator
=== CONT   Test_ThumbnailGenerator
Waiting for thumbnails to be generated
--- PASS: Test_ThumbnailGenerator (0.00s)
PASS
ok      demo      0.408s
```

```
Go Version: go1.19
```

As you can see from the test output in Listing 13.2, the test exits before the thumbnails are generated.

Our tests exit prematurely because we have not provided any mechanics to ensure that we wait for all of the thumbnail goroutines to finish before we continue.

Using a WaitGroup

To help us solve this problem, we can use a `sync.WaitGroup`,[6] Listing 13.3, to track how many goroutines are still running and notify us when they have all finished.

Listing 13.3   The `sync.WaitGroup` Type

```
$ go doc -short sync.WaitGroup

type WaitGroup struct {
        // Has unexported fields.
}
    A WaitGroup waits for a collection of goroutines to finish. The main
    ↦goroutine calls Add to set the number of goroutines to wait for. Then
    ↦each of the goroutines runs and calls Done when finished. At the same
    ↦time, Wait can be used to block until all goroutines have finished.

    A WaitGroup must not be copied after first use.

func (wg *WaitGroup) Add(delta int)
func (wg *WaitGroup) Done()
func (wg *WaitGroup) Wait()
```

Go Version: go1.19

The principle is simple: We create a `sync.WaitGroup` and use the `sync.WaitGroup.Add`[7] method to add to the `sync.WaitGroup` for each goroutine we want to wait for. When we want to wait for all of the goroutines to finish, we call the `sync.WaitGroup.Wait`[8] method. When a goroutine finishes, it calls the `sync.WaitGroup.Done`[9] method to indicate that the goroutine is finished.

The `Wait` Method

As the name suggests, a `sync.WaitGroup` is about waiting for a group of tasks, or goroutines, to finish. To do this, we need a way of blocking until all of the tasks have finished. The `sync.WaitGroup.Wait` method in Listing 13.4 does exactly that.

---

6. https://pkg.go.dev/sync#WaitGroup

7. https://pkg.go.dev/sync#WaitGroup.Add

8. https://pkg.go.dev/sync#WaitGroup.Wait

9. https://pkg.go.dev/sync#WaitGroup.Done

The sync.WaitGroup.Wait method blocks until its internal counter is zero. When the counter is zero, it means that all of the tasks have finished, and we can unblock and continue.

Listing 13.4 The sync.WaitGroup.Wait Method

```
$ go doc sync.WaitGroup.Wait

package sync // import "sync"

func (wg *WaitGroup) Wait()
    Wait blocks until the WaitGroup counter is zero.
```

Go Version: go1.19

The Add Method

For a sync.WaitGroup to know how many goroutines it needs to wait for, we need to add them to the sync.WaitGroup using the sync.WaitGroup.Add method, Listing 13.5.

Listing 13.5 The sync.WaitGroup.Add Method

```
$ go doc sync.WaitGroup.Add

package sync // import "sync"

func (wg *WaitGroup) Add(delta int)
    Add adds delta, which may be negative, to the WaitGroup counter.
    ⇥If the counter becomes zero, all goroutines blocked on Wait are released.
    ⇥If the counter goes negative, Add panics.

    Note that calls with a positive delta that occur when the counter is
    ⇥zero must happen before a Wait. Calls with a negative delta, or calls
    ⇥with a positive delta that start when the counter is greater than zero,
    ⇥may happen at any time. Typically this means the calls to Add should
    ⇥execute before the statement creating the goroutine or other event to be
    ⇥waited for. If a WaitGroup is reused to wait for several independent
    ⇥sets of events, new Add calls must happen after all previous Wait calls
    ⇥have returned. See the WaitGroup example.
```

Go Version: go1.19

The sync.WaitGroup.Add method takes a single integer argument, which is the number of goroutines to wait for. There are, however, some caveats to be aware of.

Adding a Positive Number

The sync.WaitGroup.Add method accepts an int argument, which is the number of goroutines to wait for. If we pass a positive number, the sync.WaitGroup.Add method adds that number of goroutines to the sync.WaitGroup.

As you can see from the test output in Listing 13.6, the sync.WaitGroup.Wait method blocks until the internal counter of the sync.WaitGroup reaches zero.

Listing 13.6   Adding a Positive Number of Goroutines

```go
func Test_WaitGroup_Add_Positive(t *testing.T) {
    t.Parallel()

    var completed bool

    // create a new waitgroup (count: 0)
    var wg sync.WaitGroup

    // add one to the waitgroup (count: 1)
    wg.Add(1)

    // launch a goroutine to call the Done() method
    go func(wg *sync.WaitGroup) {

        // sleep for a bit
        time.Sleep(time.Millisecond * 10)

        fmt.Println("done with waitgroup")

        completed = true

        // call the Done() method to decrement
        // the waitgroup counter (count: 0)
        wg.Done()
    }(&wg)

    fmt.Println("waiting for waitgroup to unblock")

    // wait for the waitgroup to unblock (count: 1)
    wg.Wait()
    // (count: 0)
```

(continued)

```
    fmt.Println("waitgroup is unblocked")

    if !completed {
        t.Fatal("waitgroup is not completed")
    }
}
```

```
$ go test -v -run Positive

=== RUN    Test_WaitGroup_Add_Positive
=== PAUSE Test_WaitGroup_Add_Positive
=== CONT  Test_WaitGroup_Add_Positive
waiting for waitgroup to unblock
done with waitgroup
waitgroup is unblocked
--- PASS: Test_WaitGroup_Add_Positive (0.01s)
PASS
ok      demo    0.351s
```

Go Version: go1.19

Adding a Zero Number

It is legal to call the sync.WaitGroup.Add method with a zero number, 0, Listing 13.7.
In this case, the sync.WaitGroup.Add method does nothing. The call becomes a no-op.

Listing 13.7 Adding a Zero Number of Goroutines

```
func Test_WaitGroup_Add_Zero(t *testing.T) {
    t.Parallel()

    // create a new waitgroup (count: 0)
    var wg sync.WaitGroup

    // add 0 to the waitgroup (count: 0)
    wg.Add(0)
    // (count: 0)

    fmt.Println("waiting for waitgroup to unblock")

    // wait for the waitgroup to unblock (count: 0)
    // will not block since the counter is already 0
```

(continued)

```
    wg.Wait()
    // (count: 0)

    fmt.Println("waitgroup is unblocked")
}
```

```
$ go test -v -run Zero

=== RUN    Test_WaitGroup_Add_Zero
=== PAUSE Test_WaitGroup_Add_Zero
=== CONT  Test_WaitGroup_Add_Zero
waiting for waitgroup to unblock
waitgroup is unblocked
--- PASS: Test_WaitGroup_Add_Zero (0.00s)
PASS
ok      demo    0.166s
```

Go Version: go1.19

As you can see from the test output in Listing 13.7, the sync.WaitGroup.Wait method unblocked immediately because its internal counter is already zero.

Adding a Negative Number

When calling the sync.WaitGroup.Add method with a negative number, the sync.WaitGroup.Add method panics.

As you can see from the test output in Listing 13.8, the sync.WaitGroup.Wait method was never reached because the sync.WaitGroup.Add method panicked when we tried to add a negative number of goroutines.

Listing 13.8   Adding a Negative Number of Goroutines

```
func Test_WaitGroup_Add_Negative(t *testing.T) {
    t.Parallel()

    // create a new waitgroup (count: 0)
    var wg sync.WaitGroup

    // use an anonymous function to trap the panic
    // so we can properly mark the test as a failure
    func() {

        // defer a function to catch the panic
        defer func() {
```

(continued)

```
            // recover the panic
            if r := recover(); r != nil {
                // mark the test as a failure
                t.Fatal(r)
            }
        }()

        // add a negative number to the waitgroup
        // this will panic since the counter cannot be negative
        wg.Add(-1)

        fmt.Println("waiting for waitgroup to unblock")

        // this will never be reached
        wg.Wait()

        fmt.Println("waitgroup is unblocked")
    }()

}
```

```
$ go test -v -run Negative

=== RUN   Test_WaitGroup_Add_Negative
=== PAUSE Test_WaitGroup_Add_Negative
=== CONT  Test_WaitGroup_Add_Negative
    add_test.go:92: sync: negative WaitGroup counter
--- FAIL: Test_WaitGroup_Add_Negative (0.00s)
FAIL
exit status 1
FAIL    demo    0.753s

Go Version: go1.19
```

The Done Method

Once we increase that counter by calling the sync.WaitGroup.Add method, the
sync.WaitGroup.Wait method blocks until we decrement the counter as we finish with
each goroutine.

For each item we add to the sync.WaitGroup with the sync.WaitGroup.Add method,
we need to call the sync.WaitGroup.Done method, Listing 13.9, to indicate that the
goroutine is finished.

Listing 13.9 The sync.WaitGroup.Done method

```
$ go doc sync.WaitGroup.Done

package sync // import "sync"

func (wg *WaitGroup) Done()
    Done decrements the WaitGroup counter by one.
```

Go Version: go1.19

Consider Listing 13.10, which creates N goroutines and adds N to the sync.WaitGroup using the sync.WaitGroup.Add method. Each goroutine calls the sync.WaitGroup.Done method after it finishes. We then use the sync.WaitGroup.Wait method to wait for all of the goroutines to finish.

Listing 13.10 Testing the sync.WaitGroup.Done Method

```go
func Test_WaitGroup_Done(t *testing.T) {
    t.Parallel()

    const N = 5

    // create a new waitgroup (count: 0)
    var wg sync.WaitGroup

    // add 5 to the waitgroup (count: 5)
    wg.Add(N)

    for i := 0; i < N; i++ {

        // launch a goroutine that will call the
        // waitgroup's Done method when it finishes
        go func(i int) {

            // sleep briefly
            time.Sleep(time.Millisecond * time.Duration(i))

            fmt.Println("decrementing waiting by 1")

            // call the waitgroup's Done method
            // (count: count - 1)
            wg.Done()
```

(continued)

```
        }(i + 1)
    }

    fmt.Println("waiting for waitgroup to unblock")

    wg.Wait()

    fmt.Println("waitgroup is unblocked")
}
```

```
$ go test -v -timeout 1s

=== RUN    Test_WaitGroup_Done
=== PAUSE Test_WaitGroup_Done
=== CONT  Test_WaitGroup_Done
waiting for waitgroup to unblock
decremeting waiting by 1
decremeting waiting by 1
decremeting waiting by 1
decremeting waiting by 1
decremeting waiting by 1
waitgroup is unblocked
--- PASS: Test_WaitGroup_Done (0.01s)
PASS
ok        demo    0.384s

Go Version: go1.19
```

As we can see from the test output, Listing 13.10, the `sync.WaitGroup.Wait` method unblocked after all of the goroutines finished.

Improper Usage

You *must* call `sync.WaitGroup.Done` exactly once for each number of items you add with `sync.WaitGroup.Add`.

If you don't call `sync.WaitGroup.Done` exactly once for each item you add with `sync.WaitGroup.Add`, the `sync.WaitGroup.Wait` method will block forever, which causes a deadlock and crashes your program, as shown in Listing 13.11.

Listing 13.11 Decrementing a sync.WaitGroup with the sync.WaitGroup.Done Method

```go
func Test_WaitGroup_Done(t *testing.T) {
    t.Parallel()

    const N = 5

    // create a new waitgroup (count: 0)
    var wg sync.WaitGroup

    // add 5 to the waitgroup (count: 5)
    wg.Add(N)

    for i := 0; i < N; i++ {

        // launch a goroutine that will call the
        // waitgroup's Done method when it finishes
        go func(i int) {

            // sleep briefly
            time.Sleep(time.Millisecond * time.Duration(i))

            fmt.Println("finished")

            // exiting with calling the Done method
            // (count: count)
        }(i + 1)
    }

    fmt.Println("waiting for waitgroup to unblock")

    // this will never unblock
    // because the goroutines never call Done
    // and the application will deadlock and panic
    wg.Wait()

    fmt.Println("waitgroup is unblocked")

}
```

```
$ go test -v -timeout 1s

=== RUN    Test_WaitGroup_Done
=== PAUSE Test_WaitGroup_Done
=== CONT  Test_WaitGroup_Done
```

(continued)

```
waiting for waitgroup to unblock
finished
finished
finished
finished
finished
panic: test timed out after 1s

goroutine 19 [running]:
testing.(*M).startAlarm.func1()
    /usr/local/go/src/testing/testing.go:2029 +0x8c
created by time.goFunc
    /usr/local/go/src/time/sleep.go:176 +0x3c

goroutine 1 [chan receive]:
testing.tRunner.func1()
    /usr/local/go/src/testing/testing.go:1405 +0x45c
testing.tRunner(0x140001361a0, 0x1400010fcb8)
    /usr/local/go/src/testing/testing.go:1445 +0x14c
testing.runTests(0x1400001e280?, {0x101045ea0, 0x1, 0x1},
➥{0x6e00000000000000?, 0x100e71218?, 0x10104e640?})
    /usr/local/go/src/testing/testing.go:1837 +0x3f0
testing.(*M).Run(0x1400001e280)
    /usr/local/go/src/testing/testing.go:1719 +0x500
main.main()
    _testmain.go:47 +0x1d0

goroutine 4 [semacquire]:
sync.runtime_Semacquire(0x0?)
    /usr/local/go/src/runtime/sema.go:56 +0x2c
sync.(*WaitGroup).Wait(0x14000012140)
    /usr/local/go/src/sync/waitgroup.go:136 +0x88
demo.Test_WaitGroup_Done(0x0?)
    ./done_test.go:43 0xd0
testing.tRunner(0x14000136340, 0x100fa1580)
    /usr/local/go/src/testing/testing.go:1439 +0x110
created by testing.(*T).Run
    /usr/local/go/src/testing/testing.go:1486 +0x300
exit status 2
FAIL    demo    1.225s
```

Go Version: go1.19

If you call sync.WaitGroup.Done more than the number of items you added with sync.WaitGroup.Add, the sync.WaitGroup.Done method panics, Listing 13.12. The result is the same as if you called sync.WaitGroup.Add with a negative number.

Listing 13.12   Panicking from Decrementing sync.WaitGroup Too Many Times

```go
func Test_WaitGroup_Done(t *testing.T) {
    t.Parallel()

    func() {
        // defer a function to catch the panic
        defer func() {

            // recover the panic
            if r := recover(); r != nil {
                // mark the test as a failure
                t.Fatal(r)
            }
        }()

        // create a new waitgroup (count: 0)
        var wg sync.WaitGroup

        // call done creating a negative
        // waitgroup counter
        wg.Done()

        // this line is never reached
        fmt.Println("waitgroup is unblocked")
    }()

}
```

```
$ go test -v -timeout 1s

=== RUN    Test_WaitGroup_Done
=== PAUSE Test_WaitGroup_Done
=== CONT  Test_WaitGroup_Done
    done_test.go:20: sync: negative WaitGroup counter
--- FAIL: Test_WaitGroup_Done (0.00s)
FAIL
exit status 1
FAIL    demo    0.416s
```

```
Go Version: go1.19
```

Wrapping Up Wait Groups

Using a sync.WaitGroup is a great way to manage the number of goroutines or any other number of tests that need to finish before your program can continue.

As you can see, we can effectively use a sync.WaitGroup to manage the thumbnail generator goroutines from our initial example.

In Listing 13.13, we create a new sync.WaitGroup. Then, in the for loop, we use the sync.WaitGroup.Add method to add 1 to the sync.WaitGroup. We then pass a pointer to the generateThumbnail function to sync.WaitGroup. A pointer is needed because the generateThumbnail function needs to be able to modify the sync.WaitGroup by calling the sync.WaitGroup.Done method.

Finally, we call the sync.WaitGroup.Wait method to wait for all of the goroutines to finish.

Listing 13.13 Using a sync.WaitGroup to Manage the Thumbnail Generator Goroutines

```go
func Test_ThumbnailGenerator(t *testing.T) {
    t.Parallel()

    // image that we need thumbnails for
    const image = "foo.png"

    var wg sync.WaitGroup

    // start 5 goroutines to generate thumbnails
    for i := 0; i < 5; i++ {
        wg.Add(1)

        // start a new goroutine for each thumbnail
        go generateThumbnail(&wg, image, i+1)

    }

    fmt.Println("Waiting for thumbnails to be generated")

    // wait for all goroutines to finish
    wg.Wait()

    fmt.Println("Finished generate all thumbnails")
}
```

The generateThumbnail function now receives a pointer to the sync.WaitGroup and defers a call to the sync.WaitGroup.Done method to indicate that the goroutine is finished when the function exits.

Finally, as you can see from our test output in Listing 13.14, the application now finishes successfully.

Listing 13.14   Generating Thumbnails Using a sync.WaitGroup

```go
func generateThumbnail(wg *sync.WaitGroup, image string, size int) {
    defer wg.Done()

    // thumbnail to be generated
    thumb := fmt.Sprintf("%s@%dx.png", image, size)

    fmt.Println("Generating thumbnail:", thumb)

    // wait for the thumbnail to be ready
    time.Sleep(time.Millisecond * time.Duration(size))

    fmt.Println("Finished generating thumbnail:", thumb)
}
```

```
$ go test -v

=== RUN   Test_ThumbnailGenerator
=== PAUSE Test_ThumbnailGenerator
=== CONT  Test_ThumbnailGenerator
Waiting for thumbnails to be generated
Generating thumbnail: foo.png@5x.png
Generating thumbnail: foo.png@3x.png
Generating thumbnail: foo.png@4x.png
Generating thumbnail: foo.png@2x.png
Generating thumbnail: foo.png@1x.png
Finished generating thumbnail: foo.png@1x.png
Finished generating thumbnail: foo.png@2x.png
Finished generating thumbnail: foo.png@3x.png
Finished generating thumbnail: foo.png@4x.png
Finished generating thumbnail: foo.png@5x.png
Finished generate all thumbnails
--- PASS: Test_ThumbnailGenerator (0.01s)
PASS
ok      demo    0.310s

Go Version: go1.19
```

Error Management with Error Groups

One of the downsides of the sync.WaitGroup is that it has no error management built in to capture errors that occur in the goroutines. It also has an API that requires exact implementation; otherwise, it panics.

To help address some of these issues, the golang.org/x/sync/errgroup,[10] Listing 13.15, package was introduced, providing a simpler API as well as built-in error management.

Listing 13.15 The golang.org/x/sync/errgroup Package

```
$ go doc golang.org/x/sync/errgroup

package errgroup // import "golang.org/x/sync/errgroup"

Package errgroup provides synchronization, error propagation, and Context
↪cancelation for groups of goroutines working on subtasks of a common task.

type Group struct{ ... }
    func WithContext(ctx context.Context) (*Group, context.Context)
```

```
Go Version: go1.19
```

The Problem

Consider Listing 13.16. In the example, a number of goroutines are launched to call the generateThumbnail functions. A sync.WaitGroup is used to wait for all the goroutines to finish.

Listing 13.16 Managing Goroutines with sync.WaitGroup

```go
func Test_ThumbnailGenerator(t *testing.T) {
    t.Parallel()

    // image that we need thumbnails for
    const image = "foo.png"

    var wg sync.WaitGroup

    // start 5 goroutines to generate thumbnails
    for i := 0; i < 5; i++ {
        wg.Add(1)

        // start a new goroutine for each thumbnail
        go generateThumbnail(&wg, image, i+1)

    }
```

---

10. https://pkg.go.dev/golang.org/x/sync/errgroup

```
    fmt.Println("Waiting for thumbnails to be generated")

    // wait for all goroutines to finish
    wg.Wait()

    fmt.Println("Finished generate all thumbnails")
}
```

Inside the generateThumbnail function, Listing 13.17, we see that there is an error that occurs if the size argument is divisible by 5, which causes a panic, and the application crashes.

Listing 13.17 The generateThumbnail Function

```
func generateThumbnail(wg *sync.WaitGroup, image string, size int) {
    defer wg.Done()

    // error if the size is divisible by 5
    if size%5 == 0 {
        // how do we return this error back to the main
        // goroutine without panicking?
        err := fmt.Errorf("%d is divisible by 5", size)
        panic(err)
    }

    // thumbnail to be generated
    thumb := fmt.Sprintf("%s@%dx.png", image, size)

    fmt.Println("Generating thumbnail:", thumb)

    // wait for the thumbnail to be ready
    time.Sleep(time.Millisecond * time.Duration(size))

    fmt.Println("Finished generating thumbnail:", thumb)
}
```

```
$ go test -v

=== RUN    Test_ThumbnailGenerator
=== PAUSE Test_ThumbnailGenerator
=== CONT  Test_ThumbnailGenerator
Waiting for thumbnails to be generated
panic: 5 is divisible by 5
```

(continued)

```
goroutine 9 [running]:
demo.generateThumbnail(0x0?, {0x10268ac77?, 0x0?}, 0x0?)
        ./demo_test.go:47 +0x21c
created by demo.Test_ThumbnailGenerator
        ./demo_test.go:24 +0x4c
exit status 2
FAIL    demo    0.619s
```

Go Version: go1.19

The Error Group

The errgroup.Group[11] type provides a minimal API when compared to the
sync.WaitGroup type. There are only two methods: errgroup.Group.Go[12] and
errgroup.Group.Wait.[13]

The errgroup.Group type, Listing 13.18, manages the counter for you, so there is no
need for counter management as there is with the sync.WaitGroup type.

Listing 13.18   The errgroup.Group Type

```
$ go doc golang.org/x/sync/errgroup.Group

package errgroup // import "golang.org/x/sync/errgroup"

type Group struct {
        // Has unexported fields.
}
    A Group is a collection of goroutines working on subtasks that are part
    ↪of the same overall task.

    A zero Group is valid and does not cancel on error.

func WithContext(ctx context.Context) (*Group, context.Context)
func (g *Group) Go(f func() error)
func (g *Group) Wait() error
```

Go Version: go1.19

---

11. https://pkg.go.dev/golang.org/x/sync/errgroup#Group
12. https://pkg.go.dev/golang.org/x/sync/errgroup#Group.Go
13. https://pkg.go.dev/golang.org/x/sync/errgroup#Group.Wait

The Go **Method**

You use the errgroup.Group.Go method, Listing 13.19, to launch a goroutine for the provided func() error function provided. The func() error function is executed in a goroutine. If the function returns an error, the errgroup.Group type captures the error, cancels the other goroutines, and returns the error to the caller from the errgroup.Group.Wait method.

Listing 13.19   The errgroup.Group.Go Method

```
$ go doc golang.org/x/sync/errgroup.Group.Go

package errgroup // import "golang.org/x/sync/errgroup"

func (g *Group) Go(f func() error)
    Go calls the given function in a new goroutine.

    The first call to return a non-nil error cancels the group; its error
    ↪will be returned by Wait.
```

Go Version: go1.19

The Wait **Method**

You use errgroup.Group.Wait method, Listing 13.20, to wait for all the goroutines to finish. If any of the goroutines return an error, the errgroup.Group type returns the error to the caller.

Listing 13.20   The errgroup.Group.Wait Method

```
$ go doc golang.org/x/sync/errgroup.Group.Wait

package errgroup // import "golang.org/x/sync/errgroup"

func (g *Group) Wait() error
    Wait blocks until all function calls from the Go method have returned,
    ↪then returns the first non-nil error (if any) from them.
```

Go Version: go1.19

It is important to understand the errgroup.Group.Wait method returns *only* the *first* error that occurs. Any other errors that occur are ignored. In Listing 13.21, we are calling the Go method on an errorgroup.Group 10 times. Each time we pass a function that sleeps for a random time, prints a messages, and then returns an error. From the output of the test, you can see that the error returned by the Wait method was returned from function number 4. The other nine errors are discarded.

Listing 13.21   The `errgroup.Group.Wait` Method Returns Only the First Error

```go
func Test_ErrorGroup_Multiple_Errors(t *testing.T) {
    t.Parallel()

    var wg errgroup.Group

    for i := 0; i < 10; i++ {
        i := i + 1

        wg.Go(func() error {

            time.Sleep(time.Millisecond * time.Duration(rand.Intn(10)))

            fmt.Printf("about to error from %d\n", i)

            return fmt.Errorf("error %d", i)

        })
    }

    err := wg.Wait()
    if err != nil {
        t.Fatal(err)
    }

}
```

```
$ go test -v

=== RUN    Test_ErrorGroup_Multiple_Errors
=== PAUSE Test_ErrorGroup_Multiple_Errors
=== CONT  Test_ErrorGroup_Multiple_Errors
about to error from 4
about to error from 6
about to error from 3
about to error from 1
about to error from 9
about to error from 10
about to error from 8
about to error from 5
about to error from 2
about to error from 7
    demo_test.go:38: error 4
```

```
--- FAIL: Test_ErrorGroup_Multiple_Errors (0.01s)
FAIL
exit status 1
FAIL    demo    0.263s
```

```
Go Version: go1.19
```

Listening for Error Group Cancellation

When launching a number of goroutines, it can often be useful to let others know the tasks have all completed. The errgroup.WithContext[14] function, Listing 13.22, returns a new errgroup.Group, as well as a context.Context that can be listened to for cancellation.

Listing 13.22   The errgroup.WithContext Function

```go
func Test_ErrorGroup_Context(t *testing.T) {
    t.Parallel()

    // create a new error group
    // and a context that will be canceled
    // when the group is done
    wg, ctx := errgroup.WithContext(context.Background())

    // create a quit channel for the goroutine
    // waiting for the context to be canceled
    // can close to signal the goroutine has finished
    quit := make(chan struct{})

    // launch a goroutine that will
    // wait for the errgroup context to finish
    go func() {
        fmt.Println("waiting for context to cancel")

        // wait for the context to be canceled
        <-ctx.Done()

        fmt.Println("context canceled")

        // close the quit channel so the test
        // will finish
        close(quit)
```

(continued)

---

14. https://pkg.go.dev/golang.org/x/sync/errgroup#WithContext

```go
    }()

    // add a task to the errgroup
    wg.Go(func() error {
        time.Sleep(time.Millisecond * 5)
        return nil
    })

    // wait for the errgroup to finish
    err := wg.Wait()
    if err != nil {
        t.Fatal(err)
    }

    // wait for the context goroutine to finish
    <-quit
}
```

```
$ go test -v

=== RUN    Test_ErrorGroup_Context
=== PAUSE Test_ErrorGroup_Context
=== CONT  Test_ErrorGroup_Context
waiting for context to cancel
context canceled
--- PASS: Test_ErrorGroup_Context (0.01s)
PASS
ok      demo    0.725s
```

```
Go Version: go1.19
```

Wrapping Up Error Groups

The `errgroup.Group` type provides a simpler API than the `sync.WaitGroup` type. It also provides built-in error management. This makes managing goroutines with error handling much easier. The downside is that it is not as flexible as the `sync.WaitGroup` type, where you are in charge of managing the counter.

Which type you choose to use will vary from situation to situation, so it is important to understand the tradeoffs and benefits of each before deciding which type to use.

Using a `errgroup.Group` allows you to clean up your code significantly to make it easier to understand and to manage errors.

As you can see from Listing 13.23, the `generateThumbnail` function no longer needs to take a `sync.WaitGroup` as an argument.

Listing 13.23   Update the generateThumbnail Function to use errgroup.Group

```go
func generateThumbnail(image string, size int) error {

    // error if the size is divisible by 5
    if size%5 == 0 {
        return fmt.Errorf("%d is divisible by 5", size)
    }

    // thumbnail to be generated
    thumb := fmt.Sprintf("%s@%dx.png", image, size)

    fmt.Println("Generating thumbnail:", thumb)

    // wait for the thumbnail to be ready
    time.Sleep(time.Millisecond * time.Duration(size))

    fmt.Println("Finished generating thumbnail:", thumb)

    return nil
}
```

Being able to return an error from the function means the function no longer needs to panic.

As you can see from the output, Listing 13.24, the generateThumbnail function no longer panics, and the test is now able to exit properly.

Listing 13.24   Using the errgroup.Group Type

```go
func Test_ThumbnailGenerator(t *testing.T) {
    t.Parallel()

    // image that we need thumbnails for
    const image = "foo.png"

    // create a new error group
    var wg errgroup.Group

    // start 5 goroutines to generate thumbnails
    for i := 0; i < 5; i++ {

        // capture the i to the current scope
        i := i
```

(continued)

```
    // start a new goroutine for each thumbnail
    wg.Go(func() error {

        // return the result of generateThumbnail
        return generateThumbnail(image, i)
    })

}

    fmt.Println("Waiting for thumbnails to be generated")

    // wait for all goroutines to finish
    err := wg.Wait()

    // check for any errors
    if err != nil {
        t.Fatal(err)
    }

    fmt.Println("Finished generate all thumbnails")
}
```

```
$ go test -v

=== RUN   Test_ThumbnailGenerator
=== PAUSE Test_ThumbnailGenerator
=== CONT  Test_ThumbnailGenerator
Waiting for thumbnails to be generated
Generating thumbnail: foo.png@4x.png
Generating thumbnail: foo.png@3x.png
Generating thumbnail: foo.png@1x.png
Generating thumbnail: foo.png@2x.png
Finished generating thumbnail: foo.png@1x.png
Finished generating thumbnail: foo.png@2x.png
Finished generating thumbnail: foo.png@3x.png
Finished generating thumbnail: foo.png@4x.png
    demo_test.go:43: 0 is divisible by 5
--- FAIL: Test_ThumbnailGenerator (0.00s)
FAIL
exit status 1
FAIL    demo    0.570s
```

Go Version: go1.19

Data Races

When writing concurrent applications, it is common to run into what is called a race condition.[15] A race condition occurs when two different goroutines try to access the same shared resource.

Consider Listing 13.25. There are two different goroutines. One goroutine inserts values into a map, and the other goroutine ranges over the map and prints the values.

Listing 13.25 Two Goroutines Accessing a Shared Map

```go
// launch a goroutine to
// write data in the map
go func() {
    for i := 0; i < 10; i++ {

        // loop putting data in the map
        data[i] = true

    }

    // cancel the context
    cancel()
}()

// launch a goroutine to
// read data from the map
go func() {
    // loop through the map
    // and print the keys/values
    for k, v := range data {
        fmt.Printf("%d: %v\n", k, v)
    }
}()
```

In Listing 13.26, we use those two goroutines to write a test to assert the map is written to and read from correctly.

Listing 13.26 A Passing Testing Without the Race Detector

```go
func Test_Mutex(t *testing.T) {
    t.Parallel()
```

(continued)

---

15. https://en.wikipedia.org/wiki/Race_condition

```go
// create a new cancellable context
// to stop the test when the goroutines
// are finished
ctx := context.Background()
ctx, cancel := context.WithTimeout(ctx, 20*time.Millisecond)
defer cancel()

// create a map to be used
// as a shared resource
data := map[int]bool{}

// launch a goroutine to
// write data in the map
go func() {
    for i := 0; i < 10; i++ {

        // loop putting data in the map
        data[i] = true
    }

    // cancel the context
    cancel()
}()

// launch a goroutine to
// read data from the map
go func() {
    // loop through the map
    // and print the keys/values
    for k, v := range data {
        fmt.Printf("%d: %v\n", k, v)
    }
}()

// wait for the context to be canceled
<-ctx.Done()

if len(data) != 10 {
    t.Fatalf("expected 10 items in the map, got %d", len(data))
}
}
```

```
$ go test -v

=== RUN    Test_Mutex
=== PAUSE Test_Mutex
=== CONT   Test_Mutex
--- PASS: Test_Mutex (0.00s)
PASS
ok       demo     0.471s
```

Go Version: go1.19

A quick glance at the test output, Listing 13.26, would seem to imply that the tests have passed successfully, but this is not the case.

The Race Detector

A few of the Go commands, such as `test` and `build`, have the `-race` flag exposed. When used, the `-race` flag tells the Go compiler to create a special version of the binary or test binary that will detect and report race conditions.

If we run the test again, this time with the `-race` flag, we get a *very* different result, as shown in Listing 13.27.

Listing 13.27   Tests Failing with the Race Detector

```
$ go test -v -race

=== RUN    Test_Mutex
=== PAUSE Test_Mutex
=== CONT   Test_Mutex
--- PASS: Test_Mutex (0.00s)
==================
WARNING: DATA RACE
Read at 0x00c00011c3f0 by goroutine 9:
  runtime.mapdelete()
      /usr/local/go/src/runtime/map.go:695 +0x46c
  demo.Test_Mutex.func2()
      ./demo_test.go:46 +0x50

Previous write at 0x00c00011c3f0 by goroutine 8:
  runtime.mapaccess2_fast64()
      /usr/local/go/src/runtime/map_fast64.go:53 +0x1cc
  demo.Test_Mutex.func1()
      ./demo_test.go:32 +0x50
```

(continued)

```
Goroutine 9 (running) created at:
  demo.Test_Mutex()
      ./demo_test.go:43 +0x188
  testing.tRunner()
      /usr/local/go/src/testing/testing.go:1439 +0x18c
  testing.(*T).Run.func1()
      /usr/local/go/src/testing/testing.go:1486 +0x44

Goroutine 8 (finished) created at:
  demo.Test_Mutex()
      ./demo_test.go:28 +0x124
  testing.tRunner()
      /usr/local/go/src/testing/testing.go:1439 +0x18c
  testing.(*T).Run.func1()
      /usr/local/go/src/testing/testing.go:1486 +0x44
===================
FAIL
exit status 1
FAIL    demo    0.962s
```

Go Version: go1.19

As you can see from the output, the Go race detector found a race condition in our code.

If we examine the top two entries in a race condition warning, Listing 13.28, it tells us where the two conflicting lines of code are.

Listing 13.28   Reading the Race Detector Output

```
Read at 0x00c00018204b by goroutine 9:
  demo.Test_Mutex.func2()
      problem/demo_test.go:46 +0xa5

Previous write at 0x00c00018204b by goroutine 8:
  demo.Test_Mutex.func1()
      problem/demo_test.go:32 +0x5c
```

A read of the shared resource was happening at demo_test.go:46, and a write was happening at demo_test.go:32. We need to synchronize or lock these two goroutines so that they don't both try to access the shared resource at the same time.

Most, but Not All

The Go race detector makes a simple guarantee with you (the end user).

> The Go race detector may not find *all* the race conditions in your code, but the ones it does find are *real* and *must* be fixed.

A race condition *will* panic and crash your application. If the race detector finds a race condition, you *must* fix it.

Wrapping Up the Race Detector

The race detector is an *invaluable* tool when developing Go applications. When running tests with the -race flag, you will notice a slowdown in test performance. The race detector has to do a lot of work to track those conditions.

Always enable the -race flag on your CI, such as GitHub Actions.

Once identified, the sync package, Listing 13.29, provides a number of ways that you can fix issues.

Listing 13.29   The sync Package

```
$ go doc -short sync

type Cond struct{ ... }
    func NewCond(l Locker) *Cond
type Locker interface{ ... }
type Map struct{ ... }
type Mutex struct{ ... }
type Once struct{ ... }
type Pool struct{ ... }
type RWMutex struct{ ... }
type WaitGroup struct{ ... }
```

Go Version: go1.19

Synchronizing Access with a Mutex

When you run tests with the -race flag, Go's built-in race detector can help you find data races in your code. In Listing 13.30, for example, tests that pass normally fail when run with the race detector. The failure message lists the data race found and where the reads and writes occur in our code.

Listing 13.30   Detecting Race Conditions in Tests

```
$ go test -v -race

=== RUN    Test_Mutex
=== PAUSE Test_Mutex
```

(continued)

```
=== CONT  Test_Mutex
--- PASS: Test_Mutex (0.00s)
PASS
==================
WARNING: DATA RACE
Read at 0x00c00019e3f0 by goroutine 9:
  runtime.mapdelete()
      /usr/local/go/src/runtime/map.go:695 +0x46c
  demo.Test_Mutex.func2()
      ./demo_test.go:46 +0x50

Previous write at 0x00c00019e3f0 by goroutine 8:
  runtime.mapaccess2_fast64()
      /usr/local/go/src/runtime/map_fast64.go:53 +0x1cc
  demo.Test_Mutex.func1()
      ./demo_test.go:32 +0x50

Goroutine 9 (running) created at:
  demo.Test_Mutex()
      ./demo_test.go:43 +0x188
  testing.tRunner()
      /usr/local/go/src/testing/testing.go:1439 +0x18c
  testing.(*T).Run.func1()
      /usr/local/go/src/testing/testing.go:1486 +0x44

Goroutine 8 (finished) created at:
  demo.Test_Mutex()
      ./demo_test.go:28 +0x124
  testing.tRunner()
      /usr/local/go/src/testing/testing.go:1439 +0x18c
  testing.(*T).Run.func1()
      /usr/local/go/src/testing/testing.go:1486 +0x44
==================
0: true
2: true
4: true
7: true
9: true
1: true
3: true
5: true
6: true
8: true
```

```
Found 1 data race(s)
exit status 66
FAIL    demo    0.862s
```

```
Go Version: go1.19
```

In the test in Listing 13.31, we have two different goroutines. The first is modifying a shared resource—in this case, a map. The second goroutine is ranging over the map and printing out the map's values.

In order for us to be able to fix this race condition, we need to be able to synchronize access to the shared resource.

Listing 13.31 Two Goroutines Accessing a Shared Map

```go
// launch a goroutine to
// read data from the map
go func() {
    // loop through the map
    // and print the keys/values
    for k, v := range data {
        fmt.Printf("%d: %v\n", k, v)
    }
}()

// launch a goroutine to
// put data in the map
go func() {
    for i := 0; i < 10; i++ {

        // loop putting data in the map
        data[i] = true
    }

    // cancel the context
    cancel()
}()
```

Locker

To synchronize access to the shared resource, we need to be able to lock access to the resource. By locking a shared resource, we can ensure that only one goroutine at a time can access the resource and that the resource is not modified by another goroutine while it is locked.

The sync.Locker[16] interface, Listing 13.32, defines the methods that a type must implement to be able to lock and unlock a shared resource.

Listing 13.32 The sync.Locker Interface

```
$ go doc sync.Locker

package sync // import "sync"

type Locker interface {
        Lock()
        Unlock()
}
    A Locker represents an object that can be locked and unlocked.

Go Version: go1.19
```

Locker Methods

You can use the sync.Locker.Lock[17] method, Listing 13.33, to lock the shared resource. Once a resource is locked, no other goroutine can access the resource until it is unlocked.

Listing 13.33 The sync.Locker.Lock Method

```
$ go doc sync.Mutex.Lock

package sync // import "sync"

func (m *Mutex) Lock()
    Lock locks m. If the lock is already in use, the calling goroutine blocks
    ↪until the mutex is available.

Go Version: go1.19
```

You can use the sync.Locker.Unlock[18] method, Listing 13.34, to unlock the shared resource. Once a resource is unlocked, other goroutines can access the resource.

---

16. https://pkg.go.dev/sync#Locker
17. https://pkg.go.dev/sync#Locker.Lock
18. https://pkg.go.dev/sync#Locker.Unlock

Listing 13.34   The `sync.Locker.Unlock` Method

```
$ go doc sync.Mutex.Unlock

package sync // import "sync"

func (m *Mutex) Unlock()
    Unlock unlocks m. It is a run-time error if m is not locked on entry to
    ➥Unlock.

    A locked Mutex is not associated with a particular goroutine. It is
    ➥allowed for one goroutine to lock a Mutex and then arrange for another
    ➥goroutine to unlock it.
```

Go Version: go1.19

Using a Mutex

The most basic mutex available in Go is the `sync.Mutex` type, Listing 13.35. The `sync.Mutex` uses a basic binary semaphore lock. This means that only one goroutine can access the resource at a time.

Listing 13.35   The `sync.Mutex` Type

```
$ go doc sync.Mutex

package sync // import "sync"

type Mutex struct {
        // Has unexported fields.
}
    ➥A Mutex is a mutual exclusion lock. The zero value for a Mutex is an
    ➥unlocked mutex.

    A Mutex must not be copied after first use.

func (m *Mutex) Lock()
func (m *Mutex) TryLock() bool
func (m *Mutex) Unlock()
```

Go Version: go1.19

To use a `sync.Mutex`, you need to wrap the areas of code that you want to synchronize access to by first locking the `sync.Mutex` and then unlocking it. For example, in the second goroutine in Listing 13.36, a mutex is being used to lock access around writing values into the data map.

Listing 13.36   Locking Resources with a `sync.Mutex`

```go
// launch a goroutine to
// read data from the map
go func() {
    // lock the mutex
    mu.Lock()

    // loop through the map
    // and print the keys/values
    for k, v := range data {
        fmt.Printf("%d: %v\n", k, v)
    }

    // unlock the mutex
    mu.Unlock()
}()

// launch a goroutine to
// put data in the map
go func() {

    for i := 0; i < 10; i++ {
        // lock the mutex
        mu.Lock()

        // loop putting data in the map
        data[i] = true

        // unlock the mutex
        mu.Unlock()
    }

    // cancel the context
    cancel()
}()
```

By locking access to the shared resource, you can ensure that only one goroutine at a time can access the resource. Our test output, Listing 13.37, confirms that the shared resource is only accessed by one goroutine at a time with a successful exit.

Listing 13.37 Passing Race Detector Tests

```
$ go test -v -race

=== RUN    Test_Mutex
=== PAUSE Test_Mutex
=== CONT  Test_Mutex
9: true
--- PASS: Test_Mutex (0.00s)
0: true
2: true
5: true
8: true
7: true
1: true
PASS
3: true
4: true
6: true
ok        demo       0.810s
```

Go Version: go1.19

RWMutex

Often, applications read a shared resource instead of writing to them. The sync.Mutex is a very heavy-weight locking mechanism. Access to a shared resource, whether it be a read or write, is blocked until the resource is unlocked. Only one goroutine can access a shared resource at a time.

When you want to be able to both read and write to a shared resource, you need to use a sync.RWMutex, Listing 13.38. The sync.RWMutex is a lighter-weight locking mechanism. A sync.RWMutex can allow many goroutines to read from the resource at the same time, but only one goroutine can write to the resource at a time.

Listing 13.38 The sync.RWMutex Type

```
$ go doc sync.RWMutex

package sync // import "sync"

type RWMutex struct {
        // Has unexported fields.
}
```

(continued)

> A RWMutex is a reader/writer mutual exclusion lock. The lock can be held
> ⮕by an arbitrary number of readers or a single writer. The zero value for
> ⮕a RWMutex is an unlocked mutex.
>
> A RWMutex must not be copied after first use.
>
> If a goroutine holds a RWMutex for reading and another goroutine might
> ⮕call Lock, no goroutine should expect to be able to acquire a read lock
> ⮕until the initial read lock is released. In particular, this prohibits
> ⮕recursive read locking. This is to ensure that the lock eventually
> ⮕becomes available; a blocked Lock call excludes new readers from
> ⮕acquiring the lock.

```
func (rw *RWMutex) Lock()
func (rw *RWMutex) RLock()
func (rw *RWMutex) RLocker() Locker
func (rw *RWMutex) RUnlock()
func (rw *RWMutex) TryLock() bool
func (rw *RWMutex) TryRLock() bool
func (rw *RWMutex) Unlock()
```

Go Version: go1.19

The sync.RWMutex offers two additional methods beyond those of the sync.Locker interface. You can use the sync.RWMutex.Rlock[19] and sync.RWMutex.RUnlock[20] methods to lock the resource for reading. The sync.RWMutex.Lock[21] and sync.RWMutex.Unlock[22] methods are used to lock the resource across all goroutines for writing.

In Listing 13.39, we update the goroutine that is reading the resource to use the sync.RWMutex.Rlock method instead of the sync.Mutex.Lock method. This will allow for many goroutines to read from the resource at the same time.

Listing 13.39   Using a sync.RWMutex

```go
// launch a goroutine to
// read data from the map
go func() {
    // lock the mutex
    mu.RLock()
```

19. https://pkg.go.dev/sync#RWMutex.Rlock
20. https://pkg.go.dev/sync#RWMutex.RUnlock
21. https://pkg.go.dev/sync#RWMutex.Lock
22. https://pkg.go.dev/sync#RWMutex.Unlock

```
    // loop through the map
    // and print the keys/values
    for k, v := range data {
        fmt.Printf("%d: %v\n", k, v)
    }

    // unlock the mutex
    mu.RUnlock()
}()
```

```
$ go test -v -race

=== RUN    Test_RWMutex
=== PAUSE Test_RWMutex
=== CONT  Test_RWMutex
4: true
5: true
6: true
--- PASS: Test_RWMutex (0.00s)
7: true
9: true
0: true
1: true
PASS
8: true
2: true
3: true
ok      demo    0.917s
```

```
Go Version: go1.19
```

The tests in Listing 13.39 continue to pass, but the performance of the program is improved by allowing multiple goroutines to read from the shared resource instead of arbitrarily locking all goroutines all at once.

Improper Usage

When using either sync.Mutex or sync.RWMutex, you must take care in making sure to lock and unlock in the proper order.

Consider Listing 13.40. We have a sync.Mutex, and we attempt to call sync.Mutex.Lock twice.

Listing 13.40   Attempting to Lock a sync.Mutex Twice

```go
func Test_Mutex_Locks(t *testing.T) {
    t.Parallel()

    // create a new mutex
    var mu sync.Mutex

    // lock the mutex
    mu.Lock()

    fmt.Println("locked. locking again.")

    // try to lock the mutex again
    // this will block/deadlock
    // because the mutex is already locked
    // and the lock was not released
    mu.Lock()

    fmt.Println("unlocked twice")
}
```

The result is the program will deadlock and crash, as shown in Listing 13.41. The reason is that a call to sync.Mutex.Lock blocks until the sync.Mutex.Unlock method is called. Because we have already locked the sync.Mutex, the second call to sync.Mutex.Lock blocks indefinitely because it is never unlocked.

Listing 13.41   A Panic while Trying to Unlock an Already-Unlocked sync.Mutex

```
$ go test -v -timeout 10ms

=== RUN    Test_Mutex_Locks
=== PAUSE Test_Mutex_Locks
=== CONT  Test_Mutex_Locks
locked. locking again.
panic: test timed out after 10ms

goroutine 33 [running]:
testing.(*M).startAlarm.func1()
        /usr/local/go/src/testing/testing.go:2029 +0x8c
created by time.goFunc
        /usr/local/go/src/time/sleep.go:176 +0x3c
```

```
goroutine 1 [chan receive]:
testing.tRunner.func1()
        /usr/local/go/src/testing/testing.go:1405 +0x45c
testing.tRunner(0x140001361a0, 0x1400010fcb8)
        /usr/local/go/src/testing/testing.go:1445 +0x14c
testing.runTests(0x1400001e1e0?, {0x100ec9ea0, 0x1, 0x1},
➥{0xe00000000000000?, 0x100cf5218?, 0x100ed2640?})
        /usr/local/go/src/testing/testing.go:1837 +0x3f0

testing.(*M).Run(0x1400001e1e0)
        /usr/local/go/src/testing/testing.go:1719 +0x500
main.main()
        _testmain.go:47 +0x1d0

goroutine 4 [semacquire]:
sync.runtime_SemacquireMutex(0x1400000e018?, 0x20?, 0x17?)
        /usr/local/go/src/runtime/sema.go:71 +0x28
sync.(*Mutex).lockSlow(0x14000012140)
        /usr/local/go/src/sync/mutex.go:162 +0x180
sync.(*Mutex).Lock(...)
        /usr/local/go/src/sync/mutex.go:81
demo.Test_Mutex_Locks(0x0?)
        ./demo_test.go:25 +0x130
testing.tRunner(0x14000136340, 0x100e25298)
        /usr/local/go/src/testing/testing.go:1439 +0x110
created by testing.(*T).Run
        /usr/local/go/src/testing/testing.go:1486 +0x300
exit status 2
FAIL    demo    0.527s
```

Go Version: go1.19

Worse than a deadlock caused by waiting for a lock that will never be unlocked is unlocking a lock that has not been locked.

In Listing 13.42, the result is a fatal error that crashes the application. The reason is that we have not locked the sync.Mutex before attempting to unlock it.

Listing 13.42 A Panic while Trying to Unlock an Unlocked sync.Mutex

```
func Test_Mutex_Unlock(t *testing.T) {
    t.Parallel()

    // create a new mutex
    var mu sync.Mutex
```

(continued)

```
        // unlock the mutex
        mu.Unlock()
}
```

```
$ go test -v

=== RUN   Test_Mutex_Unlock
=== PAUSE Test_Mutex_Unlock
=== CONT  Test_Mutex_Unlock
fatal error: sync: unlock of unlocked mutex

goroutine 18 [running]:
runtime.throw(0x104573b02?, 0x1400005af18?)
        /usr/local/go/src/runtime/panic.go:992 +0x50 fp=0x1400005aee0
        ↪sp=0x1400005aeb0 pc=0x1044ba9a0
sync.throw(0x104573b02?, 0x1045b6260?)
        /usr/local/go/src/runtime/panic.go:978 +0x24 fp=0x1400005af00
        ↪sp=0x1400005aee0 pc=0x1044e5664
sync.(*Mutex).unlockSlow(0x140001280b0, 0xffffffff)
        /usr/local/go/src/sync/mutex.go:220 +0x3c fp=0x1400005af30
        ↪sp=0x1400005af00 pc=0x1044ef44c
sync.(*Mutex).Unlock(...)
        /usr/local/go/src/sync/mutex.go:214
demo.Test_Mutex_Unlock(0x0?)
        ./demo_test.go:16 +0x74 fp=0x1400005af60 sp=0x1400005af30
        ↪pc=0x10456d794
testing.tRunner(0x1400010b380, 0x1045c9298)
        /usr/local/go/src/testing/testing.go:1439 +0x110 fp=0x1400005afb0
        ↪sp=0x1400005af60 pc=0x104537660
testing.(*T).Run.func1()
        /usr/local/go/src/testing/testing.go:1486 +0x30 fp=0x1400005afd0
        ↪sp=0x1400005afb0 pc=0x1045383d0
runtime.goexit()
        /usr/local/go/src/runtime/asm_arm64.s:1263 +0x4 fp=0x1400005afd0
        ↪sp=0x1400005afd0 pc=0x1044ea2a4
created by testing.(*T).Run
        /usr/local/go/src/testing/testing.go:1486 +0x300

goroutine 1 [chan receive]:
testing.tRunner.func1()
        /usr/local/go/src/testing/testing.go:1405 +0x45c
testing.tRunner(0x1400010b1e0, 0x14000131cb8)
        /usr/local/go/src/testing/testing.go:1445 +0x14c
testing.runTests(0x140001421e0?, {0x10466dea0, 0x1, 0x1}, {0xa500000000000000?,
```

```
➥0x104499218?, 0x104676640?})
        /usr/local/go/src/testing/testing.go:1837 +0x3f0
testing.(*M).Run(0x140001421e0)
        /usr/local/go/src/testing/testing.go:1719 +0x500
main.main()
        _testmain.go:47 +0x1d0


exit status 2
FAIL    demo    0.260s
```

Go Version: go1.19

Wrapping Up Read/Write Mutexes

While there are pitfalls and areas of concern when using mutexes, such as deadlocks and improper usage, sync.Mutex and sync.RWMutex are excellent tools for protecting shared resources. They are also the most commonly used locking mechanisms in Go.

Performing Tasks Only Once

There are many times when you want to perform a task only once. For example, you might want to create a database connection only once and then use it to perform a number of queries. You can use the sync.Once[23] type to do this.

As you can see from the documentation in Listing 13.43, the use of sync.Once is very simple. You just need to create a variable of type sync.Once and then call the sync.Once.Do[24] method with a function that you want to run only once.

Listing 13.43   The sync.Once Type

```
$ go doc -all sync.Once

package sync // import "sync"

type Once struct {
        // Has unexported fields.
}
    Once is an object that will perform exactly one action.

    A Once must not be copied after first use.
```

(continued)

---

23. https://pkg.go.dev/sync#Once
24. https://pkg.go.dev/sync#Once.Do

```
func (o *Once) Do(f func())
    Do calls the function f if and only if Do is being called for the first
    ➥time for this instance of Once. In other words, given

        var once Once

    if once.Do(f) is called multiple times, only the first call will invoke f,
    ➥even if f has a different value in each invocation. A new instance of
    ➥Once is required for each function to execute.

    Do is intended for initialization that must be run exactly once. Since f
    ➥is niladic, it may be necessary to use a function literal to capture the
    ➥arguments to a function to be invoked by Do:

        config.once.Do(func() { config.init(filename) })

    Because no call to Do returns until the one call to f returns, if f
    ➥causes Do to be called, it will deadlock.

    If f panics, Do considers it to have returned; future calls of Do return
    ➥without calling f.
```

Go Version: go1.19

The Problem

Often we want to use sync.Once to perform some heavy, expensive tasks only once.

Consider Listing 13.44. The Build function can be called many times, but we only want it to run once because it takes some time to complete.

Listing 13.44   The Build Method Is Slow and Should Be Called Only Once

```
type Builder struct {
    Built bool
}

func (b *Builder) Build() error {

    fmt.Print("building...")

    time.Sleep(10 * time.Millisecond)

    fmt.Println("built")
```

```
        b.Built = true

        // validate the message
        if !b.Built {
            return fmt.Errorf("expected builder to be built")
        }

        // return the b.msg and the error variable
        return nil
}
```

As you can see from the test output, Listing 13.45, every call to the `Build` function takes a long time to complete, and each call performs the same task.

Listing 13.45 Output Confirming the `Build` Function Runs Every Time It Is Called

```
func Test_Once(t *testing.T) {
    t.Parallel()

    b := &Builder{}

    for i := 0; i < 5; i++ {

        err := b.Build()
        if err != nil {
            t.Fatal(err)
        }

        fmt.Println("builder built")

        if !b.Built {
            t.Fatal("expected builder to be built")
        }
    }
}
```

```
$ go test -v

=== RUN    Test_Once
=== PAUSE  Test_Once
=== CONT   Test_Once
building...built
builder built
```

(continued)

```
building...built
builder built

building...built
builder built
building...built
builder built
building...built
builder built
--- PASS: Test_Once (0.05s)
PASS
ok      demo    0.265s
```

Go Version: go1.19

Implementing Once

As shown in Listing 13.46, you can use the `sync.Once` type inside the `Build` function to ensure that the expensive task is only performed once.

Listing 13.46 Using `sync.Once` to Run a Function Once

```go
type Builder struct {
    Built bool
    once  sync.Once
}

func (b *Builder) Build() error {

    var err error

    b.once.Do(func() {

        fmt.Print("building...")

        time.Sleep(10 * time.Millisecond)

        fmt.Println("built")

        b.Built = true

        // validate the message
        if !b.Built {
```

```
        err = fmt.Errorf("expected builder to be built")
    }
})

// return the b.msg and the error variable
return err
}
```

As you can see from the test output, Listing 13.47, the `Build` function now performs the expensive task only once, and subsequent calls to the function are very fast.

Listing 13.47   Output Confirming the `Build` Function Runs Only Once

```
$ go test -v

=== RUN    Test_Once
=== PAUSE Test_Once
=== CONT   Test_Once
building...built
builder built
builder built
builder built
builder built
builder built
--- PASS: Test_Once (0.01s)
PASS
ok      demo    0.248s

Go Version: go1.19
```

Closing Channels with Once

The `sync.Once` type is useful for closing channels. When you want to close a channel, you need to ensure that the channel is closed only once. If you try to close the channel more than once, you get a panic, and the program crashes.

Consider the example in Listing 13.48. The `Quit` method on the `Manager` is in charge of closing the `quit` channel when the `Manager` is no longer needed.

Listing 13.48 If Called Repeatedly, the Quit Function Panics and Closes an
Already-Closed Channel

```go
type Manager struct {
    quit chan struct{}
}


func (m *Manager) Quit() {
    fmt.Println("closing quit channel")
    close(m.quit)
}
```

If, however, the Quit method is called more than once, we are trying to close the
channel more than once. We get a panic, and the program crashes.

As you can see in Listing 13.49, the tests failed as a result of trying to close the channel
more than once and caused a panic.

Listing 13.49 Panicking When Trying to Close a Channel Multiple Times

```go
func Test_Closing_Channels(t *testing.T) {
    t.Parallel()

    func() {
        // defer a function to catch the panic
        defer func() {

            // recover the panic
            if r := recover(); r != nil {
                // mark the test as a failure
                t.Fatal(r)
            }
        }()

        m := &Manager{
            quit: make(chan struct{}),
        }

        // close the manager's quit channel
        m.Quit()

        // try to close the manager's quit channel again
        // this will panic
        m.Quit()
```

```
    }()
}
```

```
$ go test -v

=== RUN    Test_Closing_Channels
=== PAUSE Test_Closing_Channels
=== CONT  Test_Closing_Channels
closing quit channel
closing quit channel
    demo_test.go:31: close of closed channel
--- FAIL: Test_Closing_Channels (0.00s)
FAIL
exit status 1
FAIL    demo    0.667s
```

Go Version: go1.19

In Listing 13.50, we use the sync.Once type to ensure that the Quit method, regardless of how many times it is called, only closes the channel once.

Listing 13.50 Using sync.Once to Close a Channel Only Once

```
type Manager struct {
    quit chan struct{}
    once sync.Once
}

func (m *Manager) Quit() {

    // close the manager's quit channel
    // this will only close the channel once
    m.once.Do(func() {
        fmt.Println("closing quit channel")
        close(m.quit)
    })
}
```

As you can see from the test output, Listing 13.51, the Quit method now closes the channel only once, and subsequent calls to the Quit method have no effect.

Listing 13.51 Output Confirming the `Quit` Method Closes the Channel Only Once

```go
func Test_Closing_Channels(t *testing.T) {
    t.Parallel()

    m := &Manager{
        quit: make(chan struct{}),
    }

    // close the manager's quit channel
    m.Quit()

    // try to close the manager's quit channel again
    // this will now have no effect
    m.Quit()
}
```

```
$ go test -v

=== RUN   Test_Closing_Channels
=== PAUSE Test_Closing_Channels
=== CONT  Test_Closing_Channels

closing quit channel
--- PASS: Test_Closing_Channels (0.00s)
PASS
ok      demo    0.523s
```

Go Version: go1.19

Summary

In this chapter, we took a look at just a few of the synchronization types and functions in Go. First, we explored how to use a `sync.WaitGroup` to wait for a number of goroutines to finish. Then we explained how to use `sync.ErrGroup` to wait for a number of goroutines to finish and return an error if any of them failed. Next, we discussed how to use `sync.Mutex` and `sync.RWMutex` to synchronize access to a shared resource. Finally, we covered how to use `sync.Once` to ensure a function is only executed one time.

14

Working with Files

Working with files is a very common task in computer programming. You work with log files, HTML files, and a whole host of other file types in your programs. In this chapter, we explain how to read and write files, walk directories, use the fs[1] package, and finally, embed files into your Go binaries to create a truly self-contained application.

Directory Entries and File Information

Before you can begin using files for your programs, you first need to understand the basics of how files work in Go.

Consider the file tree in Listing 14.1. We use this file tree to help you understand files in Go. This tree contains .txt files as well as special directories testdata, _ignore, and .hidden. We cover the importance of these files and directories as we progress.

Listing 14.1   File Tree Containing Special Folders: .hidden, _ignore, and testdata

```
$ tree -a


.
|-- .hidden
|    '-- d.txt
|-- a.txt
|-- b.txt
|-- e
|   |-- f
|   |   |-- _ignore
|   |   |    '-- i.txt
|   |   |-- g.txt
|   |   '-- h.txt
|   '-- j.txt
```

(continued)

---

1. https://pkg.go.dev/fs

```
'-- testdata
    '-- c.txt

5 directories, 8 files
```

Reading a Directory

To know which files you can work with, you need to know which files are in a directory. To do this, you can use the `os.ReadDir`[2] function, Listing 14.2.

Listing 14.2 The `os.ReadDir` Function

```
$ go doc os.ReadDir

package os // import "os"

func ReadDir(name string) ([]DirEntry, error)
    ReadDir reads the named directory, returning all its directory entries
    ↪sorted by filename. If an error occurs reading the directory, ReadDir
    ↪returns the entries it was able to read before the error, along with the
    ↪error.

Go Version: go1.19
```

The `os.ReadDir` function takes a path as a parameter and returns a slice of `os.DirEntry`[3] values, Listing 14.3. Each `os.DirEntry` value represents a file or directory in the directory and contains information about the file or directory.

Listing 14.3 The `os.DirEntry` Type

```
$ go doc os.DirEntry

package os // import "os"

type DirEntry = fs.DirEntry
    A DirEntry is an entry read from a directory (using the ReadDir function
    ↪or a File's ReadDir method).

func ReadDir(name string) ([]DirEntry, error)

Go Version: go1.19
```

---

2. https://pkg.go.dev/os#ReadDir
3. https://pkg.go.dev/os#DirEntry

The `fs` package was added in go1.16, and it provides interface around the file system. The result of this was that many types were aliased to the `fs` package. This means that you may need to hunt a little further to find the deeper documentation.

For example, `os.DirEntry` was aliased to `fs.DirEntry`[4] in go1.16, Listing 14.4.

Listing 14.4 The `fs.DirEntry` Type

```
$ go doc fs.DirEntry

package fs // import "io/fs"

type DirEntry interface {
        // Name returns the name of the file (or subdirectory) described by
        ➥the entry.
        // This name is only the final element of the path (the base name),
        ➥not the entire path.
        // For example, Name would return "hello.go" not "home/gopher/
        ➥hello.go". Name() string

        // IsDir reports whether the entry describes a directory.
        ➥IsDir() bool

        // Type returns the type bits for the entry.
        // The type bits are a subset of the usual FileMode bits, those
        ➥returned by the FileMode.Type method.
        ➥Type() FileMode

        // Info returns the FileInfo for the file or subdirectory described
        ➥by the entry.
        // The returned FileInfo may be from the time of the original
        ➥directory read
        // or from the time of the call to Info. If the file has been removed
        ➥or renamed
        // since the directory read, Info may return an error satisfying
        ➥errors.Is(err, ErrNotExist).
        // If the entry denotes a symbolic link, Info reports the information
        ➥about the link itself,
        // not the link's target.
        ➥Info() (FileInfo, error)
}
    A DirEntry is an entry read from a directory (using the ReadDir function
    ➥or a ReadDirFile's ReadDir method).
```

(continued)

---

4. https://pkg.go.dev/io/fs#DirEntry

```
func FileInfoToDirEntry(info FileInfo) DirEntry
func ReadDir(fsys FS, name string) ([]DirEntry, error)
```

Go Version: go1.19

As shown in Listing 14.5, we can use the os.ReadDir function to read the contents of the data directory. We then print the names to the console. If the file is a directory, we prepend it with a ->.

Listing 14.5 Using os.ReadDir to Read the Contents of a Directory

```go
func main() {
    files, err := os.ReadDir("data")
    if err != nil {
        log.Fatal(err)
    }

    for _, file := range files {
        if file.IsDir() {
            fmt.Println("->", file.Name())
            continue
        }
        fmt.Println(file.Name())
    }
}
```

As you can see from the output in Listing 14.6, only the files in the data directory are listed. The os.ReadDir function only reads the contents of the directory and not the contents of any subdirectories. To get a full list of files, including the contents of subdirectories, we need to walk the directories ourselves. We discuss this more later in this chapter.

Listing 14.6 Output of Listing 14.5

```
$ go run .

-> .hidden
a.txt
b.txt
-> e
-> testdata
```

Go Version: go1.19

The FileInfo Interface

The main source for metadata about files is the fs.FileInfo[5] interface, Listing 14.7. In go1.16, the os.FileInfo[6] type was aliased to fs.FileInfo. From this interface, we can get the name of the file, the size of the file, the time the file was last modified, and the mode, or permissions, of the file. We can also tell whether the file is a directory or a regular file.

Listing 14.7   The fs.FileInfo Interface

```
$ go doc fs.FileInfo


package fs // import "io/fs"


type FileInfo interface {
        Name() string       // base name of the file
        Size() int64         // length in bytes for regular files;
                             ↦system-dependent for others
        Mode() FileMode      // file mode bits
        ModTime() time.Time // modification time
        IsDir() bool         // abbreviation for Mode().IsDir()
        Sys() any            // underlying data source (can return nil)
}
    A FileInfo describes a file and is returned by Stat.


func Stat(fsys FS, name string) (FileInfo, error)
```

Go Version: go1.19

Consider Listing 14.8. We read the contents of the data directory and print the mode, size, and name of each file.

Listing 14.8   Using fs.FileInfo to Print Information about Files

```
func main() {
    files, err := os.ReadDir("data")
    if err != nil {
        log.Fatal(err)
    }

    fmt.Println("Mode\t\tSize\tName")
    for _, file := range files {
```

(continued)

5. https://pkg.go.dev/io/fs#FileInfo
6. https://pkg.go.dev/os#FileInfo

```
info, err := file.Info()
if err != nil {
    log.Fatal(err)
}

fmt.Printf("%s\t%d\t\t%s\n", info.Mode(), info.Size(), info.Name())
    }
}
```

```
$ go run .

Mode          Size    Name
drwxr-xr-x    96              .hidden
-rw-r--r--    31              a.txt
-rw-r--r--    9               b.txt
drwxr-xr-x    128             e
drwxr-xr-x    96              testdata

Go Version: go1.19
```

Stating a File

The os.ReadDir function returns a slice of os.DirEntry values, from which we can get the fs.FileInfo: the os.DirEntry.Info field. To get the fs.FileInfo for a single file or directory, we can use the os.Stat[7] function, Listing 14.9.

Listing 14.9   The os.Stat Function

```
$ go doc os.Stat

package os // import "os"

func Stat(name string) (FileInfo, error)
    Stat returns a FileInfo describing the named file. If there is an error,
    ➥it will be of type *PathError.

Go Version: go1.19
```

Consider Listing 14.10, which prints the mode, size, and name of the data/a.txt file.

---

7. https://pkg.go.dev/os#Stat

Listing 14.10   Using os.Stat to Get Information about a File

```go
func main() {
    info, err := os.Stat("data/a.txt")
    if err != nil {
        log.Fatal(err)
    }

    fmt.Printf("%s\t%d\t%s\n", info.Mode(), info.Size(), info.Name())
}
```

```
$ go run .

-rw-r--r--   31  a.txt
```

```
Go Version: go1.19
```

Walking Directories

os.ReadDir does not recurse into subdirectories. To be able to do that, you need to use filepath.WalkDir,[8] Listing 14.11 to walk through all files in a directory and all subdirectories.

> filepath.WalkDir, introduced in go1.16, replaces the less efficient filepath.Walk.[9] Older examples may use filepath.Walk, but it is advised to use filepath.WalkDir instead.

Listing 14.11   The filepath.WalkDir Function

```
$ go doc filepath.WalkDir

package filepath // import "path/filepath"

func WalkDir(root string, fn fs.WalkDirFunc) error
    WalkDir walks the file tree rooted at root, calling fn for each file or
    ↪directory in the tree, including root.

    All errors that arise visiting files and directories are filtered by fn:
    ↪see the fs.WalkDirFunc documentation for details.
```

(continued)

---

8. https://pkg.go.dev/filepath#WalkDir
9. https://pkg.go.dev/filepath#Walk

> The files are walked in lexical order, which makes the output
> ➥deterministic but requires WalkDir to read an entire directory into
> ➥memory before proceeding to walk that directory.
>
> WalkDir does not follow symbolic links.
>
> _____
>
> Go Version: go1.19

To use `filepath.WalkDir`, you first need to give it a path to walk and then a function that will be called for each file. This function is the `filepath.WalkFunc`,[10] Listing 14.12.

Listing 14.12   The `fs.WalkDirFunc` Function

```
$ go doc fs.WalkDirFunc

package fs // import "io/fs"

type WalkDirFunc func(path string, d DirEntry, err error) error
    WalkDirFunc is the type of the function called by WalkDir to visit each
    ➥file or directory.

    The path argument contains the argument to WalkDir as a prefix. That is,
    ➥if WalkDir is called with root argument "dir" and finds a file named
    ➥"a" in that directory, the walk function will be called with argument
    ➥"dir/a".

    The d argument is the fs.DirEntry for the named path.

    The error result returned by the function controls how WalkDir continues.
    ➥If the function returns the special value SkipDir, WalkDir skips the
    ➥current directory (path if d.IsDir() is true, otherwise path's
    ➥parent directory). Otherwise, if the function returns a non-nil error,
    ➥WalkDir stops entirely and returns that error.

    The err argument reports an error related to path, signaling that WalkDir
    ➥will not walk into that directory. The function can decide how to handle
    ➥that error; as described earlier, returning the error will cause WalkDir
    ➥to stop walking the entire tree.

    WalkDir calls the function with a non-nil err argument in two cases.
```

_____

10. https://pkg.go.dev/filepath#WalkFunc

First, if the initial fs.Stat on the root directory fails, WalkDir calls
➥the function with path set to root, d set to nil, and err set to the
➥error from fs.Stat.

Second, if a directory's ReadDir method fails, WalkDir calls the function
➥with path set to the directory's path, d set to an fs.DirEntry
➥describing the directory, and err set to the error from ReadDir. In
➥this second case, the function is called twice with the path of the
➥directory: the first call is before the directory read is attempted and
➥has err set to nil, giving the function a chance to return SkipDir and
➥avoid the ReadDir entirely. The second call is after a failed ReadDir
➥and reports the error from ReadDir. (If ReadDir succeeds, there is no
➥second call.)

The differences between WalkDirFunc compared to filepath.WalkFunc are:

- The second argument has type fs.DirEntry instead of fs.FileInfo.
- The function is called before reading a directory, to allow SkipDir
  ➥to bypass the directory read entirely.
- If a directory read fails, the function is called a second time for
  ➥that directory to report the error.

Go Version: go1.19

Consider Listing 14.13, in which we walk through the data directory. For each file and directory, including the root directory, the filepath.WalkFunc is called.

Listing 14.13 Using filepath.WalkDir to Recurse a Directory

```go
func main() {
    err := filepath.WalkDir("data", func(path string, d fs.DirEntry, err error)
        ➥error {

        // if there was an error, return it
        // if there is an error, it is most likely
        // because an error was encountered trying
        // to read the top level directory
        if err != nil {
            return err
        }

        // if the file is a directory
        // return nil to tell walk to continue
```

(continued)

```
        // walking the directory,
        // but to no longer continue
        // operating on the directory itself
        if d.IsDir() {
            return nil
        }

        // get the file info for the file
        info, err := d.Info()
        if err != nil {
            return err
        }

        // if the file is not a directory
        // then print its mode, size, and path
        fmt.Printf("%s\t%d\t%s\n", info.Mode(), info.Size(), path)

        // return nil to tell walk to continue
        return nil
    })

    if err != nil {
        fmt.Println(err)
        os.Exit(1)
    }
}
```

First, we need to check the `error` that is passed in via the `filepath.WalkFunc` function. If this error is not `nil`, it is most likely that the root directory could not be read. In this case, we can simply return the error, and the walk stops.

If there is no error, we can then check to see if what we're dealing with is a directory or a file. If it is a directory, we can simply return `nil` to indicate that we don't want to continue processing the directory itself but walking of the directory will continue. The `fs.DirEntry.IsDir`[11] method can be used to check this, return `true` for a directory, and return `false` for a file.

Finally, we print off the mode, size, and path of the file.

As we can see from Listing 14.14, the walk function is called for each file and directory in the `data` directory. Printing out the file information is lexical order, which is the order in which the files and directories are listed in the directory.

---

11. https://pkg.go.dev/io/fs#DirEntry.IsDir

Listing 14.14 The Output of Listing 14.13

```
$ go run .

-rw-r--r--  31  data/.hidden/d.txt
-rw-r--r--  31  data/a.txt
-rw-r--r--  9   data/b.txt
-rw-r--r--  31  data/e/f/_ignore/i.json
-rw-r--r--  31  data/e/f/g.txt
-rw-r--r--  31  data/e/f/h.txt
-rw-r--r--  9   data/e/j.txt
-rw-r--r--  31  data/testdata/c.txt
```

Go Version: go1.19

Skipping Directories and Files

When walking through a directory tree, you may want to skip certain directories and files. For example, you may want to skip hidden folders like .git and .vscode or skip large folders such as node_modules. There may be other reasons to skip certain files and directories that are more specific to your application.

To illustrate this, let's look at the excerpt from the go help test command in Listing 14.15.

Listing 14.15 Excerpt from the go help test Command

```
Files whose names begin with "_" (including "_test.go") or "." are ignored.

The go tool will ignore a directory named "testdata", making it available
➥to hold ancillary data needed by the tests.
```

The documentation in Listing 14.15 says that there are certain files and directories that Go ignores when walking through a directory tree looking for test files:

- Files/directories whose names begin with . are ignored.
- Files/directories whose names begin with _ are ignored.
- The testdata directory is ignored.

Let's implement these same restrictions in our own code.

Skipping Directories

To tell Go to skip a directory, we can return `fs.SkipDir`,[12] Listing 14.16, from our
`fs.WalkFunc` function. Although technically this is an `error`[13] type, Go is using this error
as a sentinel value to indicate that the directory should be skipped. This is similar to how
`io.EOF`[14] is used to indicate that the end of a file has been reached and there is no more
data to be read.

Listing 14.16   The `fs.SkipDir` Error

```
$ go doc fs.SkipDir

package fs // import "io/fs"

var SkipDir = errors.New("skip this directory")
    SkipDir is used as a return value from WalkDirFuncs to indicate that the
    ⤶directory named in the call is to be skipped. It is not returned as
    ⤶an error by any function.
```

```
Go Version: go1.19
```

In Listing 14.17, instead of simply returning a `nil` when the `fs.DirEntry` is a directory,
we can check the name of the directory and make a decision on whether to ignore
that directory. If we want to ignore a directory, `testdata` for example, we can return
`fs.SkipDir` from our `fs.WalkFunc` function. Go then skips that directory and all
of its children.

Listing 14.17   Using `fs.SkipDir` to Skip Directories

```
package demo

import (
    "io/fs"
    "path/filepath"
    "strings"
)

func Walk() ([]string, error) {
    var entries []string

    err := filepath.WalkDir("data", func(path string, d fs.DirEntry, err error)
            ⤶error {
```

---

12. https://pkg.go.dev/io/fs#SkipDir
13. https://pkg.go.dev/builtin#error
14. https://pkg.go.dev/io#EOF

```go
        // if there was an error, return it
        // if there is an error, it is most likely
        // because an error was encountered trying
        // to read the top level directory
        if err != nil {
            return err
        }

        // if the entry is a directory, handle it
        if d.IsDir() {

            // name of the file or directory
            name := d.Name()

            // if the directory is a dot return nil
            // this may be the root directory
            if name == "." || name == ".." {
                return nil
            }

            // if the directory name is "testdata"
            // or it starts with "."
            // or it starts with "_"
            // then return filepath.SkipDir
            if name == "testdata" || strings.HasPrefix(name, ".")
            ➥|| strings.HasPrefix(name, "_") {
                return fs.SkipDir
            }

            return nil
        }

        // append the entry to the list
        entries = append(entries, path)

        // return nil to tell walk to continue
        return nil
    }))

    return entries, err
}
```

Next, in Listing 14.18, we can write a small test that asserts that the `testdata` directory and our other special directories are skipped.

Listing 14.18   Asserting Special Directories Are Skipped

```go
func Test_Walk(t *testing.T) {
    t.Parallel()

    exp := []string{
        "data/a.txt",
        "data/b.txt",
        "data/e/f/g.txt",
        "data/e/f/h.txt",
        "data/e/j.txt",
    }

    act, err := Walk()
    if err != nil {
        t.Fatal(err)
    }

    es := strings.Join(exp, ", ")
    as := strings.Join(act, ", ")

    if es != as {
        t.Fatalf("expected %s, got %s", es, as)
    }
}
```

```
$ go test -v

=== RUN    Test_Walk
=== PAUSE Test_Walk
=== CONT  Test_Walk
--- PASS: Test_Walk (0.00s)
PASS
ok      demo    0.812s
```

Go Version: go1.19

Finally, when compared to the original file listing, Listing 14.19, we see that the `testdata` directory, along with the other special directories, is no longer included in the file listing.

Listing 14.19   Original File Listing

```
$ tree -a

.
|-- .hidden
|    '-- d.txt
|-- a.txt
|-- b.txt
|-- e
|    |-- f
|    |    |-- _ignore
|    |    |    '-- i.txt
|    |    |-- g.txt
|    |    '-- h.txt
|    '-- j.txt
'-- testdata
     '-- c.txt

5 directories, 8 files
```

Creating Directories and Subdirectories

Now that we have a working test suite that asserts our `Walk` function returns the correct results, we can remove the hard-coded test data we've been using and generate the test data directly inside the test itself.

To create a single directory, we can use the `os.Mkdir`[15] function, as in Listing 14.20. The `os.Mkdir` function creates a single directory at the path specified, and with the specified permissions.

Listing 14.20   The `os.Mkdir` Function

```
$ go doc os.Mkdir

package os // import "os"

func Mkdir(name string, perm FileMode) error
    Mkdir creates a new directory with the specified name and permission bits
    ➥(before umask). If there is an error, it will be of type *PathError.
```

Go Version: go1.19

---

15. https://pkg.go.dev/os#Mkdir

To create a directory, you need to provide a set of permissions for the directory. The permissions are specified in the form of an os.FileMode[16] value, Listing 14.21. Those familiar with Unix style permissions will feel right at home here being able to use permissions such as 0755 to specify the permissions for the directory.

Listing 14.21   The os.FileMode Type

```
$ go doc os.FileMode

package os // import "os"

type FileMode = fs.FileMode
    A FileMode represents a file's mode and permission bits. The bits have
    ➥the same definition on all systems, so that information about files can
    ➥be moved from one system to another portably. Not all bits apply to
    ➥all systems. The only required bit is ModeDir for directories.
```

Go Version: go1.19

In Listing 14.22, we can create a helper that generates all of the files for us. In this helper, we first remove any test data that may have been left behind from a previous test run, by using the os.RemoveAll[17] function. This deletes the directory at the path specified; it also deletes all of its contents, including any subdirectories.

Listing 14.22   Using os.Mkdir to Create Directories on Disk

```
func createTestData(t testing.TB) {
    t.Helper()

    // remove any previous test data
    if err := os.RemoveAll("data"); err != nil {
        t.Fatal(err)
    }

    // create the data directory
    if err := os.Mkdir("data", 0755); err != nil {
        t.Fatal(err)
    }

    list := []string{
        "data/.hidden/d.txt",
        "data/a.txt",
```

---

16. https://pkg.go.dev/os#FileMode
17. https://pkg.go.dev/os#RemoveAll

```
        "data/b.txt",
        "data/e/f/_ignore/i.txt",
        "data/e/f/g.txt",
        "data/e/f/h.txt",
        "data/e/j.txt",
        "data/testdata/c.txt",
    }

    // create the test data files
    for _, path := range list {
        fmt.Println("creating:", path)
        if err := os.Mkdir(path, 0755); err != nil {
            t.Fatal(err)
        }

    }

}
```

Next, we use the os.Mkdir function to create the parent data directory, giving it the permissions 0755 that allow us to read and write to the directory.

Finally, we loop over a list of files and directories that we want to create and create each one using the os.Mkdir function.

As you can see from the test output in Listing 14.23, this approach isn't working as expected. We run into errors trying to create the necessary files and directories. The biggest problem is that we are trying to use os.Mkdir to create files instead of directories.

Listing 14.23   Error Using os.Mkdir to Create Files

```
$ go test -v

=== RUN    Test_Walk
=== PAUSE Test_Walk
=== CONT  Test_Walk
creating: data/.hidden/d.txt
    demo_test.go:52: mkdir data/.hidden/d.txt: no such file or directory
--- FAIL: Test_Walk (0.00s)
FAIL
exit status 1
FAIL    demo    0.528s
```

Go Version: go1.19

File Path Helpers

The filepath[18] package, Listing 14.24, provides a number of functions that help you manipulate file paths.

Listing 14.24   The filepath Package

```
$ go doc -short filepath

const Separator = os.PathSeparator ...
var ErrBadPattern = errors.New("syntax error in pattern")
var SkipDir error = fs.SkipDir
func Abs(path string) (string, error)
func Base(path string) string
func Clean(path string) string
func Dir(path string) string
func EvalSymlinks(path string) (string, error)
func Ext(path string) string
func FromSlash(path string) string
func Glob(pattern string) (matches []string, err error)
func HasPrefix(p, prefix string) bool
func IsAbs(path string) bool
func Join(elem ...string) string
func Match(pattern, name string) (matched bool, err error)
func Rel(basepath, targpath string) (string, error)
func Split(path string) (dir, file string)
func SplitList(path string) []string
func ToSlash(path string) string
func VolumeName(path string) string
func Walk(root string, fn WalkFunc) error
func WalkDir(root string, fn fs.WalkDirFunc) error
type WalkFunc func(path string, info fs.FileInfo, err error) error
```

Go Version: go1.19

There are three functions in particular that are going to be useful in our test suite. These are filepath.Ext,[19] filepath.Dir,[20] and filepath.Base.[21]

---

18. https://pkg.go.dev/filepath
19. https://pkg.go.dev/filepath#Ext
20. https://pkg.go.dev/filepath#Dir
21. https://pkg.go.dev/filepath#Base

Getting a File's Extension

When presented with a file path in `string` form, such as /path/to/file.txt, you need to be able to tell whether the path is a file or a directory. The easiest, although not without potential errors, way to do this is to check whether the path has a file extension. If it does, then you can assume the path to be a file; if it doesn't, then you can assume the path to be a directory. The `filepath.Ext` function, Listing 14.25, returns the file extension of a file path. If the path is /path/to/file.txt, then the function returns .txt.

Listing 14.25 The `filepath.Ext` Function

```
$ go doc filepath.Ext

package filepath // import "path/filepath"

func Ext(path string) string
    Ext returns the file name extension used by path. The extension is the
    ➡suffix beginning at the final dot in the final element of path; it is
    ➡empty if there is no dot.
```

Go Version: go1.19

Getting a File's Directory

If the `filepath.Ext` function returns an extension, such as .txt, then you can assume the path is a file. To get the directory of a file, you can use the `filepath.Dir` function, Listing 14.26. If the path is /path/to/file.txt, then the function returns /path/to.

Listing 14.26 The `filepath.Dir` Function

```
$ go doc filepath.Dir

package filepath // import "path/filepath"

func Dir(path string) string
    Dir returns all but the last element of path, typically the path's
    ➡directory. After dropping the final element, Dir calls Clean on the
    ➡path and trailing slashes are removed. If the path is empty, Dir returns
    ➡ ".". If the path consists entirely of separators, Dir returns a single
    ➡separator. The returned path does not end in a separator unless it
    ➡is the root directory.
```

Go Version: go1.19

Getting a File/Directory's Name

Regardless of whether your path has an extension, it does have a "base" name. You can use the `filepath.Base` function, shown in Listing 14.27, to return the name of the file or directory at the end of the file path. For example, if the path is /path/to/file.txt, then "base" name would be file.txt. If the path is /path/to/dir, then the "base" name would be dir.

Listing 14.27   The `filepath.Base` Function

```
$ go doc filepath.Base

package filepath // import "path/filepath"

func Base(path string) string
    Base returns the last element of path. Trailing path separators are
    ↪removed before extracting the last element. If the path is empty,
    ↪Base returns ".". If the path consists entirely of separators,
    ↪Base returns a single separator.
```

Go Version: go1.19

Using File Path Helpers

Now that you know how to find the directory, base, and extension of a file path, you can use these functions to update your helper to create *only* directories—not files. In Listing 14.28, we can use the `filepath.Dir` and `filepath.Ext` functions to parse the given file path to create the necessary folder structure on disk.

Listing 14.28   Helper Function to Create Test Folder and File Structures

```go
func createTestData(t testing.TB) {
    t.Helper()

    // remove any previous test data
    if err := os.RemoveAll("data"); err != nil {
        t.Fatal(err)
    }

    // create the data directory
    if err := os.Mkdir("data", 0755); err != nil {
        t.Fatal(err)
    }
```

```
    list := []string{
        "data/.hidden/d.txt",
        "data/a.txt",
        "data/b.txt",
        "data/e/f/_ignore/i.txt",
        "data/e/f/g.txt",
        "data/e/f/h.txt",
        "data/e/j.txt",
        "data/testdata/c.txt",
    }

    // create the test data files
    for _, path := range list {
        if ext := filepath.Ext(path); len(ext) > 0 {
            path = filepath.Dir(path)
        }

        fmt.Println("creating:", path)
        if err := os.Mkdir(path, 0755); err != nil {
            t.Fatal(err)
        }

    }

}
```

When you look at the test output, Listing 14.29, you can see that the helper function is still not working as expected. It is trying to create a directory, data, that already exists.

Listing 14.29 Test Output

```
$ go test -v

=== RUN    Test_Walk
=== PAUSE Test_Walk
=== CONT  Test_Walk
creating: data/.hidden
creating: data
    demo_test.go:57: mkdir data: file exists
--- FAIL: Test_Walk (0.00s)
FAIL
exit status 1
FAIL    demo    0.635s

Go Version: go1.19
```

Checking the Error

To try to fix our helper, we should properly check the error returned by the os.Mkdir function in Listing 14.30. If the error is not nil, we need to check whether the error is because the directory already exists. If it is, then we can ignore the error and continue. If the error is something else, then we need to return the error to the caller.

Listing 14.30   Helper Function to Check for Errors

```go
func createTestData(t testing.TB) {
    t.Helper()

    // remove any previous test data
    if err := os.RemoveAll("data"); err != nil {
        t.Fatal(err)
    }

    // create the data directory
    if err := os.Mkdir("data", 0755); err != nil {
        t.Fatal(err)
    }

    list := []string{
        "data/.hidden/d.txt",
        "data/a.txt",
        "data/b.txt",
        "data/e/f/_ignore/i.txt",
        "data/e/f/g.txt",
        "data/e/f/h.txt",
        "data/e/j.txt",
        "data/testdata/c.txt",
    }

    // create the test data files
    for _, path := range list {
        if ext := filepath.Ext(path); len(ext) > 0 {
            path = filepath.Dir(path)
        }

        fmt.Println("creating:", path)
        if err := os.Mkdir(path, 0755); err != nil {
            // ignore if the directory already exists
```

```
        if !errors.Is(err, fs.ErrExist) {
            t.Fatal(err)
        }
    }

  }

}
```

When you look at the test output, Listing 14.31, you can see that the helper function is still not working as expected, but you have moved beyond the first error to a new one. We are trying to create nested subdirectories, data/e/f/_ignore, using the os.Mkdir function that is designed to create only one directory at a time.

Listing 14.31 Using errors.Is[22] to Check for the fs.ErrExit[23] Error

```
$ go test -v

=== RUN    Test_Walk
=== PAUSE Test_Walk
=== CONT  Test_Walk
creating: data/.hidden
creating: data
creating: data
creating: data/e/f/_ignore
    demo_test.go:62: mkdir data/e/f/_ignore: no such file or directory
--- FAIL: Test_Walk (0.00s)
FAIL
exit status 1
FAIL    demo    0.761s
```

Go Version: go1.19

Creating Multiple Directories

To create multiple directories at once, you can use the os.MkdirAll[24] function, Listing 14.32. This behaves identically to os.Mkdir except that it creates all the directories in the path.

---

22. https://pkg.go.dev/errors#Is
23. https://pkg.go.dev/io/fs#ErrExit
24. https://pkg.go.dev/os#MkdirAll

Listing 14.32   The os.MkdirAll Function

```
$ go doc os.MkdirAll

package os // import "os"

func MkdirAll(path string, perm FileMode) error
    MkdirAll creates a directory named path, along with any necessary parents,
    ↪and returns nil, or else returns an error. The permission bits perm
    ↪(before umask) are used for all directories that MkdirAll creates.
    ↪If path is already a directory, MkdirAll does nothing and returns nil.
```

```
Go Version: go1.19
```

In Listing 14.33, we can update our test helper to use os.MkdirAll to create the
directories, instead of os.Mkdir, to ensure that all of the directories are created rather than
just one.

Listing 14.33   Helper Function to Create Test Folder and File Structures

```
func createTestData(t testing.TB) {
    t.Helper()

    // remove any previous test data
    if err := os.RemoveAll("data"); err != nil {
        t.Fatal(err)
    }

    // create the data directory
    if err := os.Mkdir("data", 0755); err != nil {
        t.Fatal(err)
    }

    list := []string{
        "data/.hidden/d.txt",
        "data/a.txt",
        "data/b.txt",
        "data/e/f/_ignore/i.txt",
        "data/e/f/g.txt",
        "data/e/f/h.txt",
        "data/e/j.txt",
        "data/testdata/c.txt",
    }
```

```go
    // create the test data files
    for _, path := range list {
        if ext := filepath.Ext(path); len(ext) > 0 {
            path = filepath.Dir(path)
        }

        fmt.Println("creating:", path)
        if err := os.MkdirAll(path, 0755); err != nil {
            // ignore if the directory already exists
            if !errors.Is(err, fs.ErrExist) {
                t.Fatal(err)
            }
        }
    }

}
```

```
$ go test -v

=== RUN   Test_Walk
=== PAUSE Test_Walk
=== CONT  Test_Walk
creating: data/.hidden
creating: data
creating: data
creating: data/e/f/_ignore
creating: data/e/f
creating: data/e/f
creating: data/e
creating: data/testdata
    demo_test.go:81: expected data/a.txt, data/b.txt, data/e/f/g.txt,
    ↪data/e/f/h.txt, data/e/j.txt, got
--- FAIL: Test_Walk (0.02s)
FAIL
exit status 1
FAIL    demo    0.638s
```

```
Go Version: go1.19
```

As you can see from the output in Listing 14.34, our tests are still not passing. This is because we have yet to create the necessary files.

A look at the file system itself confirms that the directories were indeed created.

Listing 14.34   The Directory Structure Created by the Test Helper

```
$ tree -a

.
|-- data
|    |-- .hidden
|    |-- e
|    |   '-- f
|    |           '-- _ignore
|    '-- testdata
|-- demo.go
|-- demo_test.go
'-- go.mod

6 directories, 3 files
```

Creating Files

Before you can read a file, you need to create it. To create a new file, you can use the os.Create[25] function, Listing 14.35. The os.Create function creates a new file at the specified path if one does not already exist. If the file already exists, the os.Create function erases, or truncates, the existing file's contents.

Listing 14.35   The os.Create Function

```
$ go doc os.Create

package os // import "os"

func Create(name string) (*File, error)
    Create creates or truncates the named file. If the file already exists,
    ↪it is truncated. If the file does not exist, it is created with mode
    ↪0666 (before umask). If successful, methods on the returned File can
    ↪be used for I/O; the associated file descriptor has mode O_RDWR. If
    ↪there is an error, it will be of type *PathError.
```

Go Version: go1.19

Consider Listing 14.36. We have a Create function that creates a new file at the specified path and writes the specified data to the file.

---

25. https://pkg.go.dev/os#Create

Listing 14.36   The Create Function

```go
func Create(name string, body []byte) error {
    // create a new file, this will
    // truncate the file if it already exists
    f, err := os.Create(name)
    if err != nil {
        return err
    }
    defer f.Close()

    // write the body to the file
    _, err = f.Write(body)
    return err
}
```

If successful, os.Create returns a os.File[26] value representing the new file. This file can then be written to and read from. In this case, we are writing the string Hello, World! to the file.

In Listing 14.37, we write a test that confirms the file was created and its contents are correct.

Listing 14.37   Testing the Create Function from Listing 14.36

```go
func Test_Create(t *testing.T) {
    t.Parallel()

    fp := "data/test.txt"

    // create test data directory
    createTestData(t)

    // assert the file does not exist
    // by trying to stat it.
    // this should return an error
    _, err := os.Stat(fp)
    if err != nil {
        if !errors.Is(err, fs.ErrNotExist) {
            t.Fatal(err)
        }
    }
```

(continued)

---

26. https://pkg.go.dev/os#File

```
body := []byte("Hello, World!")

// create the file
err = Create(fp, body)
if err != nil {
    t.Fatal(err)
}

// read the file into memory
b, err := os.ReadFile(fp)
if err != nil {
    t.Fatal(err)
}

act := string(b)
exp := string(body)

// assert the file contents are correct
if exp != act {
    t.Fatalf("expected %s, got %s", exp, act)
}

}
```

First, we need to make sure the file does not already exist. To do this, we can use the os.Stat function to check if the file exists.

Next, we can read the contents of the file using the os.ReadFile[27] function. This function reads the entire contents of the file into a byte slice. If the file does not exist, the os.ReadFile function, Listing 14.38, returns an error.

Listing 14.38   The os.ReadFile Function

```
$ go doc os.ReadFile

package os // import "os"

func ReadFile(name string) ([]byte, error)
    ReadFile reads the named file and returns the contents. A successful call
    ↪returns err == nil, not err == EOF. Because ReadFile reads the whole
    ↪file, it does not treat an EOF from Read as an error to be reported.

Go Version: go1.19
```

---

27. https://pkg.go.dev/os#ReadFile

Care must be taken when using the os.ReadFile function. If the file is very large, it may cause your program to run out of memory.

Finally, we can compare the contents of the file to the expected contents. The test output, Listing 14.39, confirms that the file was created and its contents are correct.

Listing 14.39 Test Output from Listing 14.37

```
$ go test -v

=== RUN    Test_Create
=== PAUSE Test_Create
=== CONT  Test_Create
--- PASS: Test_Create (0.00s)
PASS
ok      demo    0.390s

Go Version: go1.19
```

If we look directly at the file on disk, as shown in Listing 14.40, we can see that the file has been created and its contents are correct.

Listing 14.40 Contents of Listing 14.39

```
$ cat data/test.txt

Hello, World!
```

Truncation

If a file already exists, the os.Create function truncates the existing file's contents. This means that if a file already exists and has contents, the file is erased before the new contents are written. This can lead to unexpected results.

Consider the example in Listing 14.41. In this test, we are creating a file and setting its contents. Then, we create the file again—this time with different contents. The original contents of the file are erased and replaced with the new contents.

Listing 14.41 Using os.Create Truncates and Replaces an Existing File on Disk

```
func Test_Create(t *testing.T) {
    t.Parallel()

    fp := "data/test.txt"
```

(continued)

```
// create the file and assert
// the file should now equal the string
// "Hello, World!"
createTestFile(t, fp, []byte("Hello, World!"))

// create the file, again, and assert
// the file should now equal the string
// "Hello, Universe!"
createTestFile(t, fp, []byte("Hello, Universe!"))
}
```

To keep the test clean, we can use a helper function, Listing 14.42, to create a file, set its contents, and then assert that the contents are correct.

Listing 14.42   The `fileHelper` Function

```
func createTestFile(t testing.TB, fp string, body []byte) {
    t.Helper()

    // create test data directory
    createTestData(t)

    // assert the file does not exist
    // by trying to stat it.
    // this should return an error
    _, err := os.Stat(fp)
    if err != nil {
        if !errors.Is(err, fs.ErrNotExist) {
            t.Fatal(err)
        }
    }

    // create the file
    err = Create(fp, body)
    if err != nil {
        t.Fatal(err)
    }

    // read the file into memory
    b, err := ioutil.ReadFile(fp)
    if err != nil {
        t.Fatal(err)
    }
```

```
    act := string(b)
    exp := string(body)

    // assert the file contents are correct
    if exp != act {
        t.Fatalf("expected %s, got %s", exp, act)
    }

}
```

```
$ go test -v

=== RUN    Test_Create
=== PAUSE Test_Create
=== CONT  Test_Create
--- PASS: Test_Create (0.02s)
PASS
ok      demo    0.552s
```

```
Go Version: go1.19
```

From the test output, Listing 14.42, you can see that the original contents of the file were erased, and the new contents were written.

A look at the file on disk, Listing 14.43, confirms that the new content was written.

Listing 14.43 Contents of Listing 14.42

```
$ cat data/test.txt

Hello, Universe!
```

Fixing the Walk Tests

When we last looked at the tests for our `Walk` function, we saw that the tests were failing, Listing 14.44. Our tests are failing because we have yet to create the files necessary. We have only created the directories.

Listing 14.44 Failing Test Output

```
$ go test -v

=== RUN    Test_Walk
=== PAUSE Test_Walk
```

(continued)

```
=== CONT   Test_Walk
creating: data/.hidden
creating: data
creating: data
creating: data/e/f/_ignore
creating: data/e/f
creating: data/e/f
creating: data/e
creating: data/testdata
    demo_test.go:81: expected data/a.txt, data/b.txt, data/e/f/g.txt,
    ➥data/e/f/h.txt, data/e/j.txt, got
--- FAIL: Test_Walk (0.00s)
FAIL
exit status 1
FAIL    demo    0.318s
```
```
Go Version: go1.19
```

A look at the file system, Listing 14.45, confirms that the directories were created but the files were not.

Listing 14.45   Folders but Not Files Were Created in Listing 14.44

```
$ tree -a

.
|-- data
|   |-- .hidden
|   |-- e
|   |   '-- f
|   |       '-- _ignore
|   '-- testdata
|-- demo.go
|-- demo_test.go
'-- go.mod

6 directories, 3 files
```

Creating the Files

With knowledge of how to create files, we can now create the files necessary for our tests, Listing 14.46.

Listing 14.46   Create Files with os.Create and Directories with os.MkdirAll

```go
// create the test data files
for _, path := range list {
    dir := path
    if ext := filepath.Ext(path); len(ext) > 0 {
        dir = filepath.Dir(path)
    }

    if err := os.MkdirAll(dir, 0755); err != nil {
        // ignore if the directory already exists
        if !errors.Is(err, fs.ErrExist) {
            t.Fatal(err)
        }
    }

    fmt.Println("creating", path)
    f, err := os.Create(path)
    if err != nil {
        t.Fatal(err)
    }

    fmt.Fprint(f, strings.ToUpper(path))

    if err := f.Close(); err != nil {
        t.Fatal(err)
    }

}
```

```
$ go test -v

=== RUN    Test_Walk
=== PAUSE Test_Walk
=== CONT  Test_Walk
creating data/.hidden/d.txt
creating data/a.txt
creating data/b.txt
creating data/e/f/_ignore/i.txt
creating data/e/f/g.txt
creating data/e/f/h.txt
creating data/e/j.txt
creating data/testdata/c.txt
```

(continued)

```
--- PASS: Test_Walk (0.00s)
PASS
ok      demo     0.471s
```

```
Go Version: go1.19
```

The tests are now passing, Listing 14.47, all files and directories are created as expected, and the `Walk` function is working as expected.

Listing 14.47   The File System

```
$ tree -a


.
|-- data
|   |-- .hidden
|   |   '-- d.txt
|   |-- a.txt
|   |-- b.txt
|   |-- e
|   |   |-- f
|   |   |   |-- _ignore
|   |   |   |   '-- i.txt
|   |   |   |-- g.txt
|   |   |   '-- h.txt
|   |   '-- j.txt
|   '-- testdata
|       '-- c.txt
|-- demo.go
|-- demo_test.go
'-- go.mod

6 directories, 11 files
```

Appending to Files

When you use `os.Create` to create a file, if that file already exists, the file is overwritten. This is expected behavior when creating a new file. It would be strange to find previously written contents in a new file.

There are plenty of times when you want to append to an existing file instead of overwriting it. For example, you might want to append to a log file with new entries and not overwrite the previous log entries. In this case, you can use os.OpenFile[28] to open the file for appending, as in Listing 14.48.

Listing 14.48   The os.OpenFile Function

```
$ go doc os.OpenFile

package os // import "os"

func OpenFile(name string, flag int, perm FileMode) (*File, error)
    OpenFile is the generalized open call; most users will use Open or Create
    ➥instead. It opens the named file with specified flag (O_RDONLY etc.).
    ➥If the file does not exist, and the O_CREATE flag is passed, it is
    ➥created with mode perm (before umask). If successful, methods on the
    ➥returned File can be used for I/O. If there is an error, it will be of
    ➥type *PathError.
```

Go Version: go1.19

Consider Listing 14.49. We have an Append function that uses os.OpenFile to open the file for appending. The os.OpenFile function can be configured with flags to tell Go how to open the file. In this example, we create the file if it does not exist and append to it if it does.

Listing 14.49   The Append Function

```
func Append(name string, body []byte) error {
    // if the file doesn't exist, create it, or append to the file
    f, err := os.OpenFile(name, os.O_APPEND|os.O_CREATE|os.O_WRONLY, 0644)
    if err != nil {
        return err
    }
    defer f.Close()

    // write the body to the file
    _, err = f.Write(body)
    return err
}
```

Next, we can write a test to confirm that the file is appended to properly, Listing 14.50. We can make use of our createTestFile helper to create the initial file and fill it with some data, but we need a new helper to append to the file.

---

28. https://pkg.go.dev/os#OpenFile

Listing 14.50   Testing the Append Function

```go
func Test_Append(t *testing.T) {
    t.Parallel()

    fp := "data/test.txt"

    // create the file and assert
    // the file should now equal the string
    // "Hello, World!"
    createTestFile(t, fp, []byte("Hello, World!"))

    // create the file, again, and assert
    // the file should now equal the string
    // "Hello, Universe!"
    appendTestFile(t, fp, []byte("Hello, Universe!"))
}
```

The appendTestFile helper reads in the original contents of the file, appends the new data, and then reads the new contents of the file. Finally, we can compare to see if the new contents of the file are equal to the original contents plus the new data.

The tests in Listing 14.51 show that the file is appended to properly.

Listing 14.51   The appendTestFile Helper

```go
func appendTestFile(t testing.TB, fp string, body []byte) {
    t.Helper()

    // read the existing file into memory
    before, err := os.ReadFile(fp)
    if err != nil {
        t.Fatal(err)
    }

    // append the new data
    if err := Append(fp, body); err != nil {
        t.Fatal(err)
    }

    // read the new file into memory
    after, err := os.ReadFile(fp)
    if err != nil {
        t.Fatal(err)
```

```
    }

    // assert the new file contents
    // contain the old and new data
    // Hello, World!Hello, Universe!
    exp := string(append(before, body...))
    act := string(after)

    if exp != act {
        t.Fatalf("expected %s, got %s", exp, act)
    }
}
```

```
$ go test -v

=== RUN    Test_Append
=== PAUSE Test_Append
=== CONT   Test_Append
--- PASS: Test_Append (0.02s)
PASS
ok      demo    0.348s

Go Version: go1.19
```

Finally, a look at the file system shows that the file is appended to properly, Listing 14.52.

Listing 14.52 The Contents of the File

```
$ cat data/test.txt

Hello, World!Hello, Universe!
```

Reading Files

So far we have been reading files directly into memory using the os.ReadFile function. Although this is a very simple way to read a file, it is not the most efficient way to do so. If the file is very large, reading it into memory may not be feasible. It may also not be necessary. For example, if you have a media file, such as a video, you might only want to read its metadata at the beginning of the file and then stop reading it before you get to the actual video data.

Using interfaces, such as io.Reader and io.Writer, you can read and write files in a more efficient way.

Consider the example in Listing 14.53. We are opening a file using os.Open, which returns an os.File that implements the io.Reader[29] interface. We are passing the Read function to an io.Writer[30] as an argument. We can make use of both of these interfaces to use the io.Copy[31] function to copy the contents of the file to the io.Writer. If this io.Writer is another os.File, then io.Copy streams the data directly from one file to the other.

Listing 14.53   The Read Function

```go
func Read(fp string, w io.Writer) error {
    f, err := os.Open(fp)
    if err != nil {
        return err
    }
    defer f.Close()

    _, err = io.Copy(w, f)
    return err
}
```

In the test in Listing 14.54, we use a bytes.Buffer[32] as the io.Writer we pass to the Read function. This then allows us to assert the contents of the file were properly read.

Listing 14.54   Testing the Read Function

```go
func Test_Read(t *testing.T) {
    t.Parallel()

    bb := &bytes.Buffer{}

    err := Read("data/test.txt", bb)
    if err != nil {
        t.Fatal(err)
    }

    exp := "Hello, World!"
    act := bb.String()
```

---

29. https://pkg.go.dev/io#Reader
30. https://pkg.go.dev/io#Writer
31. https://pkg.go.dev/io#Copy
32. https://pkg.go.dev/bytes#Buffer

```
    if exp != act {
        t.Fatalf("expected %s, got %s", exp, act)
    }
}
```

```
$ go test -v

=== RUN    Test_Read
=== PAUSE  Test_Read
=== CONT   Test_Read
--- PASS: Test_Read (0.00s)
PASS
ok        demo      0.643s
```

```
Go Version: go1.19
```

Beware of Windows

When discussing file systems, special attention must be paid to Windows. Although Go has done a great job of abstracting away the differences between Windows and Unix file systems, it is still possible to run into some issues.

The largest issue is that Windows has a different file path system than Unix. In Unix, a file path is a series of directories separated by slashes, whereas in Windows, a file path is a series of directories separated by backslashes.

```
Unix:     /home/user/go/src/github.com/golang/example/
Windows:  C:\Users\user\go\src\github.com\golang\example
```

Because of this difference, whenever you want to use a nested filepath in Go, you need to use a function that converts the path to the correct format. The filepath.Join[33] function, Listing 14.55, does this.

Listing 14.55 The filepath.Join Function

```
$ go doc filepath.Join

package filepath // import "path/filepath"
```

(continued)

---

33. https://pkg.go.dev/filepath#Join

```
func Join(elem ...string) string
    Join joins any number of path elements into a single path, separating
    ↪them with an OS specific Separator. Empty elements are ignored. The
    ↪result is Cleaned. However, if the argument list is empty or all its
    ↪elements are empty, Join returns an empty string. On Windows, the result
    ↪will only be a UNC path if the first non-empty element is a UNC path.
```

Go Version: go1.19

The `filepath.Join` is a function that takes a variable number of paths and joins them together with the appropriate `filepath.Separator`.[34] The result is a string that is a valid path in the appropriate file system. In Listing 14.56, we can join multiple paths together to create a Windows or Unix file path, depending on the underlying operating system.

Listing 14.56 Using `filepath.Join` Function to Create Platform-Specific File Paths

```
path := filepath.Join("home", "user", "go", "src", "github.com", "golang",
        ↪"example")
// Unix:    /home/user/go/src/github.com/golang/example/
// Windows: C:\Users\user\go\src\github.com\golang\example
```

When we use the `fs`[35] package, we can use `/` as the separator, and the filepath is converted to the correct format for the current operating system.

The FS Package

In go1.16, the Go team wanted to introduce a long-requested feature: the ability to embed files into a Go binary. There had been a variety of third-party tools that did this, but none of them were able to do it without a lot of work.

A lot of these tools behaved in a similar way. If the file was found in their in-memory store, they would return it. If their store was empty, or didn't contain the file, the assumption was the file was in the file system, and they would read it from there. The Go team liked this approach because it was very friendly to developers. Using `go run` to start you local web server, for example, would read HTML templates from disk, allowing for live updates. But if built with `go build`, the binary would contain all of the HTML templates in memory, and the developer would have to manually update the binary to see file changes.

To enable this feature, the Go team had to introduce a new set of interfaces for working with the file system. For this, they introduced the `fs` package, Listing 14.57. Although this package was introduced to help enable the new embedding feature, it provides a common interface for working with *read-only* file systems. This allows developers to mock out the

---

34. https://pkg.go.dev/filepath#Separator
35. https://pkg.go.dev/fs

file system for testing or create their own file system implementations. For example, you can implement the fs.FS interface to create an Amazon S3 file system that is a drop-in replacement for the standard file system.

Listing 14.57 The fs Package

```
$ go doc fs

package fs // import "io/fs"

Package fs defines basic interfaces to a file system. A file system can be
➥provided by the host operating system but also by other packages.

var ErrInvalid = errInvalid() ...
var SkipDir = errors.New("skip this directory")
func Glob(fsys FS, pattern string) (matches []string, err error)
func ReadFile(fsys FS, name string) ([]byte, error)
func ValidPath(name string) bool
func WalkDir(fsys FS, root string, fn WalkDirFunc) error
type DirEntry interface{ ... }
    func FileInfoToDirEntry(info FileInfo) DirEntry
    func ReadDir(fsys FS, name string) ([]DirEntry, error)
type FS interface{ ... }
    func Sub(fsys FS, dir string) (FS, error)
type File interface{ ... }
type FileInfo interface{ ... }
    func Stat(fsys FS, name string) (FileInfo, error)
type FileMode uint32
    const ModeDir FileMode = 1 << (32 - 1 - iota) ...
type GlobFS interface{ ... }
type PathError struct{ ... }
type ReadDirFS interface{ ... }
type ReadDirFile interface{ ... }
type ReadFileFS interface{ ... }
type StatFS interface{ ... }
type SubFS interface{ ... }
type WalkDirFunc func(path string, d DirEntry, err error) error
```

Go Version: go1.19

The fs package is for working with a "read-only" file system. It does not provide any methods for writing to the file system. You continue to use the previously discussed methods for creating files and directories.

The FS Interface

At the core of the `fs` package are two interfaces: the `fs.FS`[36] interface and the `fs.File`[37] interface.

The `fs.FS` interface is used to define a file system, Listing 14.58. To implement this interface, you must define a method, named `Open`, that accepts a path and returns an `fs.File` interface and a potential error.

Listing 14.58   The `fs.FS` Interface

```
$ go doc fs.FS

package fs // import "io/fs"

type FS interface {
        // Open opens the named file.
        //
        // When Open returns an error, it should be of type *PathError
        // with the Op field set to "open", the Path field set to name,
        // and the Err field describing the problem.
        //
        // Open should reject attempts to open names that do not satisfy
        // ValidPath(name), returning a *PathError with Err set to
        // ErrInvalid or ErrNotExist.
        Open(name string) (File, error)
}
    An FS provides access to a hierarchical file system.

    The FS interface is the minimum implementation required of the file
    ⮕system. A file system may implement additional interfaces, such as
    ⮕ReadFileFS, to provide additional or optimized functionality.

func Sub(fsys FS, dir string) (FS, error)


Go Version: go1.19
```

There are already examples of the `fs.FS` interface in the standard library, such as `os.DirFS`,[38] `fstest.MapFS`,[39] and `embed.FS`.[40]

---

36. https://pkg.go.dev/io/fs#FS
37. https://pkg.go.dev/io/fs#File
38. https://pkg.go.dev/os#DirFS
39. https://pkg.go.dev/testing/fstest#MapFS
40. https://pkg.go.dev/embed#FS

The File Interface

The fs.File interface is used to define a file, Listing 14.59. While the interface for fs.FS is very simple, the fs.File interface is more complex. A file needs to be able to be read, closed, and able to return its own fs.FileInfo.[41]

Listing 14.59   The fs.File Interface

```
$ go doc fs.File

package fs // import "io/fs"

type File interface {
        Stat() (FileInfo, error)
        Read([]byte) (int, error)
        Close() error
}
    A File provides access to a single file. The File interface is the minimum
    ↦implementation required of the file. Directory files should also
    ↦implement ReadDirFile. A file may implement io.ReaderAt or io.Seeker as
    ↦optimizations.
```

Go Version: go1.19

There are examples of fs.File in the standard library already, such as os.File and fstest.MapFile,[42] Listing 14.60.

Listing 14.60   The fstest.MapFile Implements fs.File

```
$ go doc fstest.MapFile

package fstest // import "testing/fstest"

type MapFile struct {
        Data    []byte        // file content
        Mode    fs.FileMode   // FileInfo.Mode
        ModTime time.Time     // FileInfo.ModTime
        Sys     any           // FileInfo.Sys
}
    A MapFile describes a single file in a MapFS.
```

Go Version: go1.19

---

41. https://pkg.go.dev/io/fs#FileInfo
42. https://pkg.go.dev/testing/fstest#MapFile

Using the FS Interface

Previously, we had been using `filepath.WalkDir` to walk the directory tree. This worked by walking the file system directly. As a result, we have to make sure that the file system is in the correct state before we can use it. As we have seen, this can cause a lot of setup work to be done. Either we have to keep completely different folders for each test scenario we have, or we have to create all of the files and folders at the start of the test before we begin. This is a lot of work and is often prone to errors.

The `filepath.WalkDir` function works directly with the underlying file system, whereas the `fs.WalkDir` function takes an `fs.FS` implementation. By using `fs.WalkDir` instead, as shown in Listing 14.61, we can easily create in-memory `fs.FS` implementations for testing.

Listing 14.61 The fs.WalkDir[43] Function

```
$ go doc fs.WalkDir

package fs // import "io/fs"

func WalkDir(fsys FS, root string, fn WalkDirFunc) error
    WalkDir walks the file tree rooted at root, calling fn for each file or
    ➥directory in the tree, including root.

    All errors that arise visiting files and directories are filtered by fn:
    ➥see the fs.WalkDirFunc documentation for details.

    The files are walked in lexical order, which makes the output
    ➥deterministic but requires WalkDir to read an entire directory into
    ➥memory before proceeding to walk that directory.

    WalkDir does not follow symbolic links found in directories, but if root
    ➥itself is a symbolic link, its target will be walked.
```

Go Version: go1.19

In Listing 14.62, we can continue to use the same code inside of the `fs.WalkFunc`[44] function as we did before. Our test code only needs two small changes to make it work. The first is we need an implementation of the `fs.FS` interface to pass to the `Walk` function. For now, we can use the `os.DirFS` function, Listing 14.63. The implementation will be backed directly by the file system.

---

43. https://pkg.go.dev/io/fs#WalkDir
44. https://pkg.go.dev/io/fs#WalkFunc

Listing 14.62 Using the fs.WalkDir Function

```go
func Walk(cab fs.FS) ([]string, error) {
    var entries []string

    err := fs.WalkDir(cab, ".", func(path string, d fs.DirEntry, err error)
        ↪error {

        // if there was an error, return it
        // if there is an error, it is most likely
        // because an error was encountered trying
        // to read the top level directory
        if err != nil {
            return err
        }

        // if the entry is a directory, handle it
        if d.IsDir() {

            // name of the file or directory
            name := d.Name()

            // if the directory is a dot return nil
            // this may be the root directory
            if name == "." || name == ".." {
                return nil
            }

            // if the directory name is "testdata"
            // or it starts with "."
            // or it starts with "_"
            // then return filepath.SkipDir
            if name == "testdata" || strings.HasPrefix(name, ".") ||
            ↪strings.HasPrefix(name, "_") {
                return fs.SkipDir
            }

            return nil
        }

        // append the entry to the list
        entries = append(entries, path)
```

(continued)

```
        // return nil to tell walk to continue
        return nil
    })

    return entries, err
}
```

Listing 14.63   The os.DirFS Function

```
$ go doc os.DirFS

package os // import "os"

func DirFS(dir string) fs.FS
    DirFS returns a file system (an fs.FS) for the tree of files rooted at
    ➥the directory dir.

    Note that DirFS("/prefix") only guarantees that the Open calls
    ➥it makes to the operating system will begin with "/prefix":
    ➥DirFS("/prefix").Open("file") is the same as os.Open("/prefix/file").
    ➥So if /prefix/file is a symbolic link pointing outside the /prefix tree,
    ➥then using DirFS does not stop the access any more than using os.Open
    ➥does. DirFS is therefore not a general substitute for a chroot-style
    ➥security mechanism when the directory tree contains arbitrary content.
```

Go Version: go1.19

File Paths

The other change we need to make is the expected paths. Before, we were expecting paths such as /data/a.txt returned from our Walk function. However, when working with fs.FS implementations, the paths returned are relative to the root of the implementation. In this case, we are using os.DirFS("data") to create the fs.FS implementation. This places data at the root of the file system implementation and paths returned from the Walk function will be relative to this root.

> Paths are expected to use / as the path separator, regardless of the operating system.

We need to update our test code for the relative paths, a.txt, to be returned instead of /data/a.txt.

As you can see from the test output in Listing 14.64, we have successfully updated our code to use the fs.FS interface.

Listing 14.64 Testing the Walk Function

```go
func Test_Walk(t *testing.T) {
    t.Parallel()

    exp := []string{
        "a.txt",
        "b.txt",
        "e/f/g.txt",
        "e/f/h.txt",
        "e/j.txt",
    }

    cab := os.DirFS("data")

    act, err := Walk(cab)
    if err != nil {
        t.Fatal(err)
    }

    es := strings.Join(exp, ", ")
    as := strings.Join(act, ", ")

    if es != as {
        t.Fatalf("expected %s, got %s", es, as)
    }
}
```

```
$ go test -v

=== RUN    Test_Walk
=== PAUSE Test_Walk
=== CONT   Test_Walk
--- PASS: Test_Walk (0.00s)
PASS
ok        demo      0.704s
```

Go Version: go1.19

Mocking a File System

One of the biggest advantages of having interfaces for the file system is that it allows us to mock it out for testing. We no longer need to either have the files already on disk or have to create them before we can test our code. Instead, we just need to provide an interface that has that information already in it.

To help make testing easier, we can use the `fstest` package. In particular, we can use the `fstest.MapFS` type, Listing 14.65, to mock out a file system using a map.

Listing 14.65   The `fstest.MapFS` Type

```
$ go doc fstest.MapFS

package fstest // import "testing/fstest"

type MapFS map[string]*MapFile
    A MapFS is a simple in-memory file system for use in tests, represented
    ↪as a map from path names (arguments to Open) to information about the
    ↪files or directories they represent.

    The map need not include parent directories for files contained in the
    ↪map; those will be synthesized if needed. But a directory can still be
    ↪included by setting the MapFile.Mode's ModeDir bit; this may be
    ↪necessary for detailed control over the directory's FileInfo or to
    ↪create an empty directory.

    File system operations read directly from the map, so that the file
    ↪system can be changed by editing the map as needed. An implication is
    ↪that file system operations must not run concurrently with changes to
    ↪the map, which would be a race. Another implication is that opening or
    ↪reading a directory requires iterating over the entire map, so a MapFS
    ↪should typically be used with not more than a few hundred entries or
    ↪directory reads.

func (fsys MapFS) Glob(pattern string) ([]string, error)
func (fsys MapFS) Open(name string) (fs.File, error)
func (fsys MapFS) ReadDir(name string) ([]fs.DirEntry, error)
func (fsys MapFS) ReadFile(name string) ([]byte, error)
func (fsys MapFS) Stat(name string) (fs.FileInfo, error)
func (fsys MapFS) Sub(dir string) (fs.FS, error)
```

Go Version: go1.19

The `fstest.MapFile` type, Listing 14.66, is provided to help with creating files in memory and implementing the `fs.File` interface.

Listing 14.66 The `fstest.MapFile` Type

```
$ go doc fstest.MapFile

package fstest // import "testing/fstest"

type MapFile struct {
        Data    []byte      // file content
        Mode    fs.FileMode // FileInfo.Mode
        ModTime time.Time   // FileInfo.ModTime
        Sys     any         // FileInfo.Sys
}
    A MapFile describes a single file in a MapFS.
```

Go Version: go1.19

Using MapFS

Because the `Walk` function already takes the `fs.FS` interface, we can use the `fstest.MapFS` type to create a file system that has the files we need for our test in it.

In Listing 14.67, we create a helper function that creates a new `fstest.MapFS` type, Listing 14.68, and fills it with the files we need.

Listing 14.67 Creating a Helper Function to Populate a `fstest.MapFS`

```
func createTestFS(t testing.TB) fstest.MapFS {
    t.Helper()

    cab := fstest.MapFS{}

    files := []string{
        ".hidden/d.txt",
        "a.txt",
        "b.txt",
        "e/f/_ignore/i.txt",
        "e/f/g.txt",
        "e/f/h.txt",
        "e/j.txt",
        "testdata/c.txt",
    }

    for _, path := range files {
        cab[path] = &fstest.MapFile{
            Data: []byte(strings.ToUpper(path)),
```

(continued)

```
        }
    }
    return cab
}
```

If we look at the file system directly, we can see that there are no additional files on disk for us to use in our tests. We are relying on the `fstest.MapFS` type, Listing 14.68, to provide the files we need.

Listing 14.68   No Additional Test Files Needed When Using `fstest.MapFS`

```
$ tree -a

.
|-- demo.go
|-- demo_test.go
'-- go.mod

0 directories, 3 files
```

Inside of the test itself, we can use the helper function to get the `fstest.MapFS` and pass that to the `Walk` function instead of the `os.DirFS` implementation we were using before.

As you can see from our test output, Listing 14.69, we are now able to test our code without having to worry about the files on disk.

Listing 14.69   Using the Helper Function to Get the `fstest.MapFS`

```
func Test_Walk(t *testing.T) {
    t.Parallel()

    cab := createTestFS(t)

    exp := []string{
        "a.txt",
        "b.txt",
        "e/f/g.txt",
        "e/f/h.txt",
        "e/j.txt",
    }

    act, err := Walk(cab)
    if err != nil {
        t.Fatal(err)
    }
```

```
    es := strings.Join(exp, ", ")
    as := strings.Join(act, ", ")

    if es != as {
        t.Fatalf("expected %s, got %s", es, as)
    }
}
```

```
$ go test -v

=== RUN    Test_Walk
=== PAUSE  Test_Walk
=== CONT   Test_Walk
--- PASS: Test_Walk (0.00s)
PASS
ok      demo      0.272s
```

Go Version: go1.19

Embedding Files

As was mentioned earlier, the `fs` package and the subsequent changes to the standard library were added to allow for the embedding of files, such as HTML, JavaScript, and CSS, into the final binary.

To use this feature, you can use the `embed` package and the `//go:embed` directive to define which file or files to embed, Listing 14.70.

Listing 14.70   The embed Package

```
$ go doc embed

package embed // import "embed"

Package embed provides access to files embedded in the running Go program.

Go source files that import "embed" can use the //go:embed directive to
➥initialize a variable of type string, []byte, or FS with the contents of
➥files read from the package directory or subdirectories at compile time.
➥...
```

Go Version: go1.19

Using Embedded Files

Per the documentation, we can embed a single file as either a `string` or a `[]byte`. For our purposes, and more often than not, we will be embedding multiple files, so we need a `fs.FS` implementation to hold the files. The `embed.FS` type, Listing 14.71, implements the `fs.FS` interface and provides a read-only file system for the embedded files.

Listing 14.71   The `embed.FS` Type

```
$ go doc embed.FS

package embed // import "embed"

type FS struct {
        // Has unexported fields.
}
    An FS is a read-only collection of files, usually initialized with a
    //go:embed directive. When declared without a //go:embed directive, an
    FS is an empty file system.

    An FS is a read-only value, so it is safe to use from multiple goroutines
    simultaneously and also safe to assign values of type FS to each other.

    FS implements fs.FS, so it can be used with any package that understands
    file system interfaces, including net/http, text/template, and
    html/template.

    See the package documentation for more details about initializing an FS.

func (f FS) Open(name string) (fs.File, error)
func (f FS) ReadDir(name string) ([]fs.DirEntry, error)
func (f FS) ReadFile(name string) ([]byte, error)

Go Version: go1.19
```

In Listing 14.72, we can define a global variable of type `embed.FS` and use the `//go:embed` directive to define the directories and files to embed.

Listing 14.72   The `//go:embed` Directive

```
//go:embed data
var DataFS embed.FS
```

The `//go:embed data` directive tells Go to fill the `DataFS` variable with the contents of the `data` directory. Files beginning with `.` and `_` are ignored by the `//go:embed` directive.

In the tests, Listing 14.73, we can use the `DataFS` variable to pass to the `Walk` function.

Listing 14.73   Testing Using the `embed.FS` as an `fs.FS`

```go
func Test_Walk(t *testing.T) {
    t.Parallel()

    exp := []string{
        "data/a.txt",
        "data/b.txt",
        "data/e/f/g.txt",
        "data/e/f/h.txt",
        "data/e/j.txt",
    }

    act, err := Walk(DataFS)
    if err != nil {
        t.Fatal(err)
    }

    es := strings.Join(exp, ", ")
    as := strings.Join(act, ", ")

    if es != as {
        t.Fatalf("expected %s, got %s", es, as)
    }
}
```

As you can see from the test output in Listing 14.74, the files we wanted were successfully embedded and added to the `DataFS` variable.

Listing 14.74   Successful Test Output Using an `embed.FS`

```
$ go test -v

=== RUN    Test_Walk
=== PAUSE Test_Walk
=== CONT  Test_Walk
--- PASS: Test_Walk (0.00s)
PASS
ok       demo    0.869s

Go Version: go1.19
```

Embedded Files in a Binary

To see the embedding in action, we can write a small application that uses our application.

Consider Listing 14.75. We are calling our demo.Walk function from the main function, using the demo.DataFS variable, which is an embed.FS implementation. We then print out the results of the Walk function.

Listing 14.75   The main Function

```go
func main() {
    files, err := demo.Walk(demo.DataFS)
    if err != nil {
        log.Fatal(err)
    }

    for _, file := range files {
        fmt.Println(file)
    }
}
```

When we use go run to run the application, Listing 14.76, we see that the output is as expected.

Listing 14.76   The go run Output

```
$ go run .

data/a.txt
data/b.txt
data/e/f/g.txt
data/e/f/h.txt
data/e/j.txt
```

```
Go Version: go1.19
```

In Listing 14.77, we compile a binary of our application. We use the go build command and output the binary to the bin directory.

Listing 14.77   Building a Binary with Embedded Files

```
$ go build -o bin/demo
```

```
Go Version: go1.19
```

Finally, when we run the binary, Listing 14.78, we see that the output is as expected. Our application is able to successfully embed the files we defined. We now have a fully self-contained application that can contain not just the necessary runtime needed to execute the binary on the desired GOOS and GOARCH combinations but also the files we defined.

Listing 14.78   Files Embedded in the Binary

```
$ bin/demo

data/a.txt
data/b.txt
data/e/f/g.txt
data/e/f/h.txt
data/e/j.txt
```

Modifying Embedded Files

While we only needed to embed one directory, we can also embed multiple directories and files. We can do this by using the //go:embed directive multiple times, as in Listing 14.79.

Listing 14.79   The //go:embed Directive

```
//go:embed data
//go:embed cmd
//go:embed go.mod
var DataFS embed.FS
```

As you can see from the test output, Listing 14.80, the extra //go:embed directives embedded the files we did not want, and, as a result, the test failed.

Listing 14.80   Using Multiple //go:embed Directives

```
$ go test -v

=== RUN   Test_Walk
=== PAUSE Test_Walk
=== CONT  Test_Walk
    demo_test.go:29: expected data/a.txt,
        data/b.txt,
        data/e/f/g.txt,
        data/e/f/h.txt,
        data/e/j.txt, got cmd/demo/main.go,
```

(continued)

```
        data/a.txt,
        data/b.txt,
        data/e/f/g.txt,
        data/e/f/h.txt,
        data/e/j.txt,
        go.mod
--- FAIL: Test_Walk (0.00s)
FAIL
exit status 1
FAIL    demo    0.303s
```

Go Version: go1.19

Embedding Files as a String or Byte Slice

In addition to embedding files and directories to a embed.FS, we can also embed the contents of a file as a string or []byte, as shown in Listing 14.81. This makes gaining access to the contents of a file easier.

Listing 14.81   The //go:embed Directive with a string and a []byte

```
package demo

import _ "embed"

//go:embed data/LICENSE
var LICENSE string

//go:embed data/LICENSE
var LICENSE_BYTES []byte
```

Summary

In this chapter, we delved deep into using files with Go. We showed you how to create, read, and append to files. We discussed the fs.FS and fs.File interfaces that make working with readonly file systems easier. We covered how to mock out file systems for testing. We also explained how to read and walk directories. Finally, we covered how to use the embed package to embed files into our Go binaries.

Index

D

E

Z